Handbook of Behavioral Assessment *edited by Anthony R. Cimi~   ~ S. Calhoun, and Henry E. Adams*

Counseling and Psychotherapy: A Behavioral *~*

Dimensions of Personality *edited by ~*

The Mental Health Industry: A *~* ~ert Gripp, *David McDowell, and Ivan W. ~*

Nonverbal Communication: The S~ *~, Arthur N. Weins, and Joseph D. Matarazzo*

Alcoholism and Treatment *by David ~ ~nael Polich, and Harriet B. Stambul*

A Biodevelopmental Approach to Cli~ ~ Child Psychology: Cognitive Controls and Cognitive Control Theory *by Sebastiano Santostefano*

Handbook of Infant Development *edited by Joy D. Osofsky*

Understanding the Rape Victim: A Synthesis of Research Findings *by Sedelle Katz and Mary Ann Mazur*

Childhood Pathology and Later Adjustment: The Question of Prediction *by Loretta K. Cass and Carolyn B. Thomas*

Intelligent Testing with the WISC-R *by Alan S. Kaufman*

Adaptation in Schizophrenia: The Theory of Segmental Set *by David Shakow*

Psychotherapy: An Eclectic Approach *by Sol L. Garfield*

Handbook of Minimal Brain Dysfunctions *edited by Herbert E. Rie and Ellen D. Rie*

Handbook of Behavioral Interventions: A Clinical Guide *edited by Alan Goldstein and Edna B. Foa*

Art Psychotherapy *by Harriet Wadeson*

Handbook of Adolescent Psychology *edited by Joseph Adelson*

Psychotherapy Supervision: Theory, Research and Practice *edited by Allen K. Hess*

Psychology and Psychiatry in Courts and Corrections: Controversy and Change *by Ellsworth A. Fersch, Jr.*

Restricted Environmental Stimulation: Research and Clinical Applications *by Peter Suedfeld*

Personal Construct Psychology: Psychotherapy and Personality *edited by Alvin W. Landfield and Larry M. Leitner*

Mothers, Grandmothers, and Daughters: Personality and Child Care in Three-Generation Families *by Bertram J. Cohler and Henry U. Grunebaum*

Further Explorations in Personality *edited by A.I. Rabin, Joel Aronoff, Andrew M. Barclay, and Robert A. Zucker*

Hypnosis and Relaxation: Modern Verification of an Old Equation *by William E. Edmonston, Jr.*

Handbook of Clinical Behavior Therapy *edited by Samuel M. Turner, Karen S. Calhoun, and Henry E. Adams*

Handbook of Clinical Neuropsychology *edited by Susan B. Filskov and Thomas J. Boll*

The Course of Alcoholism: Four Years After Treatment *by J. Michael Polich, David J. Armor, and Harriet B. Braiker*

Handbook of Innovative Psychotherapies *edited by Raymond J. Corsini*

The Role of the Father in Child Development (Second Edition) *edited by Michael E. Lamb*

Behavioral Medicine: Clinical Applications *by Susan S. Pinkerton, Howard Hughes, and W.W. Wenrich*

Handbook for the Practice of Pediatric Psychology *edited by June M. Tuma*

Change Through Interaction: Social Psychological Processes of Counseling and Psychotherapy *by Stanley R. Strong and Charles D. Claiborn*

Drugs and Behavior (Second Edition) *by Fred Leavitt*

(*continued on back*)

PSYCHOSOCIAL ASPECTS OF DISASTER

Psychosocial Aspects of Disaster

Edited by

RICHARD GIST

BERNARD LUBIN

WILEY

JOHN WILEY & SONS

New York • Chichester • Brisbane • Toronto • Singapore

This publication is designed to provide accurate and
authoritative information in regard to the subject
matter covered. It is sold with the understanding that
the publisher is not engaged in rendering legal, accounting,
or other professional service. If legal advice or other
expert assistance is required, the services of a competent
professional person should be sought. *From a Declaration
of Principles jointly adopted by a Committee of the
American Bar Association and a Committee of Publishers.*

ISBN 0-471-84894-8

Printed in the United States of America

10 9 8 7 6 5 4 3 2 1

To the memory of Rene A. Ruiz,
whose friendship and insight
remain a part of all we do

Contributors

Danny Axsom, PhD
Assistant Professor of Psychology
Virginia Polytechnic Institute
Blacksburg, Virginia

Allan Beigel, MD
Vice President for External
  Relations
University of Arizona
Tucson, Arizona

Michael R. Berren, PhD
Director of Research and
  Psychological Services
Kino Community Hospital
Tucson, Arizona

Leonard Bickman, PhD
Professor of Psychology
Director, Program Evaluation
  Laboratory
Peabody College/Vanderbilt
  University
Nashville, Tennessee

Robert Bolin, PhD
Associate Professor of Sociology
New Mexico State University
Las Cruces, New Mexico

Evelyn J. Bromet, PhD
Professor of Psychiatry and
  Behavioral Science
State University of New York at
  Stony Brook
Stony Brook, New York

James Neal Butcher, PhD
Professor of Psychology
University of Minnesota
Minneapolis, Minnesota

Laurie A. Dunn, BA
Doctoral Candidate
Clinical Psychology Program
University of Minnesota
Minneapolis, Minnesota

Richard Gist, PhD
Consulting Community
  Psychologist
Kansas City, Missouri Health
  Department
Kansas City, Missouri

Don M. Hartsough, PhD
Director of Clinical Psychology
  Training
Purdue University
West Lafayette, Indiana

George Howe, PhD
Research Associate Professor
Department of Psychiatry
George Washington University
  School of Medicine
Washington, District of Columbia

Morty Lebedun, PhD, MSW
Mental Health Consultant
Kansas City, Missouri

Bernard Lubin, PhD
Professor of Psychology and
  Medicine
University of Missouri at
  Kansas City
Kansas City, Missouri

Diane Garaventa Myers, RN, MSN
Program Manager for Adult
  Outpatient Services
Marin County Community Mental
  Health Services
Marin County, California

Jose M. Santiago, MD
Chairman, Department of
  Psychiatry
Kino Community Hospital
Clinical Professor of Psychology
University of Arizona
Tucson, Arizona

Susan D. Solomon, PhD
Coordinator, Emergency/Disaster
  Research Program
National Institute of Mental Health
Rockville, Maryland

Kathleen J. Tierney, PhD
Adjunct Assistant Professor
Institute of Safety and Systems
  Management
University of Southern California
University Park, California

Sue A. Timmons, BA
Graduate Student in Clinical
  Psychology
University of Arizona
Tucson, Arizona

Enrique Vera, MD
Director of Residency Training
Greater Kansas City Mental Health
  Foundation
Associate Professor of Psychiatry
University of Missouri at
  Kansas City
School of Medicine
Kansas City, Missouri

Charles B. Wilkinson, MD
Executive Director
Greater Kansas City Mental Health
  Foundation
Professor of Psychiatry
University of Missouri at
  Kansas City
School of Medicine
Kansas City, Missouri

Karl E. Wilson, MD
Executive Director
Four County Mental Health
  Services
St. Charles, Missouri

Suzanne Yates, PhD
Assistant Professor of Psychology
Lehman College of the City
  University of New York
Bronx, New York

Marlene A. Young, PhD, JD
Executive Director
National Association for Victim
  Assistance
Washington, District of Columbia

Series Preface

This series of books is addressed to behavioral scientists interested in the nature of human personality. Its scope should prove pertinent to personality theorists and researchers as well as to clinicians concerned with applying an understanding of personality processes to the amelioration of emotional difficulties in living. To this end, the series provides a scholarly integration of theoretical formulations, empirical data, and practical recommendations.

Six major aspects of studying and learning about human personality can be designated: personality theory, personality structure and dynamics, personality development, personality assessment, personality change, and personality adjustment. In exploring these aspects of personality, the books in the series discuss a number of distinct but related subject areas: the nature and implications of various theories of personality; personality characteristics that account for consistencies and variations in human behavior; the emergence of personality processes in children and adolescents; the use of interviewing and testing procedures to evaluate individual differences in personality; efforts to modify personality styles through psychotherapy, counseling, behavior therapy, and other methods of influence; and patterns of abnormal personality functioning that impair individual competence.

IRVING B. WEINER

Fairleigh Dickinson University
Rutherford, New Jersey

Preface

Disasters, by definition, are castastrophic events that disrupt entire communities. It should not be surprising, then, that community psychologists have taken particular interest in researching, evaluating, and attempting to ameliorate their effects. But disaster intervention represents more than just a specific area of inquiry and application; in many respects, the development of mental health responses to disaster reflects the discipline's evolution from a collection of loosely aggregated activities into an integrated body of theory and practice.

The history of community psychology might easily serve as a case study in the evolution of social movements. Born of the spirit of radical change and charismatic consensus that typified the community mental health ideology of the 1960s, its initial phases were marked in part by an egalitarian notion that almost any undertaking might appropriately fall under its aegis—provided, of course, that it was of a suitably nontraditional nature.

A quarter century of maturation has brought a variety of changes to the discipline. Perhaps most significant has been a series of subtle shifts from the characteristics of a social cause to those of a social science. There is now a clearer understanding of how and where particular viewpoints best fit in the broader picture of psychology and human services. Community psychologists have learned, both from successes and failures, what it is they do well and what is better done by others.

Such lessons from the field, many learned in communities recovering from disaster, have contributed to the development of a more focused body of research and practice. Significant strides have been made in identifying the factors that differentiate strengths from failings, and in molding from this knowledge the constructs of a cogent interactionist viewpoint. An ecological framework has also emerged to provide a contextual model for the operation of those constructs. These developments hold significant promise for organizing and directing future endeavors.

This volume brings together observations from a number of active researchers and practitioners in disaster intervention and presents their current thinking along lines drawn by the editors' ecological perspectives. Credit for the quality of the work and thought reflected in these chapters belongs exclusively to the contributors; all responsibility for the organization and presentation of the material—always a difficult chore, and never one that does justice to the components—must be placed squarely at the feet of the editors.

We do, however, owe several outstanding debts to persons whose unique contributions have done so much to shape these and other efforts we have undertaken, both individually and together. To Shirley McKnight and Alice Lubin we owe the gratitude consistently earned by the spouses of "Type A" academics, but too rarely expressed by their task-driven partners. To our colleagues at the University of Missouri, Kansas City, and the Kansas City, Missouri, Health Department, we owe thanks, for both the direct contributions involved in review and discussion of our work and the daily interaction that has helped shape our direction and commitment to the field. Tricia Falk and Sally Conrad, loyal friends and able assistants for many years, have rescued us time and again from assorted faults and foibles.

The most specific debt of scholars and academics, however, is owed to students. By preventing the basic questions of any discipline from slipping away, students keep the process of inquiry alive and grounded. As editors of this volume we are the students of the contributors; we hope our product proves worthy of their tutelage.

RICHARD GIST
BERNARD LUBIN

Kansas City, Missouri
December 1988

Contents

PSYCHOSOCIAL ASPECTS OF DISASTER

PSYCHOLOGICAL ASPECTS OF STRESS

INTRODUCTION

Ecological and Community Perspectives on Disaster Intervention

RICHARD GIST AND BERNARD LUBIN

Probably no single statement is as often quoted, by psychologists in general and by community psychologists in particular, as the maxim first attributed to Kurt Lewin: "There's nothing so practical as good theory." Good theory serves first to frame and focus systematic inquiry; it leads to recognition of the salient features of observations and to derivation of prudent and fruitful hypotheses from observed relationships. Good theory guides the examination of those hypotheses through objective evaluation of their adequacy in predicting, inventing, preventing, explaining, and comprehending the actual events of the empirical world. Good theory also provides a self-correcting vehicle through which the results of inquiry refine in turn the theory that directed it.

Any sound attempt to examine the psychosocial aspects of disaster must therefore begin, implicitly or explicitly, with at least a general set of assumptions about the nature of human behavior and some notions about the principles that influence human behavior under the conditions disaster may impose. The framework reflected in this volume is an ecological viewpoint with an explicitly community-based orientation (O'Connor & Lubin, 1984). Although the major focus of the text is on the practical application of intervention principles by mental health personnel in the field, it begins with a basic discussion of the viewpoint that binds the material and guides its organization.

THE EVOLUTION OF PSYCHOLOGICAL THEORY

Many of the central issues in contemporary study of human behavior might best be described as matters of context. Humans are, first and foremost, complex biological entities; human behavior may be accordingly expected to be both limited and directed by the biological heritage of the species. But just as the expression of the biological possibilities afforded an organism

1

through its genetic inheritance will be controlled in large measure by the nature of the environment within which that organism develops and functions, so also will the expressions of human behavior be largely determined by environmental contexts.

Traditional viewpoints in psychology—biological, behavioral, psychodynamic—have concentrated primarily on individual-level variables in their attempts to uncover and explain the mechanisms of behavior. The organism has been seen primarily as a reactive element within its environment, its behavior comprised of determined responses to events and experiences. Much as physical sciences have sought to decipher the processes governing inanimate behavior through examination of the systematic reactions of matter to forces and conditions acting upon it, these approaches to psychological inquiry have sought to uncover similar types of processes governing the behavior of organisms.

Gergen (1982, 1985) has termed this epistemological disposition an *exogenic perspective,* descriptive of models derived from logical empiricist assumptions regarding the structure of nature and the meanings of knowledge concerning that structure. These assumptions hold the essential determinants of knowledge and behavior to exist independently of any apprehension by or assertion of the organism, leading to attempts to explain human behavior as the necessary and sufficient consequences of invariant external processes. This line of construction leaves such critical issues as volition and cultural relativity—irrelevant to the explanation of inanimate behavior but potentially crucial in the determination of human activity—difficult to reconcile (cf. Howard & Conway, 1986).

As an opposite epistemological pole, Gergen described an *endogenic perspective,* derived from rationalist traditions and typified in approaches such as the field theories of Kurt Lewin (cf. Lewin, 1951). Contemporary directions in social psychology, particularly in the areas of social cognition and social perception, suggest the ascendance of viewpoints that hold human actions to depend more on beliefs about the nature of one's world than on direct knowledge of its empirical structure. These constructions face limitations at least equal in consequence to the ones confronted by exogenic orientations, their logical extension yielding an unfortunate solipsism that must struggle to accommodate such critical issues as the evolution of complex cognitive behavior or its developmental emergence within the individual (Gergen, 1985).

Theoretical Imperatives in Community Psychology

Psychology's seeming inability to reconcile its disparate epistemological frameworks has led to an enduring schism with far-reaching implications. Kimble (1984) has described the result as the emergence of separate cultures, one characterized by the more deterministic exogenic viewpoints, the other characterized by a more endogenic phenomonological humanism. The former viewpoint has provided the tradition for much of scientific and academic psychology, leading often to theoretical positions that may appear conceptually divorced from the pragmatic world of the practitioner. In contrast, traditions of the practitioner have been more strongly influenced by the endogenic orientation, a framework generally eschewed by academics and scientists.

Despite the pervasiveness of a scientist-practitioner archetype crafted with the intent of diminishing such divisions, the gap between these traditions has continued to grow. Community psychology, generated as the discipline's response to the imperatives of the community mental health movement of the mid-1960s, was steeped in a tradition encompassing social action through the scientist-practitioner ethic. Originally a subfield geared more toward method and context than toward development of unique theoretical viewpoints, many of the crucial activities its early practitioners elected to pursue forced them to address the implications of the endogenic-exogenic dichotomy.

Needs assessment and program development activities, for example, require the application of systematic approaches to the diagnosis of problems at both individual and community levels, the establishment of priorities among identified issues, and the selection of intervention approaches that hold promise for solution of priority issues (Stewart, 1979). Attempts to describe such problems by objective, exogenic standards alone have consistently proven problematic, particularly to the extent that subjective and/or sociocultural decisions regarding deviance comprise major aspects of their contextual definitions (cf. Schact, 1985). Furthermore, the establishment of intervention priorities demands the effective blending of social, cultural, political, and economic agendas with the more familiar clinical imperatives. Community psychology's orientation toward preventive and consultative approaches drives the community practitioner toward modes of intervention that, because they must usually be executed within the constraints of a delivery system dominated by explicitly exogenic medical models, tend to keep these epistemological conflicts in sharpened focus (cf. Rappaport & Chinsky, 1974).

Program evaluation presents another example. This activity was initially conceived as entailing somewhat atheoretical post hoc assessments of programmatic efficacy, intended to provide patently objective information for administrative and political decision making (Weiss, 1972). It soon became apparent, however, that the nature and goals of evaluation research gave the enterprise a character profoundly different from typical academic inquiry. The conduct of evaluation studies proved to be inextricably intertwined with the social and political contexts in which they were conceived and executed. Evaluation activities were repeatedly shown to be strongly shaped by a number of contextual variables; their findings, however, rarely seemed to exert substantial influence on the social and political systems they were intended to guide (Weiss, 1975).

The process of evaluation, before it could achieve any level of coherent utility, had to be reconceptualized within an interactive framework that could encompass the disparate conventions of the evaluator's competing constituencies. Building a productive role for evaluation research in political decision making, for example, required translating a substantial portion of the conceptual models from strictly academic paradigms to ones that could address the values and imperatives of the political system while maintaining the analytic integrity of traditional approaches to research (Chelimsky, 1987). Frequently, however, objective analyses of social issues have resulted in disaffirmation of entrenched views, leaving the evaluator—who often thought his or her objective data would provide clear and welcome solutions—an equally disenfranchised outsider among colleagues, constituents, and consumers (Rossi, 1987).

In Search of Cogency

Resolution of these functional dilemmas has taken community psychology through a series of methodological and epistemological metamorphoses. The early effort by Caplan (1964) to transport certain concepts of public health into the community mental health arena provided a useful starting point, but its reliance upon implicitly exogenic medical metaphors failed to provide an adequate structure through which to accommodate the broad range of interactive behavioral phenomena it sought to encompass. Barker's (1968) ecological concepts provided an alternative schema for the interactive analysis of community functioning, whereas Rappaport's (1981) concept of empowerment supplied an alternative to the disease-based notion of prevention.

Definitions of community psychology, initially dominated by descriptions of its component activities, began to reflect interactionist imperatives. Heller and Monahan (1977), for example, organized their community psychology text along a model that described points and types of intervention in accordance with discrete ecological levels. Gottfredson (1984) advanced the principle that program evaluation should be used to generate and empirically validate hypotheses relating to the theoretical underpinnings of the interventions under scrutiny. Yet despite the accumulation of applied examples, articulation of a cogent theoretical position was slow to appear.

Emergence of an Interactionist Framework

Bry (1985) cited the emergence of a coherent interactionist viewpoint in O'Connor and Lubin (1984) as "a watershed in community psychology" (p. 951). She summarized the major elements of consensus among its contributors as entailing a series of assumptions about person-environment interactions as the most salient locus of analysis, with the ecological or systems perspective on those interactions being the most productive approach to their explanation and study. Much like Bandura's (1977) concept of reciprocal determinism, these assumptions posit that the construction of reality an individual employs to guide his or her behavior is both a consequence of that individual's apprehensions and experiences and a determinant of the future behavior of that individual and others. The social and environmental contexts of these determinants establish the norms and settings for individual and community behavior, thereby defining both accepted and pathological patterns of individual action (Marsella, 1984).

Cronkite, Moos, and Finney (1984) and Bechtel (1984) have presented complementary discussions of the mechanisms through which these factors exert their influences on behavior. Each construction argued that certain role expectations and behavioral norms exist as a part of an individual's comprehension of a given setting, and that those norms and expectations prescribe behavioral possibilities afforded the individual by participation in that setting. The reinforcements directed toward behavior emitted in a given setting in turn dictate the probability that specific behavioral possibilities will be enacted or repeated, usually based upon the actors' and observers' cognitive evaluations of those environmental reactions. In this fashion, the social constructionist perspective advanced by Gergen (1985) sees some realization, in that the individual's endogenic construction of reality is given a primary role in determining behavior but is said to be formed through exogenically describable principles of social learning. It is these elements *acting together* that are posited to ultimately yield observable behavior.

COMMUNITIES IN DISASTER

Disaster, by almost any of its essential definitions, is a community-level event, but it is also an event with profound implications for functioning at all subordinate levels of analysis. The disruption of regular environments and normal social networks can place extraordinary stress upon victims (cf. Pattison & Hurd, 1984) and can exert substantial pathognomonic influences on the perceived quality of life in a community (Goodhart & Zautra, 1984).

Clearly, the majority of persons impacted by disaster will not suffer long-term catastrophic or pathological responses, though most may experience some symptoms related to situational stress (Helzer, Robins, & McEvoy, 1987). Efforts to intervene with these populations may therefore be more productively guided by models that employ ecological concepts of dysfunction and intervention.

Ecological Perspectives in Disaster Intervention

Gist and Stolz (1982) described one such circumstance in which community adjustment following a major building collapse was enhanced through a series of interventions designed to identify and augment natural helping systems. Anticipatory guidance and mutual support mechanisms formed the major components of the intervention, with mental health personnel serving primarily as informational resources working through vehicles as diverse and diffuse as broadcast media and self-selected support group participants.

Such approaches contrast sharply with traditional "waiting modes" of intervention (Rappaport & Chinsky, 1974). They are in essence preventive models, seeking both to strengthen the capacity of individuals to withstand the inevitable stresses of catacylsmic life events and to improve the capacity of both the natural and the structured helping systems that assist those endeavors. The distress experienced by disaster victims is viewed as a normal reaction to abnormal circumstances, rather than as a manifestation of dispositional pathology. Crisis intervention, rather than protracted therapeutic engagement, dominates the kind of direct service approaches that may evolve.

BUILDING AN UNDERSTANDING

The first effort in the design of this text is to provide a framework for the examination and discussion of the major issues to be addressed. Consistent with the focus on ecological perspectives, the volume begins by framing the nature of disaster and responses to it in terms of communities and the systems they embody.

Disasters, of course, do not represent any singular type of phenomenon. In marked contrast to natural disasters, the proverbial "acts of God," stand mass transportation accidents, technological catastrophes, and deliberate acts of violence or terrorism. It is clear that the nature of these various events will profoundly influence the social construction of the disaster and its impact and hence yield substantially different imperatives for the planning and execution of interventions. Accordingly, typologies for the study of disaster are examined next.

Much can be learned from the experience of researchers and practitioners in addressing various types of disaster. Part Two reviews several major categories of cataclysmic events a community might face—natural disasters, airline accidents, technological failures, and criminal acts, violence, or terrorism. It is possible to draw from these reviews some insight into both the features common across all responses to disaster and the distinctive features of reactions to each.

Ecological approaches, as established earlier, prescribe multilevel strategies for preventive and supportive activity. Part Three explores a model of help seeking in disaster and considers models for both the prevention and remediation of crisis-engendered reactions to situational stress. It also describes the organizational aspects of planning and executing disaster responses.

The final section returns the focus to more theoretical issues. The growing knowledge of human responses to disaster has also generated a new arena for litigation; Part Four considers first, then, the legal implications of disaster-induced reactions. An extensive review of current research directions in the study of psychosocial responses to disaster follows, and the volume concludes with some thoughts on the implications of disaster work for the future of community psychology.

COMMENTS FOR THE READER

The design of this text represents an attempt to provide a creditable overview of both theoretical and practical elements of mental health involvement in disasters. As is the case with most compromise positions, certain sacrifices were made. Some duplication was left in a number of chapters by design, primarily so that the reader with a very specific interest in the content of one particular chapter would be able to make quick and efficient use of that reference. Great diversity in the definition of key terms and concepts was allowed and even encouraged to better reflect the evolving nature of disaster research and practice. Minor stylistic variations were also imposed to enhance the readability of text and the ease of locating references.

Overall, the editors have tried to keep a consistent focus on bringing together the best of current thinking and practice and on organizing that information in accordance with a coherent, clearly articulated theoretical viewpoint. It is certainly hoped that the finished volume serves both to mark the state of the art at one particular moment and to help shape the agenda for subsequent investigation.

REFERENCES

Bandura, A. (1977). *Social learning theory.* Englewood Cliffs, NJ: Prentice-Hall.

Barker, R. G. (1968). *Ecological psychology.* Stanford, CA: Stanford University Press.

Bechtel, R. B. (1984). Patient and community, the ecological bond. In W. A. O'Connor & B. Lubin (Eds.), *Ecological approaches to clinical and community psychology* (pp. 216–231). New York: Wiley.

Bry, B. H. (1985). Community psychology comes of age: Distinctive theoretical frameworks. [Review of *Ecological approaches to clinical and community psychology*]. *Contemporary Psychology, 30,* 950–951.

Caplan, G. (1964). *Principles of preventive psychiatry.* New York: Basic Books.

Chelimsky, E. (1987). The politics of program evaluation. *Society, 25*(1), 24–32.

Cronkite, R. C., Moos, R. H., & Finney, J. W. (1984). The context of adaptation: An integrative perspective on community and treatment environments. In W. A. O'Connor & B. Lubin (Eds.), *Ecological approaches to clinical and community psychology* (pp. 189–215). New York: Wiley.

Gergen, K. J. (1982). *Toward transformation in social knowledge.* New York: Springer-Verlag.

Gergen, K. J. (1985). The social constructionist movement in modern psychology. *American Psychologist, 40,* 266–275.

Gist, R., & Stolz, S. B. (1982). Mental health promotion and the media: Community response to the Kansas City hotel disaster. *American Psychologist, 37,* 1136–1139.

Goodhart, D. E., & Zautra, A. (1984). Assessing quality of life in the community: An ecological approach. In W. A. O'Connor & B. Lubin (Eds.), *Ecological approaches to clinical and community psychology* (pp. 251–290). New York: Wiley.

Gottfredson, G. D. (1984). A theory-ridden approach to program evaluation. *American Psychologist, 39,* 1101–1112.

Heller, K., & Monahan, J. (1977). *Psychology and community change.* Homewood, IL: Dorsey Press.

Helzer, J. E., Robins, L. N., & McEvoy, L. (1987). Post-traumatic stress disorder in the general population: Findings of the Epidemiologic Catchment Area Survey. *New England Journal of Medicine, 317,* 1630–1634.

Howard, G. S., & Conway, C. G. (1986). Can there be an empirical science of volitional action? *American Psychologist, 41,* 1241–1251.

Kimble, G. A. (1984). Psychology's two cultures. *American Psychologist, 39,* 833–839.

Lewin, K. (1951). *Field theory in social science.* New York: Harper & Row.

Marsella, A. J. (1984). An interactional model of psychopathology. In W. A. O'Connor & B. Lubin (Eds.), *Ecological approaches to clinical and community psychology* (pp. 232–250). New York: Wiley.

O'Connor, W. A., & Lubin, B. (Eds.). (1984). *Ecological approaches to clinical and community psychology.* New York: Wiley.

Pattison, E. M., & Hurd, G. S. (1984). The social network paradigm as a basis for social intervention strategies. In W. A. O'Connor & B. Lubin (Eds.), *Ecological approaches to clinical and community psychology* (pp. 145–188). New York: Wiley.

Rappaport, J. (1981). In praise of paradox: A social policy of empowerment over prevention. *American Journal of Community Psychology, 9,* 1–26.

Rappaport, J., & Chinsky, J. M. (1974). Models for delivery of service from a historical and conceptual perspective. *Professional Psychology, 5,* 42–50.

Rossi, P. H. (1987). No good applied social research goes unpunished. *Society, 25*(1), 74–79.

Schact, T. E. (1985). DSM-III and the politics of truth. *American Psychologist, 40,* 513–521.

Stewart, R. (1979). The nature of needs assessment in community mental health. *Community Mental Health Journal, 15,* 287–295.

Weiss, C. H. (1972). *Evaluation research: Methods for assessing program effectiveness.* Englewood Cliffs, NJ: Prentice-Hall.

Weiss, C. H. (1975). Evaluation research in the political context. In E. Struening & M. Guttentag (Eds.), *Handbook of evaluation research* (pp. 13–26). Beverly Hills, CA: Sage Publications.

PART 1

Foundations for the Study of Disaster

The behavior of individuals can never be completely understood outside the context of the settings and systems from their daily lives. This is especially true with respect to disaster victims who, in addition to weathering often catastrophic personal consequences, must also adapt to rapid and severe changes in the social fabric of their communities. Many important connections to family, friends, and supportive social systems are likely to be disrupted in the wake of disaster; many new connections, however, may emerge as those systems respond to the challenges of reaction, recovery, and reconstruction.

This section begins with Tierney's examination of the dynamics of community systems as they attempt to respond to the challenges imposed by disaster. Disaster preparedness and response is in some respects a political issue, in some areas an issue of resource management, in yet other aspects a collection of issues in organization development. The ability of community systems, both formal and informal, to cope with each phase of disaster response exerts a substantial influence on the capacity of their constituents to achieve productive resolutions.

Disaster, however, cannot be treated as a generic concept when applied to issues of intervention, evaluation, or research. Although all disasters share the common element of cataclysmic disruption, the unique features of each event make most generalizations somewhat suspect and may render many counterproductive.

Berren, Santiago, Beigel, and Timmons have evolved the schema for the classification of disasters presented in Chapter 2. Their approach considers several dimensions—type of disaster; its temporal and geographic scope; the extent of its personal impact; the presence and nature of identifiable low points; and the size of the disaster in terms of individuals, systems, and communities affected by impact and response. When taken together, these dimensions yield a more-or-less factorial assessment of the critical features pertinent to a particular disaster event and lead both the researcher and the interventionist toward the most salient aspects of victim reactions and needs in the given situation.

CHAPTER 1

The Social and Community Contexts of Disaster

KATHLEEN J. TIERNEY

The delivery of mental health services following disasters differs from everyday service delivery, in part because the social context is different. Disasters produce a number of significant changes at the community, organizational, and individual levels. In addition to increasing the stress on individuals, families, and organizations, disasters can also affect the ability of the community and the mental health system to respond to victims' needs. A disaster can be detrimental to the individual's social support network, reducing its stress-buffering effect; at the same time, however, it can lead to unprecedented levels of public agency involvement in the provision of assistance to victims, which can have positive consequences for mental health. Understanding disaster-related social processes can help mental health workers know what to expect in community emergencies so that they can devise appropriate programs to meet disaster-related needs.

This chapter reviews some of the empirical research on disasters by social scientists concerning how communities, organizations, and groups adapt in crisis situations. No effort is made to present studies in depth; instead, major trends and emphases in the field are reviewed, and findings from earlier research are summarized and synthesized. The chapter also provides information on the sociopolitical context of emergency management that should help readers better understand why emergency preparedness and response activities are often fraught with difficulty. The outline of research findings is followed by a section that discusses the implications of disaster-generated community changes for organized attempts to provide mental health services.

CONCEPTUALIZING DISASTER

Any discussion of the impact of disasters on communities must begin with an understanding of what is meant by the term *disaster*. The word is used in several different ways by members of the general public, researchers, and practitioners; in fact, lack of agreement on what types of events to include under the disaster label is one of the roots of the ongoing debate on how disasters affect mental health (Quarantelli, 1985; Tierney, 1986b).

The concept of disaster used in this chapter follows the classic formulation developed by sociologist Charles Fritz (1961), who defined a disaster as:

> an event, concentrated in time and space, in which a society, or a relatively self-sufficient subdivision of a society, undergoes severe danger and incurs such losses to its members and physical appurtenances that the social structure is disrupted and the fulfillment of all or some of the essential functions of the society is prevented. (p. 655)

Disasters are commonly thought of as merely physical events or acts of God. However, in thinking about the concept of disaster, it is important to keep in mind a point made by Kreps (1984) about the social dimension of disasters: "Both the causes and consequences of these events are related to the social structures and processes of societies or their subunits" (p. 312). In other words, human behavior and social processes affect every stage of the "hazard chain," from the predisaster period through impact and recovery.

This point seems obvious when technological disasters are considered, but it is equally true for natural hazards. For example, earthquakes of comparable magnitudes are not equally damaging, disruptive, or disastrous in all parts of the world, because some societies and communities have been more effective in mitigating the earthquake hazard—for example, by constructing buildings that are earthquake resistant—and are more capable than others of launching an effective emergency response to earthquakes when they occur. These capabilities are, in general, related to the society's level of economic development. The social disruption that follows major earthquakes is more the result of economic factors and predisaster policies and practices than of the earth tremors themselves.

As used here, then, the term disasters refers to *collective stress situations that happen (or at least manifest themselves) relatively suddenly in a particular geographic area, involve some degree of loss, interfere with the ongoing social life of the community, and are subject to human management.*

Disasters differ in their characteristics and effects; several subtypes and classifications have been suggested. Dynes (1970) suggests that disaster agents—the physical phenomena that create disaster impacts—can be classified along nine dimensions: (1) frequency, (2) predictability, (3) controlliability, (4) cause, (5) speed of onset, (6) length of possible warning, (7) duration, (8) scope of impact, and (9) destructive potential. Other investigators (Quarantelli, 1970; Stallings, 1973; Warheit, 1976) distinguish between collective crises in which there is community consensus (e.g., natural disasters) and those in which there is dissensus (e.g., civil disturbances).

Quarantelli (1985) notes that within the broad category of collective stress situations, some situations can be considered disasters and others, such as riots and hostage incidents, are more appropriately categorized as conflicts. Within the disaster subcategory, only some events are community disasters, while others, such as transportation accidents, should be viewed as different types of events because they do not actually disrupt community life. A distinction is also increasingly made with respect to the social impact of natural and technological disaster agents (Kasperson & Pijawka, 1985). It is important to keep in mind these kinds of distinctions because they are likely to be related to the social response to and consequences of the crisis event.

THE DISASTER RESEARCH TRADITION

Drabek (1986) suggested that the first social scientific study of disaster was probably Samuel Prince's doctoral dissertation, which concerned a marine accident and explosion in 1917 near Halifax, Nova Scotia (Prince, 1920). Some social science studies of community crises were conducted during World War II (see Janis, 1951). However, the disaster research tradition in the social sciences did not really begin until the early 1950s. The main focus of these early research activities was to generate findings on human behavior under situations of collective stress that could be extrapolated to conditions of war. The federal government, which sponsored this early research, wanted to be able to predict how the public would respond during and after nuclear attack; disaster events were seen as a natural laboratory in which patterns of human response could be discovered.

The first large-scale sociological investigations of community crises were conducted at the National Opinion Research Center (NORC) at the University of Chicago roughly between 1950 and 1954. The NORC research focused on individual and group behavior in numerous natural and technological emergencies (see Fritz & Marks, 1954, for a discussion of this work). Another major research effort was launched in the mid-1950s by the Disaster Research Group of the National Academy of Sciences and the National Research Council. Summaries and assessments of much of this early research can be found in Fritz (1961), Barton (1969), Dynes (1970), and Kreps (1981). Dynes suggested that this early research had three main foci or levels of analysis: mass behavior, or the reactions of the general public in emergency situations; individual perceptions and actions in crises; and organizational response.

The Disaster Research Center (DRC), established in 1963 at the Ohio State University, has made important contributions to the understanding of community emergency preparedness and response. Now located at the University of Delaware, the DRC is headed and staffed by sociologists, and its research tends to focus primarily on the activities of community sectors, interorganizational networks, organizations, and groups (as opposed to individuals) in disasters and other community crises. The DRC has conducted numerous studies of natural disasters, technological emergencies, student and civil disturbances, and other large-scale community crises. Over the years, various topics have received emphasis in DRC research: organizational adaptation, communication, and decision making in crisis situations (Brouillette & Quarantelli, 1971; Drabek & Haas, 1969; Dynes & Quarantelli, 1977; McLuckie, 1970); disaster as a factor in organizational change (Anderson, 1966; 1972; Kreps, 1973); disaster response by crisis-relevant organizations and groups (Anderson, 1970; Warheit, 1970); emergency medical services and mental health service delivery in disasters (Taylor, 1977; Taylor, Ross, & Quarantelli, 1976; Tierney & Taylor, 1977; Quarantelli, 1983); community preparations for and response to chemical emergencies (Tierney, 1980; Quarantelli, 1984); and emergent groups in disaster preparedness and response (Stallings & Quarantelli, 1985).

Other organizations and disciplines have been actively involved in studies of the social aspects of disasters. Researchers affiliated with the Natural Hazards Research and Applications Information Center at the University of Colorado in Boulder represent a variety of academic fields, including geography, sociology, and economics. The Colorado researchers have tended to focus on the broader topic of how societies and communities perceive and "adjust" (their term) to hazards, rather than on disaster impacts in the immediate emergency period. A range of adjustments is considered in the work of the Natural Hazards group, including land use management, technological interventions, warning systems, disaster insurance, and postdisaster relief and rehabilitation (White & Haas, 1975). Their studies have tended to focus on individual hazards (e.g., flood, earthquake, hurricane, tornado) and on natural, rather than technological agents. Studies by University of Colorado researchers include large-scale surveys of the magnitude of natural hazards and on alternative adjustment strategies (White, 1974); studies on the phases involved in long-term community recovery from natural disasters (Haas, Kates, & Bowden, 1977); cross-cultural studies of hazard vulnerability and management strategies (Burton, Kates, & White, 1978); and research on the economic impact of disasters (Cochrane, 1975). Through its workshops, held annually for the past 11 years, its extensive publications program, and its newsletter, *Natural Hazards Observer,* the University of Colorado group is also a major disseminator of research on disasters.

Another perspective on disasters and hazards has recently been developing at the Center for Technology, Environment, and Development (CENTED) at Clark University in Worchester, Massachusetts. As a result of the 1979 Three Mile Island accident and the Love Canal (New York) and Times Beach (Missouri) toxic episodes—and, more recently, Chernobyl— more and more attention is being paid to technological hazards. Problems related to new and potentially hazardous technologies are a major emphasis in the work of the Clark University group, composed mainly of geographers and academics trained in the area of public policy. Their work is fundamentally concerned with the social construction of risk and the social response to risky technologies; the title of a recent publication by researchers affiliated with CENTED, *Perilous Progress: Managing the Hazard of Technology* (Kates, Hohenemser, & Kasperson, 1985) illustrates the group's research interests. CENTED recently completed a study of the Bhopal catastrophe (Bowonder, Kasperson, & Kasperson, 1985) and is currently conducting research on the Chernobyl disaster (Goble, Hohenemser, & Kasperson, 1987).

New research units continue to form as the field of disaster research expands and as people trained by the first generation of disaster researchers develop their own careers. Several faculty members from different social science disciplines have formed the Office of Hazard Studies in the School of Public Affairs at Arizona State University and have conducted studies on a number of topics, including warning and evacuation processes in disasters (Perry, 1983; Perry & Mushkatel, 1984) and various aspects of the earthquake problem. A considerable amount of research is also being done by researchers in the Department of Sociology at Colorado State University (Mileti, Hartsough, Madson, & Hufnagel, 1984; Mileti, Hutton, & Sorensen, 1981).

As a result of these research activities, there is now a rather extensive knowledge base concerning a number of facets of the social response to hazards and disasters. Major attempts have been made over the years to systematically summarize that information. Among the most important recent efforts at review and codification are those of Mileti, Drabek, & Haas (1975), Quarantelli and Dynes (1977), and Drabek (1986). The sections that follow focus on some of the key findings in the literature.

Researchers and policy makers tend to agree on a convention that divides the disaster problem and its management into four phases: (1) *mitigation*, or activities designed to reduce the probability of disaster occurrence or the magnitude of disaster impacts; (2) *preparedness*, which includes activities such as the preparation of plans, public education, and responder training, designed to increase the capacity of social units to respond in the event of an emergency; (3) *response*, or the performance of disaster-related tasks such as evacuation, search and rescue, care of persons who are injured, and the provision of emergency assistance; and (4) *recovery*, or longer term efforts to rebuild the disaster-stricken community and its institutions. Although activities in each of these four phases are potentially relevant to mental health and the delivery of mental health services, the response and recovery phases hold the most direct implications for the conduct of disaster mental health programs. Therefore, this discussion will focus more on those two postdisaster phases than on the predisaster community context, although some relevant topics in that area will be covered. The focus will be strongly on community, organizational, and household impacts (rather than individual responses).

HAZARD AWARENESS, MITIGATION, AND PREPAREDNESS IN U.S. COMMUNITIES

Earlier, in discussing the concept of disaster, it was noted that human activity and social processes play a major role in creating disasters. Much of what occurs after the impact of the disaster agent reflects predisaster policies and patterns of behavior. The manner in which disaster management is defined and implemented in U.S. society is related to the losses, social disruption, and recovery problems communities experience. Four important aspects of the predisaster setting will be discussed here.

Political Salience of Disaster Preparedness

Some studies of public views on disaster preparedness (e.g., Turner, Nigg, Paz, & Young, 1980) have indicated that the general public accepts the need for disaster planning and believes hazard management is an appropriate role for government. However, other research (Rossi, Wright, & Weber-Burdin, 1982) has suggested that disasters are a very low priority for most of the public, when compared to other community problems such as crime, air pollution, and unemployment. This same research indicated that hazard management issues are not considered important by local and state decision makers, when compared to many other functions government is expected to perform. In short, while hazard mitigation and preparedness are approved of in principle, they are not viewed as high-priority political issues.

Organized support for disaster programs tends to be weak in most communities. Issues are put on the public agenda at all governmental levels because constituencies and organized interest groups exist to push those issues, and this type of support for hazard management seems to be missing in many communities. There are, of course, exceptions to this pattern. Disaster experience can help put hazard management on the political agenda, at least temporarily creating opportunities for increasing public safety. In California, for example, many of the important ordinances and laws to mitigate earthquake hazards were initiated or enacted just after major damaging earthquakes. By and large, however, hazard mitigation and emergency preparedness are not major issues in most U.S. communities during noncrisis times.

Resources and Prestige of Local Emergency Organizations

For organizations, effective performance tends to be associated with control of necessary resources and with linkages to other organizations and institutions important for performance of organizational tasks. In general, community emergency management (or civil defense) organizations lack these characteristics, and thus many are less effective than they could be. While the situation is changing as the field of emergency services becomes more professionalized (Petak, 1984), these agencies still tend to be relatively low in organizational prestige, underfunded, understaffed, and far removed from political decision makers (Quarantelli & Tierney, 1979). The responsibilities of local emergency management offices are broad and their tasks are obviously important, but frequently they lack the means to launch effective programs.

Governmental Approaches to Hazard Management

Inconsistent Policies and Regulations

In the early 1980s, the Federal Emergency Management Agency (FEMA) began promoting the Integrated Emergency Management System (IEMS), an approach that attempts to coordinate the activities of all governmental levels in all four disaster phases (mitigation, preparedness, response, recovery) for all types of hazards. One objective of IEMS is to stimulate communities to take into consideration the entire range of hazards they face and to develop comprehensive management strategies (McLoughlin, 1985). Like other comprehensive "rational-system" sets of guidelines, IEMS is logically sound, but it is actually quite difficult to implement in the current policy context. Numerous agencies at the federal, state, regional, and local level, as well as private entities such as the insurance industry, have responsibilities that relate to hazard management, making coordination very difficult (Petak & Atkisson, 1982).

Policies and programs in the hazards area have developed in a piecemeal fashion and contain many inconsistencies. The management of sudden toxic chemical releases is a case in point. At present, effective handling of chemical emergencies involving community residents is impeded by the fact that overall responsibility for such incidents is still unclear (Zimmerman, 1985). There is no federal legislation that mandates preparedness planning for chemical emergencies, and there is no counterpart to FEMA in the chemical hazards area. Although it has produced emergency planning guidelines (Federal Emergency Management Agency, 1981) and assisted in the relocation of seriously contaminated communities, FEMA actually has no statutory authority for planning for and responding to chemical disasters. Until the Superfund reauthorization in 1986, there were no existing federal regulations designed to mitigate, prepare for, or respond to sudden, large-scale emergencies at chemical facilities. The role of the Environmental Protection Agency centered primarily on monitoring routine, rather than catastrophic, toxic emissions. This kind of confusion complicates attempts to deal with hazards comprehensively.

Emphasis on Postdisaster Relief

In general, government policies and local emergency management agency practices have placed most emphasis on increasing emergency response capability and providing assistance to disaster victims, rather than on long-term hazard mitigation or ensuring community recovery from disasters. To make an analogy with the public health and mental health fields, programs have sought to provide remedies for disorders when they develop, rather than to engage in prevention. In some ways, this has given both local governments and residents little incentive to be concerned about hazards. The pattern has changed somewhat in recent years for some hazards, such as floods; through the National Flood Insurance Program, the government tries to encourage both communities and households to obtain protection against flood losses (Kunreuther, 1978). However, there is still relatively little emphasis placed on encouraging actions in the predisaster period that could reduce disaster-related losses.

Another reason mitigation is underemphasized is that attempts to manage disaster agents typically involve debates about locally important issues such as land use and building codes. It is difficult to restrict development in flood plains and on hillsides that are subject to landslides, because people like to build in such areas. Efforts to reduce hazards may be opposed by powerful local interest groups, such as industry and real estate organizations. Support for proposed programs can also vanish if people are told the programs will lead to the loss of jobs, depress property values, or hurt the local economy.

Attempts to launch hazard mitigation programs often fail. From the standpoint of the local elected official, doing little to address hazards and requesting state and federal disaster assistance after occurrence of an event may appear less costly than attempting to mitigate the problem.

Preparedness efforts such as public education, training of emergency personnel, mobilization of disaster-relevant resources, and the development of preparedness plans tend to be less costly and controversial than attempts to mitigate hazards. Nevertheless, these kinds of activities are also underemphasized in most communities.

Intensive preparedness activities often are confined to a small core of emergency-relevant organizations. Comprehensive interorganizational preparedness efforts are still relatively rare, despite the growing awareness of their importance. Disaster experience tends to stimulate local preparedness efforts, but mainly for the most recent and salient disaster agent, not for other hazards (Mileti et al., 1975). For example, a flood-prone community may have extensive planning for flood emergencies, but not for tornadoes or hazardous materials releases.

Public Awareness and Preparedness

Researchers are beginning to get a better understanding of how objective conditions of risk, hazard perception, and self-protective decisions are related and what factors influence actions people take with respect to hazards. High levels of objective risk are not necessarily associated with subjective risk perception (Drabek, Mushkatel, & Kilijanek, 1983; Mushkatel & Nigg,

1987); studies suggest that residents of disaster-prone communities may not be any more concerned about hazards than those who live in safer areas.

Awareness is generally higher for disaster agents that recur frequently, such as floods, compared with those that occur less often. For example, many people in the central United States are doubtless aware of tornado and flood hazards but are probably not aware of or concerned about the earthquake threat, although very large earthquakes have occurred and will recur in that area. Personal experience with a hazard generally causes hazard perception to be more accurate (Mileti et al., 1975). Concern with particular kinds of hazards can increase as a result of mass media attention or a major emergency; for example, the 1984 Bhopal chemical disaster increased public awareness of chemical hazards and stimulated considerable activity aimed at reducing those hazards.

Even when community residents are aware of natural or technological hazards, this awareness does not necessarily translate into preparedness activity. For example, research on household preparedness for earthquakes in Southern California, an area where awareness of the earthquake hazard is high, indicated that the overwhelming majority of residents had done relatively little to prepare for earthquakes. Less than 10% of those surveyed had engaged in activities such as storing food and water, rearranging kitchen cabinets to prevent spills and breakage, or getting together with neighbors to plan what to do if an earthquake should occur. Only about 13% of the homeowners in the sample had purchased earthquake insurance (Turner et al., 1980).

One possible reason for this lack of willingness to prepare is that people believe that the probability of the hazard actually affecting them is too low to warrant the effort. Other matters that are more pressing on a day-to-day basis take priority. Kunreuther (1978) came to this conclusion after studying decision making with respect to the purchase of flood insurance. Unfortunately, many hazards that contemporary society faces, such as major earthquakes, are in this category of "low probability/high consequence" events, and motivating people to take protective measures with respect to these hazards is difficult.

Another reason that hazard awareness doesn't always lead to preparedness may be that people aren't knowledgeable about potentially effective preparedness strategies. To cope with the probability of disaster, one has to know what to do to lessen the risk; many people simply lack such information. The Kunreuther insurance study (1978), for example, found that most of the persons surveyed knew of the existence of flood and earthquake insurance but also found that nearly two thirds of the residents in high-risk areas didn't know that they were eligible to purchase coverage. A majority of those surveyed did not have accurate information about rates and deductibles for hazard insurance.

The knowledge people have about hazards is derived from a variety of different sources, including folk tales, electronic and print media, government agencies, and scientific sources (Turner et al., 1980). How much people know about specific protective strategies is based in part on the content of the messages they receive from these sources. This demonstrates the importance of increasing accurate reporting about hazards and supporting governmental public education efforts.

A related point is that hazard awareness and emergency preparedness are associated with sociodemographic characteristics, such as income, education, and ethnicity. Studies suggest that, in general, nonminorities and persons with higher socioeconomic status tend to be better prepared for disasters than others (Sims & Baumann, 1972; Turner et al., 1980). On the basis of their review of the literature on minorities and disasters, Perry and Mushkatel (1984) note:

> . . . minorities experience greater relative difficulties than Whites because they have lower incomes and money reserves, are more likely to be unemployed, less likely to have disaster insurance, and more likely to have problems communicating with institutional providers of information about disaster risks and post-impact relief. (p. 35)

When a disaster occurs, low-income and minority households and neighborhoods may thus suffer higher proportional losses (that is, relative to their financial and material resources) and more disruption, and they may find it more difficult to recover.

SOCIAL ASPECTS OF EMERGENCY RESPONSE

Understanding Behavior in Emergencies: Reality versus Myth

The social activities and processes that occur in a community stricken by disaster are very different from popular representations. Social scientists have documented extensively what actually happens in community crises and have contrasted these facts with widespread beliefs about how people behave (see Quarantelli & Dynes, 1972; Wenger, Dykes, Sebok, & Neff, 1975; Wenger, James, and Faupel, 1985). Three of the most significant of these disaster myths will be outlined briefly and juxtaposed with more accurate information.

Panic

Popular conceptions of disaster indicate that panic flight is common among residents in the stricken area. Mass media reports and disaster films typically depict community residents as engaging in irrational, headlong flight to avoid danger. In actuality, panic flight (as opposed to anxiety or subjective feelings of peril) is very rare in disaster situations. Summarizing the literature on this topic, Mileti et al. (1975) conclude, "Most persons confronting natural disasters do not suddenly become wildly disorganized and irrational; in immediate danger they may flee, but that hardly justifies the stereotype'' (p. 58).

Where panicky activity does develop, it occurs as a result of a very specific set of circumstances (Quarantelli, 1954; 1981) that are likely to be present in a very small number of situations. Panic has been reported in many disasters, but when investigated empirically, such reports have often proved unfounded. The 1977 Beverly Hills nightclub fire is a well-known case in point, and many others could be cited (see Sime, 1980). Contrary to the myth, most people react quite rationally in disaster situations; they do not behave in an asocial, irrational manner as the "panic" image suggests.

Helplessness and Dependence on Outside Assistance

Another commonly held belief about communities in disaster is that residents in the stricken area go through a period of being so stunned and shocked following disaster impact that they are out of touch with events and unable to engage in meaningful self-help activity. Conversely, it is frequently thought that without assistance from outside sources, victims will be unable to engage in necessary disaster tasks such as search and rescue. An event such as a large explosion or the Hyatt Regency skywalk collapse can certainly create considerable short-term shock and anxiety among victims. However, even in such extreme cases, victims quickly become active and behave in an altruistic and highly adaptive manner. On this issue, Wenger et al. (1985) note:

> The disaster literature is replete with findings indicating that the initial search and rescue activity, casualty care, and restoration of services are accomplished by the victims themselves, with the assistance of people and organizations from the immediate filter area . . . the immediate emergency period is epitomized by adaptive behavior, intense activity, and the formation of new groups. (pp. 36, 37)

Similarly, it is typically assumed that disaster victims and evacuees are dependent on government and private agencies for provision of postdisaster shelter. In actuality, the vast majority of displaced disaster victims—up to 90%—do not use public shelters; they prefer instead to stay with relatives and friends.

The proportion of persons who use public shelters in disasters can vary as a function of factors such as the size of the disaster event and the level of community preparedness, but the percentage is never large (Perry, Lindell, & Green, 1981). For example, following the 1983 Coalinga, California earthquake, which left approximately 1,000 persons (out of a population of 6,500) temporarily homeless, very few victims used the public shelter. They chose to stay with friends, neighbors, and relatives or in tents and campers on their own property (Tierney, 1985).

Looting

Disasters are widely assumed to bring out the worst in people. For example, looting or the necessity for taking precautions against looting are almost always reported following major natural disasters, and disaster victims are typically worried about its occurrence. Contrary to this notion, in the United States looting has been found to be extremely uncommon in natural disasters (Dynes & Quarantelli, 1968: Quarantelli & Dynes, 1972) but much more widespread in civil disturbances such as those that occurred in the 1960s. In the small number of cases where looting does occur in disasters, it tends to be the work of individuals from outside the community, acting alone, who seize upon a momentary opportunity for gain. Community residents strongly condemn this behavior. In contrast, looting in civil disorders is typically a collective activity that is engaged in by community members with community approval (Quarantelli & Dynes, 1969).

Wenger et al., (1975) studied the prevalence of these and other erroneous beliefs in a random sample of Delaware residents and found it to be very high. For example, 83% of the respondents in that study believed panic to be a major problem in disasters, and almost 75% agreed with the idea that victims are dazed and helpless after disaster. Wenger et al (1985) replicated the survey in three other communities. They found that misconceptions—particularly the myths about panic and looting behavior—were widespread, *even in communities with extensive disaster experience*. To their surprise, they also found local officials with emergency responsibilities to be only slightly better informed than community residents.

One of the things these researchers discovered is that people in our society base their impressions about disaster behavior mainly on mass media accounts. The more respondents found the mass media salient as sources of information, the more likely they were to hold erroneous conceptions about social behavior in disasters. Even where individuals have been through a disaster and have experienced what actually happens, they tend to discount their experience as atypical.

The prevalence of these beliefs means that they can influence the behavior of disaster victims and emergency organizations in disaster situations. Wenger et al. (1985) point out that when officials hold erroneous beliefs, problems such as the following can occur:

> Organizational resources may be allocated toward solving unrealistic problems. Necessary warning and protective information may not be distributed in fear of panicking the residents. . . . Valuable personnel and resources may be wasted in unused shelters. Local organizations may not be prepared to integrate their relief and rescue activity with the ongoing, emergency patterned activity of the victims. Equally important, it is likely that disaster planning will not be based upon factual assumptions of social behavior. (p. 225)

Common Patterns of Community and Organizational Response

Studies of disaster-stricken communities have discovered a number of basic patterns and processes that recur during the emergency response period. These include (1) intense community mobilization, (2) increased community consensus, (3) convergence, and (4) organizational adaptation and innovation.

Community Mobilization

Immediately following disaster impact, community participation is very high as people become intensely involved in addressing disaster-generated needs. In his classic book *Communities in Disaster* (1969), Allen Barton refers to a postimpact pattern termed "informal mass assault," consisting of mutual assistance by primary groups (e.g., families) and community-oriented activities by both individuals and groups. This mass mobilization, at first relatively spontaneous and uncoordinated, tends to focus on the most immediate priorities—saving lives and caring for injured persons.

Even in the most severe disasters, nonvictims typically outnumber victims, so the community retains the ability to provide for itself. In natural disasters and multiple-casualty incidents, for example, it is typically community residents and not formally designated emergency care providers who first assist victims and transport them to hospitals and first-aid stations (Quarantelli, 1983). The 1985 earthquake in Mexico City graphically illustrated this pattern of intense community mobilization and helping behavior. If the emergency period is of long duration or if preemergency planning was extensive, these spontaneous helping activities become more routinized and coordinated over time (see Organizational Adaptation to Crisis, in this chapter).

Community Consensus

During nondisaster times, residents' time and energy are devoted to a number of different activities, and their lives tend to be relatively compartmentalized. Communities also typically experience some degree of manifest and latent conflict; community life is accompanied by ongoing debates about how resources should be distributed and which issues should have priority, and some stakeholder groups with more power than others may dominate the decision-making process.

In contrast, the emergency period in communitywide disasters is characterized by agreement on community priorities and the suspension of conflicts. There is a high level of consensus on values and norms. This emergency consensus centers on newly developed priorities that include care for disaster victims (the most important priority); restoration of essential community services (e.g., utilities, hospital services); and the maintenance of public order and community morale (Dynes, 1970). Other important community activities such as education, the production of goods, and the provision of nonessential services may be temporarily suspended as all residents focus on emergency tasks. Conflict and competition among community groups, typically accepted and even expected during nondisaster times, are reduced as a result of emergent norms that emphasize doing as much as possible to help disaster victims and the community in general. Community participation increases dramatically following disaster impact as residents try to do anything they can to provide assistance.

This broad emergency consensus does not, of course, extend to all aspects of the disaster response, nor does it continue indefinitely. Although the community agrees on goals and priorities, it is quite common for responding organizations to be unclear about their disaster roles (see discussion below on organizational adaptation in crisis), and this can lead to disputes. As the community returns to normal, predisaster conflicts reemerge. After the immediate crisis passes, it is also not unusual for bitterness to develop between residents of the stricken community and extracommunity agencies that provide assistance. Despite such occurrences, there is a period of time immediately after the disaster when social solidarity and social participation are extremely high, and all the energies of community residents are focused on common goals.

Convergence

Although erroneous popular images focus on the flight of people *out of* the stricken area, a major problem communities actually face in disasters is convergence, or the movement of people and resources *into* the stricken area. The convergence problem was first identified by Fritz and Mathewson (1957) and has been extensively documented in disasters. Individuals and groups who become part of the convergence phenomenon include those who want to offer assistance or find out about loved ones in the disaster community, members of the press, and curiosity seekers who just want to see what is going on. Extracommunity organizations (e.g., ambulance companies) wishing to provide emergency assistance also converge on the site, regardless of whether they are actually asked to help. Ironically, mass media efforts to provide timely information about the disaster and to urge people not to enter the area may have the opposite effect.

There is a natural tendency for members of our society to provide material assistance to disaster victims, but managing all these additional resources can become a problem for local emergency officials. Unfortunately, many of the resources that converge on disaster-stricken communities—food, medicines, and clothing—may not be needed (Dynes, 1970).

The convergence phenomenon is also apparent in the area of communications. People inside and outside of the community want information about the event; emergency organizations are typically inundated with requests for information. Telephone systems in the stricken area are usually overloaded by this excess demand; they may not function properly for some time after disaster impact. The amount of information that emergency organizations must process greatly escalates in the postimpact phase, leading to increased stress on emergency personnel.

In federally declared disasters, shortly after the immediate emergency period concludes (usually within 3 or 4 days after impact), another more formalized type of convergence begins as representatives of federal agencies and other relief organizations come to the community to offer various kinds of disaster assistance. The provision of disaster assistance does not always go smoothly, and conflicts can develop during this period. Typically, community residents begin receiving large volumes of new, unfamiliar, and sometimes contradictory information about disaster assistance. They tend to become impatient with what they perceive as the overly bureaucratic perspective of government relief agencies. Residents may also be quite surprised when they discover that the terms under which some relief is offered are not entirely favorable and could actually leave them worse off (see Tierney, 1985, for an example of California earthquake victims' dismay about the loans offered by the Small Business Administration).

Organizational Adaptation to Crisis

A key feature of disasters is that they create a very high demand for a range of activities (e.g., life-saving, medical care, the provision of social support, debris removal) that exceeds the community's normal response capability. Under such high levels of social system stress, system subunits—organizations, groups, and individuals—must adapt. For organizations, adaptation means undergoing changes in structure and functioning which enable them to perform disaster-related tasks more effectively.

One typology of organizational adaptation to stress that has been used extensively (see Dynes, 1970; Stallings, 1978) classifies community organizations according to two dimensions—tasks and structure—and according to whether or not either dimension undergoes change during the emergency period. This classification yields four types of organizational response to disaster (see Figure 1.1). Type I organizations, which are termed *established* organizations, are those that perform the same tasks for which they are responsible during nondisaster times, with basically the same organizational structure. Relatively specialized and highly structured, these organizations do not attempt to take on new tasks or incorporate new members. They simply do more of the same things they were doing before the disaster. Examples of established organizations include coroners' offices that take charge of improvised morgues and utility companies that engage in emergency repairs to restore service.

Type II, or *expanding,* organizations include organizations that tend to be small and comparatively inactive during nondisaster times but increase in size during the emergency, and which also become involved in activities different from their everyday, nondisaster tasks. The Red Cross and the Salvation Army are examples of organizations that expand in disasters. Such organizations can experience difficulty in adapting, because their structure

Tasks

		Routine	Nonroutine
Organizational Structure	*Same as Predisaster*	*Type I* *Established*	*Type III* *Extending*
	New	*Type II* *Expanding*	*Type IV* *Emergent*

Figure 1.1 Forms of organizational adaptation in disasters. Based on illustration in Dynes, 1970.

changes at the same time that they are required to engage in relatively unfamiliar and complex tasks.

Type III, or *extending,* organizations retain their predisaster structure but engage in disaster-related tasks that are new for those organizations. What changes for these organizations is what they are doing in the emergency period, not their membership or authority structure. Examples include community service organizations that mobilize to assist disaster victims and business enterprises that provide needed resources and personnel.

Type IV, or *emergent,* groups are "private citizens who work together in pursuit of collective goals relevant to actual or potential disasters but whose organization has not yet become institutionalized" (Stallings & Quarantelli, 1985). Emergent groups develop in part out of the shared belief that there are disaster-related needs that are not being met by community responders. Such groups devise new structures that address these needs, engaging in tasks that are nonroutine for their members. At least initially, these groups tend to be informal and structurally undifferentiated. Amateur radio operators that organize to provide communications resources for emergency agencies and community residents and the volunteer teams that assisted trapped earthquake victims in Mexico City are examples of Type IV groups.

The presence of these new, adaptive organizational forms is one of the reasons that achieving overall coordination in the emergency response period is difficult. People are anxious to provide assistance, and they mobilize collectively to do so, but many disaster tasks are unfamiliar and participants in the emergency response may lack a clear idea of which organizations and groups are responsible for which activities.

Mental health service providers can be better prepared to work with community organizations following a major disaster if they understand the kinds of adaptive changes organizations are likely to undergo. They should be prepared for "turf" misunderstandings arising as a result of altered organization roles. Workers may find themselves coming into contact with organizational personnel who seem unsure of their disaster roles or appear to lack an awareness of the division of labor in the disaster response. Needless to say, such changes and ambiguities are stressful for organizational members.

It is also likely that organizations that provide mental health services will themselves undergo at least some degree of change in their structure or functioning at the time of a disaster. For example, a mental health center may find itself following a Type II or Type III pattern rather than continuing with its predisaster mode of operations. It will be necessary for workers to understand and adjust to their new crisis roles, which can produce stress.

Factors Affecting Community Crisis Management

It may appear that the community emergency response is uniform across disaster events and communities, but this is not the case. A number of factors can influence the emergency response. Among the most significant factors are disaster experience, predisaster preparedness, and agent characteristics.

Disaster Experience and Predisaster Preparedness

Communities, organizations, and groups learn from experience, incorporating lessons from earlier emergencies into disaster-planning procedures. In general, communities with a history of disasters are better able to respond to those agents.

Some communities are regularly stricken or threatened by particular disaster agents. As a result, "disaster subcultures" can develop, built around knowledge, behavioral practices, and resources intended to increase community and household response capability. In communities where disaster subcultures exist, the emergency response with respect to the focal disaster agent is usually more rapid and more easily coordinated (Weller & Wenger, 1973). These subcultures are most likely to develop with respect to agents that allow for a warning period (e.g., riverine floods and hurricanes) and that have caused extensive damage in the community—particularly to high-status groups who then develop an interest in promoting preparedness (Wenger, 1978).

Disaster subcultures unfortunately tend to be agent-specific. Communities that are very conscious of and well-prepared for one particular agent may still experience problems responding to other kinds of disasters. It cannot be assumed that because a community has developed effective measures for responding to the most common threats that it is well prepared for all potential emergencies.

Research suggests that community preparedness activities do pay off when the event actually occurs. When organizations have a clear understanding of their disaster roles and when good working relationships are established in the predisaster period, the emergency response is less problematic (Mileti, et al., 1975; Quarantelli, 1980).

At the household level, planning also has a positive effect on postimpact behavior. For example, Perry and Mushkatel (1984) found that black and white households that had a plan for evacuating in emergencies were more likely than nonplanners to comply with emergency evacuation orders.

Disaster Agent Characteristics

As stated in an earlier section, disaster agents can be classified in terms of various dimensions, such as predictability and the length of the warning period, and certain kinds of disasters create greater challenges for communities than do other types. (Recall also that these characteristics are, for the most part, not inherent properties of disaster agents as physical events, but are socially determined. The extent to which a disaster can be predicted, for example, depends not so much on the agent as on knowledge of the hazard and the precision of prediction technology.) If a disaster can be forecasted, and if the period of warning is sufficiently long, then the community has a better chance to institute protective measures and coordinate the emergency response. There may thus be fewer deaths and injuries, and less damage and social disruption. Obviously, a disaster with a relatively narrow scope of impact is not as disruptive and difficult to manage as one that affects an entire region; in the former case, more local resources are available for emergency assistance. The severity of the damage produced by an agent also affects response and recovery potential.

Some disaster agents, such as fires and tornadoes, have a one-time impact; they strike, but they do not recur. The community does not face an ongoing threat over a long period of time. Other agents can have a long period of impact (e.g., droughts) or can recur. In some cases, the danger period associated with an agent can last for months or even years. While this gives the community time to adapt, it also means that social disruption lasts longer and residents are subjected to a long-term stressor.

The earthquake hazard is a case in point. The reason major earthquakes are viewed as such a serious hazard, warranting extensive mitigation and preparedness efforts, is related to several characteristics: At present, they cannot be accurately predicted; they occur without warning; they affect a large geographic area; and they have tremendous destructive potential. In the case of great earthquakes (Richter magnitude 8 and higher), aftershocks may go on for months, increasing damage and injuries and demoralizing the population.

Technological disasters may produce distinctive community effects. Some technological disasters, such as nuclear accidents, are greatly feared by the public (Slovic, Fischoff, & Lichtenstein, 1979). This can influence postimpact behavior. For example, getting residents to evacuate for their own safety in response to an official order is typically very difficult in natural disasters. In the 1979 Three Mile Island nuclear accident, however, about 144,000 persons voluntarily left the area around the nuclear plant, even though a general evacuation order had not been issued (Stallings, 1984).

In natural disasters, people comply with evacuation orders because they view government messages about potential danger as credible; one reason people left their homes during the Three Mile Island accident is because they *didn't* trust official messages (Stallings, 1984). Kasperson and Pijawka (1985) suggest that technological events differ from natural disasters in their community impact because they are more unfamiliar and more feared by the public, because their long-term effects on health are not well understood, and because they can involve higher levels of postevent community conflict and a lower level of supportive community mobilization than natural disasters.

THE COMMUNITY IN THE POSTDISASTER RECOVERY PERIOD

The emergency response period is followed by what researchers have called the short-term recovery or restoration period. At this point, the community begins to return to normal. Schools and businesses open, debris is removed, and utilities and community services are restored. This period is succeeded by a reconstruction phase, in which damaged structures are replaced and social and economic activities reach optimal levels (Haas, Kates, & Bowden, 1977).

Relatively few studies of long-term recovery have been undertaken, compared to the volume of data developed on emergency response. However, several general propositions about social processes and disaster impacts in the recovery period have received considerable empirical support. Some of these findings are discussed in the sections that follow.

Significance of Emergency and Restoration Period Decisions

In the aftermath of a major disaster, there is understandably a very strong desire on the part of residents to return to their normal predisaster routines as quickly as possible. Residents want to get back into their homes or rebuild and get on with their lives, and businesses need to resume their activities to avoid serious financial difficulties. Officials responsible for recovery management can find themselves under considerable pressure to make important decisions, sometimes with little supportive data and few guidelines.

The necessity for making major decisions quickly can commit a community to a course of action that presents long-term drawbacks or one that achieves some benefits at the expense of others. For example, following the

1983 Coalinga earthquake, the community faced major decisions, such as how to provide housing for several hundred families whose homes had been destroyed, what to do about seriously damaged commercial buildings in the downtown area, how to provide facilities for displaced businesses, and how to finance community reconstruction. Answers to some very complex questions were required within a matter of weeks, despite a nearly complete lack of experience in recovery planning. Some of the decisions reached may end up having unanticipated negative consequences for the community (Tierney, 1986a).

Major damaging disasters highlight the need for better hazard mitigation. As noted in an earlier section, it is often only after a disaster occurs that residents and officials begin to support changes in land use and building practices or other hazard management strategies. However, mitigation of future disaster damage is not always considered in the recovery process. Other considerations, such as the desire to rebuild the community as it was before the disaster and to finish reconstruction as quickly as possible, can take priority.

Rubin, Saperstein, and Barbee (1985) studied the recovery process in 14 communities that had experienced disasters since 1980 and found variations in the quality of recovery decision making. To manage recovery efficiently, they argue, communities need three general resources: knowledge (e.g., of government assistance program requirements); leadership; and the ability to act—that is, technical and management expertise.

Researchers concur that recovery decisions are made more difficult for communities because so little time and effort are devoted to predisaster recovery planning. Rebuilding after a disaster involves a number of value choices and trade-offs that require detailed study and public debate (Haas et al., 1977), and communities have a better chance of making sound recovery decisions if their recovery goals are articulated and strategies developed before the event occurs. The crisis period that follows a disaster is not the best time to start such discussions.

Household Recovery

The recovery of households, businesses, and other social units is, of course, closely linked to overall community recovery. The main generalization that can be made about families in disaster is that one should be very cautious about making any generalizations. The literature suggests that, just as there are many types of families, there are many ways in which disasters can affect families. For example, disasters appear to be followed by changes in both the internal dynamics of families and in their relationships with outside sources of social support, such as kinship networks (Drabek & Key, 1976; Drabek, Key, Erickson, & Crowe, 1975). While the disaster experience can increase family solidarity and marital satisfaction (Bates, Fogleman, Parenton, Pittman, & Tracy, 1963; Taylor, 1977), it can also disrupt the household and create considerable stress.

Some families appear to be more vulnerable than others to this stress. Determining which families will experience the most difficulty recovering from disasters and what factors encourage recovery is a complex task that researchers have only recently begun to address. As Bolin (1982) notes, family recovery is influenced by many factors, including family characteristics, social support, governmental aid, and insurance coverage.

Two points from the literature on household impacts seem especially relevant to mental health outcomes. First, some studies (e.g., Bolin, 1982; Drabek & Key, 1984; Mileti et al., 1975) suggest that, other things being equal, families with low socioeconomic status and those who are socially marginal (e.g., elderly persons) are more likely than other groups to experience economic problems in the recovery period. Second, the manner in which postdisaster assistance is managed can be a major source of stress for families. For example, the housing provided for displaced families—specifically mobile homes placed in group sites—can add to family stress, disruption, and social isolation (Bolin, Erikson, 1976; Gleser, Green, & Winget, 1981; Hall & Landreth, 1975).

Government disaster assistance can help the family replace lost goods, giving the appearance of economic recovery, but at the same time it may significantly increase the family's indebtedness (Rossi, Wright, Weber-Burdin, & Pereira, 1983; Vinso, 1977). As noted earlier, the traditional approach to dealing with disasters has been to compensate victims, rather than to reduce losses through mitigation projects, increased community and household preparedness, or mandated disaster insurance coverage. However, the conditions for disaster assistance have in recent times become more stringent and less advantageous to recipients. Thus, while victims' homes and possessions may be restored (and may in fact be better) after a disaster, the owners may also be saddled with additional debts.

Community Conflict in the Recovery Period

The recovery period following major disasters tends to be marked by conflict and disillusionment. Predisaster political and interest group rivalries re-emerge, and old issues are reactivated. Additionally, the recovery process itself can become a topic of intense debate. Reconstruction typically involves decisions on issues such as zoning and land use that mobilize community interest groups. Should the community be rebuilt as it was before the disaster, or should it be different? Should reconstruction occur as rapidly as possible, or should there be a moratorium on building so the community has time to plan more comprehensively? If victims were living in structures that did not conform to the zoning laws before the disaster, should they be allowed to rebuild a similar structure on the same site? Conflict can rage over such issues. Conflicts between governmental levels (local, state, and federal) are also not unusual following disasters. Disputes may be particularly rancorous when officials at different levels represent opposing political parties (Quarantelli & Dynes, 1976).

The volume of work and the number of decisions local officials face in the recovery period are greatly increased; decisions are made rapidly, and the usual procedures are sometimes bypassed. This can lead residents to feel that they are not being adequately consulted and informed about governmental actions; questions of equity and fairness in recovery programs typically arise. After the 1983 Coalinga earthquake, respondents in a random sample of households were asked for their assessments of governmental activities at two different points: 6 weeks after the earthquake, and 1 year later. Approval ratings, which were high at first, dropped in the second survey, particularly for local and federal government performance (Tierney, 1985). Discontent may be particularly high among recipients of disaster assistance. Bolin (1982), for example, has extensively documented the negative opinions of tornado victims concerning the management of disaster programs, especially FEMA housing and Small Business Administration loans.

CONCLUSIONS AND IMPLICATIONS

The foregoing sections have attempted to give an overview of research on the social and organizational aspects of the preimpact, emergency, and recovery periods in major disasters. A number of points have been made about social processes that are typical for communities facing the reality or the threat of disaster (e.g., that emergent groups are common during the emergency period) and about what not to expect (e.g., panic). Using this material as a background, the chapter concludes with a list of recommendations on actions mental health service providers can take to help reduce the negative impacts of disasters.

1. *The best way to reduce postdisaster community stress is to prevent it from happening.* Disruption of family and work life, grief over the loss of loved ones, and nostalgia for lost homes and possessions are major factors in victim stress. These negative effects can be eliminated or substantially reduced through the adoption of better mitigation and preparedness measures. Mental health workers and organizations should be active in efforts to reduce disaster losses.

2. *Making mental health an element in the disaster preparedness process will ensure better postdisaster coordination.* Comprehensive preparedness planning can help communities respond more efficiently and effectively to disaster impact. If mental health workers expect to coordinate with other emergency organizations such as emergency medical service providers,

emergency management organizations, and fire and police departments when a disaster occurs, they should establish linkages with these organizations during normal times.

3. *Mental health service providers should have a role in community educational programs.* Campaigns to inform the public about disasters tend to consist mainly of lists of "dos and don'ts": "Make sure you have a flashlight"; "Store water"; "Turn off the gas if you think you have a leak"; and the like. While valuable, such directives do not address the range of concerns that community residents have with regard to disasters. Mental health workers are the appropriate persons to provide information on human behavior and social processes in emergencies and to tell residents what to expect when disaster strikes. Service providers should also attempt to communicate with public officials about such issues, to be sure that the planned emergency actions are based on correct assumptions about how the public will react to a community crisis.

4. *Mental health organizations should be prepared to adapt in emergencies and to work with both existing community organizations and emergent groups.* The organizational structure and division of labor that exist in mental health organizations during nondisaster times may not be well suited for emergency operations. Mental health workers should consider how their organizations are likely to be affected by a disaster and plan accordingly. Some of the changes that can be anticipated include shifting from a 9-to-5 to a 24-hours-a-day schedule, providing services at sites that are different from the usual settings, taking on local volunteers and/or mental health workers from other communities, and becoming involved in tasks that are not usually considered part of the service provider role.

At the same time, workers should be aware that the structures, roles, and activities of other organizations will also change. They should be prepared for a certain amount of ambiguity and confusion in the postimpact period. As in the predisaster phase, it is important that mental health organizations establish linkages with those organizations that are responsible for coordinating emergency activities—for example, by having a representative at the emergency operations center (EOC). Contacts should also be established with emergent groups; such groups will likely be an important source of information on the needs of disaster victims and on developing problems.

5. *Postdisaster mental health interventions should build upon community strengths.* Disasters mobilize latent community resources and contribute to the emergence of social support networks. Rather than attempting to operate separately, disaster mental health programs should identify and attempt to coordinate with these supportive groupings, and they should facilitate the development of mutual-help networks where they do not exist.

6. *Advocating on behalf of community residents is an appropriate mental health activity.* The negative psychological reactions people manifest following disasters can be traced in part to legitimate grievances about the way

their problems are being handled by persons in authority and to feelings of powerlessness. Actions that mental health workers take on behalf of disaster victims to help them get needed assistance have a positive mental health function. Mental health workers should be prepared to act as advocates for victims in their dealings with administrators of disaster assistance and in their interactions with community leaders.

Keeping in mind that the prevention of disaster-related mental health problems should receive higher priority, it is also appropriate for providers of mental health services to advocate for and work with community residents with respect to predisaster hazard mitigation and preparedness activities. The management of hazards associated with toxic chemicals is a case in point. Because of recent events such as the Bhopal catastrophe, community residents have become increasily concerned about assessing and mitigating chemical hazards, pointing out the need for community right-to-know legislation and improved hazard reduction programs. Working to help such groups gain legitimacy and access to community leaders is the kind of activity that could reduce stress and increase residents' coping capacities.

REFERENCES

Anderson, W. A. (1966). *Disaster and organizational change: A study of some of the long-term consequences of the March 27, 1964 Alaska earthquake.* Unpublished doctoral dissertation, Ohio State University, Columbus.

Anderson, W. A. (1970). Military organizations in natural disaster: Established and emergent norms. *American Behavioral Scientist, 13,* 415–422.

Anderson, W. A. (1972). DRC studies of organizational change. In *Proceedings of the Japan–United States Disaster Research Seminar.* Newark: University of Delaware, Disaster Research Center.

Barton, A. H. (1969). *Communities in disaster: A sociological study of collective stress situations.* Garden City, NJ: Doubleday.

Bates, F. L., Fogleman, C. W., Parenton, V. J., Pittman, R. H., & Tracy, G. S. (1963). *The social and psychological consequences of a natural disaster.* National Research Council Disaster Study No. 18. Washington, DC: National Academy of Sciences.

Bolin, R. C. (1982). *Long-term family recovery from disaster.* Boulder: Institute of Behavioral Science, University of Colorado.

Bowonder, B., Kasperson, J. X., & Kasperson, R. E. (1985). Avoiding future Bhopals. *Environment, 27,* 6–13; 31–37.

Brouillette, J. R., & Quarantelli, E. L. (1971). Types of patterned variation in bureaucratic adaptations to organizational stress. *Sociological Quarterly, 41,* 39–46.

Burton, I., Kates, R. W., & White, G. F. (1978). *The environment as hazard.* New York: Oxford University Press.

Cochrane, H. C. (1975). *Natural hazards and their distributive effects.* Boulder: University of Colorado, Institute of Behavioral Science.

Drabek, T. E. (1986). *Human system responses to disaster: An inventory of sociological findings.* New York: Springer-Verlag.

Drabek, T. E., & Haas, J. E. (1969). Laboratory simulation of organizational stress. *American Sociological Review, 34,* 223–238.

Drabek, T. E., & Key, W. H. (1976). The impact of disaster on primary group linkages. *Mass Emergencies, 1,* 89–105.

Drabek, T. E., & Key, W. H. (1984). *Conquering disaster: family recovery and long-term consequences.* New York: Irvington.

Drabek, T. E., Key, W. H., Erickson, B. E., & Crowe, J. L. (1975). The impact of disaster on kin relationships. *Journal of Marriage and the Family, 37,* 481–494.

Drabek, T. E., Mushkatel, A. H., & Kilijanek, T. S. (1983). *Earthquake mitigation policy: The experience of two states.* Boulder: University of Colorado, Institute of Behavioral Science.

Dynes, R. R. (1970). *Organized behavior in disaster.* Lexington, MA: D. C. Heath.

Dynes, R. R., & Quarantelli, E. L. (1968). Redefinition of property norms in community emergencies. *International Journal of Legal Research, 3,* 100–112.

Dynes, R. R., & Quarantelli, E. L. (1977). *Organizational communications and decision making in crises.* Newark: University of Delaware, Disaster Research Center.

Erikson, K. T. (1976). *Everything in its path.* New York: Simon & Schuster.

Federal Emergency Management Agency. (1981). *Disaster operations: A handbook for local governments,* (CPG-16). Washington, DC: Author.

Fritz, C. E. (1961). Disasters. In R. K. Merton & R. A. Nisbet (Eds.), *Contemporary social problems* (pp. 651–694). New York: Harcourt.

Fritz, C. E., & Marks, E. S. (1954). The NORC studies of human behavior in disaster. *Journal of Social Issues, 10,* 26–41.

Fritz, C. E., & Mathewson, J. H. (1957). *Convergence behavior in disasters.* National Research Council Disaster Study No. 9. Washington, DC: National Academy of Sciences.

Gleser, G. C., Green, B. L., & Winget, C. N. (1981). *Prolonged psychosocial effects of disaster: A study of Buffalo Creek.* New York: Academic Press.

Goble, R., Hohenemser, C., & Kasperson, R. E. (1987, February 14–18). *Nuclear emergency management after Chernobyl.* Paper presented at the 153rd annual meeting of the American Association for the Advancement of Science, Chicago.

Haas, J. E., Kates, R. W., & Bowden, M. J. (1977). *Reconstruction following disaster.* Cambridge, MIT Press.

Hall, P. S., & Landreth, P. W. (1975). Assessing some long-term consequences of a natural disaster. *Mass Emergencies, 1,* 55–61.

Janis, I. L. (1951). *Air war and emotional stress: Psychological studies of bombings and civilian defense.* New York: McGraw-Hill.

Kasperson, R. E., & Pijawka, K. D. (1985). Societal response to hazards and major hazard events: Comparing natural and technological hazards. *Public Administration Review* (Special Issue), *45,* 7–18.

Kates, R. W., Hohenemser, C., & Kasperson, J. X. (Eds.). (1985). *Perilous progress: Managing the hazards of technology.* Boulder, CO: Westview Press.

Kreps, G. A. (1973). *Decision making under conditions of uncertainty: Civil distur-bance and organizational change in urban police and fire departments.* Newark: University of Delaware, Disaster Research Center.

Kreps, G. A. (1981). The worth of the NAS-NRC and DRC studies of individual and social responses to disasters. In J. D. Wright & P. H. Rossi (Eds.), *Social science and natural hazards* (pp. 91–121). Cambridge, MA: Abt Publishing.

Kreps, G. A. (1984). Sociological inquiry and disaster research. *Annual Review of Sociology, 10,* 309–330.

Kunreuther, H. (1978). *Disaster insurance protection: Public policy lessons.* New York: Wiley.

McLoughlin, D. (1985). A framework for integrated emergency management. *Public Administration Review,* (Special Issue), *45,* 145–172.

McLuckie, B. F. (1970). A study of functional response to stress in three societies. Unpublished doctoral dissertation, Ohio State University, Columbus.

Mileti, D. S., Drabek, T. E., & Haas, J. E. (1975). *Human systems in extreme environments: A sociological perspective.* Boulder: University of Colorado, Institute of Behavioral Science.

Mileti, D. S., Hartsough, D. M., Madson, P., & Hufnagel, R. (1984). The Three Mile Island incident: A study of behavioral indicators of human stress. *International Journal of Mass Emergencies and Disasters, 2,* 89–113.

Mileti, D. S., Hutton, J. R., & Sorensen, J. H. (1981). *Earthquake prediction response and options for public policy.* Boulder: University of Colorado, Institute of Behavioral Science.

Mushkatel, A. H., & Nigg, J. M. (1987). The effect of objective risk on key actor support for seismic mitigation policy. *Environmental Management. II,* 77–86.

Perry, R. W. (1983). *Comprehensive emergency management: Evacuating threatened populations.* Greenwich, CT: JAI Press.

Perry, R. W., Lindell, M. K., & Green, M. R. (1981). *The implications of natural hazard evacuation warning studies for crisis relocation planning.* Seattle, WA: Battelle Human Affairs Research Centers.

Perry, R. W., & Mushkatel, A. H. (1984). *Disaster management: Warning response and community relocation.* Westport, CT: Quorum Books.

Petak, W. J. (1984). Natural hazard mitigation: professionalization of the policy-making process. *International Journal of Mass Emergencies and Disasters, 2,* 285–302.

Petak, W. J., & Atkisson, A. A. (1982). *Natural hazard risk assessment and public policy: Anticipating the unexpected.* New York: Springer-Verlag.

Prince, S. H. (1920). *Catastrophe and social change, based upon a sociological study of the Halifax disaster.* Doctoral dissertation, Columbia University, Department of Political Science, New York.

Quarantelli, E. L. (1954). The nature and conditions of panic. *American Journal of Sociology, 60,* 267–275.

Quarantelli, E. L. (1970). Emergent accommodation groups: Beyond current collective behavior typologies. In T. Shebutani (Ed.), *Human nature and collective behavior: Papers in honor of Herbert Blumer* (pp. 111–123). Englewood Cliffs. NJ: Prentice-Hall.

Quarantelli, E. L. (1980). *Evacuation behavior and problems: Findings and implications from the research literature.* Newark: University of Delaware, Disaster Research Center.

Quarantelli, E. L. (1981). Panic behavior in fire situations: Findings and a model from the English language research literature. In *Proceedings of the Fourth Joint Panel Meeting; U.J.N.R. Panel on Fire Research and Safety.* Tokyo: Building Research Institute.

Quarantelli, E. L. (1983). *Delivery of emergency medical services in disasters: Assumptions and realities.* New York: Irvington.

Quarantelli, E. L. (1984). *Sociobehavioral responses to chemical hazards: Preparation for and responses to acute emergencies at the local community level* (Book and Monograph Series No. 17). Newark: University of Delaware, Disaster Research Center.

Quarantelli, E. L. (1985). An assessment of conflicting views on mental health: The consequences of traumatic events. In C. Figley (Ed.), *Trauma and its wake: The study of treatment of post-traumatic stress disorder* (pp. 173–215). New York: Brunner/Mazel.

Quarantelli, E. L., & Dynes, R. R. (1969). Dissensus and consensus in community emergencies: Patterns of looting and property norms. *Il Politico, 34,* 276–291.

Quarantelli, E. L., & Dynes, R. R. (1972). When disaster strikes (it isn't much like what you've heard and read about). *Psychology Today, 5,* 66–70.

Quarantelli, E. L., & Dynes, R. R. (1976). Community conflict: Its absence and its presence in natural disasters. *Mass Emergencies, 1,* 139–152.

Quarantelli, E. L., & Dynes, R. R. (1977). Response to social crisis and disaster. *Annual Review of Sociology, 3,* 23–49.

Quarantelli, E. L., & Tierney, K. J. (1979). Disaster preparation planning. In *Fire safety and disaster preparedness* (AAAS Pub. No. 79-R-3). Washington, DC: Office of Public Sector Programs, American Association for the Advancement of Science.

Rossi, P. H., Wright, J. D., & Weber-Burdin, E. (1982). *Natural hazards and public choice: The state and local politics of hazard mitigation.* New York: Academic Press.

Rossi, P. H., Wright, J. D., Weber-Burdin, E., & Pereira, J. (1983). *Victims of the environment: Loss from natural hazards in the United States, 1970–1980.* New York: Plenum.

Rubin, C. B., with Saperstein, M. D., & Barbee, D. G. (1985). *Community recovery from a major natural disaster.* Boulder: Institute of Behavioral Science, University of Colorado.

Sime, J. D. (1980). The concept of panic. In D. Canter (Ed.), *Fires and human behaviour* (pp. 63–81). London: Wiley.

Sims, J. H., & Baumann, D. D. (1972). The tornado threat: Coping styles of the North and South. *Science, 176,* 1386–1392.

Slovic, P., Fischoff, B., & Lichtenstein, S. (1979). Rating the risks. *Environment, 21,* 14–20; 36–39.

Stallings, R. (1973). The community context of crisis management. *American Behavioral Scientist, 16,* 312–325.

Stallings, R. A. (1978). The structural patterns of four types of organizations in disaster. In E. L. Quarantelli (Ed.), *Disasters: Theory and research* (pp. 87–103). Beverly Hills: Sage.

Stallings, R. (1984). Evacuation behavior at Three Mile Island. *International Journal of Mass Emergencies and Disasters, 2,* 11–26.

Stallings, R. A., & Quarantelli, E. L. (1985). Emergent citizen groups and emergency management. *Public Administration Review* (Special Issue), *45,* 93–100.

Taylor, V. A. (1977). Good news about disaster. *Psychology Today, 11,* 93–94; 124–126.

Taylor, V. A., Ross, G. A., & Quarantelli, E. L. (1976). *Delivery of mental health services in disasters; The Xenia tornado and some implications* (Book and Monograph Series No. 11). Newark: University of Delaware, Disaster Research Center.

Tierney, K. J. (1980). *A primer for preparedness for acute chemical emergencies* (Book and Monograph Series No. 14). Newark: University of Delaware, Disaster Research Center.

Tierney, K. J. (1985). *Report on the Coalinga Earthquake of May 2, 1983.* Sacramento: California Seismic Safety Commission (SSC Report #85-01).

Tierney, K. J. (1986a). Dilemmas in post-earthquake recovery: The case of the 1983 Coalinga, California earthquake. In *Proceedings of the Third U.S. National Conference on Earthquake Engineering* (pp. 2401–2411). El Cerrito, CA: Earthquake Engineering Research Institute.

Tierney, K. J. (1986b, October 5–10). *Disasters and mental health: A critical look at knowledge and practice.* Paper presented at the Italy–United States Conference on Disaster Research, University of Delaware, Disaster Research Center, Newark.

Tierney, K. J., & Taylor, V. A. (1977). EMS Delivery in mass emergencies: preliminary research findings. *Mass Emergencies. 2,* 151–157.

Turner, R. H., Nigg, J. M., Paz, D. H., & Young, B. S. (1980). *Community response to the earthquake threat in Southern California.* Los Angeles: University of California Institute for Social Science Research.

Vinso, J. D. (1977). Financial implications of natural disasters: Some preliminary indications. *Mass Emergencies, 2,* 205–217.

Warheit, G. J. (1970). Fire departments: Operations during major emergencies. *American Behavioral Scientist, 13,* 362–368.

Warheit, G. J. (1976). A note on natural disasters and civil disturbances: Similarities and differences. *Mass Emergencies, 1,* 131–137.

Weller, J. M., & Wenger, D. E. (1973, May). *Disaster subcultures: The cultural residues of community disasters.* Paper presented at the annual meeting of the North Central Sociological Association, Cincinnati.

Wenger, D. E. (1978). Community response to disaster: Functional and structural alterations. In E. L. Quarantelli (Ed.), *Disasters: Theory and research* (pp. 17–47). Beverly Hills: Sage.

Wenger, D. E., Dykes, J., Sebok, T., & Neff, J. (1975). It's a matter of myths: An empirical examination of individual insight into disaster response. *Mass Emergencies, 1,* 33–46.

Wenger, D. E., James, T. F., & Faupel, C. E. (1985). *Disaster beliefs and emergency planning.* New York: Irvington.

White, G. F. (Ed.) (1974). *Natural hazards: Local, national, global.* New York: Oxford University Press.

White, G. F., & Haas, J. E. (1975). *Assessment of research on natural hazards.* Cambridge, MIT Press.

Zimmerman, R. (1985). The relationship of emergency management to governmental policies on man-made technological disasters. *Public Administration Review* (Special Issue), *45,* 29–39.

CHAPTER 2

A Classification Scheme for Disasters

MICHAEL R. BERREN, JOSE M. SANTIAGO, ALLAN BEIGEL,
AND SUE A. TIMMONS

"Kindly let me help you before you drown," said the monkey as he placed the fish safely up in the tree.

ALAN WATTS

This lesson, symbolically presented by Alan Watts, has great significance in thinking about disasters and the planning for disaster intervention. A common, but not empirically supported, assumption is that following major disasters, victims develop psychoses or other major mental health disorders. Based upon the expectation of mass psychoses and disabling anxiety and depression, a logical conclusion would be to ensure readily accessible psychiatric/psychological services for the victims of disasters. These services would include crisis intervention, short- and long-term counseling, psychotropic medications, and such. As pointed out by Baisden and Quarantelli (1981) of the Disaster Research Center at Ohio State University, however:

> To assume this approach, or to set up programs with a basically medical, one-to-one delivery model, is to focus on the *wrong* techniques by the *wrong* providers, for the *wrong* clients, or at least for the *wrong* problems of the clients. (p. 197)

The reason that medical, one-to-one service delivery intervention is inappropriate is that the literature (despite some methodological flaws to be discussed later) indicates that severe disaster-related psychiatric disorders rarely occur (Baum, 1985). And the few victims who do experience clinically significant symptoms can almost always be served through the existing public and private clinical services (Baisden & Quarantelli, 1981).

Two authors of this chapter learned this lesson firsthand while working at the large community Mental Health Center, Tucson, Arizona. In 1978 a plane crash occurred about one-half mile from the Center. The 7-D Corsair II jet fighter crashed in the street approximately 100 feet from the fence that surrounded a local junior high school (Berren, Beigel, & Ghertner, 1980). Upon impact, the aircraft ignited into a wall of flames several stories high. Two university students were burned to death in their cars and six others received second- and third-degree burns. The crash and subsequent incineration of the victims were witnessed by at least 100 students who were outside eating lunch at the time. The explosion and fire resulted in many students and teachers running hysterically through the school yard and school building.

Within hours after the crash, plans were already established to have clinical staff from the Mental Health Center go to the school the next morning. The basic strategy was to provide crisis counseling and possibly to establish the groundwork for more long-term counseling to those many students who it seemed certain would develop anxiety and depressive symptoms over the next few weeks. The well-intentioned effort, however, was in vain.

The assumption that there would be a flood of psychiatric emergencies was incorrect. Students and teachers wanted information about what had happened, who was to blame, and how likely it was that it might happen again. The students who had physiological reactions, for example, vomiting, at the time of the crash seemed most interested in discussing why they reacted the way they did. Their primary interest was in information. But the anticipated acute anxiety, sleep disturbances, and the like simply never developed. Despite the fact that school personnel and parents were well aware that the Mental Health Center was equipped to deal with problems that students might be having, not one student was ever officially identified as having any difficulties that indicated a need for psychological counseling. (Given the Center's excellent relationship with school officials and positive regard in the community, it is assumed that lack of referrals was not a function of reluctance to come to the mental health center.) Admittedly, this was a small disaster, but it was a learning experience in that the preconceived idea of the victims' needs was inaccurate.

The purpose of this chapter is to compare and contrast various types of disasters, and in doing so, to describe a model for conceptualizing the different disasters that have been reported in the literature. The reason for developing such a scheme is simple. On the one hand, a great deal has been written under the rubric of disaster. And by default, much of the literature discusses the disaster events as if they were a unidimensional phenomenon. On the other hand, the resulting impact on individual victims and systems described in these same articles is often quite diverse. Some research suggests minimal adverse emotional consequences following a disaster (e.g., Acquire, 1980; Baisden & Quarantelli, 1981; Fairley, 1986). Other research suggests significant emotional consequences (e.g., Green, 1982; Logue & Hansen, 1980; Newman, 1977). And as might be expected, there are articles that suggest moderate and short-term consequences, but nothing of major significance (e.g., Poulshock & Cohen, 1975). For a thorough analysis, Hartsough (1985) is an excellent resource for the measurement of the psychological consequences of disaster.

For example, most literature concerning the disaster at Buffalo Creek, West Virginia, has reported severe, widespread, and long-term psychological consequences following the collapse of the dam (e.g., Titchner & Kapp, 1976). In another example, victims of the Mount St. Helens Volcano were symptomatic up to 3 years after the eruptions (Murphy, 1986). According to Baisden and Quarantelli (1981), however, most problems faced by disaster victims can be termed *problems in living,* rather than psychiatric problems. These problems in living are generally transient and do not usually impair social functioning.

A primary reason that the reported emotional consequences to disasters differ in terms of severity and duration is that the disaster events described are generally quite different from one another. About all that the events have in common is that they carry the common label "disaster." The fact is, the emotional consequences following a disaster are a function of the specific type of event that has occurred. And since disasters are not cookie-cutter replicas of each other, it is not surprising that these emotional consequences differ.

The investigation and comparison of consequences following disasters is a very difficult task. In addition to being generally unprepared to collect adequate data following a disaster, researchers eventually employ methodologies and instruments that are often unique to the situation and vary significantly across disaster studies. Unlike other areas of psychological research, where there is a generally accepted methodology, disaster research often follows the specific situation. As such, it is difficult, if not impossible, to compare and contrast the findings of one study with the findings of another study. Given any two investigations of disasters, it is quite likely that (1) the instruments used to measure the emotional consequences are different, (2) the time frames in which consequences are measured probably differ, and (3) the sample populations on which data were collected differ.

As a matter of fact, it is quite likely that not only do the methodologies differ, but also the issues being investigated differ. This becomes quite clear if one reviews the data in Green's (1982) article comparing various disasters. Thus, research tends to show dissimilar outcomes and, to some degree, those differences are a function of the fact that the research itself generally is not comparable. In a more recent review, Melick (1985) reviews approaches to measurement and findings in a variety of disasters.

Methodological concerns aside, research does seem to suggest that the degree of emotional consequences from events labeled disasters is often not the same. The assumption in writing this chapter is that researchers involved in the various disaster investigations have collected reasonably reliable data, which fairly accurately reflect the state of the postdisaster situation. It is further assumed that the differences in the outcomes are, in large part, a function of the fact that the victims of the reported disasters were victims of significantly different types of events. The lack of a conceptual model and of adequate descriptive terms has resulted in the uniform treatment of all these dissimilar events.

Without an understanding of the variables that differentiate disasters and how these variables can act individually and in concert, it is difficult to predict the behavioral consequences of disasters. And the prediction of behavior is essential for planning effective services (and likewise, for preventing plans for unnecessary services).

CHARACTERISTICS OF DISASTER

Before exploring the differences between various types of disasters, it is necessary first to identify the characteristics of, or to define, a disaster. Therefore, the strategy in this chapter will be to first identify the common links that make events disasters. After identifying these links, the next step will be to explore what it is about the events described as disasters that differentiates them from one another.

Fritz (1961) defines a disaster as:

> an event, concentrated in time and space, in which a society, or a relatively self-sufficient subdivision of a society, undergoes severe danger and incurs such losses to its members and physical appurtenances that the social structure is disrupted and the fulfillment of all or some of the essential functions of the society is prevented. Viewed in this way, a disaster is an event that disturbs the vital functioning of a society. It affects the system of biological survival (subsistence, shelter, health, reproduction), the system order (division of labor, authority patterns, cultural norms, social roles), the system of meaning (values, shared definitions of reality, communication mechanisms), and the motivation of the actors within all of these systems. (p. 655)

A somewhat similar definition by McCaughey (1984) defines a disaster as:

> an event that occurs suddenly, unexpectedly, and uncontrollably, that is catastrophic in nature, involves threatened or actual loss of life or property, disrupts the sense of community, and often results in adverse psychological consequences for the survivors. (p. 84)

Another definition (Shah, 1985) describes a disaster as:

> the impinging upon a structured community, by an external force capable of destroying human life or its resources for survival, on a scale wide enough to excite public alarm, to disrupt normal patterns of behavior, to impair or overload any of the central services necessary to conduct normal affairs or for the prevention or alleviation of suffering and loss. (p. 462)

In a somewhat circular definition, Slaby, Lieb, and Tancredi (1981) quote the Disaster Relief Act of 1974 definition of a disaster as:

> a hurricane, tornado, storm, flood, high-water, wind-driven water, tidal wave, tsunami, earthquake, volcanic eruption, landslide, snowstorm, fire . . . which causes damage of sufficient severity and magnitude to warrant disaster assistance. (p. 261)

A common element in all of these definitions of disaster is that the impact of the tragic event is felt by a large (none of the definitions, however, give specific operational measures for "large") group. That is, the crash of a jetliner would probably be classified by most definitions as a disaster, whereas the crash of a single-engine plane with one person aboard (however tragic for the family of the victim), would not be so classified. The fact is, however, that the behavioral/emotional consequences to victims of violence or families of victims of small plane crashes or small fires, and so forth, are every bit as significant as the consequences to victims of large tornadoes or families of victims of major air disasters.

One might reasonably argue that victims of tragedies where there are no other victims face more difficult situations than do victims who are part of a larger group. Groups allow for affiliation and cohesion, which can often be facilitative in the healing process. Thus, for purposes of this chapter, the number of victims will *not* be used to discriminate a disaster from a non-disaster. Rather, the size of the group affected will be used as a variable to differentiate *types* of disasters.

Baum (1985), in one of the best conceptualizations of the topic, suggests that perhaps a stress theory would be best for determining long- and short-term consequences (emotional consequences). As Baum points out, the advantage of a stress theory is that since there is a body of knowledge about stress (and its consequences), knowing how disasters impact on stress will in turn provide a basis for best understanding the emotional consequences of disasters.

For purposes of this chapter, a disaster is defined as *any event that stresses a society, a portion of that society, or even an individual family beyond the normal limits of daily living*. This definition is obviously far more liberal and inclusive (in what is included as a disaster) than the definitions previously cited. It can encompass anything from the death of a spouse in a car accident to the devastation caused by an earthquake. Not included in the definition are events that fall within the realm of stresses of day-to-day living, that is, job layoffs, divorce, broken washing machines, and so forth.

Definitions such as those presented by Fritz (1961) not only limit disasters to events affecting large groups but also exclude events like the accident at the Chernobyl nuclear power plant or toxic waste disasters. That is, Fritz defines a disaster as being confined to a particular time and space. In our new technological society, with its problems of toxic waste, acid rain, and potential nuclear accidents, it is quite plausible that many disasters of the future will no longer be confined either in time or space. The recent accident at Chernobyl, in the Soviet Union, will potentially affect hundreds of thousands of individuals over millions of square miles, for possibly many years. Early reports of the accident suggest that the rates of certain kinds of cancer might increase for years to come. Individuals not yet born may be the major victims of technological disasters such as this.

The same is true of toxic waste problems. Results of toxic waste disasters are not limited in either time or space. The consequences may be years in coming and may affect individuals not living within a confined area. As toxic waste seeps into water supplies and that water either travels or is used in irrigation, the scope of the possible disaster spreads. Thus, as with size of an event, factors involving time and space are not being used in this chapter as criteria for a disaster. Rather, like size, time–space confinement (scope) becomes one of the criteria to differentiate types of disasters.

Establishing a Model

An article by Berren, Beigel, and Ghertner (1980) identified five primary factors that could be utilized to distinguish one disaster from another: (1) type of disaster (natural vs. man-made), (2) duration, (3) degree of personal impact, (4) potential for recurrence, and (5) control over future impact. That article pointed out that all disasters could be rated on each of the five criteria. The five factors were not based upon a statistical analysis, but rather on clinical and system perspectives for what had occurred in these various situations. It was believed that a step needed to be taken to be more specific and precise in the use of the term disaster.

Following that paper, Berren, Beigel, and Barker (1982) have discussed implications of the typology for intervention and Beigel and Berren (1985) have elaborated on the implications of human-induced disasters. Additionally, other researchers have used this model and others in their own analyses of disasters.

Since the original paper, society has witnessed the inevitable occurrence of more disasters. However, in addition to traditional disasters (i.e., earthquakes, floods, tornadoes, plane crashes, etc.), disasters that are specific to our highly technological society and do not fit in the earlier typology have begun to happen.

The clearest example is the nuclear accident that occurred at Chernobyl as this chapter was in preparation. This event (like the ones at Three Mile Island and Love Canal) is of a totally different type from previous disasters, not necessarily in terms of potential size and impact, but rather in terms of the unknown. Unlike the destruction caused by a tornado, which is immediately apparent, the impact of high-technology disasters is often more difficult to see. The impact is not necessarily confined to a particular community or time. Accordingly, there is a need to modify our typology.

The modified model of disasters, seen in Figure 2.1, incorporates much of the older model presented in earlier writings. The variables of (1) "type of disaster" (natural vs. human induced) and (2) "degree of personal impact," remain the same. The third variable, "scope," includes both temporal and geographic dimensions of disasters. The fourth variable in the modified model involves whether or not there is an identifiable "low point" (Baum, 1985). The low point, not considered in the previous model, is now regarded as one of the most critical aspects of classifying a disaster. It will certainly become a factor of concern over the next few decades as breakdowns begin to occur in our technological society. The final variable, "disaster size," is one that initially tends to affect systems to a greater extent than it does individuals. But as systems are affected, secondary victims will be impacted, and as a consequence, the size of a disaster does not become a very important issue.

Two variables have been removed from the model—"duration" and "control" over future impact—not because they are no longer important, but rather because they seem to collapse quite well within other variables. Additionally, the variable, "probability of future recurrence," was removed because it seemed less related to behavioral and emotional consequences than it does to system planning for the future.

The reason for only including five variables or factors is the need to limit the list at some point. The purpose in classifying disasters is to provide a conceptual framework for better understanding of the phenomenon. Identifying variables helps in the clarification process, but too many variables may be more than one can cognitively handle. The always present normal curve is a reminder that, adding too many variables to the clarification process may serve to muddy the waters rather than to clear them.

As can be seen in Figure 2.1, the model theoretically allows for 32 different types of disasters. In reality, however, certain combinations are implausible, if not impossible. For example, natural disasters that are large but have a limited scope, that is, a typical large tornado, are by definition going to have a low point. Therefore, rather than resembling a model akin to the periodic table in chemistry, that is, one that has an objectifiable reality, this model includes five variables that seem to help in the understanding of those events that generally receive the label of disaster.

Having some common language will enable those persons involved in disaster interventions to become more cognizant of the subtleties not generally discussed; hence, language is a very important part of the classification scheme. It has been demonstrated quite clearly by Whorf (1956) that language directly affects the limits of perception. For example, one who has only one or two words for snow, has limited perception of the nuances that make one type of snow different from another. A culture that has a language with dozens of words for various types of snow will be better able to perceive these subtle differences.

The same holds true for disasters. Using the global term *disaster* tends

		Human Induced		Natural		Limited Scope	High Scope
		Large	*Small*	*Large*	*Small*		
No Low Point	*Low Personal Impact*						
	High Personal Impact						
Low Point	*Low Personal Impact*						
	High Personal Impact						

Figure 2.1. Disaster typology. *Source:* Frederick (1980).

to create blindness to the subtle (and not so subtle) differences among those events. The use of a classification scheme like the one proposed here should facilitate the identification of these differences.

TYPE OF DISASTER (NATURAL VERSUS HUMAN-INDUCED DISASTERS)

The first criterion by which disasters can be differentiated is whether they are natural or human-induced. At one end of the continuum are disasters like tornados, hurricanes, and earthquakes, and at the other end are events of terrorism. Frederick (1980), recognizing that the two types of disasters are not equivalent, compared the consequences to victims. He suggests that the victims of the two types of disasters differ in terms of (1) the emotional stages they pass through, (2) the psychological symptoms they suffer, and (3) the social processes they encounter.

One of the basic reasons for the differences is the *perceived involvement* of the victims. According to Frederick (1980), victims of natural disasters are perceived as victims of events totally beyond their control. Victims of human-induced violence, on the other hand, are often perceived as being partially responsible for their fate. The specific differences, as conceived by Frederick, are presented in the left side of Figure 2.2.

Review of the literature in the area of human-induced disasters leads one

Natural Disasters	Human Induced	Probable Impact of No Low Point
Phases	*Phases*	*Phases*
1. Initial impact	1. Initial impact	Anticipation of impact
2. Heroism	2. Acceptance	
3. Honeymoon	3. Interaction with perpetrators	
4. Disillusionment	4. Disintegration	
5. Reorganization	5. Acquiescence/surrender	
Psychological Symptoms	*Psychological Symptoms*	*Psychological Symptoms*
Anxiety	Anxiety	Anxiety
Phobias concerning event	Phobias concerning event	Depression
Little guilt concerning other victims	Guilt concerning others	Depression
Paranoia concerning government officials	Mild annoyance concerning government officials	Paranoia
Social Processes	*Social Processes*	*Social Processes*
Feelings of loss	Feelings of loss	Feelings of nonresolution
Acceptance by others	Rejection by others	Doubt by others concerning genuineness of complaints
No humiliation	Humiliation	Lack of cohesion
No doubt by others concerning genuineness of complaints	Doubt by others concerning genuineness of complaints	
Short-term cohesion	Long-term cohesion	

Figure 2.2. Consequences of disaster.

to the conclusion that the term is synonymous with acts of violence such as kidnappings and terrorism. There are, however, many human-induced disasters that have nothing to do with terrorism. Events such as accidents in nuclear power plants and toxic spills are certainly within the realm of human-induced disasters and occur with equal, if not greater, frequency than terrorism. Other examples of human error resulting in disasters are airline crashes involving human error and faulty building construction resulting in exacerbation of earthquake damage. Additionally, as pointed out by Beigel and Berren (1985), the distinction between a natural and human-induced disaster is not always clear.

In cases of terrorism or mass kidnappings, a human-induced conclusion is straightforward. Often, however, the disaster is a function of both natural occurrences and human error or human involvement. For example, the worst airline disaster in history was a function of both fog (a natural phenomenon) and miscommunication (human error) between the control tower and the planes ("Airline Officials Speculate," 1977). Similarly, buildings with inadequate smoke alarm systems or poor designs are potentially going to intensify the consequences of a natural disaster. A recent example occurred in Mexico City in 1985. The reports following the earthquake suggest that building codes and faulty construction resulted in much of the tragedy ("Heavy Damage," 1985).

Two Types of Human-Induced Disasters

Just as disasters can be distinguished as natural or human-induced, human-induced disasters can be further subdivided into the ones that are acts of omission versus the ones that result from acts of commission.

Acts of Omission

Acts of omission are generally not the kind of human-induced disaster reported in the literature. They are, however, the type of disaster likely to occur at ever-increasing rates in the years to come. These disasters result not necessarily because of malevolent intent, but rather because of poor planning or attempts to save money, resources, or time. Negligence is often a term associated with acts of omission.

As evidence that acts of omission can cause significant problems, there are presently 802 cities and towns designated for toxic waste cleanup by the Environmental Protection Agency (Federal Register, 1987). The specific problems range from contaminated groundwater to asbestos contamination. The toxicity is often caused by the dumping of chemicals. And the dumping is not an act of terrorism, but rather a cost savings or convenience to various companies. Other examples of acts of omission occur in flooding, earthquakes, and fire (Beigel & Berren, 1985).

A distinguishing aspect of omission disasters is the time frame within which they occur. Unlike natural disasters and acts of terrorism, which are often immediate, disasters resulting from acts of omission are often preceded by a "ticking time bomb" effect. An example is Buffalo Creek, which was, at least partially, a result of an act of omission. The years preceding the eventual disaster were filled with anticipation of what was to come (Rangell, 1976).

Acts of Commission

Disasters under this category include terrorism, mass kidnappings, and other purposeful violence. A graphic example would be the mass kidnapping that occurred in Chowchilla, California (Terr, 1979). On July 15, 1976, children on a school bus were kidnapped and buried alive for 27 hours. Eventually the ordeal ended with no physical harm to the children. After the ordeal, however, reports of nightmares came from the children, and reports of guilt came from the parents.

Just as natural disasters differ from human-induced disasters, acts of commission can be distinguished from acts of omission in terms of (1) the phases victims pass through, (2) the symptoms that might develop, and (3) the social processes that are involved.

The primary difference between an act of omission and one of commission is in terms of the initial impact. With acts of omission, the initial impact is significantly different from both acts of commission and natural disasters. With many acts of omission, the initial impact follows a public report of the precipitating events as opposed to the events themselves. Unlike victims of natural disasters or mass terrorism, victims of acts of omission often do not know they are victims until they have been so informed. Newspaper and governmental reports are commonly the symbolic initial impact.

Not only is the initial impact different in the way that awareness develops, it is different in that there is often conflicting evidence as to whether or not the disaster even occurred. The actual effects of chemicals in the water or radiation in the atmosphere may not appear for years or even generations. An extreme example of this nebulous initial impact was displayed in a lawsuit by numerous individuals in Nevada and Utah claiming to have been affected by the testing of atomic bombs in the 1950s. The decision as to whether or not they were actually victims became a legal issue as opposed to something that was self-evident.

This diffusion of initial impact in acts of omission results in a far smaller role for other stages. A Johns Hopkins University team ("Toxic Towns," 1983) reports that two phases occur after individuals learn that they have been potential victims of chemical dumping: (1) learning to live with the risk (acceptance), and (2) coping with the anger (at all parties, including government) for allowing the situation to develop (acquiescence). A primary difference between acts of commission and acts of omission is to whom the victims acquiesce. Victims of acts of omission tend to develop large-scale, generalized mistrust. Victims of acts of commission are more specific in their acquiescence to the perpetrator.

In terms of psychological symptoms, anger and frustration seem to be much higher in victims of acts of omission than in victims of acts of commission. A major problem in dealing with the anger is that it is not directed at any one individual or group. It is a diffuse anger at the system.

In this respect, the response is similar in victims of natural disasters. The major difference between the two types of disasters, however, concerns the perceived role of government officials. Victims of natural disasters often tend to perceive government officials (the system) negatively because of their inability to act swiftly in resolving the disaster. Red tape and delays exacerbate the distress of the victims (Murphy, 1986). Victims of acts of omission, however, perceive government as more than a hindrance. Victims are likely to perceive government as being at least partly responsible for the disaster by allowing it to happen. This perceived responsibility results in distrust and polarization.

Finally, the social processes for victims of acts of omission are similar to those for victims of acts of commission. Both groups tend to receive less emotional support than do victims of natural disasters. There is, however, one major difference. Victims of acts of omission are often perceived as *causing new problems.*

For example, it was pointed out that while victims of an asbestos problem were waiting for the red tape to clear, many residents of the larger community began to blame those same victims for complaining to the federal government about the problem (Beigel & Berren, 1985). It was a "blaming the messenger for the message" phenomenon. The more the victims voiced their concern, the more severe was the blot on the community. For individuals with a vested interest in maintaining the community's good name, the image of the problem (caused by the victims) was seen as worse than the problem itself. Similarly, using case study data, Cuthbertson and Nigg (1987), argue that with technological disasters the classic therapeutic community is unlikely to develop. The reasons for lack of a therapeutic community include the formation of victim clusters and questions, as well as disagreements as to who are the true victims.

The major point to keep in mind is that just as the consequences of natural disasters differ from those of human-induced disasters, the type of human-induced disaster also affects consequences.

LOW POINT VERSUS NO LOW POINT DISASTERS

Thinking about or picturing disasters generally conjures up images of mass destruction: buildings that have crumbled, houses that have been destroyed, the remains of the fuselage from a large commercial airplane that has crashed, or the like. As indicated earlier, even the Disaster Relief Act of 1974 (Slaby et al., 1981) defines a disaster as "a hurricane, tornado, storm, flood, high-water, wind-driven water, tidal wave, tsunami, earthquake, volcanic eruption, landslide, snowstorm, fire . . . *which causes damage of sufficient severity* [italics added].'' The fact is, however, that as a side-effect of technological and industrial advances, many recent events that might be classified as disasters no longer fit the stereotypic notion of visible mass destruction. And even though many such disasters are going to be human-induced acts of omission, the topic is important enough to be discussed separately.

The most recent, and largest, such disaster concerns the accident at the Chernobyl nuclear power plant in May 1986. Apparently, the main unit at the Chernobyl Plant had caught fire and, due to a variety of design and human errors, resulted in leakage of massive amounts of radiation. Because of difficulty with news coverage, initial reports were quite unclear as to the actual and potential impact of the disaster.

Over the months, however, specifics of the disaster and its possible consequences became more clear. For one thing, news media estimates of the initial death toll were significantly exaggerated. The scope of the effects, however, was quite dispersed, not only in terms of geography but also time.

Dairy farmers, hundreds of miles form the disaster, were forced to dispose of their milk, and individuals not impacted by the initial disaster must live with the knowledge that they are at an increased risk for developing leukemia or other forms of cancer. And even if higher mortality rates for leukemia do not occur over the next decade, there will still be concern and anxiety by potential victims over the *possibility* of the consequences.

In Chernobyl, however, there were no pictures of mass destruction befitting the consequences that could potentially occur. It is not just because the accident happened in the Soviet Union and news coverage was limited. Similar occurrences in the United States (for example, Three Mile Island and Love Canal), were not amenable to horrifying pictures. As Baum (1985) indicates, other than pictures of technological workers wearing uniforms reminiscent of science fiction, there is no immediate visible evidence of the disaster.

The manner in which the electronic media presented ''evidence'' of the disaster at Chernobyl is interesting. Given that radiation is invisible and that the television medium customarily presents pictures of disasters, the network news showed mock versions of Geiger counters as narrators explained what had happened and where the radiation was spreading.

Thus, a new generation of disasters has been defined. Despite their potentially catastrophic nature, they are not necessarily perceivable via the five senses. Instruments and detectors are needed to reveal that they have occurred, how large they are, what their geographic scope is, and how long they will be having an impact. We might refer to these disasters as *disasters without a footprint*.

The ''footprint'' concerns both space and time. Just as dairy farmers in Eastern Europe could not see the radiation, so too, the consequences of Chernobyl will most likely travel over time, causing illness and possibly premature death to thousands who presently feel fine. And what of future generations? It is not inconceivable that a nuclear or toxic disaster might have as much as or more of an impact on a future generation than it had on the generation alive during the primary phase of the disaster.

This new type of invisible disaster is significant because the emotional consequences are probably different from those experienced in more traditional disasters. The impact of not having a low point can be seen on the right side of Figure 2.2. In those more traditional visible disasters, victims have been described as going through certain emotional stages: (1) initial impact, (2) heroism, (3) honeymoon, (4) disillusionment, and (5) reorganization (Frederick, 1980). In a typical disaster, such as an earthquake or tornado, there is immediate evidence to everyone that a disaster has occurred. There is the impact and ensuing low point. Immediately following this initial impact, acts of heroism are often witnessed—workers digging babies out of rubble, rescue workers and medical staff working day and night, and so forth. It is not uncommon to hear stories of volunteers doing extraordinary things.

In situations like the ones at Chernobyl and Three Mile Island, where there is no perceptible evidence of the disaster (with the possible exception of fire or heat damage and a change in activity level in the immediate vicinity), there is no impact in the traditional sense (Baum, 1985). There is no low point. And without a low point, there is really very little opportunity for acts of heroism. The primary impact of nuclear and toxic waste disasters is something that might be years away.

Rather than being able to go through the various emotional stages, individuals are, in a sense, suspended in a stage of anticipation. The victims are told through the media and other sources that it may take years for consequences to be known. There is no immediate closure to the situation. And lack of closure in a stressful situation results in unresolved anxiety and tension.

In an attempt to create their own closure, individuals may utilize a defense mechanism such as denial, or they may just continue to ruminate about the possible consequences. In either case, without some sort of actual closure, a healthy psychological resolution will be extremely difficult. Additionally, without closure and an identifiable low point, victims will not have the opportunity to pass through the healing emotional stages. They will be fixated in a stage far short of resolution.

SCOPE OF DISASTER

Some disasters, whether they are characterized as human induced or natural, or whether they have or do not have a low point, are local and impact the residents of a geographically limited area. An example would be a tornado in West Texas or a hurricane somewhere along the Gulf Coast. Although tourists or others who are passing through may be affected, the majority of victims are local.

Other disasters, however, are very dispersed in their impact and affect individuals from many areas. The most straightforward example is the major airline crash. Although there may be some on the ground who are victims and some destruction to local property, by and large the victims, those suffering the most, are families of the individuals who died in the crash. These families, in most cases, are spread all over the country or even the globe.

Although many differences may be present, one primary difference to victims of local disasters, as opposed to victims of dispersed disasters, is the cohesion and support factor. As seen on countless occasions, disasters often serve to tie the community together. This is particularly true following natural disasters. One aspect that seems to aid in the healing process is the shared suffering phenomenon. When individuals suffer together, they tend to form a cohesive bond.

The cohesive bond and its healing power, however, are missing in the airline accident where the victims' families might reside in any number of communities. In such disasters, the situation to be dealt with is very similar to the crisis intervention that might occur following any tragic death. Even though the airline crash itself may have been a disaster, the diffusion of the suffering results in a situation where there really is no focal point. It will be up to individual counselors in various locales to provide what is typically provided to individuals who are facing tragic crisis situations. In terms of the community where the crash has taken place, the individuals most impacted by the disaster are probably the workers who have had to carry the dead, often mutilated, bodies off the plane.

As mentioned in the previous section, the scope of disaster is certainly influenced by the technological society. Disasters where the geographic and time scopes are not specifically limited will undoubtedly continue to occur.

SIZE OF DISASTER

The very large disaster has implications, not so much for the emotional consequences to any one victim, but rather for the cumulative negative effects it has on systems. The effect the large disaster has on various systems (e.g., health care, social welfare, housing), can both increase the number of secondary victims and exacerbate the problems already faced by primary victims. Suppose, for example, a small but lethal fire causes damage to four houses on a neighborhood block. The damage to two of the houses is significant, and in fact, one of the houses is completely destroyed. Suppose further that for one of those families there was loss of life of a family member. The disaster will impact on all four of the families. Anxiety, depression, grief, and other sequelae, will almost certainly occur, even if not at clinically significant levels. All other things being equal, it is safe to assume greatest emotional consequences to the families with the greatest loss. Additionally, the families will have to deal with the realities of rebuilding houses, filing insurance, gaining temporary shelter, and the other predictable consequences of their experience.

Now imagine a much larger disaster, such as a tornado that destroys 20 times as much property as the fire. Eighty houses are affected, dozens are injured, and seven deaths occur. A local community shelter, a shopping center, several churches, and part of a highway have been destroyed.

Initially, the impact of loss of house and life should be the same for the victims of this disaster as in the smaller disaster. There are just more victims. Secondary effects are likely, however, to have a rippling effect and magnify whatever has already occurred. A rippling effect can be predicted in that the greater the number of victims, the greater will be the demand for services. And the greater the demand for services, the greater the number of individuals involved in the response. In small disasters, only those initially impacted are generally going to be victims. In larger disasters, the number of secondary victims is going to increase as a function of the size of the disaster.

Following disasters there is tendency for victims to compete for limited resources. Although this competition does not necessarily occur in a malicious manner, competition for resources in situations wherein resources are limited can lead to noncooperative behavior. In large disasters, not only will there be more competition for services, and hence more secondary victims, but it is likely that services themselves will also have been adversely affected. In a large disaster, there will be many victims competing for resources from a system that even in good times is often taxed. And following the large disaster, the system itself is probably not functioning well, irrespective of demand. The rippling and magnification will thus work together to make the large disaster worse.

An important issue to consider in determining the size of a disaster is the *size of the community* in which the disaster has occurred. Size is a relative concept. Two tornadoes causing equal absolute destruction in Dallas and Brownfield, Texas, are really quite different in relative size. The tornado that does major destruction to property in Brownfield, and significantly taxes the community's ability to deal with the disaster, might be of much less impact in a large metroplex. As we have pointed out previously, the initial impact to primary victims will be quite similar in both situations. The difference between the two disasters is the impact the large disaster will have on secondary victims and on the system itself. This additional stress can, in turn, affect the primary victims' abilities to cope.

DEGREE OF PERSONAL IMPACT

Who is a victim of a disaster? Although it should perhaps be asked first, this question has been saved for last. Most persons would probably agree that members of a family who have lost their home in a flood are victims of a disaster. Likewise, the individuals who have lost their lives in an airplane crash are obviously victims of a disaster. But what about the family members of the airline disaster victims? Are they also victims? And what about individuals who live in a community where a flood has destroyed the homes of friends? Does the concept of victimization apply even to those whose exposure to disaster is passing or indirect?

Just as disasters differ in degree and type, so do victims differ in *extent* and *type* of the disaster's impact upon them. And the extent and type of impact to any one individual is not necessarily perfectly related to the type or size of a disaster. It makes sense to assume that there are small disasters where a small number of victims are impacted to a significantly greater extent than are some victims of other, much larger disasters.

Thus, in thinking about victims, it is necessary to recognize that the personal impact on any one victim is *not* necessarily a function of the size of the disaster. Personal impact is the extent to which the disaster affects someone *regardless* of the size or scope of the disaster. In any disaster, there will be a high impact on some individuals. Even though many others might ultimately be affected to some extent, those at the outer edges of the ripple are less immediately affected. In terms of the earlier question, both the individual whose house has been destroyed, *and* the individual who merely lives in the community, are victims. One, however, has certainly had a greater personal impact.

One thing not included in this discussion of personal impact is the phenomenology of the individual. While it is true that a victim's personality, support systems, ability to deal with stress, and the like, will affect his or her perception of the situation and hence the personal impact, in this chapter the term *personal impact* is being applied from a more external perspective. Someone who has lost a home or loved one is impacted to a greater extent than someone who has merely been inconvenienced by the disaster.

Personal impact does correlate with size of disaster in the increasing number of secondary or lower impact victims that will exist in a large disaster. The larger the disaster, the greater the impact on the community itself, and the greater the number of individuals who are inconvenienced.

A second dimension of personal impact is whether a victim was directly involved in the disaster or has lost loved ones in a disaster. Major airline crashes best exemplify this point. Even though the family of an individual who dies in a plane crash might not have been involved in the crash itself, it would be hard not to consider them as victims. Their victimization is different from that of the family who has lost their home in a flood that has done major destruction to their hometown. They are, however, certainly victims. As was pointed out previously, disagreements about who the true victims are can significantly affect a community's ability to create support systems. This is especially true for technological disasters (Cuthbertson & Nigg, 1987).

This discussion has now gone full circle, from classifying disasters to indicating that, regardless of the nature of the disaster, the persons affected are impacted on an individual and unique basis.

CONCLUSION

The question now is: What can be gained by classifying disasters and by recognizing that impact on victims is not uniform? Ideally, it will help professionals gain the sensitivity that comes with awareness. The greater the awareness of what has actually happened and how it is likely to affect individuals, the more appropriate will be the interventions (or avoidance of interventions, as the case may be). It is beyond the scope of this chapter to suggest how one goes about setting up interventions. And as it is, much is already available on crisis intervention and intervention with systems. The purpose of this chapter and the conceptual framework presented is to put the role of professionals into perspective. Before volunteering to provide any services to victims, the first task should be to recognize what it is those victims need. After all, does the monkey really need to rescue the fish from drowning?

REFERENCES

Acquire, B. E. (1980). The long-term effects of major natural disasters on marriage and divorce: An ecological study. *Victimology, 5,* 298–307.

Airline officials speculate on causes of 747 jet crash. (1977, March 30). *Los Angeles Times,* p. 1.

Baisden, B., & Quarantelli, E. L. (1981). The delivery of mental health services in community disasters: An outline of research findings. *Journal of Community Psychology, 9,* 195–203.

Baum, A. S. (Speaker). (1985). *Toxins, technology, and natural disaster* (Cassette Recording No. 154-297-86A). Washington, DC: American Psychological Association.

Beigel, A., & Berren, M. R. (1985). Human induced disasters. *Psychiatric Annals, 15,* 143–150.

Berren, M. R., Beigel, A., & Barker, G. (1982). A typology for the classification of disasters: Implications for intervention. *Community Mental Health Journal, 18,* 120–135.

Berren, M. R., Beigel, A., & Ghertner, S. (1980). A typology for the classification of disasters. *Community Mental Health Journal, 16,* 103–111.

Cuthbertson, B. H., & Nigg, J. M. (1987). Technological disaster and the nontherapeutic community: A question of true victimization. *Environment & Behavior, 19,* 462–483.

Fairley, M. (1986). Psychological and physical morbidity in the aftermath of a cyclone. *Psychological Medicine, 16,* 671–676.

Federal Register (1987, July 22). Vol. 52, No. 40.

Frederick, C. (1980). Effects of natural vs. human induced violence upon victims. *Evaluation and Change,* Special Issue, 71–75.

Fritz, L. E. (1961). Disaster. In R. K. Merton & R. A. Nisbet (Eds.), *Contemporary social problems* (pp. 651–694). New York: Harcourt.

Green, B. L. (1982). Assessing levels of psychological impairment following disaster. *The Journal of Nervous and Mental Disease, 70,* 544–552.

Hartsough, D. M. (1985). Measurement of the psychological effects of disaster. In S. Loube & S. Murphy (Eds.), *Perspectives on disaster recovery* (pp. 22–60). Norwalk, CT: Appleton-Century-Crofts.

Heavy damage inflicted upon Mexico City. (1985, September 23). *New York Times,* Section I, p. 5.

Logue, J. N., & Hansen, H. (1980). A case-control study of hypertensive women in a post-disaster community: Wyoming Valley, PA. *Journal of Human Stress, 6,* 28–34.

McCaughey, B. G. (1984). U.S. naval disaster: The psychological symptomatology. *U.S. Naval Research Center Report, 84*(2), 8.

Melick, M. E. (1985). The health of post-disaster populations: A review of literature and case study. In Sloube & Murphy (Eds.), *Perspectives on disaster recovery* (pp. 179–209). Norwalk, CT: Appleton-Century-Crofts.

Murphy, S. (1986). Perceptions of stress, coping, and recovery one and three years after a natural disaster. *Issues in Mental Health Nursing, 8,* 63–77.

Newman, C. J. (1977). Children of disaster: Clinical observations of Buffalo Creek. *Annual Progress in Child Psychiatry and Clinical Development, 10,* 149–161.

Poulshock, S. W., & Cohen, E. S. (1975). The elderly in the aftermath of a disaster. *Gerontologist, 15,* 357–361.

Rangell, L. (1976). Discussion of the Buffalo Creek disaster: The course of psychic trauma. *American Journal of Psychiatry, 133,* 313–316.

Shah, G. (1985). Social work in disaster. *Indian Journal of Social Work, 45,* 462–471.

Slaby, A. E., Lieb, J., & Tancredi, L. R. (1981). *Handbook of psychiatric disorders.* Garden City, NY: Medical Examination Publishing Co.

Terr, L. (1979). A study of psychic trauma. *Psychoanalytic Study of the Child, 34,* 547–623.

Titchner, J. L., and Kapp, F. T. (1976). Family and character change at Buffalo Creek. *American Journal of Psychiatry, 133,* 295–299.

Toxic towns. (1983, Oct. 23). *Arizona Daily Star,* Section B, p. 8.

Whorf, B. L. (1956). Science and Linguistics. In J. Carroll (Ed.), *Language, thought, and reality* (pp. 207–219). Cambridge, MA: M.I.T. Press.

PART 2

Types of Disaster

Berren, Santiago, Beigel, and Timmons have made clear a number of different issues imposed by the various sorts of cataclysmic events contemplated under the general rubric *disaster*. Each type of event poses a unique set of challenges, and each demands different approaches to response and intervention.

For most people, the prototypical disaster is the act of God, such as a tornado, hurricane, earthquake, or flood. Such events are capable of causing extensive damage to lives and property with amazing quickness, leaving disruptions of community and support that may endure for months or even years. The impact of natural disasters on individual and community functioning is reviewed in Chapter 3 by Bolin, along with avenues for intervention.

Another prototype for disaster is the airline crash. In contrast to natural disasters, where property loss is often extreme, these events are most often characterized by extensive loss of life. Similarly, the disruption to a defined community typical of natural disaster is likely to be much less in these cases, where victims ordinarily share few strong connections.

The enormous scale of many of these catastrophes presents unique challenges with respect to mobilization of response, coordination of efforts, and targets of interventions. Butcher and Dunn discuss these issues in Chapter 4.

A third type of event, characterized by insidious effects over extended periods rather than by violent and immediate impact, is examined by Bromet in Chapter 5. Technological failures, such as at Three Mile Island, Chernobyl, and Bhopal, present new and profound challenges for the community interventionist. These challenges can be even more difficult, in that many of the possible effects may remain purely speculative for decades, leaving few clear courses for specific action. Social action, community empowerment, and prevention accordingly become major themes for persons focusing on this type of problem.

Crime, violence, and terrorism have become significant sources of community concern. Particularly in cases where multiple homicides or mass violence are involved, entire communities may experience effects quite similar to other types of disaster. The deliberate nature of such acts, however, adds an element of disequilibrium that demands special attention. These topics are treated by Young in Chapter 6.

CHAPTER 3

Natural Disasters

ROBERT BOLIN

Natural disasters constitute a category of environmental events that periodically, and with varying degrees of intensity, subject human systems to a
wide range of disruptions and stress. It is, however, not always simple to
distinguish a natural disaster from a disaster occasion in which human agency
plays a part. Technological hazards and disasters (toxic waste spills, nuclear
power plant accidents, transportation disasters, urban fires, dam breaks,
etc.) are, with increasing frequency, also impacting human populations. The
goal in this chapter is to focus on the particular impacts of natural disasters
as environmental stress agents. Other authors in this volume address the
range of "non-natural" disasters, as well as the psychosocial impacts of
those agents and events.

The introduction discusses what appear to be some of the more important
differences between natural and technological disasters. By contrasting technological hazards with natural disasters, the specific features of the latter
that are related to psychosocial stress may be better understood. As a sociologist, my concern will be to focus on the interplay of the environmental
stress agent, the impacted populations (individuals, families, kin groups,
communities), and the social responses to the disaster.

The treatment of the topic will be guided by a general "open systems"
or ecological perspective. This perspective will be briefly reviewed, in order
to provide an interpretive framework for understanding findings from the
research literature on natural disasters. Because disasters impact existing
social systems, each with its unique historical dynamics, social responses
to natural disasters flow from the predisaster characteristics of the impacted
individuals and social groupings. While predisaster characteristics can determine levels of vulnerability to the stressor, they can also determine the
nature of responses.

Social responses to natural disasters are a category of secondary stresses
that expose victims to long-term response-generated demands. Distinguishing between disaster-produced stress and response-generated demands
(Quarantelli, 1985) is important in anticipating the types and extent of mental
health services that will be necessary in the aftermath. Accordingly, part of

this chapter will examine to what extent social responses to natural disasters may, in themselves, produce psychosocial disturbances.

Both the physical characteristics of the event and the social responses to the event can engender or exacerbate psychosocial stresses within victim populations. A systemic approach calls attention to the social context of the impacted individuals and groups, as well as to actual impact-generated demands. As collective stress events, natural disasters appear to create social dynamics through their impacts that are different from the ones caused by other agents. The chapter will conclude with a brief review of suggested intervention strategies in light of the prevailing characteristics of natural disasters.

CHARACTERISTICS OF NATURAL DISASTERS

As a natural agent of victimization, disasters share certain generic features with other cataclysmic phenomena such as war and technological disaster. Quarantelli (1985) has suggested that it is beneficial from the point of view of the social sciences to focus on the features that all types of disasters have in common. In the discussion to follow, the important generic feature of cataclysmic events, whether from natural sources, the failure of technological systems, or the intentional acts of collective violence by organizations, is that they subject human systems to extraordinary demand levels. Quarantelli (1985) suggests that disaster be defined as a crisis event in which the demands being placed on a human system by the event exceed the system's capacity to respond (cf. Drabek & Key, 1984; Haas & Drabek, 1973). Lazarus and Cohen (1977) group natural disasters with stress events referred to as ". . . sudden, unique and powerful single life-events requiring major adaptive responses from the groups sharing the experience" (p. 91).

Natural agents such as tornadoes, hurricanes, droughts, blizzards, lightning, hailstorms, forest fires, earthquakes, floods, seismic sea waves, and volcanic eruptions clearly fall into a category of "Acts of God." They can be categorized according to a number of agent characteristics such as speed of onset, scope of impact, duration of impact, predictability, intensity of impact, and threat of recurrence (cf. Barton, 1970; Berren, Beigel, & Ghertner, 1980; Mileti, Drabek, & Haas, 1975; Perry & Lindell, 1978).

It is not unusual, however, for natural agents and their impacts to precipitate further environmental disruptions that are not so clearly natural. An earthquake, for example, can trigger massive urban fires while also disrupting the means of fighting those fires (Haas, Kates, & Bowden, 1977). A flood can wash toxic wastes such as dioxin from a dump site into people's homes, thereby rendering them uninhabitable (e.g., Smith, 1984). Practitioners and researchers alike must be alert to the sometimes fuzzy distinction between truly natural and human-made disasters. Some disaster occasions appear to combine natural forces and human acts or technologies.

These gray areas notwithstanding, it is useful to try to distinguish unique characteristics of natural disasters, both to better anticipate potential mental health impacts and to understand the nature of social and psychological responses to them. Natural disasters are typically preceded by some warnings or environmental cues as to their imminent impact (although extent of warning varies by agent), result in physical destruction of property, often cause traumatic injury and death, and can threaten victim populations with a potential for recurrence (particularly in the case of earthquakes and volcanoes). Even with this list of broad characteristics, it must be recognized that there are various slow onset types of disasters (droughts, crop blights) that don't share these characteristics and expose victims to much more protracted types of stressors.

As Baum, Fleming, and Davidson (1983) note, an important characteristic of natural disaster, not typically shared by technological and related catastrophes, is a "low point." They argue that, at the low point of a natural disaster, there is a shift in victim appraisal from the threat of the agent's impact to the losses it caused. After the low point, restoration activities begin, and environmental conditions usually begin to improve. To the extent that human-caused disasters share such characteristics, social and psychological responses to them will be similar. In contrast, many types of technological disasters (e.g., toxic waste dump site leaks; nuclear power plant accidents) have neither obvious physical impacts or a clearly identifiable low point. Thus Baum et al. (1983) suggest that they result in different types of psychosocial impacts than do natural disasters, their argument being that technological disasters are intrinsically more stressful.

The issue of controllability of the disaster agent is also significant. Natural disasters are, by definition, uncontrollable, although with adequate warning victims can prepare in various ways for impact. Technological and related human-caused disasters signify a breakdown of human control, giving victims a focus for blame and resentment (cf. Erikson, 1976; Gleser, Green, & Winget, 1981; Levine, 1982). Natural disasters tend to involve no victim concern (or at least less concern) with affixing blame for cause.

The lack of a comprehensive typology of disaster characteristics and impacts (cf. Drabek, 1986; Quarantelli, 1985) leaves researchers having to make qualifying statements when distinguishing between disaster types. The reader should keep in mind that each disaster event has both unique and generic characteristics.

A CONCEPTUAL FRAMEWORK

To most fruitfully interpret the complex interplay of natural disaster characteristics with their disruptive sequelae on human systems, a general ecological or systems approach is useful (cf. Drabek & Key, 1984; O'Connor & Lubin, 1984). In this orientation, human systems are characterized by a complex interpenetrated and somewhat integrated network of social units (individuals, small groups, families, interpersonal networks, communities, macrolevel collectivities) that exist within a physical, material environment (Jasnowski, 1984).

Natural disasters are major negative environmental inputs that disrupt these systems by subjecting them to sets of demands that typically require at least temporary reorganization and the restructuring of intersystemic linkages (Haas & Drabek, 1973). The restructuring is both disruptive of the predisaster state and a way for human systems to cope with the disaster-induced qualitative and quantitative changes in demands. When disaster-related demands exceed system response capabilities, the social unit in question experiences a condition of stress (Baum & Davidson, 1985; Quarantelli, 1985).

To understand the nature of stress produced by natural disasters, it is necessary to consider individual victim characteristics, their interpersonal relationships (including family), social structure, and the cultural context, in addition to the actual geophysical environment (Warheit, 1985). Human systems at all levels of complexity will exhibit endogenous characteristics that will determine their vulnerability to the disruptions of disaster. Systems with preexisting maladaptive tendencies will be the most likely to exhibit deleterious effects from disaster impact, whether those negative effects are psychosocial disturbances, family disorganization, or long-term community decline (Pelanda, 1982).

Existing research clearly indicates that the ability to externalize losses to higher system levels is a key coping strategy for responding to natural disaster (Bolin & Bolton, 1986; Drabek & Key, 1984). Thus the individual under disaster-induced stress will typically turn to family (spouse, children) first. If the forthcoming aid and support are inadequate, additional social linkages are usually established to higher order systems (Bolin, 1982). If intrafamilial social support does not sufficiently augment coping capacity, the extended kin group or similar interpersonal networks may be drawn upon (Bolton, 1979). In response to disaster in the United States, linkages are commonly established with formal aid givers to augment recovery capacity (Drabek, 1986). These formal aid givers provide the victim with access to resources of the larger society.

The extension of linkages to environing systems embeds the victim in social support networks, both formal and informal in nature. Social support, from whatever sources, has been found to have a stress-buffering effect by providing victims with additional material and affective resources to augment coping capacities (Bolin, 1983; Kahn & Antonucci, 1980; Lindy & Grace, 1985).

At an analytical level, then, the psychosocial impacts of natural disaster are consequences of a complex process of social and environmental interaction. Such impacts are determined by the interactive outcome of disaster event characteristics and individual, interpersonal, and community (social structure) characteristics (Warheit, 1985). It is not just event characteristics, then, but the social responses to the event and its aftermath that affect the psychosocial impacts of the event.

Potential mental health impacts are the outcome of a complex web of physical, psychological, social, and material factors in mutually contingent interaction. Natural disasters are environmental events that create an array of existential demands to which individuals and collectivities must respond. Failure to cope with demands creates stress situations that may produce psychological disturbances.

DISASTER PHASES

In discussing issues pertinent to natural disasters, a generally accepted starting point is to examine the phases of disaster from the issuance of warning to impact, emergency period responses, rehabilitation, and the recovery phases. This section identifies elements of each phase that have been found to be associated with increased stress levels. It should be recognized that stress implies a condition in which the victim has inadequate resources to cope with the demands of the disaster. Stress is not intrinsic as to the event but as to the interplay between demand levels and response capacities (Quarantelli, 1985).

Warnings

One of the chief characteristics of many types of natural disasters is that they allow preimpact warnings to be disseminated. In contrast, technological disasters are frequently sudden, with no environmental cues as to their onset. In the realm of natural-occurring disasters, such as tornadoes, floods, and hurricanes, watches and warnings can be issued from hours to days in advance. Floods in particular can often be predicted days or weeks in advance, and threatened populations can be suitably alerted. Similarly, with current technologies hurricanes can be tracked, and areas threatened by landfall can be warned or evacuated. In any case, the ability to issue warnings allows persons to take action to mitigate potential impacts to themselves or their property (cf. Drabek, 1986).

The major exception regarding the issuance of warnings is in the case of earthquakes and earthquake-related phenomena (e.g., tsunamis). Earthquake prediction has in the last decade become the focus of a great deal of scientific research, both in the United States and other earthquake-prone areas such as China and Japan (Turner, 1983; Turner, Nigg, & Paz, 1986). Unlike other types of disaster warnings, earthquake prediction cannot currently meet criteria of specifying quake magnitude, place, time, and probability of occurrence (Nigg, 1986). Thus current practice typically involves announcing that a destructive quake is likely in the next X number of years in a general region or area (Nigg, 1986). As technologies and techniques are developed, more refined earthquake warnings will increase.

When natural disasters are preceded by a warning period of hours or days, such as in the case of hurricanes and slow onset floods (Bates, Fogleman, Parenton, Pittman & Tracy, 1963; Hannigan & Kueneman, 1978), they are often not associated with significant psychosocial disturbances unless the intensity of impact or the scope of destruction is very high (Bolin, 1985). Warning of a possible disaster does, in itself, have the potential of creating a lengthy period of perceived threat (Lazarus, 1966). There is, however, little in the literature to suggest that, in natural disaster, such a warning period produces psychological sequelae. Certainly there is a substantial body of literature indicating that panic behavior as the result of disaster warnings is extremely rare and is best considered as a disaster myth (Quarantelli, 1979). If anything, the research on warning for natural disaster suggests that disbelief of initial warnings, rather than panic, is the most common individual response (Mileti, Drabek, & Haas, 1975; Perry, Lindell, & Green, 1980).

Generally, an adequate warning period allows a measure of anticipatory socialization to occur, which in turn has the potential for reducing the stressfulness of the impact of the agent, should it occur (Drabek, 1986; Kessler, 1979; Pearlin & Schooler, 1978). Similarly, in areas with a history of natural disasters, sociocultural adjustments to the hazards often become institutionalized. Consequently, the previous disaster experiences of individuals and collectivities may increase their repertoires of coping behaviors and reduce the stressfulness of the event. Such sociocultural adjustments are referred to in the literature as "disaster subcultures" (Hannigan & Kueneman, 1978; Weller & Wenger, 1973) and may be identified in communities with a continuing or cyclical threat of natural disaster. Of course, in the absence of preexisting norms to guide behaviors, coping responses are problematic until new situationally based norms emerge (Boyd, 1981; Drabek, 1968; Hufnagel & Perry, 1982).

Threat and Risk Perception

With respect to the warning phase of natural disaster, the existence of a disaster subculture or of victims with significant previous experience with a particular disaster agent will reduce the likelihood of psychological disruptions related to short-term impact. A phenomenon conceptually related to preimpact warning is that of threat and the perception of risk. One of the key characteristics of natural as opposed to human-caused disasters is that the former can be described objectively and accurately as to the speed of onset, scope, intensity, and possible impact duration (Mileti et al., 1975). Of course, scientific description of the impending event may have little to do with how individuals perceive it (Mileti, 1980; Turner et al., 1986; Van Arsdol, Sabagh, & Alexander, 1964).

It is well documented that individuals tend to underestimate the hazardous features of their physical environment (Covello, 1983). Nevertheless, threat and risk perception are part of the social-psychological milieu of victims in the preimpact and impact phases of natural disaster. It has been suggested that the tendency of persons to interpret impending disaster situations as nonhazardous is a psychological strategy that reduces the dissonance involved in being in a high-risk situation. As Kinston and Rosser (1974) have indicated, denial of threat can be violently negated by the impact of a disaster, resulting in psychological stresses (cf. Withey, 1964).

If environmental cues of a threatened disaster event are ambiguous, coping problems and stress levels may increase (cf. Baum & Davidson, 1985; Drabek, 1986; Lazarus, 1966). However, in the case of natural disasters there tends to be less ambiguity and uncertainty regarding threat than there is in technological disasters (Baum & Davidson, 1985). As with some technological hazards, several types of natural disasters are accompanied by a threat of recurrence. This is particularly true of earthquakes, volcanic activity, and, to a lesser extent, cyclonic activity such as tornadoes.

It is important to consider that the potential for recurrence is both a characteristic of the agent *and* a subjective assessment by survivors (Green, 1985). Living with the often frequent aftershocks of a major earthquake or the smoking summit of an active volcano can constitute a chronic threat and a prolonged stressor, both of which are phenomena associated with certain types of psychological distress (Gleser et al., 1981; Lang & Lang, 1964; Schorr, Goldsteen, & Carter, 1982). Most of the evidence, in this regard, is from technological disasters (e.g., Three Mile Island, Bromet & Dunn, 1981) or disasters caused by human activities (e.g., the Buffalo Creek dam break in West Virginia, Erikson, 1976).

Agent Impact Characteristics

Moving from the warning–threat phase of natural disaster, a number of typological dimensions of agent impact characteristics may be considered in attempting to anticipate psychological distress among victims (e.g., Berren et al., 1980; Quarantelli, 1985; Warheit, 1985). Duration, intensity, and scope of impact are three that have particular salience for natural disasters. Of course, individual victim experiences with the agent can differ considerably from victim to victim and each, in turn, can differ from a general description of the event's impacts. An earthquake can be a very intense and violent event lasting only a minute. But if a victim is trapped in a collapsed building for 24 hours, he or she may experience the impact as lasting that long, not the mere 60 seconds registered on a seismograph. Clearly individual experience is a key consideration in attempting to anticipate possible negative psychological consequences of the event.

In general, it is the dramatic natural disasters—those with intense, short-term impacts with proportionately large impact zones—that, on the face of it, are more likely to be associated with psychosocial stresses among victims

(Ahearn & Castellon, 1979; Bolin, 1985; Leik, Leik, Ekker, & Gifford, 1982). As always, in attempting to conceptualize relatively complex social systems, there are a number of conditional factors that must be considered. Such factors can include victim characteristics (age, race, sex, social class, previous disaster experience, etc.), social context variables, and the nature of social responses to the disaster impact.

Acute stressors, such as those associated with the impact of tornadoes, hurricanes, and flash floods, may engender intense psychological reactions, but often those reactions are short-lived and disappear once the environmental stressors subside (Baum et al., 1983). Earthquakes, on the other hand, may involve an intense impact phase of short duration followed by intermittent aftershocks that can function as chronic stressors on victims experiencing them (Ahearn, 1981; Greenson & Mintz, 1972). Such prolonged exposure to environmental stresses and long-term threat may be disruptive of recovery processes and may produce enduring symptoms of stress for some (Bolin, 1982).

The nature and extent of the damage produced by a natural disaster is a significant indicator of potential psychological sequelae among victims. Personal losses, including injury and death among family, kin, and acquaintances, are the most obvious type of damage or losses that suggest the need for mental health services. However, other losses, including the home and pets, may be a significant source of stress and grief (Bolin, 1986a; Fried, 1963; Sowder, 1985). Grief, bereavement, and role stress as well as economic and social disruption accompany injury and death in disaster, adding to adjustment problems that survivors may face.

Violent disasters, particularly earthquakes, flash floods, and tornadoes, expose some victims to acutely threatening situations. The force with which such agents strike can subject victims to extreme life-threatening conditions. This exposure to the terror of the disaster may be associated with subsequent psychological impairment (Gleser et al., 1981). However, studies documenting mental health problems associated with extreme impact characteristics suggest that it is not so much the threat to one's life that is particularly traumatizing; it is rather one's exposure to the death of others. This is especially pronounced if the disaster agent mutilates or disfigures bodies as in the case of earthquakes and floods (Bolin, 1985; Sowder, 1985), where exposure to such sights further accentuates the horror of the impact's physical effects.

Another dimension of disasters pertinent in estimating potential for psychological stresses is the geographic scope of impact. The concept of a disaster as an imbalance in the demand/capability ratio of a social system suggests that the wider the scope of impact, the more disastrous or stressful the event will be to the stricken social systems (Quarantelli, 1985). Imbalance between demands and response capabilities is an indicator of stress for individuals and social collectivities (Drabek & Key, 1984). Some natural disaster agents can have widespread impacts, leaving little of an impacted community undamaged. This may be observed in earthquakes, volcanic disasters, and hurricanes in particular (e.g., Haas, Kates, & Bowden, 1977; White & Haas, 1975).

The Buffalo Creek flood is perhaps the best researched disaster in which virtually not one of the impacted communities was left undamaged. This wide-scale destruction deprived victims of a familiar, unaffected part of the community in which to seek refuge and support. This resulted in prolonged exposure to post-disaster stress (Erikson, 1976; Gleser et al., 1981; Lifton and Olson, 1976). In general, if a large proportion of a local population is involved, the disaster is likely to be accompanied by psychological distress (Quarantelli, 1985).

In summarizing to this point, several general findings may be highlighted:

1. Disasters that expose victims to life-threatening situations or that expose them to the death or injury of primary group members are more likely to produce psychological distress. Chief agents here would be earthquakes, flash floods, volcanoes, and, in some instances, tornadoes.
2. Disaster agents that are accompanied by long periods of threat or the threat of recurrence after an initial intense impact may be particularly stressful. In general, postimpact threat of recurrence will be more stressful than preimpact stress. As noted earlier, earthquakes, volcanoes, and tornadoes are frequently accompanied by threats of recurrence (e.g., Bolin, 1982; Bolin & Bolton, 1986; Leik et al., 1982).
3. When combined with an intense impact, disasters with a high ratio of damaged to undamaged community are associated with mental health sequelae. This would involve agents such as earthquakes, some flood events, and major tornadoes. Of course, impact ratio is dependent on the size of the community as well as on the natural dimensions of the disaster (Bolin, 1985).
4. Disaster agents with a sudden and unanticipated onset (e.g., earthquakes) will be more stressful than anticipated events (Quarantelli, 1985).
5. Disaster events with which victims are unfamiliar are more likely to be psychologically disturbing. Previous experience, individually or collectively, as in the case of disaster subcultures, mitigates the stress effects of natural disaster agents (Mileti et al., 1975).

POSTIMPACT EFFECTS

These observations constitute only one element in the complex of determinant factors (e.g., Warheit, 1985). The second set of factors involves stresses generated by individual and collective responses to natural disasters, rather than agent characteristics per se. Response-generated demands that are common in natural disaster include evacuation behavior, temporary sheltering, temporary housing, and recovery activities (Bolin & Bolton, 1986; Dynes, Quarantelli, & Kreps, 1981; Quarantelli, 1982).

While both natural and technological disasters may result in mass evacuations (e.g., hurricanes, floods, toxic leaks, nuclear power plant accidents), natural disasters are much more frequently associated with temporary housing and long-term reconstruction activities (e.g., Haas et al., 1977). Social responses to natural disaster create distinct demands on victims which are separate from, and in addition to, the event's physical impact characteristics (Bolin, 1986b; Dynes et al., 1981).

Evacuation

Evacuation is a complex social process that occurs as a result of warnings or actual impact. It involves the withdrawal of persons from a potential impact area, the temporary sheltering of those persons, and their return to their homes (Quarantelli, 1982). Families typically evacuate as a unit and usually seek temporary shelter with kin or friends. More affluent families may evacuate to motels or second homes outside the impact area (Bolin, 1986b; Drabek, 1969). Typically, poorer families are the most likely to use mass shelters such as the ones often established by the Red Cross.

Because families usually evacuate as a unit and frequently go to the homes of friends, they are able to maintain a supportive social context. In general, evacuation and emergency sheltering do not lead to extensive psychological distress in natural disasters. Exceptions to this occur in instances where families are not able to evacuate as a whole or are not able to stay together in emergency shelters (Drabek & Boggs, 1968; Instituut voor Sociaal Onderzoek, 1955). In such instances, evacuation can be associated with mental health stresses. However, most of the literature documenting evacuation-related stresses is from research based on technological disasters with their ambiguous threats (Bromet et al., 1980).

Research recently conducted following a flood disaster in California illustrates circumstances under which evacuation can be problematic for victims (Bolin, 1986b). In the study site, victims were first given shelter in a public building in the community. As the Russian River continued to rise, the evacuees were forced out of the first shelter into a second shelter on higher ground. The flooding river cut off the town before evacuees could be removed to a safer area and the resultant isolation resulted in food scarcity in the mass shelter.

After two days of increasing anxieties and frustrations, victims were evacuated from the flood zone by helicopter. That evacuation involved hours of standing in a cold rain, with victims being uncertain as to how much longer it would take to be removed from the flood zone. After the evacuation was completed, many victims spent hours or days in a mass shelter in another town, uncertain as to when they would be able to return to their homes or what they would find when they got there. Victims, many of whom made a total of three evacuation trips before being helicoptered to safety, found their experiences anxiety producing and demoralizing because of the persistent uncertainties, charges of human mismanagement, and prolonged exposure to environmental threats (Bolin, 1986b).

The sheltering of populations evacuating a disaster site is not an area which has been extensively studied (Quarantelli, 1982), thus observations concerning its effects must be considered preliminary. As noted, mass shelters are disproportionately utilized by lower socioeconomic status victims; there is some indication that middle- and upper-income victims find public shelters stigmatizing (Quarantelli, 1982). Because in many natural disaster situations (e.g., hurricanes) the stay in public shelter is short, the experience is generally not, of itself, stressful to those who utilize it. However, when evacuation and temporary sheltering become protracted, then psychosocial stress can mount significantly (Parker, 1977).

Because postimpact sheltering and temporary housing are relatively common social responses to natural disasters, it is important to establish the conditions under which they contribute to psychosocial stress experienced by victims. Since most victims of natural disaster seek temporary shelter with kin or friends, which gives them access to social support in a familiar surrounding, this phase is rarely problematic.

In research on flooding in California (Bolin, 1986b), problems were identified that emerged in the mass sheltering phase. In particular, instances of interpersonal violence and threatening behavior occurred, resulting in the need to have law enforcement personnel present to keep order. Victims interviewed in that study, particularly those with young children in the shelter, found their shelter stay as a significant stressor in their overall disaster experience (Bolin, 1986b).

As one respondent reported in that study:

> I was stuck in three different shelters. . . . I was hungry, I got wet and cold, and spent a lot of time not knowing what was going on. Some people around me were drunk or stoned and . . . I was pretty damned scared of them. At times I thought the flood was the least of my problems. (Bolin, 1986b, pp. 22–23)

The local mental health outreach program placed counselors in the shelter to help victims work out hostilities and to reduce tensions among occupants.

The Therapeutic Community

One of the distinguishing features of natural disasters is that often they are followed by a period of heightened altruism, social support, and helping behavior. This phase is referred to in the natural disaster literature as the "therapeutic community" (Barton, 1970). During this therapeutic period, aid is made available to victims by official sources, and helping behavior is common from individuals and voluntary organizations, both locally and from outside the impacted community.

From a systems perspective, it is during the therapeutic community phase that new linkages are established between systems, new organizations emerge, and interorganizational networks are created (Haas & Drabek, 1973). Families establish or modify ties with their primary groups and with formal aid givers, just as communities establish ties with state and national agencies that can provide aid and organizational expertise. These links become conduits of need resources for families and community organizations (e.g., Drabek, 1986; Drabek & Key, 1984).

The therapeutic community becomes the social context for the response and recovery activities of victims (Golec, 1983). To the extent that it emerges and is maintained, this altruistic phase can be expected to mitigate the stress effects of the disaster for victims (Lindy & Grace, 1985).

Temporary Housing and Relocation

In instances of temporary or permanent relocation, access to social support and the therapeutic community can be disrupted and psychosocial stress can become more pronounced (Miller, Turner, & Kimball, 1981; Milne, 1977; Parker, 1977; Tierney & Baisden, 1979). In natural disasters, where large numbers of homes are destroyed, temporary housing programs are instituted as part of routine federal disaster response (Bolin & Bolton, 1986). Temporary housing is often located away from the disaster's impact area, and it is often away from established transportation routes (Bolton, 1979; Davis, 1975). This type of geographical isolation can cut victims off from the positive elements of their support networks (Western & Milne, 1979).

In mass disasters in the United States, mobile homes are sometimes used as temporary housing, where existing housing stock is inadequate to absorb the displaced victim population (Quarantelli, 1982). The use of these trailers appears to be a problematic form of temporary housing and has been found to be associated with psychosocial stress among victims living in them. The negative effects of the trailers on the mental health status of occupants seems heightened when the trailers are clustered into "parks" or camps solely for disaster victims (Bolin, 1976; Erikson, 1976). The trailer courts are often highly heterogeneous socially, creating a sense of alienation among some residents and inhibiting their reintegration into a socially supportive context (Trainer & Bolin, 1976).

The trailers, because of their placement and their typically flimsy construction, can also create a sense of vulnerability and a heightened fear of disaster recurrence among victims (Bolin, 1982; Gleser et al., 1981). They often complain of such temporary housing as being crowded (Bolin, 1982) and culturally inappropriate (Bolton, 1979, Hogg, 1980), and as requiring too much red tape and bureaucratic intrusions (Bolin, 1982). Viewed in this context temporary housing can both disrupt support networks and create a set of stresses or demands completely independent of the disaster agent's impacts.

Studies of a major cyclone that destroyed Darwin, Australia, provide additional evidence of the potential negative psychosocial impacts of victim relocation. The large-scale evacuation of Darwin resulted in what Parker (1977) referred to as "relocation stressors." Such stressors include the disruption of familiar neighborhood patterns, the impairment of support network effectiveness, and increased financial costs (Garrison, 1985). As documented in studies of the Darwin relocation experience, evacuees who could not return to the impacted community exhibited the highest stress levels and the greatest incidence of related psychosocial problems (Western & Milne, 1979). Such victims were cut off from a familiar physical environment and from a supportive social environment as well, factors which appear to prolong the stress effects of a disaster (Milne, 1977; Milne 1979).

Frequent residential changes while in temporary housing have also been associated with a higher incidence of emotional stress and family adjustment problems (Bolin & Bolton, 1986; Gleser et al., 1981). The evidence is clear that victims who fail to establish stable temporary housing, particularly if they become geographically isolated, will be more likely to exhibit negative psychosocial sequelae (Lindy, Grace, and Green, 1981).

Because relocation and temporary housing can increase the financial burdens that families bear, those with the fewest resources are likely to experience the greatest stresses. Disasters tend to exacerbate preexisting trends and conditions whether at the individual or collective level. Poorer persons are more likely to report depressive symptoms over disaster-induced increases in indebtedness and to exhibit declines in self-esteem as a consequence (Pearlin & Schooler, 1978). Increased financial strains as a result of relocation and reconstruction inhibit psychosocial recovery from disaster (Bolin, 1982).

The effects of relocation, the disruption of social support, loss of home, personal injury, financial burdens, and so forth are additive and interactive. In terms of psychosocial stress, the cumulative effects can be expected to produce psychosocial disturbances, particularly for those victims with the fewest coping resources. From this perspective, social responses such as relocation not only increase stresses but can also reduce available coping resources by cutting victims off from the stress-buffering effects of social support.

As Garrison (1985) notes in the context of relocation, the psychological effects can be compounded when victims do not feel in control of the relocation process. Because in some natural disasters (and many technological ones) victims are not allowed to rebuild at their former home sites (e.g., Haas et al., 1977), they objectively lack the ability to control the situation. It has been suggested that under such circumstances depression and a sense of helplessness may emerge. (Folkman, 1984). On the other hand, victims who rebuild in their former neighborhoods and can avail themselves of the support available in the community as it reconstructs are less likely to experience such psychosocial reactions.

Research on the 1986 flooding in California (Bolin, 1986b) serves to illustrate the preceding points. Victims in that disaster were evacuated from their flood-damaged town to a neighboring community 30 miles away. A number of evacuees sought temporary shelter with friends or family in that community. Some victims, primarily those with lower income, had no support networks available to them in the host community and had to stay in a public shelter established by the local chapter of the Red Cross.

While staying in public shelters was found to be stressful by a number of victims who were interviewed, they also experienced several additional demands and problems. Because of their low income they generally had lived in rental properties in the impacted community. Following the flood, landlords were raising rents to pay for flood damages, creating severe financial burdens for some of the victims. The housing problem was intensified by the destruction of much of the available low-income housing in the community, exacerbating the predisaster housing shortage. The lack of available housing resulted in stays of up to 1 month in public shelters for some of the individuals and families that were interviewed. Because the public shelter was a considerable distance from the impacted community, victims without cars were not able to return to that community to access the support and aid available there.

For some, then, there was a compounding of stressors that resulted in depression and heightened anxiety, particularly among families in lower socioeconomic strata (Bolin, 1986b). Poorer victims faced uncertainties as to where they would eventually live. Many had to stay in public shelters for an extended period. The ones who found new housing in the community, often found it to be more expensive than their old housing, increasing their financial strain. A number faced the uncertainty as to whether they would even be able to return to the community; some had trouble acquiring government aid for housing and the replacement of lost possessions. Few had extensive support networks to augment their coping resources. These response-generated demands must be viewed in context of the initial stresses of the disaster's impact and the protracted evacuation experience described previously (Bolin, 1986b).

This case study illustrates the multiple stresses that accrue from the interaction of victim characteristics (poverty, lack of support networks), event characteristics (protracted impact, destruction of personal possessions), and response-generated stresses (evacuation, temporary shelter problems, financial strains, housing uncertainties). In contrast, middle-income families in that study tended to have more extensive support networks, owned their homes (thus qualifying for more extensive government aid), and faced fewer of the uncertainties regarding their long-term prospects in the community (Bolin, 1986a).

Relocation, of course, is not unique to natural disasters as the recent events at Love Canal, New York (Levine, 1982), Times Beach, Missouri (Smith, 1984), and Chernobyl in the Ukraine (Dudley, 1986), have demonstrated. However, relocation of populations is more common as a response to major natural disasters. The Disaster Relief Act of 1974, authorizing federal aid in response to disasters, is intended primarily to aid the victims of natural disaster. It is a major element in mitigating long-term negative effects of disasters by providing response and recovery aid, allowing stricken systems (families, organizations, communities) to externalize their losses to the national system (Bolin, 1982; Drabek, 1986).

Reconstruction and Recovery

Natural disasters with intense and violent impacts producing significant widespread property damage give rise to recovery and reconstruction activity in the impacted community. Reconstruction at the community level can result in major alterations of the postdisaster environment (Haas et al., 1977). Except in isolated cases of dam breaks and urban fires, most technological disasters do not produce extensive reconstruction activities. Rather, the abandonment of a community and resettlement of victims elsewhere (e.g., Levine, 1982) is a more likely consequence.

Like relocation, recovery and reconstruction can create continuing stresses on victims of natural disaster (Bolin, 1982; Bolin & Bolton, 1986). Many of these societally generated demands are a continuation of the ones experienced in the earlier phases of disaster response: postdisaster residential changes, increased financial burdens, job interruptions, lack of time for recreation and visitation, problems in rebuilding damaged homes, and adjustments to new or altered neighborhoods (Trainer & Bolin, 1976).

These demands, while variable in nature, may occur in addition to psychosocial strains created by death or injury within primary networks and grief over a destroyed home (e.g., Fried, 1982; Garrison, 1985). As yet, little is known about the cumulative and interactive effects of multiple problems in living and daily hassles that typically accompany the postdisaster reconstruction of home and community.

Where a large portion of a community is impacted, the distinction between victims and nonvictims is often blurred (Dudasik, 1980; Taylor, Ross, & Quarantelli, 1976). In such instances, the social and physical disruptions within the community can be stressful for nonvictims as well as the individuals directly impacted (Bolin, 1982; Erikson, 1976). In cases of massive disruption and destruction, the possibility of a supportive and altruistic environment (the therapeutic community) is negated, and the potential for psychological distress among survivors is heightened (Erikson; Lifton, 1967).

The central factor in the stress potential of the later phases of natural disaster is the character and quality of the emergent and institutionalized social responses to the event. Whether from kin and friends, local voluntary organizations, the state, the federal government, or a combination, the aid and support available is of considerable significance in determining whether the event will have long-term mental health consequences for victims (cf. Bolin & Bolton, 1986; Drabek, 1986; Lindy & Grace, 1985).

In two separate studies of family recovery from disaster, the utilization of state and federal aid was found to be positively correlated with both economic and psychosocial recovery (Bolin, 1982a; Bolin, 1986a). Victims who either could not or did not receive financial, housing, and material aid were consistently slower to recover and more likely to report emotional strains persisting 15 months after disaster impact (Bolin, 1982). The data also disclosed that there was differential use of formal aid programs. Poorer victims, older victims, and blacks were less likely to receive adequate aid and, as a result, were slower to recover (Bolin, 1986a; Bolin & Klenow, 1983). Blacks, victims from lower socioeconomic strata, and those with more than three minor dependents exhibited higher levels of reported emotional disruptions and were slower than others to reestablish permanent housing (Bolin & Bolton, 1986).

Financial stresses associated with the recovery process were most pronounced for those categories of victims who were already financially disadvantaged. Disasters and the responses to them were found to create financial, emotional, and instrumental demands in excess of the coping capacities of some victims. While the event was also followed by a therapeutic response in which new sources of aid became available, the accumulation of post-disaster demands had its greatest negative effect on minorities and the poor, the victims who received the least aid (Bolin & Bolton, 1986).

The long-term psychosocial impacts of natural disasters will be affected not only by event and victim characteristics, but by the patterns of aid distribution and the differential access to that aid. In addition, the nature of community reconstruction can affect the psychosocial recovery of victims. The process of reconstruction can alter the spatial arrangement of neighborhoods and businesses, thereby disrupting behavioral routines (Trainer & Bolin, 1976). If there is widespread alteration of predisaster community patterns, victims may experience chronic stresses, especially if the alterations disrupt social support networks and access to the therapeutic community (Bolin, 1982; Milne, 1977).

In natural disasters such as earthquakes, the potential is high for major change in the postdisaster community (e.g., Bolton, 1979; Dudasik, 1980). If the impacted community or region is transformed in the reconstruction process, it may create additional long-range adjustment demands for persons in that community.

Because community reconstruction can continue long after the therapeutic community has faded, disruptions tolerated during the initial response period may, if they persist, become far more burdensome to victims (Bolin, 1982). In general, the pace of reconstruction is faster for business and community structures than it is for individual families. Victims may still be coping with recovery demands long after the community per se is recovered. The psychological effects of coping with recovery demands after the physical signs of the disaster have been erased has not been extensively studied (cf. Green, 1985). However, recovery research does suggest natural disasters and the responses to them may create stresses that persist well beyond the therapeutic community and the heightened social support that accompanies it (Bolin, 1982; Golec, 1983; Haas et al., 1977).

SUMMARY AND CONCLUSIONS

The issue of the psychosocial impacts of natural disasters is embedded in the interplay of agent impact characteristics, victim characteristics, and social responses to the event. From a systems perspective, a disaster creates sets of demands on the impacted systems, often in excess of the response capacity of those systems. The individual victim turns to the residential family first; families may seek help from extended kin networks. At the community level, linkages are often established with the state or national government. These linkages constitute a process of systemic reorganization in order to cope with demands in excess of capacity.

To understand the psychosocial impacts of natural disaster, it is necessary to consider a number of factors. One set of variables, victim characteristics (age, race, sex, socioeconomic status), has only been alluded to here, because it is a part of predisaster system qualities and is discussed in accompanying chapters. Although as stress events, many types of disasters share generic features, some of the unique elements of natural disaster have been noted. Agent characteristics and social responses to natural disaster have been discussed as the two areas in which some of these unique elements can be identified.

Of course, for any agent characteristic (scope, speed of onset, duration, severity) of natural disaster, an analogue may be identified in the realm of technological–human-caused disasters. Unlike technological disasters, natural disasters always have observable physical impacts, resulting in material destruction of some part of a social system. Consequently, natural disasters always create response and recovery demands.

Because they always engender immediate social response (except in the case of droughts), they are accompanied by response-generated demands (evacuation, relocation, temporary sheltering, rebuilding, reestablishing neighborhoods and businesses, etc.) All phases of natural disaster, from the preimpact warning phase through impact, restoration, and recovery, can create stresses on victims. Some of these stresses are from impact characteristics, and some are from social reponses to the disaster.

Natural disasters often give rise to a period of altruism and heightened social support afterwards. This therapeutic community phase can be a significant factor in reducing the psychosocial stresses of disaster, through the empathy and support that may be forthcoming to the survivors. However, the reconstruction and recovery process often outlasts the therapeutic phase, and long-term psychosocial stresses may manifest themselves only after the postdisaster altruism declines (Bolin, 1982).

Victims who are denied access to social support, whether through evacuation, relocation, or alteration of the community during reconstruction, are more likely to experience psychosocial strains. A supportive social environment acts as a stress buffer for survivors and mitigates potential mental health impacts.

Mental health intervention programs must pay attention to complexities of individual experiences with the disaster and with the social environment of the victims (Dynes & Quarantelli, 1976; Lindy & Grace, 1985). Disaster response at all levels is a process, and as such, response-generated demands change qualitatively and quantitatively over time. Community responses can alter the recovery environment, creating or reducing psychological stresses on victims. Changes that disrupt support networks are critical in producing or exacerbating psychosocial disturbances.

That natural disaster agents are familiar to many does not negate their disruptive effects on ongoing human systems. Sudden, wide-scale impacts, particularly ones that cannot be avoided, increase stress levels. Communities that lack adequate material and organizational skills to respond effectively will increase the potential stress effects of the disaster on the individual and his or her family. Community responses that disrupt social support networks and that result in significant alterations in the postdisaster environment will increase the risk of mental health problems for some individuals. Natural disasters, more than most other types, are likely to produce physical effects to which victims may be exposed for extended periods, creating the potential for persistent stresses.

Thus, natural disasters can create a paradoxical situation. On the one hand they can produce a range of event-related demands and social response demands. On the other they can create a supportive environment of heightened social solidarity and altruism that can buffer the negative effects of impact and response stresses. Clearly, the natural disasters most likely to be associated with mental health problems are the ones that create major impact demands (death, injury, large-scale property loss), along with response demands (relocation, sheltering problems), but that fail to give rise to an adequate therapeutic response at the community level.

Intervention strategies for mental health practitioners must be based first on a recognition of the impact and social response characteristics that are most likely to create high levels of psychosocial stress. Situations in which there is widespread use of temporary housing, particularly trailers, or significant relocation of populations, are likely to produce continuing psychological strains. Any impact characteristic or societal response that disrupts existing support networks or established behavioral routines (work, school, shopping, visitation) has the potential for creating persistent emotional stresses.

Outreach programs following natural disasters are a useful way of disseminating information to victims about available aid and services, particularly if indigenous workers can be utilized. The stationing of outreach workers in Disaster Application Centers to help victims fill out aid forms can also be used to familiarize victims with local mental health programs and workers, reducing victim reluctance to use counseling services (Baisden, 1979; Cohen & Ahearn, 1980).

Because victims' mental health problems are often a result of stress created by the countless response and recovery problems with which they must deal, mobilizing support networks can be an important mitigating factor. Mental health workers can act as facilitators, helping victims activate both informal and formal support networks and reducing the level of demands that victims must confront. Victims typically need both instrumental assistance and emotional support in a setting where familiar sources of help may be difficult to access. Mental health professionals should focus on helping victims to establish links with new sources of aid, as well as to restore ties to informal support networks that may have been disrupted (Frederick, 1977; Heffron, 1977; Solomon, 1985).

Because natural disasters can create long-term alterations in the community setting and can subject victims to extended stays in temporary housing, mental health professionals should also be alert to the lingering stresses that some victims may experience. Long after many in a stricken community may have forgotten about the disaster, some victims may still be living in temporary housing or attempting to pay off disaster reconstruction loans. Victims can experience frustrations and anxieties over knowing that although the rest of the community has recovered, the effects of the disaster continue for them (Golec, 1983).

Outreach efforts shouldn't stop simply because the more visible features of impact have been repaired. Victims may continue to experience elevated demand levels and can benefit from the continuing availability of disaster-relevant support services (Hartsough, 1982; Zusman, 1976). Because natural disasters can create community-wide disruptions, even when their zone of destruction is limited, outreach and related mental health services should emphasize that their assistance is not just for those directly impacted.

It is not unusual for persons outside the impact zone to experience varying degrees of emotional distress through being exposed to the results of the disaster or by knowing victims of the disaster. It has been shown that these secondary victims (Golec, 1983) may be very reluctant to utilize mental health services, because they feel the services are there for "real" victims (e.g., Bolin, 1982). Outreach programs should legitimize their presence in the community and emphasize that their services are available for all who are experiencing difficulties in coping with disaster-related problems. Effective mental health interventions will be grounded in an awareness of the specific disaster-induced demands being faced by victims and on a cognizance of the problems created in the social responses to natural disasters.

REFERENCES

Ahearn, F. (1981). Disaster mental health: A pre-post and post-earthquake comparison of psychiatric admission rates. *The Urban and Social Change Review, 14*(2), 22–28.

Ahearn, F., & Castellon, S. (1979). Mental health problems following a disaster situation. *Acta Psiquiatrica y Psicologica de America Latina, 25,* 58–68.

Baisden, B. (1979). Social factors affecting mental health delivery: The case of disasters. In E. Lewis, L. Nelson, D. Scully, J. Scully, & J. Williams (Eds.), *Sociological Research Symposium IX* (pp. 238–241). Virginia Commonwealth University: Richmond.

Barton, A. (1970). *Communities in disaster.* Garden City, NY: Doubleday.

Bates, F., Fogleman C., Parenton V., Pittman R., & Tracy, G. (1963). *The social and psychological consequences of a natural disaster.* National Research Council Disaster Study No. 18. Washington, DC: National Academy of Science.

Baum, A., Fleming, R., & Davidson, K. (1983). Natural disaster and technological catastrophe. *Environment and Behavior, 15,* 333–354.

Baum, A., & Davidson, L. (1985). A suggested framework for studying factors that contribute to trauma in disaster. In B. Sowder (ed.), *Disasters and mental health: Selected contemporary perspectives* (DHHS Publication No. ADM 85-1421, pp. 29–40). Washington, DC: U.S. Government Printing Office.

Berren, M., Beigel, A., & Ghertner, S. (1980). A typology for the classification of disasters. *Community Mental Health Journal, 16,* 103–120.

Bolin, R. (1976). Family recovery from natural disaster: A preliminary model. *Mass Emergencies, 1,* 267–277.

Bolin, R. (1982). *Long-term family recovery from disaster,* Boulder: University of Colorado, Institute of Behavioral Science.

Bolin, R. (1983, April 21–23). *Social support and psychosocial stress in disaster.* Paper presented at the meeting of the Western Social Science Association, Albuquerque, NM.

Bolin, R. (1985). Disaster characteristics and psychosocial impacts. In B. Sowder (Ed.), *Disasters and mental health: Selected contemporary perspectives* (DHHS Publication No. 85-1421, pp. 3–28). Washington, DC: U.S. Government Printing Office.

Bolin, R. (1986a). Impact and recovery: A comparison of black and white disaster victims. *Mass Emergencies and Disasters, 4,* 35–50.

Bolin, R. (1986b). *A quick response study of the 1986 California floods.* Report to the Natural Hazards Information Center, University of Colorado, Boulder.

Bolin, R., & Bolton, P. (1986). *Race, religion, and ethnicity in disaster recovery.* Boulder: University of Colorado, Institute of Behavioral Science.

Bolin, R., & Klenow, D. (1983). Response of the elderly to disaster: An age-stratified analysis. *International Journal of Aging and Human Development, 16,* 283–296.

Bolton, P. (1979). *Family recovery following disaster: The case of Managua, Nicaragua.* Unpublished doctoral dissertation, University of Colorado, Boulder.

Boyd, S. (1981). Psychological reactions of disaster victims. *South African Medical Journal, 60,* 744–748.

Bromet, E., & Dunn, L. (1981). Mental health of mothers nine months after the Three Mile Island accident. *The Urban and Social Change Review, 14,* 12–15.

Bromet, E., Schulberg, H. C., Dunn, L., & Gondek, P. (1980). *Three Mile Island: Mental health findings.* Rockville, MD: National Institute of Mental Health.

Cohen, R. E., & Ahearn, F. (1980). *Handbook for mental health care of disaster victims.* Baltimore: The Johns Hopkins University Press.

Covello, V. (1983). The perception of technological risk: A literature review. *Technological Forecasting and Social Change, 23,* 285–297.

Davis, I. (1975, January). Disaster housing: A case study of Managua. *Architectural Design,* 42–47.

Drabek, T. (1968). *Disaster in aisle 13.* Columbus: Ohio State University.

Drabek, T. (1969). Social processes in disaster: Family evacuation. *Social Problems, 16,* 336–349.

Drabek, T. (1986). *Human system responses to disaster.* New York: Springer-Verlag.

Drabek, T., & Boggs, K. (1968). Families in disaster: Reactions and relatives. *Journal of Marriage and the Family, 30,* 443–451.

Drabek, T., & Key, W. (1984). *Conquering disaster: Family recovery and long-term consequence.* New York: Irvington.

Dudasik, S. (1980). Victimization in natural disaster. *Disasters, 4,* 329–338.

Dudley, E. (1986). In the aftermath of Chernobyl: Contamination, upheaval and loss. *Nucleus, 8*(3), 3–5.

Dynes, R., & Quarantelli, E. (1976). The family and community context of individual reactions to disaster. In H. Parad, H. Resnik, & L. Parad (Eds.), *Emergency and disaster management: A mental health sourcebook* (pp. 231–245). Bowie, MD: Charles Press.

Dynes, R., Quarantelli, E., & Kreps, G. (1981). *A perspective on disaster planning.* (Report Series No. 11). Newark: University of Delaware, Disaster Research Center.

Erikson, K. (1976). *Everything in its path.* New York: Simon & Schuster.

Folkman, S. (1984). Personal control and stress and coping processes: A theoretical analysis. *Journal of Personality and Social Psychology, 46,* 839–852.

Frederick, C. (1977). Current thinking about crisis or psychological intervention in United States disasters. *Mass Emergencies, 2,* 43–50.

Fried, M. (1963). Grieving for a lost home. In J. Duhl (Ed.), *The urban condition: People and policy in the metropolis.* (pp. 151–171). New York: Basic Books.

Fried, M. (1982). Endemic stress: The psychology of resignation and the politics of scarcity. *American Journal of Orthopsychiatry, 52,* 4–19.

Garrison, J. (1985). Mental health implication of disaster relocation in the United States. *Journal of Mass Emergencies and Disasters, 3,* (2), 49–66.

Gleser, G., Green, B., & Winget, C. (1981). *Prolonged psychosocial effects of disaster: A Study of Buffalo Creek.* New York: Academic Press.

Golec, J. (1983). A contextual approach to the social psychological study of disaster recovery. *Journal of Mass Emergencies and Disasters, 1,* 255–276.

Green, B. (1985). Conceptual and methodological issues in assessing the psychological impact of disaster. In B. Sowder (Ed.), *Mental health and disaster: Selected contemporary perspectives* (DHHS Publication No. ADM 85-1421). Washington, DC: U.S. Government Printing Office.

Greenson, R., & Mintz, T. (1972). California earthquake 1971: Some psychoanalytic observations. *International Journal of Psychoanalytic Psychotherapy, 1,* 7–23.

Haas, J., & Drabek, T. (1973). *Complex organizations.* New York: Macmillan.

Haas, J., Kates, R., & Bowden, M. (1977). *Reconstruction following disaster.* Cambridge: M.I.T. Press.

Hannigan, J., & Kueneman, R. (1978). Anticipating flood emergencies: A case study of Canadian disaster subculture. In E. Quarantelli (Ed.), *Disasters: Theory and research* (pp. 129–146). Beverly Hills: Sage.

Hartsough, D. (1982). Planning for disaster: A new community outreach program for mental health centers. *Journal of Community Psychology, 10,* 255–264.

Heffron, E. (1977). Project outreach: Crisis intervention following natural disaster. *Journal of Community Psychology, 5,* 103–111.

Hogg, R. (1980). Pastoralism and impoverishment: The case of the Isolo Boran of Northern Kenya. *Disasters, 4,* 299–310.

Hufnagel, R., & Perry, R. (1982, April 14–16). *Collective behavior: Implications for disaster planning.* Paper presented at the meeting of the Pacific Sociological Association Meeting, San Diego.

Instituut voor Sociaal Onderzoek van het Nederlandse Volk Amsterdam. (1955). *Studies in the Holland flood disaster 1953.* National Academy of Science–National Research Council, Volumes I–IV. Washington, DC: National Academy of Sciences.

Jasnowski, M. (1984). The ecosystemic perspective in clinical assessment and intervention. In W. A. O'Connor & B. Lubin (Eds.), *Ecological approaches to clinical and community psychology* (pp. 41–56). New York: Wiley.

Kahn, R., & Antonucci, T. (1980). Convoys over the life course: Attachment roles and social support. In P. Baltes & P. Brim (Eds.), *Life span and development* (pp. 381–412). Boston: Lexington.

Kessler, R. (1979). A strategy for studying differential vulnerability to the psychological consequences of stress. *Journal of Health and Social Behavior, 20,* 100–108.

Kinston, W., & Rosser, R. (1974). Disaster: Effects on mental and physical state. *Journal of Psychosomatic Research, 18,* 437–456.

Lang, K., & Lang, G. (1964). Collective responses to the threat of disaster. In G. Grosser, H. Wechsler, M. Greenblatt (Eds.), *The threat of impending disaster.* (pp. 50–73). Cambridge: M.I.T. Press.

Lazarus, R. (1966). *Psychological stress and the coping process.* New York: McGraw-Hill.

Lazarus, R., & Cohen, J. (1977). Environmental stress. In I. Altman & J. Wohlwill (Eds.), *Human behavior and enviroment: Current theory and research* (pp. 89–127). New York: Plenum.

Leik, R. K., Leik, S. A., Ekker, K., & Gifford, G. A. (1982). *Under the threat of Mount St. Helens: A study of chronic family stress.* Minneapolis: University of Minnesota, Family Study Center.

Levine, A. (1982). *Love Canal: Science, politics and people.* Toronto: Lexington.

Lifton, R. J. (1967). *Survivors of Hiroshima: Death in life.* New York: Random House.

Lifton, R. J., & Olson, E. (1976). The human meaning of total disaster. *Psychiatry, 39,* 1–18.

Lindy, J. D., & Grace, M. (1985). The recovery environment: Continuing stressor versus a healing psychosocial space. In B. Sowder (Ed.), *Disasters and mental health: Selected contemporary perspectives* (DHHS Publication No. ADM 85-1421, pp. 137–149). Washington, DC: U.S. Government Printing Office.

Lindy, J. D., Grace, M. C., & Green, B. L. (1981). Survivors: Outreach to a reluctant population. *American Journal of Orthopsychiatry, 5,* 468–478.

Mileti, D. (1980). Human adjustment to the risk of environmental extremes. *Sociology and Social Research, 64,* 328–347.

Mileti, D., Drabek, T. E., & Haas, J. E. (1975). *Human systems in extreme environments.* Boulder: University of Colorado, Institute of Behavioral Science.

Miller, J. A., Turner, J. G., Kimball, E. (1981). Big Thompson flood victims: One year later. *Family Relations, 30,* 111–116.

Milne, G. (1977). Cyclone Tracy: Some consequences of the evacuation for adult victims. *Australian Psychologist, 12,* 39–54.

Milne, G. (1979). Cyclone Tracy: Psychological and social consequences. In J. I. Reid (Ed.), *Planning for people in natural disaster* (pp. 116–123). Townsville, Queensland, Australia: James Cook University of N. Queensland.

Nigg, J. (1986, October 10–15). *The issuance of earthquake "predictions": Information diffusion and public response.* Paper presented at the Italy–U.S. Conference on Disaster Research. University of Delaware, Disaster Research Center, Newark.

O'Connor, W., & Lubin, B. (Eds.), (1984). *Ecological approaches to clinical and community psychology.* New York: Wiley.

Parker, G. (1975). Psychological disturbance in Darwin evacuees following cyclone Tracy. *Medical Journal of Australia, 1,* 650–652.

Parker, G. (1977). Cyclone Tracy and Darwin evacuees: On the restoration of the species. *British Journal of Psychiatry, 130,* 548–555.

Pearlin, L. I., & Schooler, C. (1978). The structure of coping. *Journal of Health and Social Behavior, 16,* 2–21.

Pelanda, C. (1982, August 12–17). *Disaster and order: Theoretical problems in disaster research.* Paper presented at the Tenth World Congress of Sociology, Mexico City.

Perry, R. W., & Lindell, M. K. (1978). The psychological consequences of natural disaster: A review of research on American communities. *Mass Emergencies, 3,* 105–115.

Perry, R. W., Lindell, M., & Green, M. (1980). *The implications of natural hazard evacuation warning studies for crisis relocation planning.* Seattle, WA: Battelle Human Affairs Research Center.

Quarantelli, E. (1979). *The consequences of disasters for mental health: Conflicting views* (Monograph #62). Columbus: Ohio State University, Disaster Research Center.

Quarantelli, E. (1982). *Sheltering and housing after major community disaster: Case studies and general conclusions.* Columbus: Ohio State University, Disaster Research Center.

Quarantelli, E. (1985). Social support systems: Some behavioral patterns in the context of mass evacuation activities. In B. Sowder (Ed.), *Disasters and mental health: Selected contemporary perspectives* (DHHS Publication No. ADM 85-1421, pp. 122–136). Washington, DC: U.S. Government Printing Office.

Schorr, J. K., Goldsteen, R., & Carter, C. H. (1982, August 12–17). *The long-term impact of man-made disasters: A sociological examination of a small town in the aftermath of the Three Mile Island nuclear reactor accident.* Paper presented at the Tenth World Congress of Sociology, Mexico City.

Smith, E. (1984). *Chronology of disaster in Eastern Missouri.* (Contract No. 83md525181) Report for the National Institute of Mental Health.

Solomon, S. (1985). Enhancing social support for disaster victims. In B. Sowder (Ed.), *Disasters and mental health: Selected contemporary perspectives* (DHHS Publication No. 14-8521, pp. 107–121). Washington, DC: U.S. Government Printing Office.

Sowder, B. (1985). Some mental health impacts of loss and injury: A look outside the disaster field. In B. Sowder (Ed.), *Disasters and mental health: Selected contemporary perspectives* (DHHS Publication No. ADM 14-8521, pp. 74–106). Washington, DC: U.S. Government Printing Office.

Taylor, V., Ross, G. A., & Quarantelli, E. (1976). *Delivery of mental health services in disasters: The Xenia tornado and some applications* (Book and Monograph Series, Vol. II). Columbus: Ohio State University, Disaster Research Center.

Tierney, K. J., & Baisden, B. (1979). *Crisis intervention programs for disaster victims: A source book and manual for small communities.* Rockville, MD: National Institute of Mental Health.

Trainer, P., & Bolin, R. (1976). Persistent effects of disasters on daily activities. *Mass Emergencies, 1,* 279–290.

Turner, R. H., (1983). Waiting for disaster: Changing reactions to earthquake forecasts in Southern California. *Mass Emergencies and Disasters,1,* 307–334.

Turner, R. H., Nigg, J., & Paz, D. (1986). *Waiting for disaster.* Berkeley: University of California Press.

Van Arsdol, M. G., Sabagh, D. & Alexander, F. (1964). Reality and the perception of environmental hazards. *Journal of Health and Human Behavior, 5,* 144–155.

Warheit, G. (1985). A propositional paradigm for estimating the impact of disasters on mental health. *Mass Emergencies and Disasters, 3,* 29–48.

Weller, J., & Wenger, D. (1973, April 4–6). *Disaster subcultures: The cultural residues of community disasters.* Paper presented at the meeting of the North Central Sociological Society, Cincinnati, OH.

Western, J. S., & Milne, G. (1979). Some social effects of a natural hazard: Darwin residents and Cyclone Tracy. In R. L. Heathcote & B. G. Thom (Eds.), *Natural hazards in Australia* (pp. 448–502). Canberra: Australian Academy of Science.

White, G., & Haas G. (1975). *Assessment of research on natural hazards.* Boulder: University of Colorado, Insitute of Behavioral Science.

Withey, S. (1964). Reaction to uncertain threat. In G. Grosser, H. Wechsler, & M. Greenblatt (Eds.), *The threat of impending disaster* (pp. 105–114). Cambridge: M.I.T. Press.

Wolfenstein, M. (1957). Causal attribution and personal control. In J. Harvey, W. Ickers, & R. Kidd (Eds.), *New directions in attribution research.* (pp. 56–67). Hillsdale, NJ: Erlbaum.

Zusman, J. (1976). Meeting mental health needs in a disaster: A public health view. In J. Parad, H. L. P. Reznik, & L. G. Parad (Eds.), *Emergency and disaster management: A mental health sourcebook* (pp. 159–167). Bowie, MD: Charles Press.

CHAPTER 4

Human Responses and Treatment Needs in Airline Disasters

JAMES NEAL BUTCHER AND LAURIE A. DUNN

Airline crashes and airline-targeted terrorist attacks are among the most feared and dreaded disasters in contemporary civilization. In 1985, nearly 2,000 people were victims of airplane crashes around the world, making it the deadliest year in civil aviation history. Not only are those who fly potential victims of an air disaster, but people on the ground can also be seriously impacted by airplane crashes due to loss of life and extensive property or environmental damage. This situation occurred in 1978 when an inbound PSA flight, after a midair collision with another aircraft, ploughed through a San Diego suburb. Twenty-two homes were destroyed, and 9 people on the ground in addition to the 137 airline passengers were killed. Repercussions of a major air disaster can extend beyond the immediate effects of the crash into the community as a whole. Productivity may decline because of jobs lost and because of loss of faith in both the transportation industries and government agencies that are charged with preventing these terrible mishaps.[1]

The impact that aircraft disasters can have on human adjustment is great, yet most communities and airports have not planned for the possibility of such disasters or have not incorporated a psychological intervention program into their disaster response planning efforts. This chapter addresses several

We would like to thank Dr. Carolyn Williams for comments she made on an earlier draft of the manuscript.

[1]Although these tragedies and statistics are sobering, they are not presented here to undermine the importance of the air industry to consumers or its favorable overall safety record. Air travel is a comparatively safe way to travel. Far more lives are lost on American highways, where an estimated 43,000 traffic fatalities occur every year (Greenwald, 1986). On a mile-for-mile basis, a person is 100 times more likely to be killed in an automobile than in an airplane. Nonetheless, the impact of air disasters—both psychological and economic—is enormous, and for those who have been directly affected by them through death of loved ones or enduring emotional distress, such statistics give small comfort.

aspects of aircraft disasters and their impact on human adaptation. The disaster syndrome, as manifested by victims of airline disasters, will be discussed, and important efforts at reducing the ensuing psychological adjustment problems will be considered.

POTENTIAL CAUSES OF CONTEMPORARY AIR DISASTERS

In the early days of aviation, disasters were perhaps more easily understood in light of the incipient state of aviation technology. Flying the early airways involved known risks: Our ability to monitor and predict adverse weather conditions and to communicate this vital information to pilots was far less advanced; fatal mistakes were sometimes made in the design and construction of early aircraft and were only corrected after a tragic experience; there was little or no pilot screening for medical and psychological problems; pilot training was sparse; and pilot certification was nonexistent.

In the 1980s, great strides were made in assuring that the aircraft, the airways, and the flight crews were worthy of carrying passengers. One might assume that the traditional lethal factors of inclement weather, pilot error, flawed and unsafe aircraft, and faulty communication would have been all but eliminated as contemporary causes of air mishaps. Yet many of the traditional problems (along with some new ones) continue to affect air travel today:

1. *Weather.* One of the worst crashes in 1985 was caused by a poorly understood and difficult-to-predict weather phenomenon called "wind shear" when the aircraft attempted to land at the Dallas–Fort Worth Airport, killing 134 passengers. Few airports or airliners today have the expensive radar equipment capable of detecting this subtle but hazardous condition.

2. *Aircraft Design Problems.* Design flaws in aircraft still slip through Federal Aviation Administration (FAA) inspection, as in the case of a DC-10 cargo door that could be closed improperly by baggage handlers. The door could then blow out under pressure changes during flight, causing rapid depressurization and a dangerous flying condition. This slippage occurs in part, because the ones most qualified to inspect designs are the engineers who designed the craft in the first place. These individuals may serve dual roles as company designers and FAA inspectors (Nance, 1986). Potential hazards in design may be missed until the craft has already gone into production.

3. *Increased Air Traffic and Air Traffic Control Problems.* Poor communication between crew members and ground controllers continues to be cited as a causal or contributory factor to accidents. In 1977 one of the most costly crashes in terms of human life took place when two jumbo jets collided at the airport in Tenerife, Canary Islands, because the pilots of one 747 misunderstood the air controller's instructions and believed they had been cleared for takeoff. In the poor visibility, the jet literally ran over another

747 ahead of it on the runway as both prepared for takeoff using the same runway.

The U.S. air traffic control system has been considered weak, especially in the years following the air traffic controller's strike and the subsequent firing of several thousand air traffic controllers. There have been numerous reported near misses and some collisions as a result of air traffic controller errors or of confusion in the system. In June 1986, a midair collision took the lives of all crew and passengers on two charter flights over the Grand Canyon because of inadequate air traffic control. On August 31, 1986, two airplanes collided over the city of Los Angeles, killing all passengers aboard and numerous people on the ground; the accident was due, in part, to air traffic congestion.

4. *Failures in Crew Coordination.* Poor crew coordination practices may also result from the subtle but entrenched communication system that exists in the cockpit (Foushee, 1982). Subordinate flight members are often reluctant to assert themselves over the captain's authority, even when a potentially dangerous situation arises. Subordinate crew members may fail to speak up when questions arise in their minds about the safety of the operation, assuming that the captain has already registered the threat and determined it innocuous. Or, if they do raise queries, crew members may hesitate to pursue the point forcefully when the captain seems not to have understood the seriousness of the condition, has dismissed it too soon, or has not acknowledged that the information was heard.

There have been several instances in which flight recorders recovered at crash sites have documented doubts raised by crew members about the flight that went unheeded until it was too late (e.g., National Transportation and Safety Board [NTSB] Blue Cover Accident Rep. No. NTSB-AAR-80-1; NTSB-AAR-82-8; NTSB-AAR-74-4). Effective crew coordination and information transfer are critical, since large carriers employ thousands of pilots who are often unfamiliar with each other's style and ability, and, if they are new to the airline, with the special features of certain aircraft or of that company's operations.

5. *Airline-Targeted Terrorism.* The rash of terrorist attacks over the past several decades has added a new danger to the airways and other transportation systems (e.g., trains or cruise liners) in which hundreds of people can be taken hostage (Crelinsten & Szabo, 1979; Jacobs, Ramp, & Breay, 1979). In his book on terrorism, Netanyahu (1986) points out that terrorist attacks, a popular political weapon, have increased tenfold in the 1970s and 1980s. Although terrorist attack remains a very slim possibility for the average traveler, it remains an especially reprehensible threat and appears to be on the increase in the world.

6. *Economic Pressures on the Airlines and the Possibility of Ignored Maintenance.* Deregulation of the airline industry may have added to the potential for air disaster (Nance, 1986). Charter companies, and even major

airlines threatened by take-over from new companies and by ever-changing economic pressures, may possibly cut corners wherever feasible. Paperwork may go ignored or be faked in rapid start-up operations or in mergers of carriers. Pilots shuffled between companies may not always be properly trained on the types of aircraft they fly. Mechanics may not be familiar with the different planes acquired by their companies when airlines are merged.

For airline management, remaining solvent has become a major concern; for the company's employees, jobs are on the line. Thus, in the air transportation business, as in any business, winning against the competitor comes down to an economic yardstick in the end. Human safety may become another cost accountable item, and what increases safety in the air is not always what increases profit. Of course, for the sake of business an airline must maintain an acceptable flying record without accidents to mar its reputation, or it will risk losing its passengers. Most reputable airlines follow the legal guidelines for safety; however, the cost-cutting practices of some carriers may have created a game of chance for the passenger who boards a plane as unsafe conditions build up (Nance, 1986).[2]

UNIQUE ASPECTS OF AIR DISASTERS

The psychological impact of air disasters can be appreciated when one considers that airline crashes almost always result in fatalities and that dozens to hundreds of individuals may be involved at a time. There is frequently little warning of disaster, and even if danger is recognized, the crew and passengers are often helpless to avert the disaster once it becomes imminent. The victims of air crashes are usually strangers to each other from widely differing backgrounds and so encounter an "almost total lack of community" (Frederick, 1981, p. 17) during the immediate postdisaster period. An even greater sense of disorientation and isolation may ensue if the crash occurs on an international flight among peoples of other nationalities or on foreign soil where the language, customs, and laws may be alien.

Following the crash, the survivors usually disperse quickly. Thus, a sense of sharing or social support, which is present at the site of some disasters, may not develop to provide reassurance to survivors, nor may the passengers have the chance to vent their feelings and to receive psychological first aid at the crash site. Satisfactory resolution of the crisis experience may be delayed or preempted. If the disaster occurs far from home, victims tend to go away quickly so long-term follow-up care and assessment of ongoing needs is difficult. Others who have not suffered or been injured themselves may not be able to relate to the particular trauma of the victims when they return to their communities. The injuries of survivors may be quite severe and may leave lifelong disfigurement, as well as physical and emotional scars.

[2]At the time of this writing, the accident and near-miss rate of recent years has prompted the Congress of the United States to introduce new regulation proposals for the airline industry.

Even air crashes without death or serious injury can result in severe trauma among survivors. Sloan (1986) followed up 32 survivors of a charter plane crash and administered several psychological tests in the months following the accident. He reported that there were intense levels of stress among the survivors, which decreased over time.

Besides the impact to the survivors, the aftermath of a crash can be quite traumatic to relief workers and other official personnel who must recover the evidence relating to the cause of the accident, as well as gather and identify human remains. The families of victims may be barraged by unwanted media attention and by lawyers who seek to instigate litigation on the survivors' behalf. Finally, in many instances, an aircraft disaster represents a betrayal of public trust (Nance, 1986). Unlike natural disasters such as tornadoes, floods, or other acts of God, many air disasters are ultimately the result of human error, whether it be due to faulty aircraft design; to poor airline management practices in terms of maintenance, crew training, and safety precautions; or to pilot error. In any event, the long-term mental health impact for all involved can be enormous.

RESPONSIBILITY FOR MANAGING HUMAN PROBLEMS FOLLOWING AN AIR DISASTER

Aircraft manufacturers and airlines have traditionally applied their efforts to reducing the likelihood of accidents or to limiting the negative consequences of crashes through improved aircraft design and safe operating procedures. Neither party has focused much attention upon managing the problems that develop *when* an aircraft accident occurs.[3]

Generally, the response of airline management to the specter of potential disaster is to deny that any problems exist. Even when faced with undeniable figures such as the death toll in 1985, airlines and aircraft manufacturers may suggest that the numbers represent nothing more than a statistical aberration. Different aircraft and airlines were involved, so no common target for blame can be identified. Additionally, the reasons cited for the crashes are dissimilar and range from weather conditions to mechanical malfunction to a suspected bomb. Furthermore, airline accidents are relatively rare. In the past 25 years, fewer than 140 fatal crashes have occurred among the civilian airlines of Western countries (Greenwald, 1986).

The complacency of airports in preparing to cope with a major disaster may also be due to poorly defined limits of responsibility and the lack of an

---

[3]Not all airlines have ignored the important problem of managing human problems that follow an aircraft disaster. For example, Republic Airlines (1986) incorporated a crisis intervention component into their Emergency Manual and arranged for professional psychologists to serve on the Go Team responding to emergencies. This program was discontinued after the company merged with another carrier.

organized consumer group to seek remediation and action from airport management, airline management, or government agencies (Barbash, Yoeli, Ruskin, & Moeller, 1986). Jones (1982) suggests that the accident investigation process may itself contribute to the problem of mass denial on the part of airline management. The investigation team is seen "working long hours and expending a great deal of emotional energy to prove that this accident was preventable" (Jones, 1982, p. 597). All factors that contributed to the crash—psychological, physical, mechanical, aerodynamic, managerial—are accounted for and explained. This may contribute to further denial on the part of airport management, airline administrators, and air crew who can now tell themselves, "Since the cause of the accident is identified and can therefore be controlled against, it will not happen again [or, at least, not to *us*]."

But, accidents *will* continue to occur. And it is believed by some experts that the threat of disasters of major proportion is increasing. Since the deregulation of the airline industry in 1978, the number of flights and passengers has increased dramatically. About 30,000 flights take off each day in the United States, which is a more than 10% increase (Greenwald, 1986). Only 36 airlines had interstate routes in 1978; the figure stood at nearly 100 interstate airlines in 1985 (Alexander, 1986). The number of near collisions between aircraft was 592 in 1984, a new record (Greenwald).

With the increase in air traffic and nonconcomitant increase in air traffic controllers and other airport personnel to handle the traffic, this dubious record may be surpassed. According to Federal Aviation Commission statistics, the percentage change in the number of FAA-certified airlines since deregulation is + 150% compared to a percentage change in the number of FAA inspectors of only + 2% ("Harper's Index," 1986). Prior to 1985, the greatest number of lives lost in a single year was just over 1,000 in 1974. This has climbed to the nearly 2,000 people killed from crashes in 1985 ("A Bad Start," 1986).

FEDERAL REQUIREMENTS FOR DISASTER RESPONSE

For certification and permission to operate, the Federal Aviation Administration (FAA) does require basic emergency preparedness on the part of airports (Federal Aviation Regulations, Title 14, C.F.R., Part 139). Airports must demonstrate that they possess "an emergency plan that insures prompt response to all emergencies and other unusual conditions in order to minimize the possibility and extent of personal and property damage on the airport." This plan must include the following items: (1) instruction of relevant personnel in how to respond to general aircraft accidents, bomb incidents, fires, natural disasters, sabotage, radiation, or nuclear attack; (2) medical services in the form of basic medical supplies and assistance, information on local hospital capabilities and on-call personnel, and transportation to appropriate facilities; (3) names and contact information of rescue squads, ambulances, "go team" or disaster response team members, and other immediate aid agencies; (4) buildings (if the accident occurs on airport property) for the accommodation of the injured and deceased until appropriate transfer can be arranged; and (5) procedures for crowd control.

In short, each airport must show that it has a coordinated emergency plan with law enforcement agencies, firefighters, rescue units, medical facilities, and key public officials. Notably, drills to ascertain the effectiveness of the plan in operation or to prepare the emergency workers are *not* required.

THE NEGLECTED ENTITY: HUMAN VICTIMS OF AIR DISASTERS

Airport operators are responsible for monitoring safe operations of their airport and for developing procedures for responding to aircraft accidents on their field. However, in the face of other demands, disaster response programs are often given low priority. Typically, the first people on the scene of a major disaster are the fire, rescue, and law enforcement/security workers. The firefighters must extricate and remove the victims and survivors as quickly as possible while suppressing any existing blaze. Rescue workers must stabilize survivors at the scene and prepare them for transport to more elaborate medical care facilities. The police must cordon off the area from onlookers, media, and other individuals who may obstruct the work of the rescuers, as well as ensure that an unimpeded route to medical facilities is maintained. The focus is on first aid and emergency services, the crash site, and the accident.

For the most part, little attention is given to the potential psychological trauma of survivors or the relatives of victims. Survivors are usually dealt with by investigators, media, airline representatives and, if needed, medical personnel. Psychological help is seldom available. Airline personnel, relief units, fire departments, and law officials on the scene may provide the only psychological first aid the victims receive.

Since multiple factors (e.g., expanding air traffic, terrorist threat) now operate to make air disasters increasingly probable, the need to prepare for the psychological sequelae of such disasters in the survivors and other affected persons cannot be ignored. Greater preparedness on the part of the airlines, airports, and disaster relief agencies is needed.

The next section discusses the treatment needs of individuals who experience trauma associated with air and other major disasters. The particular needs of air disaster victims will be addressed, and a plan of preparedness that takes these elements into account will be illustrated. An existing model of such a disaster response plan at a major international airport will also be described.

PSYCHOLOGICAL RESPONSE TO AIR DISASTER

The First Trauma: The Crash and Its Aftermath

Everyone involved in an air crash suffers some form of stress, whether it be from grief over lost loved ones, from injury or psychological distress, from property or environmental damage, or from hassles of the legal system (Frederick, 1981). Furthermore, the closer one is to the crash impact area (for example, if one experiences firsthand the horror of people dying), the greater the impact of the disaster will be (Bolin, 1985) and the more likely it is that psychological adjustment problems will result (Souder, 1985).

> Of the five people who survived the crash of a Boeing 737 into an icy Potomac River in 1985, passenger Joe Stiley suffered doubly. A veteran flyer and pilot himself, he knew something did not feel right about the plane's operations, but it was not until the plane had taxied onto the runway for take-off that he realized proper de-icing procedures had not been followed. By now he wanted off the plane, but it was too late. While the others retrospectively reported apprehension as the plane began to shake violently after liftoff, Stiley knew beyond a doubt that a crash was coming, yet he was helpless to stop it. All he could do was instruct his co-worker next to him to brace for impact and wait. Everything seemed to go in slow motion as the seat legs buckled beneath him and crushed his legs. At the final impact, after the plane had already hit the traffic-choked bridge and just before he lost consciousness, he told himself that he was dead. (Adapted from Nance, 1986, pp. 195–230)

Stiley did, in fact, survive, although for six months afterwards he lived with his legs in a painful brace and had to learn to walk again. His co-worker, whose legs were also crushed, goes through life with one leg shorter than the other. They and the other three survivors—a businessman who never lost consciousness in the impact, a flight attendant, and a woman who screamed in desperation for her baby and husband lost somewhere beneath the water—were haunted by memories of the crash.

A man who escaped from the inferno caused by the collision of the jets in Tenerife reported considerable guilt and subsequent self-blame because of his inability to save his wife:

> He sat stunned and motionless for some 25 seconds after the [other plane] hit. He saw nothing but fire and smoke in the aisles, but he roused himself and led his wife to a jagged hole above and behind his seat. Martin climbed out onto the wing and reached down and took hold of his wife's hand, but, "an explosion from within literally blew her out of my hands and pushed me back and down onto the wing." He reached the runway, turned to go back after her, but the plane blew up seconds later. . . .
>
> [Five months later] Martin was depressed and bored, had "wild dreams," a short temper and became easily confused and irritated. "What I saw there will

terrify me forever," he says. He . . . avoided television and movies, because he couldn't know when a frightening scene would appear. (Perlberg, 1979, pp. 49–50)

The helplessness of crew and passengers alike was expressed by survivors of a 727 flight from Rome to Athens on which a terrorist's bomb exploded, sucking four passengers out a gaping hole near the right wing:

One passenger recalled that "I was talking with my wife when we heard the explosion. Suddenly my chair sank. The man sitting next to me at the window, I don't know what happened to him. He disappeared. My foot went through the cabin floor. I caught hold of my wife's seat and held on hard." Another passenger said "The plane shook, as it would in turbulence. In front of me, I saw a sort of green lightning. I thought I was dying." A wind filled the cabin and debris below about; some terrified passengers grabbed their hand baggage and told flight attendants that they wanted to leave the plane. The captain, believing that a window had blown out, began an immediate descent into the Athens airport and told his passengers "Please don't panic. Our engines are O.K. We'll be landing in about ten minutes if nothing else goes wrong." The captain did land safely amid cheers from the crew and passengers. He later admitted his concern in the last few minutes of the flight because "you wonder if you have your brakes and your hydraulic system. . . . Even though it shows on the instruments, you never know." (Adapted from Smith, 1986)

Although only four lives were lost in this terrorist attack, it demonstrated the chilling fact that governments and airlines have not yet found a way to counteract this threat to safety. Even though passengers and luggage were inspected and a private security firm performed a spot check of the airliner before takeoff, a terrorist's accomplice was still able to plant a plastic explosive (which could not be picked up by metal detectors) beneath a seat during an earlier flight.

Family and friends also suffer feelings of impotence when they are unable to help with search and rescue of loved ones. Immediately following any disaster, rumors and lack of information abound. Those in the waiting area of flight terminals are often the neglected victims of an air disaster. After a United Airlines flight crashed in a Portland surburb in 1978, a nurse who went to the airport to offer aid said that she "helped relatives track down family members who were believed to be aboard the plane. Some anxious relatives would just sit there and stare blankly at the wall, and we would give them some kind of snack and try to get them to talk." ("Nurses Join in Rescue," 1979, p. 3).

Families who lose their fliers . . . are exposed, with little warning, to a long-dreaded and long-feared actuality which mandates a total change in their lives. . . . In addition to [their] mourning, [they] may feel anger at the dead flier for abandoning [them] or for continuing a career that they [all] knew was so dangerous. This anger may be complicated by the guilt that [they] feel over the anger, by the depression at [their] loss, and by . . . fears for the future. Furthermore, the family of crew may be subjected through speculative newscasts and gossip to ". . . subtle belittling of the dead [crew's] flying ability, reasons why [they] should not have been flying that day, rehashing of the events so that everyone understands what the *right* thing to do would have been. . . . When the cause of the mishap is directly attributed to "pilot error," the effects of guilt, anger, and blame on the crew's family may be especially intense. (Adapted from Jones, 1982, p. 596)

Other support personnel directly or indirectly involved in an accident can also be adversely affected and may suffer postaccident anxiety (Popplow, 1984). This includes the designers of the craft, service and maintenance technicians, tower controllers, flight instructors, and management, some of whom may feel an immediate sense of responsibility. Other pilots may have lost friends in the disaster and may suffer from fear that the same thing will happen to them. It is not uncommon that they, too, may experience vague guilt that the tragedy happened to someone else while they were spared. The stunning realization that a terrible disaster has occurred on an airliner may result in poor morale, anger, feelings of futility, apathy, and a host of other psychological problems for airline personnel who must work in an environment in which blame for the disaster may reside.

Problems Experienced by Relief and Rescue Workers

Relief workers suffer from stress stemming from critical decisions, confrontation with human carnage, mass destruction to property or environment, distraught relatives or survivors, pressure from their own families who want them home, and sometimes interference from media and other onlookers, as they struggle to do their difficult job. Even experienced health care workers may be unprepared for the grim reality of a mass casualty situation. Rescue teams must often deal with situations for which they are not trained or prepared, and frequently they will be plagued by doubts about their decisions and ability to handle the job. Outside help sent into devastated communities may also become convenient scapegoats of victims' anger at the destruction that has occurred. The necessary distancing from the emotional and sometimes physical aspects of the disaster that workers must adopt in order to maintain their equilibrium and do their jobs may be misinterpreted as a sign of uncaring and insensitivity by the distraught victims, and they may be harshly rebuked for this perceived callousness.

STAGES OF PSYCHOLOGICAL ADAPTATION TO DISASTER

The foregoing accounts and descriptions typify individuals who have experienced catastrophe firsthand. The stages through which victims pass after a disaster seem to follow a prescribed pattern as well.

Reactions to disaster were first systematically assessed by Lindemann (1944) following a fire that swept through the crowded Cocoanut Grove nightclub in Boston, leaving 493 people dead. Before this, no investigator had documented so comprehensively the acute grief process through which victims passed or the impact brief psychotherapy had on this process (Bloom, 1984). Lindemann described an initial grief reaction that consisted of waves of psychological and physical distress triggered by stimuli that reminded the victim of the trauma or lost loved one(s); feelings of derealization and depersonalization; preoccupation with images of the deceased; feelings of guilt, hostility, and anger; emotional distancing from others; lack of initiative for everyday tasks; depression; anhedonia; compulsion to talk about the event; agitation; and dependency on those who could motivate the victim to action. Later, the victim entered a period during which he or she separated psychologicaly from the deceased, readjusted to life without the deceased, and began to form new relationships.

Two important observations Lindemann made at this time were that the therapist's facilitation of grief expression in the survivors led to a more rapid resolution of the intense grief phase and to an increased ability to look ahead to the future. Additionally, both underreactions or overreactions to the loss needed to be addressed by the mental health professional, as they sometimes reflected possible pathological adjustment.

Research on disaster response in recent years has suggested a typical pattern of human reaction through which many victims pass. The "disaster syndrome," as it is called, comprises several overlapping phases. Historically, disasters were divided into the phases of warning, period of threat, impact, inventory, rescue, remedy, and recovery (Powell & Rayner, 1952). Of course, not all disasters occur in the same manner or with the same features, so not all of these stages will be observed in every case. In many disasters, for instance, there is little if any prior warning.

Contemporary writers generally attend to three phases which correspond to the traumatic experience itself, the immediate postdisaster reactions, and long-term complications. These were labeled the periods of impact, recoil, and posttrauma by Tyhurst (1951) and have been described in detail by others as well (e.g., Farberow, 1978; Frederick, 1978; Horowitz, 1976). First, the relatively uniform reactions observed when a prior risk is known—the preimpact or warning phase—will be discussed.

Preimpact

If a preimpact period can be delineated and threat perceived, people generally try to prepare for impact. Nonetheless, some victims of the Buffalo Creek Flood in 1972, an event which destroyed 4,000 homes and left 125 dead when a dam burst, had lived for years in the shadow of the dam with the knowledge that it might give way (Titchener & Kapp, 1976). They had not, however, prepared for that possibility. Valent (1984) explained in his account of the

Ash Wednesday bushfires in Australia that took 72 lives, destroyed over 2,000 homes, and caused property damage valued at almost 3 hundred million dollars, that anxiety about impending fires after years of drought only facilitated preparation to a point. When it became too much and threatened people's security, they resorted to denial. "While this was adaptive in preventing mental functioning from being overwhelmed, it was maladaptive when it did not fit reality. Thus, only a handful of families acknowledged the danger sufficiently to evacuate some hours before the fire" (Valent, p. 292).

Maladaptive responses at this phase include minimizing impending danger by denial of warning signs, exaggerating the self's invulnerability, and reinterpreting events as benign (Proctor, 1984). Contrary to popular misconceptions, panic behavior during this period is not the norm and most people can handle the immediate situation without disorganization.

Impact

During impact, some people suffer a great disruption in normal functioning. Many survivors also suffer from shock, disbelief, disorientation, and confusion. Tyhurst (1951) estimated that approximately three fourths of any population of catastrophe victims will become stunned and that the symptoms might last from minutes to hours before gradually giving way to emotional expression, which may be intense. Another 15–25% of victims will remain cool and collected during the impact of disaster, while the remaining 10–25% show lasting impairment with persistent disorientation, immobilization and numbing, or a feeling of being out of control of their emotions. When action is taken, survival and protection of one's self and loved ones are primary concerns. Individuals will take an inventory of the situation and resources at their disposal and then use these in their rescue attempts. The acute reactions begin immediately upon disaster impact and last as long as the disaster itself. In the case of human-induced disasters, such as airplane crashes or building collapse, the impact phase may last from only minutes to hours. The impact of natural disasters may be more prolonged, as in the case of hurricanes, forest fires, or floods.

Recoil

In the recoil phase, survivors begin a period of readjustment to life as it exists after the disaster. They must attempt to resume normal activities and put the disaster into perspective, a process which may take many months. If the people have had to be evacuated from their homes, individual reactions are further complicated.

Researchers at the Disaster Research Center of Ohio State University have found that the distinctly individualistic responses to disaster revealed at disaster impact are also quite evident during recoil (Quarantelli, 1980).

However, as a rule, the most chaotic part of the evacuation experience occurs when people return to their devastated environment and begin to face their losses.

At this point, feelings of mastery may emerge if the person feels satisfied with his or her behavior during the height of the disaster; conversely, beliefs that one inadequately coped with the stress of impact may lead to low self-esteem, depression, helplessness, and hopelessness. Negative self-evaluations formed at this time may haunt the survivor, even if the overall outcome is successful. Psychotherapy with a survivor of the Beverly Hills Supper Club Fire in 1977 illustrates this fact:

> Nine months after the fire Mr. K. was experiencing symptoms of irritability, recurrent nightmares of being in the fire, three precipitous job changes, decreased libido, and a general attitudinal change from a dedicated family man to one who could "only take one day at a time." . . . He recounted that as smoke billowed into the room, Mr. K. lost contact with his wife. . . . He . . . concluded he could not make it out and would face almost certain death unless something miraculous were to happen. He then suddenly found himself walking across the tops of booths bypassing the blocked passage way. As a result, he was among the last patrons to leave the fire safely. But once outside, he realized that he had saved his own life without tending to his wife's safety. He anticipated intense shame when his children would ask why mother was not out safely with him. Three hours later, he learned his wife had been carried to safety through a separate exit, and an emotional reunion followed. The treatment session was the first time he had shared these intense emotions with anyone. . . . The therapist linked the current rage and self-recrimination to hopelessness and shame during the fire. Mr. K. chastised himself because he had failed to risk going back in . . . to pull bodies from the blaze. Mr. K. seemed to be pressing for, yet fearing he would not gain, the doctor's understanding and acceptance of his behavior in the fire. (Lindy, Green, Grace, & Titchener, 1983, p. 603)

The initial symptoms of post-traumatic stress disorder may manifest themselves at this time and might include reexperiencing of the event, numbness, apathy, withdrawal, constriction of emotions, cognitive or vegetative somatic signs, and guilt. Those who have denied or suppressed their emotional reactions to the death of loved ones and destruction of what is meaningful in their lives through turning their attention to others may begin to break down during this period, and experience their feelings as overwhelming. Gradually, the period of recoil evolves into the final phase of posttrauma, during which recovery and reconstruction from the full trauma may take years, if not the rest of the person's life.

Posttrauma

The final stage has been further subdivided into the honeymoon, disillusionment, and reconstruction phases. In cases of community destruction, a sense of cooperation and generosity takes hold in which those who have been spared great loss help those who have suffered. Although there may be a sense of euphoria (mixed with guilt) over being spared and of pride in one's mastery over the immediate aftermath of disaster, frustration and apathy generally become manifest as the extent of the damage is slowly appreciated and allowed into awareness.

When the disaster results from human negligence, intent, or error, the natural anger that attends loss of a sense of invulnerability and inviolacy is heightened. Titchener and Kapp (1976) describe "a feeling of impotent rage over the destruction of life, property, and a way of life. . . . The victim has little outlet for his anger or hope of satisfaction" (p. 297). Legal proceedings, insurance claims, bureaucratic hassles, and forms take time away from rebuilding and may only accentuate the belief in human callousness after a human-induced disaster. The disillusionment may continue into severe depression, lack of interest in rebuilding one's life, and despair that one's life may never again be the same. Severe and unresolved anxiety or depression, chronic fatigue, or prolonged survivor guilt or bereavement are maladaptive reactions that may persist unless treated.

FACTORS DETERMINING SEVERITY AND EXTENT OF PSYCHOLOGICAL SUFFERING

A study of evacuees after Cyclone Tracy destroyed a city in Australia revealed that marked psychological dysfunction which was present at impact had returned to baseline levels for that population at 14 months following the disaster (Parker, 1977). The author concluded that the high initial level of dysfunction was associated with a "mortality stressor"—the fear of injury or death—whereas later levels of maladjustment were associated with a "relocation stressor"—loss of possessions and place after the cyclone's destruction.

Parker's (1977) inability to find an increased prevalence of psychological sequelae a year postdisaster is not typical. Ninety percent of the survivors of the Buffalo Creek flood interviewed more than 2 years later evidenced disabling psychological symptoms such as character change, lifestyle change, anxiety, depression, and—in children—developmental problems (Titchener & Kapp, 1976). The cyclone victims' better adjustment may be because this city was primarily a transient population, and most evacuees elected not to return since they had resources and ties elsewhere. Returning to a community that may never be fully reconstructed and where there are constant reminders of what once existed but now is gone is almost invariably accompanied by considerable psychological morbidity (Kinston & Rosser, 1974; Parker, 1977).

Particularly difficult readjustment was noted among victims of the Wilkes-Barre (Richard, 1974) and Buffalo Creek floods (Lifton & Olson, 1976), in which most victims were evacuated and housed among strangers in makeshift housing for long periods. These difficulties have been attributed to the disruption of family patterns and social systems; unfamiliarity of new surroundings; loss of support of neighbors, friends, and traditional community resources; loss of familiar landmarks; and perceived government ineptitude and indifference in relocation and reconstruction efforts. It is difficult to appraise the extent to which the long period of litigation following the Buffalo Creek Flood served to maintain the expression of psychological symptoms among survivors of the flood.

Although victims of air disasters usually do not face the loss of community experienced by victims of many natural disasters, they also lack the therapeutic sense of camaraderie formed when groups who have faced a common danger attempt to rebuild. Since air catastrophes often involve human responsibility, victims may need to contend with intense anger and subsequent feelings of futility stemming from the belief that a potentially *preventable* disaster was allowed to occur and that they became its innocent victims. Furthermore, the majority of the flying public comprises persons who are in the prime of their lives, are active in careers and family life, and have good health and long futures. The severe disablement that often accompanies survival from a plane crash may increase their outrage over the event.

Nance (1986), who spent years researching the effects of deregulation on air safety, cogently summed up the catastrophic effect air disasters have on individual lives:

> It is sobering to realize that survivors such as Joe Stiley will never be completely free of the scars, the back pain, and other physical and psychological manifestations resulting from survival of an airline crash. We hear that people have survived a crash, and we tend to assume that they will fully recover. Few, in fact, do. For those who live, the following years may be another nightmare of pain and operations, broken bones and casts, therapy and all too often despair, coupled with the recurrent questions: "Why me, Lord? Why did I survive, while the others died?"
>
> And for the friends and relatives of those who did not make it, the psychological pain is all too real, and all too lasting. (p. 388)

The Second Trauma: The News Media

The problems may not be over when the air crash and immediate aftermath have ended. A frequent occurrence experienced by crash survivors, family members, or disaster workers—what might be called the second trauma—involves intrusive harassment by print, radio, and television journalists.

Air disasters, because of the extent of their horror in the minds of most people, are usually well attended by the press. Many newspaper and television news services monitor emergency frequencies and become aware of disasters almost immediately. It is not unusual for news personnel to arrive on the scene of an accident before the debris settles. Fire and rescue personnel and law enforcement officers frequently encounter media personnel while they are responding to an emergency.

Many emergency personnel have come to terms with the problem of handling the press as a result of previous incidents. In some disaster programs, there are prearranged Press Rooms set up to house and to some extent contain or lessen the impact of reporters while the business of rescue and initial disaster management are undertaken. As time passes, however, and as the news void persists, the pressure for information becomes greater. In such circumstances it often becomes more difficult for standard operating procedures to effectively lessen the intrusive presence of reporters who have deadlines to meet and who need information.

Victims of air crashes or family members of victims are generally not accustomed to dealing with the press. Reporters, in search of a story, have sometimes imposed harshly upon grieving family or friends or upon a victim in a state of shock. This situation is often very difficult for the individual to handle. Seemingly opportunistic journalists may attempt to capture the experience of a tragedy for their viewer or reader at the expense of the victim.

The desire on the part of a television journalist, for example, to capture for the 6 o'clock news some images of family members' faces as they learn of the tragedy can lead to deplorable consequences. One patient, being seen in therapy following a family member's death in an air crash, told of repeated and insensitive invasions of privacy by a television station to do stories on the patient's adaptation problem. In the hours immediately following the crash, the patient reluctantly consented to being interviewed while in a confused and vulnerable state. As the repeated follow-up requests persisted (this case seemingly had great public interest), the patient became more bothered by the invasions. Finally, with the return of self-confidence after a period of time, the patient began refusing further interviews.

A balance must be struck between the public's right to know and the vulnerable individual's right to privacy and solitude during moments of grief. An effective disaster response program will involve a component to lessen the negative impact of press coverage of the disaster.

Properly managed, however, the media can be an ally in disaster management programs through providing accurate information to the public (Gist & Stole, 1982).

The Third Trauma: The "Ambulance-Chasing" Attorney

A third major trauma following airline disasters may be the swarm of attorneys wishing to represent the survivor in the litigation that invariably ensues. Airline crashes, unlike natural disasters, typically involve the question of human responsibility and potential blame for the accident. Consequently, there is a legal vulnerability on the part of the air carrier(s). Attorneys are often on the scene of an accident very soon after it occurs.

While legal representation is often very important to individuals who have been injured or victimized by another party, it is not unusual to find over-aggressive attorneys seeking clients before there is a recognized need for representation by the individuals themselves or while the victims are still in a state of shock. Grieving family members may, while having to deal with the loss, be asked to participate in legal action. Under such circumstances, the litigation may actually serve to intensify their frustration and initial anger over the loss of their loved one.

Long-term adjustment can actually be made more difficult or soured by the process of litigation. It is difficult for victims of a disaster to put aside their problems and go on with life as long as legal battles continue. Passengers or crew members of airline crashes who have not been physically injured or psychologically disrupted by the accident, may still remain psychologically unsettled throughout the period of litigation.

The manner in which the legal aspects of a disaster are dealt with can be detrimental to the adjustment process. Consequently, it behooves the crisis intervention specialist who is attempting to deal with the psychological problems of the victim to be aware of this complicating, though seemingly necessary, element.

Failure to Plan

National Transportation and Safety Board statistics show that most (85%) civil aviation accidents in the United States occur during takeoff or landing, or within a 5-mile radius of the airport (Dove, Del Guercio, Stahl, Star, & Abelson, 1982). Therefore, it is important for airports, especially major airports with frequent operations, to develop procedures for handling victims. Frederick (1981) recently noted that, although procedures now exist to handle the mental health needs of victims of natural disasters since enactment of the Disaster Relief Act of 1974, no such plan was in place to deal with the special needs that arise following an air disaster.

Although the unique features of air disasters and their victims may make the provision of aid more difficult to arrange, they do not preclude the incorporation of a psychological intervention component into the disaster response procedures already established at FAA-certified airports. Community mental health centers could encourage the needed integration through crisis intervention training of flight and ground personnel. On their part, airports can make their required resources for medical and/or logistical aid for crash victims available to community agencies and volunteer response groups for use in disaster training drills. Major hospitals are required to enact mock disasters (if not faced with an actual one) at least once per year in order to maintain accreditation (Clark, 1975); therefore, area hospitals and volunteer associates of the airport disaster response team can work toward the completion of mutual goals.

Disaster response plans at airports typically do not incorporate a crisis intervention component. Duffy (1978) conjectured that most airport disaster response programs are "complete failures in terms of meeting the human needs of all those individuals who are part of the disaster scene" (p. 1004). The reluctance of airports to develop an integrated, community-wide response which includes psychological attention to survivor/victims is partially because air disasters are relatively rare. Airlines may also fear adverse publicity if they openly encourage or support disaster planning and training exercises (Dove et al., 1982). For these and other reasons, pressure to incorporate these plans traditionally has come from dedicated individuals within the airport management field or from professionals in the community.

Some communities have taken rather drastic steps to reduce the impact and perhaps probability of human-induced air disasters. For example, one community pressured the local Air Force unit into changing its flight landing pattern after a jet crashed near a junior high school (Berren, Beigel, & Barker, 1982). In another community, after three crashes had occurred in quick succession, angry citizens threatened to destroy an airport if officials would not close it (Edwards, 1976). Some writers have charged that there is no good reason why the same technologies used to develop the aviation industry should not be applied to the care of accident victims and survivors (Dove et al., 1982). This sentiment was strongly expressed by Healy (1977): "Whether lack of disaster planning is caused by the press of daily problems or from apathy is not important if an emergency situation develops, because the result may be the same—catastrophe" (p. 18).

Assessment of Psychological Intervention Needs Following a Disaster

An accurate assessment of treatment needs must take into account differences in disasters and in the individuals and community involved. Berren, Beigel, and Ghertner's (1980) model for the classification of disasters may be used as one basis for planning and determining intervention strategies to systematize relief efforts. First of all, disasters differ in their degree of personal impact. "Other things being equal, the greater the personal impact of the disaster, the greater will be the overall consequences" (Berren et al., 1980, p. 126). A more extensive network must be designed to deal with the wider array of problems that will ensue and the greater number of individuals who could benefit from intervention. Consultation should be available to service providers who are overwhelmed by the strain placed on them in the wake of major, mass-casualty disasters. Educational services designed to inform victims how to solve practical problems of living and to help non-victims facilitate recovery of victims may be mandated.

The type and extent of disaster influences the treatment needs of the victims. For example, following human-induced disasters such as terrorism, people may face, in addition to the common symptoms of trauma (anxiety, depression, insomnia, guilt), other obstacles not encountered by victims of natural disasters. The perception by others that the victims were partially responsible for what happened to them might lead to rejection or withdrawal by others and an accentuation of emotional distress (Frederick, 1981). If there is the potential for recurrence of the disaster, Berren, Beigel, & Barker (1982) assert that "at a minimum consultation with community organizations and didactic informational services to the community are necessities" (p.

129). These may especially aid in prevention of possible problems such as those produced by unresponsive agencies from whom victims seek aid and legal advice, the so-called secondary disasters. In natural disasters where future occurrences are inevitable, one can reduce the impact of negative consequences through community preparation in the form of disaster plans, warning systems, upgraded standards for buildings, or emergency care. The duration of disaster may be lessened by prompt and sincere response by the airlines and airport management.

　　1. *Outreach.* Outreach psychological services to victims of airline accidents is important because victims generally do not look upon themselves as psychological casualties (Heffron, 1977). Many have never needed mental health services and therefore do not know about available existing services or how to obtain them. The natural tendency in crisis situations is to turn to trusted others first for help and support. This can be problematic if they, too, were victims. A substantial number will also want to avoid reminders of the disaster. For these reasons, many survivor/victims may be reluctant to seek or accept psychological aid.

　　As a rule, outreach aid should be made as accessible and as palatable as possible. Heffron (1977) reports that when workers refrained from referring to themselves as mental health workers but called themselves outreach counselors instead, resistance to therapeutic intervention attempts disappeared. Outreach programs must also be tailored to the particular disaster circumstances. Lindy, Grace, and Green (1981) point out that in centrifugal disasters, such as plane crashes where specific spaces or vehicles are destroyed without affecting more extensive areas, outreach workers may be seen as intrusive to the protective groups that form around survivor/victims. In larger disasters, the entire community often shares in grief with the victim. In these cases, outreach workers partly derived from the community may encounter less hostility or resistance to intervention attempts as they are part of the natural support group. According to Lindy, Grace, and Green's review, outreach performed within the first 3 months following disaster seems optimal. Thus, there may be ample time for recruitment and training of outreach workers following some disasters.

　　A recent outreach effort illustrates the preventive function of outreach services. Project Outreach (Heffron, 1977) was designed to provide mobile mental health services to victims of the 1972 Agnes flood disaster that destroyed 400 homes and caused 80,000 people to evacuate the area. This direct intervention approach was intended to prevent the development of long-term mental dysfunction. Outreach workers gave direct intervention instead of locating cases for referral and helped strengthen victims' existing coping skills and/or develop new coping techniques to deal with problems stemming from the disaster.

　　An important feature of this program is that *nonprofessionals from the community* who represented a cross-section of the population (and who themselves were victims of the disaster) were trained and supervised by professionals. Training lasted one week, and lay counselors worked in pairs for mutual support. Daily meetings with supervisors gave workers a chance to ventilate their feelings and seek advice. Frequent inservice training sessions were held throughout the 32-month program.

Other researchers (Lindy et al., 1981) have found that outreach via printed (educative) material was rated as far superior to visual media by survivors of the Beverly Hills Supper Club fire. Survivors explained that unexpected messages or images on television were frightening and intrusive, disturbing their need to contain fearful thoughts or images relating to the experience. Printed matter, on the other hand, could be laid aside or discarded until the individual was better able to cope with the material.

Because the aim of outreach programs is the prevention of long-term psychological distress, it is impossible to measure the effectiveness of such programs in decreasing the amount of psychological morbidity following disasters. However, it is a well-documented observation in the disaster literature that serious maladjustment to catastrophe is to be expected in a proportion of victims. It is likely that many of these cases are preventable if detected promptly following the trauma.

McFarlane (1984, 1986) strongly emphasizes the need for psychiatric consultation teams who work in conjunction with disaster relief programs as a preventive measure. He treated many cases of post-traumatic stress disorder that occurred in people over a year after they had been exposed to the Ash Wednesday bushfires in Australia. Most of these cases had been misdiagnosed or overlooked by their general practitioners and health care workers who had had previous contact with them. Suggested reasons for the low detection rate of psychological impairment include the following: (1) Symptoms presented as physical rather than psychological distress (sleep disturbance, respiratory problems, etc.); (2) disaster response workers were not adequately trained to recognize symptoms; (3) delayed-onset post-traumatic stress disorder does not emerge immediately but only after many months when the victims have resettled; and (4) distress and preoccupation with the disaster then reappear in the recovery phase.

2. *Victims.* Preparedness planning must take into account variations in victims' personalities and the prototypical responses of some (Frederick, 1981). Persons who resort to denial or avoidance as a primary defense against the personality disruption of sudden trauma will have an intense need to avoid the reexperiencing of the event and may require a more active role on the part of care providers. Others with basic trust issues may exhibit pronounced distrust of or hostility toward helping professionals. Victims who have unresolved issues concerning self-esteem or personal effectiveness may experience troublesome doubts about their role in the crisis, which may lead to disabling guilt or anxiety. Overwhelming feelings of helplessness and

vulnerability are likely in those with high dependency needs. Those who have suffered injury or death of loved ones may feel resentfulness toward those spared death or maiming.

Workers must be cautioned that it is unwise to give false reassurance to victims. Instead, they must encourage them to face reality. If things will not be as they were before the disaster, the victim must face this and adjust to life under new conditions. Otherwise, there is greater danger of psychological maladjustment as the denial defense fails. False hope may also cause increased resistance in the victim to therapeutic intervention (Heffron, 1977). Increased alcohol and sedative use in the recovery period has also been observed (Erikson, 1976; Logue, Hanse, & Struening, 1979). Professionals must be aware of signs of drug abuse, as it can complicate treatment.

Certain populations have emerged as high-risk groups to the development of adjustment problems following disaster. The elderly often show persistent depression, hopelessness, and apathy in rebuilding their lives. Many are reluctant to seek help due to fear of asking for help from strangers. Many live alone and no longer have family. Their isolation may compound their feelings of loss, as well as make them more difficult to locate for treatment. Children represent another high-risk group because of their inability to understand the traumatic event and their feelings of powerlessness. They may manifest school problems, phobias and fears, separation anxiety, sleep disturbance, and disruptive behavior. Finally, those who are especially vulnerable from previous stressful life events or the presence of psychopathology must be carefully observed for signs of emotional maladjustment.

3. *Air Crew Personnel.* Airline personnel are often treated by the airline medical staff who may or may not offer psychological intervention. Psychological counseling and support may be delayed because of the confusion following the disaster at the airport. Preaccident training in crisis-management may help crew members in handling their own responses and those of others who are traumatized by the disaster. This type of training should include the flight crew because they must deal with precrash emergency management of passengers. Warning generally makes a disaster more manageable psychologically, and the skill with which the flight crew readies the passengers may attenuate precrash fear and confusion, perhaps decreasing the anger and guilt experienced by survivors. Crisis training for air personnel who must deal with the public should include techniques on how to inform the family of the deceased with the least pain possible and how to combat the spread of rumors that abound immediately after the crash.

4. *Disaster Response Workers.* Disaster relief workers not infrequently become secondary victims of emotional trauma because of their close and sometimes protracted contract with the results of major disasters. They are under pressure to know what to do with respect to life and death decisions and must dare to do it (Burkle, 1983). The nature of their work may also

make it impossible for them to talk freely with family and typical support systems. Rayner (1958) described maladaptive responses that she observed in emergency care nurses: overintellectualization of the experience, which may impede expression of emotions later; a sense of urgency leading to ineffective treatment; and rigid or reflexive performance of duties, which narrows awareness and may block out information necessary for optimal functioning and decision making (see also Davidson, 1979).

In order to minimize maladaptive behavior in workers, supervisors should screen recruits beforehand, if possible, for the ones who are most adaptable to stress and uncertain situations; those who are less adaptable should be assigned to different duties (Frederick, 1978). Jones (1985), who studied reactions of personnel who had to identify and recover human remains of the Jonestown tragedy, suggested assigning younger workers to less trauma-inducing tasks. When this is not possible, they should be paired with older, more experienced workers. Job rotation and backup to relieve workers when they feel they have had enough also goes a long way toward reducing burn-out.

Daily emotional support should be available, perhaps in group sessions that allow expression of the common reactions, so that inexperienced and even seasoned workers do not feel alone. Groups can provide reassurance that revulsion, anger, and flashbacks of distressing scenes are normal re-actions and are to be expected. Jones (1985) also recommends the use of humor to relieve stress and formal termination for members, which includes a sensitive debriefing, recognition by valued authority for their grueling labor, and provision of follow-up as needed.

It is important for superiors to stress that each person has his or her limitations and that it is healthy to recognize this. Beliefs of personal heroism on the part of disaster workers must be realistic (Frederick, 1978). Team members should also be warned that shifts in their usual ego-organization are to be expected (Burkle, 1983). In the short run, many can remain dis-tanced and objective. But denial of the disaster's impact cannot be effective for long periods and should be discouraged and guarded against.

The negative impact of disaster relief work on disaster workers can be great. Bartone, Ursano, Ingraham, and Saczynski-Wright (1987) found that even professional military officers accustomed to rigorous duty can be se-verely impacted for months following an air crash clean-up operation. Many officers who assisted in the identification of remains of military personnel killed in the U.S. Army charter crash in Newfoundland reported extensive psychological symptoms which actually increased in severity 12 months after the operation had terminated.

The psychological distress of disaster workers can be reduced if appro-priate intervention measures are taken. Mitchell (1982) reported on effective debriefing procedures for aiding disaster workers to manage their symptoms in the aftermath of air crashes.

REQUIREMENTS OF A WORKABLE DISASTER PLAN

An effective disaster response protocol requires simplicity, clarity, flexibility, practice, communication, and coordination (Patterson, 1981; Winch, Hines, Booker, & Ferrar, 1976). Given the complexity of a mass-casualty disaster, the number of individuals involved in the rescue and treatment, and the many unpredictable and unique variables involved in an air disaster, it follows that simpler and more exact steps will have a greater chance of being carried out successfully. The sheer intensity of a major accident can make the following of orders difficult for even experienced personnel. Thus, the number of set rules and procedures should be kept to a minimum. Simplicity also allows greater flexibility for those in charge when making decisions based on the particular circumstances and needs.

The disaster plan should be practiced before an actual crisis situation occurs. Its effectiveness and shortcomings will be apparent only with a trial run. Unfortunately, only 24% of the certified airports in the United States have conducted disaster drills in the last 3 years (Barbash et al., 1986). One misconception impeding the use of drills is overestimation of the cost. But in reality, disaster simulations are not costly. Cooperation of participating agencies is usually granted freely. Furthermore, knowledge gained through the employment of disaster response procedures, in both simulated and actual crises at some airports, has made the development of workable plans easier and less costly for other airports because of fewer mistakes by new users.

Gerace (1979) details several other ways in which the benefits of a mock disaster far outweigh its cost: (1) It allows correction of deficiencies in the plan which, in the event of actual disaster, could result in unnecessary complications; (2) it allows participants to reevaluate their roles and examine both their reactions to and readiness for a crisis, as studies have shown that reactions to mock disasters not uncommonly mirror the reactions seen in true disasters (Sanner & Wolcott, 1983); and (3) careful study of mock airline disasters can provide the community and other localities with information to apply in planning for other crisis conditions. The success and effectiveness of drills at some airports has generated support for an FAA requirement that such drills be conducted.

Communication is also a vital ingredient in effective disaster plans. An accurate inventory and communication of resources at one's disposal allows the greatest flexibility and most responsible decision making. On-site emergency teams must be able to assess local care facilities for their resources and treatment capabilities when making decisions on where to evacuate victims.

Implementation difficulties in a disaster drill mainly involve coordination and training of the various groups that volunteer to serve in the program. Although the groups may know general crisis intervention or disaster response techniques, familiarity with the procedures and operations of the airport and of the multiple response units who will be involved in a real disaster necessitates integrated training and practice runs. Orientation and guidance for incoming workers should be established. For instance, a principal marshalling area should be designated beforehand for workers to gather from which they will be escorted to the crash site. "Recruitment of outside agencies without processing them through detailed training programs is a certain recipe for chaos in the event of a disaster" (Barbash et al., 1986, p. 81).

In actual emergencies, the major problems are logistical and not medical (Dove et al., 1982). For example, after the Hyatt Regency skywalk collapse, problems discovered were lack of bystander control; poor on-site communication; and difficulty identifying key personnel, which hindered coordination at the scene (Orr & Robinson, 1983). It is extremely important to establish good flow patterns for transportation of victims and clearly defined priorities for victim treatment prior to an actual crisis situation.

Many (e.g., Dove et al., 1982; Naggan, 1976) stress that primary treatment and stabilization as close to the site and time of disaster as possible is more important than evacuation. Airports must be prepared with adequately trained personnel, a practiced response plan, and on-site facilities to minimize loss of life when many potential victims and massive injuries are likely. Emergency care can then be given immediately, with care continuing throughout evacuation. Easton (1977) estimated that 3–20% of deaths that occur in the "therapeutic vacuum" (within 20 minutes after injury or collapse) could be prevented with proper resuscitation techniques. The larger aircraft built today carry a greater number of passengers, thus creating a potentially greater number of survivors with serious injuries (Dove et al., 1982). Airports should plan for mass injuries instead of mass casualties (Bergot, 1971) and ensure accommodations for the worst situation possible (i.e., one involving the type of airliner that has the maximum passenger capacity for that airport). If the airport plan envisions Mobile-Assistance Teams who fly in from area hospitals to provide on-site professional treatment of the injured prior to evacuation, the teams could also be used for other emergency conditions to make them more cost-effective. Airport disaster programs relying upon mobile air rescue operations should have alternative plans in case weather conditions necessitate closing the airport.

Because affected individuals leave the disaster site quickly, mobile emergency assistance is important. Go-teams should include mental health professionals to deal with short-term sequelae. Care must continue beyond the immediate postcrash period in the form of support, education in common reactions, and information on where to seek additional aid if needed.

Immediate intervention steps can be taken to alleviate the impact of the following stressful experiences that occur in the days following disaster: contact with the authorities for information during the investigation process, expression and communication of feelings and thoughts concerning the experience, support in dealing with an altered reality, and long-term assistance (e.g., support and therapy). It would be beneficial to clarify to the survivor–victim what to expect from long-term contact with various agencies, such as normative information, level of support to be expected, possible time factors or delays, and the amount of effort required on their part to achieve their ends. Attention must also be paid to pathological predictors (e.g., whether the victim is a member of a high risk group) and individual response modes to extreme stress.

Other practical considerations that must be taken into account in the work-up of a general disaster response plan include the extent of expected health effects, the size and vulnerability of population at risk, the likelihood of prolonged effects, cost, the spead with which answers concerning the disaster will be needed, generalizability of answers to other situations, and the importance of feedback to the public relating to disasters and their likelihood (Buist, Martin, Shore, Butler, & Lybarger, 1986).

Two examples of disaster plans illustrate how the preceding points may be modified to fit particular needs. Following the crash of a 727 in 1975, John F. Kennedy Airport developed a disaster plan in which the hospital personnel and resources were brought to the scene when the traditional response system was shown to be inadequate (Dove et al., 1982). Because of its location in a metropolitan area and the attention such a disaster brought, ground transportation was hopelessly jammed within 30 minutes following the crash. It was impossible to get victims to area hospitals in a timely fashion.

Now prearranged teams are airlifted in by helicopter to supplement the airport's existing medical teams. Suitable facilities are available to provide immediate and intensive care to the most severely injured until they can be transported to hospital facilities in an ever-widening radius, with most serious cases transported to the nearest hospitals so as not to overload any facility. Backup staff for the first-response teams are also airlifted in. Kennedy Airport management has sponsored a mock disaster exercise annually since 1971 (Star, Abelson, Del Guercio, & Pritchett, 1980).

Barbash et al. (1986), on the other hand, believe that bringing the hospital to the airport may be inefficient or unfeasible, except in cases in which evacuation proposes harm. They believe the most important objective is stabilization and prevention of death enroute to evacuation, as hospitals will always be better equipped to deal with injuries than airport medical facilities. An emphasis on evacuation, then, might place the heaviest demands on police and security to keep access lanes open. Each airport must develop its own plan to fit its structure.

CRISIS INTERVENTION

In crisis intervention therapy, the therapist does not follow a disease model of psychopathology—viewing the symptoms as a sign of an underlying process of personality deterioration. Rather, the individual is viewed as experiencing a period of transition in which the symptoms will dissipate, even if untreated, in a brief span of time—about 6 weeks. The focus of crisis intervention is to reduce the present stress level and enable the individual to reestablish psychological equilibrium thereby promoting better adaptation. The primary goal is to assist the individual to manage the immediate stressful life situation. An additional goal of crisis therapy is to foster the development of skills to deal with future stress.

It is important that crisis intervention disaster programs not become defined or viewed as "services for the mentally ill." Stress-induced psychological problems are naturally occurring and transitory states, which usually do not require traditional mental health services. Victims of disasters, even those individuals experiencing extremely high stress, may avoid psychiatric help because they do not view themselves as mentally ill. An important goal in disaster recovery is to provide for the temporary management of psychosocial needs of victims and to encourage the individual to use appropriate community resources as the primary means of problem resolution. Individuals undergoing acute stress-related problems may be receptive to outside intervention and may be quite motivated for behavior change.

Individuals with previous psychological adjustment problems may experience an exaggeration of those problems under stress. In some instances, these individuals may gain insight into their previous problems and learn more adaptive coping techniques that result in a posttrauma adjustment better than before the disaster. People experiencing post-traumatic stress disorder usually feel overwhelmed—they are anxious; they often feel intense physiological symptoms; or they may become quite angry or acutely agitated.

The primary goal of crisis intervention is symptom relief. The therapist attempts to provide structure to the individual, who is perhaps in a confused and bewildered state, offering the victim opportunity to ventilate feelings and to relive the trauma. The therapist serves as an objective reality for the possibly irrational individual and provides a balanced perspective on the present situation and upon what the individual may experience in the future. The crisis intervention specialist may help provide organization to the individual's perceived chaotic situation with facts to supplement confusion and rumor, realistic reassurance to balance the frequent feelings of discouragement, and viable alternatives to the feelings of immobilization.

A Prototypical Program for Air Disaster Crisis Intervention

A model disaster response program for major airports was developed by the Metropolitan Airports Commission at the Minneapolis–St. Paul International Airport. The overall disaster response program has evolved over the past 10 years and employs both paid airport, fire, police, and ambulance personnel and volunteer service professionals including physicians, nurses, and clinical psychologists. The primary aim is to employ existing community resources to ensure that human psychological needs following a disaster will be met.

The medical staff of the Airport Medical Clinic, located on the airport grounds, developed an emergency medical response program employing both regular staff physicans and nurses and a number of volunteer medical specialists from the community. The goal of the Medical Disaster Response Program is to provide immediate first aid to the injured and to facilitate transfer to local hospitals (Webb, 1980). The medical service team has developed a 240-bed field hospital at the airport terminal which includes four operating rooms that could be put into operation moments following a disaster. The medical service space at the airport is committed as a triage center and is not used for other purposes. In addition to the medical-surgical area, the Triage Center includes a crisis intervention room where crash survivors could be seen by a professional psychologist or psychiatrist. The crisis center adjacent to the field hospital ward area would be staffed with trained psychologists and psychiatrists who are included in the emergency call-up in the event of a crash. The Crisis Intervention Program includes a family waiting room area in the terminal where it would be accessible from passenger gates.

The Metropolitan Airport Disaster Crisis Intervention Program is designed to provide immediate crisis intervention therapy for surviving victims, family members, and disaster personnel who may need help following a disaster. The crisis intervention program was developed to provide brief psychotherapy or crisis intervention therapy to individuals as soon as practical after a crash. The goals of this counseling program are to provide victims the opportunity to talk over their problems with a trained professional psychologist or psychiatrist, to provide symptom relief, to aid in the restoration of the individual's adaptive techniques to the precrisis level, and to help individuals arrive at adaptive ways of dealing with life situations brought on by the crisis (Butcher, 1980).

The Crisis Intervention Program was designed to be activated immediately following the report of an air disaster at the Minneapolis–St. Paul airport. Some crisis intervention personnel would report to designated areas at the airport terminal while others, standby counselors, would await referrals. The Crisis Intervention Program includes the following three elements.

Point A—Triage Center

A major goal of the Crisis Intervention Program is to provide emergency psychological counseling services to victims of a disaster near the site of a disaster. Several crisis volunteers are assigned as disaster personnel who would report to the Triage Center at the initial report of an air disaster. These volunteers would be stationed in the area of the Triage Center designated for survivors who do not or no longer require medical first aid. Crisis intervention volunteers in the Triage Center area might, as time and circumstances warrant, provide telephone counseling to families of disaster victims or assist in helping individuals obtain information about their families.

The major focus of counseling at Point A would be to allow crash victims to relate their experiences and concerns and to provide emotional support to individuals disturbed by the situation. Referral for follow-up therapy to a standby counselor might be made if the individual is in need of more extensive psychological attention.

Point B—Family Area

A second goal of the Crisis Intervention Program is to provide emergency counseling to waiting families and friends of disaster victims in the terminal area. Volunteers would be called immediately following a disaster and would report to a designated area of the terminal building. These volunteers would be available for counseling with family members or disaster workers and would be available to receive telephone inquires from family members away from the airport. In addition, these volunteers might, if time permits, make telephone calls to relatives of crash victims.

Point C—Standby Counselors

An important goal of the Crisis Intervention Program is to provide free, immediately accessible mental health services to disaster victims and emergency personnel in need of attention in the aftermath of a disaster. Standby counselors are mental health professionals who volunteer to serve as therapists for a period of about 6 weeks following a disaster. These counselors would be initially contacted, as needed, by administrative personnel or crisis counselors from the Triage Center or Family Counseling Center at the terminal and alerted to the possibility of emergency referrals. The standby counselors should provide up-to-date scheduling information and indicate how many cases they could manage.

A listing of volunteer mental health professionals is periodically updated and kept in a file with the disaster plan administrative staff (Butcher, 1980). The Metropolitan Airport Disaster Program is tested annually with a drill to assure that personnel are familiar with the facilities, resources, and procedures. At the time of this writing, the general disaster program has not had an emergency that required full activation of the disaster system. However, one part of the program, the Crisis Intervention Program, was activated partially in response to the crash of an inbound charter plane at the Reno Airport in 1985. Most of the passengers who were killed in the crash were from the Twin Cities area. Crisis intervention therapy was offered at no charge to family members from this accident.

The crisis intervention team was also mobilized to provide psychological services for families of passengers and for airline personnel for Northwest Airlines following the crash of Flight 255 in Detroit in August 1987.

CONCLUSIONS

Psychological adjustment following airline disasters shares many characteristics of other disasters—both human and natural. The adjustment problems typically are transitory and usually dissipate in the months following the accident. The form of disorder that results is usually less debilitating than major mental health disorders (such as major affective disorder or schizophrenia), and seldom does it require psychiatric hospitalization. Some individuals may experience prolonged or delayed stress as a result of particularly severe trauma, losses that require extreme environmental readjustment, such as severe injuries, burns, or the like, or complications caused by premorbid adjustment problems.

Several features of airline disasters involve unique elements of psychological adaptations. Airline accidents typically are sudden, unexpected events that involve loss of life and the experience of horror—all of which appear to add to the acuteness of the trauma. Airline disasters, by their newsworthy nature, are apt to be replayed for several days (and sometimes for months), serving to keep the images vividly emblazened in victim's memories. In addition, reporters may serve as an unwanted provocation with survivors or family members in the period following an accident. Because airplane accidents often involve the possibility of human responsibility somewhere in the causal chain, litigation and attorneys are frequently elements with which survivors must contend in the months following an accident. These proceedings typically keep the situation emotionally charged for a long period of time until the court settlements are made. Even individuals who have not been seriously injured or affected by the crash may show psychological symptoms for months following an accident in cases where compensation hearings are pending. Airline disasters also differ in that the social structure of flights is usually not organized in a social network. People do not know each other. This lack of community results in a more traumatic situation because there is not a social support system.

Airport Disaster Response Programs developed to deal with the aftermath of an airline crash generally do not include a psychological intervention component. There is a need to develop effective disaster response programs that incorporate elements of psychological intervention at major airports.

The symptoms and typical course of the disaster syndrome are well known. Disaster planners and mental health personnel need to consider the following psychological adjustment problems that may occur in the aftermath of an airline disaster:

1. *Symptoms of immediate shock* such as psychic numbness and anxiety are usually present.

2. *Symptoms of post-traumatic stress disorder* such as intrusive and recurring thoughts are commonly present, and there is often a need for

the individual to reexperience the trauma in an effort to master the situation.

3. *Depressive reactions* such as low mood, feelings of hopelessness, social or occupational ineffectiveness, and an inability to deal with day-to-day hassles, problems in concentration, and health concerns are psychological symptoms that are likely to occur in the weeks following a disaster.

4. *Confusion and disorganization* that typically follow a disaster may need to be given special attention with survivors of air crashes, since the usual social support system that operates in natural disasters may not be present.

5. *Survivors of airline disasters may be particularly vulnerable to adaptational problems* occurring after the initial disaster and resulting from intrusive reporters or eager attorneys. Assistance in managing these hassles during a period of grief may facilitate postdisaster adjustment.

6. *There may be a need for the survivor or family member to discuss adaptational problems* of readjustment and the postdisaster demands with a crisis intervention specialist in order to facilitate problem resolution.

7. *Aftercare,* including psychological intervention, may be required for disaster workers in the period following an air disaster.

REFERENCES

A bad start for 1986. (1986, January 27). *Time,* p. 35.

Alexander, C. P. (1986, January 13). Super savings in the skies. *Time,* pp. 40–45.

Barbash, G. I., Yoeli, N., Ruskin, S. M., & Moeller, D. W. (1986). Airport preparedness for mass diaster: A proposed schematic plan. *Aviation, Space, and Environmental Medicine, 57,* 77–81.

Bartone, P., Ursano, R. J., Ingraham, L. H., & Saczynski-Wright, K. (1987, August). *The impact of military air disaster on family assistance workers.* Paper presented at the meeting of the American Psychological Association, New York.

Bergot, G. P. (1971). Disaster planning at major airports. *Aerospace Medicine, 42,* 449–455.

Berren, M. R., Beigel, A., & Barker, G. (1982). A typology for the classification of disaster: Implications for intervention. *Community Mental Health Journal, 18,* 120–134.

Berren, M. R., Beigel, A., & Ghertner, S. (1980). A typology for the classification of disaster. *Community Mental Health Journal, 16,* 102–120.

Bloom, B. L. (1984). *Community mental health: A general introduction* (2nd ed.). Monterey, CA Books/Cole.

Bolin, R. (1985). Disaster characteristics and psychosocial impact. In B. J. Sowder

(Ed.), *Disasters and mental health: Selected contemporary perspectives* (pp. 3–28). Rockville, MD: U.S. Department of Health and Human Services, National Institute of Mental Health.

Buist, A. S., Martin, T. R., Shore, J. H., Butler, J., & Lybarger, J. A. (1986). The development of a multidisciplinary plan for evaluation of the long-term health effects of the Mount St. Helens eruption. *American Journal of Public Health, 76* (Suppl.), 39–44.

Burkle, F. M. (1983). Coping with stress under conditions of disaster and refugee care. *Military Medicine, 148,* 800–803.

Butcher, J. N. (1980). The role of crisis intervention in an airport disaster plan. *Aviation, Space, and Environmental Medicine, 51,* 1260–1261.

Clark, C. D. (1975). The need for mock major accidents. *Resuscitation, 4,* 283–284.

Crelinsten, R. D., & Szabo, D. (1979). *Hostage-taking.* Lexington, MA: D. C. Heath.

Davidson, A. D. (1979). Coping with stress reactions in rescue workers: A program that worked. *Police Stress.*

Dove, D. B., Del Guercio, L. R. L. M., Stahl, W. M., Star, L. D., & Abelson, L. C. (1982). A metropolitan airport disaster plan: Coordination of a multihospital response to provide on-site resuscitation and stabilization before evacuation. *Journal of Trauma, 22,* 550–559.

Duffy, V. C. (1978). Emergency mental health services during and after a major aircraft accident. *Aviation, Space, and Environmental Medicine, 49,* 1004–1008.

Easton, K. (1977). In K. Easton (Ed.), *Rescue emergency care* (p. 147). London: Heinemann Medical Books.

Edwards, V. G. (1976). Psychiatric aspects of civilian disasters. *British Medical Journal, 1,* 944–947.

Erikson, K. T. (1976). Disaster at Buffalo Creek: Loss of communality at Buffalo Creek. *American Journal of Psychiatry, 133,* 302–305.

Farberow, N. L. (Ed.). (1978). *The training manual for human service workers in major disasters* (DHEW Publication No. ADM 77–538). Washington, DC: U.S. Government Printing Office.

Federal Aviation Regulations. (1979). Title 14, C.F.R., Part 139. Washington, DC: Federal Aviation Administration.

Foushee, H. C. (1982). The role of communications, sociopsychological, and personality factors in the maintenance of crew coordination. *Aviation, Space, and Environmental Medicine, 53,* 1062–1066.

Frederick, C. (Ed.). (1978). *Training manual for human service workers in major disasters.* Rockville, MD: National Institute of Mental Health.

Frederick, C. (Ed.). (1981). *Aircraft accidents: Emergency mental health problems* (DHHS Publication No. ADM 81-956). Washington, DC: U.S. Government Printing Office.

Gerace, R. V. (1979). Role of medical teams in a community disaster plan. *CMA Journal, 120,* 923–928.

Gist, R., & Stole, S. (1982). Mental health promotion and the media: Community response to the Kansas City Hotel disaster. *American Psychologist, 37,* 1136–1139.

Greenwald, V. (1986, January 13). Is there cause for fear of flying? *Time,* pp. 49–51.

Harper's Index (1986, April). *Harper's*, p. 11.

Healy, R. J. (1977). Emergency and disaster planning. *Professional Safety, 22*(10), 16–20.

Heffron, E. F. (1977). Project outreach: Crisis intervention following natural disaster. *Journal of Community Psychology, 5,* 103–111.

Horowitz, M. (1976). *Stress response syndromes.* New York: Jason Aronson.

Jacobs, L. M., Ramp, J. M., Breay, J. M. (1979). An emergency medical system approach to disaster planning. *Journal of Trauma, 19,* 157–162.

Jones, D. R. (1982). Emotional reactions to military aircraft accidents. *Aviation, Space, and Environmental Medicine, 53,* 595–598.

Jones, D. R. (1985). Secondary disaster victims: The emotional effects of recovering and identifying human remains. *American Journal of Psychiatry, 142,* 303–307.

Kinston, W., & Rosser, R. (1974). Disaster: Effects on mental and physical state. *Journal of Psychosomatic Research, 18,* 437–456.

Lifton, R. J., & Olson, E. (1976). The human meaning of total disaster: The Buffalo Creek experience, *Psychiatry, 39,* 1–18.

Lindemann, E. (1944). Symptomatology and management of acute grief. *American Journal of Psychiatry, 101,* 141–148.

Lindy, J. D., Grace, M. C., & Green, B. L. (1981). Survivors: Outreach to a reluctant operation. *American Journal of Orthopsychiatry, 51,* 468–478.

Lindy, J. D., Green, B. L., Grace, M., & Titchener, J. (1983). Psychotherapy with survivors of the Beverly Hills Supper Club fire. *American Journal of Psychotherapy, 37,* 593–610.

Logue, J. N., Hansen, H., & Struening, E. (1979). Emotional and physical distress following Hurricane Agnes in Wyoming Valley of Pennsylvania. *Public Health Reports, 94,* 496–502.

McFarlane, A. C. (1984). The Ash Wednesday bushfires in South Australia: Implications for planning for future post-disaster services. *Medical Journal of Australia, 141,* 286–291.

McFarlane, A. C. (1986). Posttraumatic morbidity of a disaster: A study of cases presenting for psychiatric treatment. *Journal of Nervous and Mental Disease, 174,* 4–14.

Mitchell, J. T. (1982). The psychological impact of the Air Florida 90 disaster on fire-rescue, paramedic, and police officer personnel. In Crowley, R. A. (Ed.), *Mass casualties: A lessons learned approach.* (DOT Pub No. HS 806302, pp. 239–244) Washington, DC: U.S. Government Printing Office.

Naggan, L. (1976). Medical planning for disaster in Israel. *Injury, 7,* 279–285.

Nance, J. (1986). *Blind trust: The human crisis in airline safety.* New York: Morrow.

National Transportation Safety Board. *Aircraft Accident Report.* Report No. NTSB-AAR-80-1.

National Transportation Safety Board. *Aircraft Accident Report.* Report No. NTSB-AAR-82-8.

National Transportation Safety Board. *Aircraft Accident Report.* Report No. NTSB-AAR-74-4.

Netanyahu, B. (1986). *Terrorism: How the West can win.* New York: Farrar, Straus, & Giroux.

Nurses join in rescue efforts for Portland disaster victims. (1979, January 20). *American Nurse,* p. 3.

Orr, S. M., & Robinson, W. A. (1983). The Hyatt Regency skywalk collapse: An EMS-based disaster response. *Annals of Emergency Medicine, 12,* 601–605.

Parker, G. (1977). Cyclone Tracy and Darwin evacuees: On the restoration of the species. *British Journal of Psychiatry, 130,* 548–555.

Patterson, P. (1981). Operating room staffs respond to Hyatt casualties. *AORN Journal, 34,* 411–416.

Perlberg, M. (1979, April) Trauma at Tenerife: The psychic aftershocks of a jet disaster. *Human Behavior,* pp. 49–50.

Popplow, V. R. (1984). After the fire-ball. *Aviation, Space, and Environmental Medicine, 55,* 337–338.

Powell, J. W., & Rayner, J. (1952). *Progress notes: Disaster investigation July 1, 1951–June 30, 1952.* Edgewood, MD: Army Chemical Center, Chemical Corps Medical Laboratories.

Proctor, M. R. (1984). Psychological management of disaster victims. In E. L. Bassuk & A. W. Birk (Eds.), *Emergency psychiatry: Concepts, methods, and practices,* (pp. 263–270). New York: Plenum.

Quarantelli, E. L. (1980). *Evacuation behavior and problems: Findings and implications for the research literature.* Columbus: Ohio Disaster Research Center, Ohio State University.

Rayner, J. F. (1958). How do nurses behave in disaster? *Nursing Outlook, 6,* 572–576.

Republic Airlines (1986). *Emergency manual: Accident procedures.* Minneapolis: Unpublished manual.

Richard, W. (1974). Crisis intervention services following natural disaster: The Pennsylvania Recovery Project. *Journal of Community Psychology, 2,* 211–219.

Sannes, P. H., & Walcott, B. W. (1983). Stress reactions among participants in mass casualty simulations. *Annals of Emergency Medicine, 12,* 426–428.

Sloan, P. (1986). *Post-traumatic stress in survivors of an airplane crash-landing.* Paper given at the meeting of the American Psychological Association, Washington, DC.

Smith, W. E. (1986, April 14). Explosion on Flight 840. *Time,* pp. 34–37.

Sowder, B. J. (1985). Some mental health impacts of "loss" and injury: A look outside the disaster field. In B. J. Sowder (Ed.), *Disasters and mental health: Selected contemporary perspectives.* (DHHS Publication No. ADM 85-142D, pp. 74–103), Rockville, MD: U.S. Department of Health and Human Services, National Institute of Mental Health.

Star, L. D., Abelson, L. C., Del Guercio, R. M., & Pritchett, C. (1980). Mobilization of trauma teams for aircraft disasters. *Aviation, Space, and Environmental Medicine, 51,* 1262–1269.

Titchener, J. L., & Kapp, F. T. (1976). Family and character change at Buffalo Creek, *American Journal of Psychiatry, 133,* 295–299.

Tyhurst, J. S. (1951). Individual reactions to community disaster: Natural history of psychiatric phenomena. *American Journal of Psychiatry, 107,* 764–769.

Valent, P. (1984). The Ash Wednesday bushfires in Australia: *Medical Journal of Australia, 141,* 291–300.

Webb, A. C. (1980). Medical coordination in airport disasters, *Aviation, Space, and Environmental Medicine, 51,* 1256–1258.

Winch, R. D., Hines, K. C., Booker, H. T., & Ferrar, J. M. (1976). Disaster procedures report. Report following the Moorgate train crash on 28 February. *Injury, 7,* 288–291.

CHAPTER 5

The Nature and Effects of Technological Failures

EVELYN J. BROMET

Technological catastrophes, such as the malfunctioning at the Three Mile Island (TMI) and Chernobyl nuclear power plants or the toxic chemical leak in Bhopal, India, occur with considerably less frequency than other types of human-induced disasters, such as fires, airplane crashes, and train crashes. Clearly, such catastrophes are especially rare when compared to natural disasters like floods, tornadoes, or earthquakes. However, when these events occur, their impact is felt not just on the surrounding community but on the world at large.

Recent epidemiologic research on the mental health effects of disaster and evaluation studies of effectiveness of crisis intervention programs have made important theoretical and pragmatic contributions to the understanding of acute stress. Because technological disasters are protracted, the application of research into their psychological effects has conceptual and practical implications for the understanding of chronic stress. Moreover, because in widespread technological emergencies the exposure can impact upon care givers as well as recipients, unique difficulties arise in implementing clinical intervention programs. Thus, this chapter considers (1) the unique characteristics of technological versus other types of human-induced and natural disasters, and the implications of these unique characteristics for health and mental health research; (2) the psychosocial effects on community residents and TMI workers of the most extensively studied technological catastrophe to date, namely, the accident at the TMI nuclear power plant; and (3) unique issues in the design of clinical intervention programs in the aftermath of technological catastrophes.

This chapter was based in part on research funded by NIMH Contract No. 278-79-0048 (SM) and Grant No. 35425 and by funds from the William T. Grant Foundation.

CHARACTERISTICS OF TECHNOLOGICAL DISASTERS

Perhaps the major conclusion to be drawn from disaster research in general is that no two disasters are alike. Disasters differ along a variety of dimensions, and even the rubrics—natural, human-made, or technological (Baum, Fleming & Davison, 1983)—encompass disasters that are as heterogeneous within such categories as among them. Thus technological disasters such as nuclear power plant accidents or leakage from toxic waste dumps (e.g., Love Canal; Levine, 1982) differ from each other in several significant ways that have major implications for studying their aftermath, as well as for generalizing to other disaster situations.

Like other natural and human-induced disasters, each technological catastrophe is unique with respect to (1) type, (2) onset and duration of exposure, (3) level of toxicity or severity, and (4) the extent to which the population has control over future similar events (Berren, Beigel, & Ghertner, 1980).

With respect to type natural disasters (e.g., floods or tornadoes) or other human-induced occurrences (e.g., train crashes) differ in obvious ways. Within the rubric of technological catastrophes, different types of events have also occurred. Examples include a failure at the Chernobyl nuclear power plant that impacted upon millions of people across several continents, and by contrast, recent reports of toxic exposures from hazardous waste facilities that affect more circumscribed areas (Bachrach & Zautra, 1985). *A unique thread, however, links the different types of technological disasters, namely, long-term threat to health resulting from exposure to toxic elements that are potentially carcinogenic.* A recent report in the *Bulletin of the World Health Organization* pointed out that, with the exception of earthquakes, the survivors of natural disasters rarely incur serious health consequences (Lechat, 1979). By contrast, individuals exposed to lethal technological disasters, such as the escape of toxic chemicals from the Union Carbide plant in Bhopal, India, which left more than 2,000 people dead and many others blind, ill, or dying (Raphael, 1986), share an unfortunate uncertainty, namely, the potential for developing a chronic or fatal disease. Thus any discussion of the different types of technological disasters must be cognizant of this common characteristic.

The onset and duration of technological disasters also differ across circumstances in ways that are much the same with other types of disasters. Natural and human-made disasters may occur suddenly or develop more gradually; similarly technological disasters may have sudden or insidious onsets. Regardless of the actual length of onset, a technological event may take a community by surprise. For example, at Times Beach, Missouri, oil mixed with dioxin had been sprayed in the early 1970s. However, it was not until the winter of 1982 that residents of Times Beach experienced a double disaster when they were temporarily evacuated following a series of devastating floods and then forced to permanently relocate when the dioxin contamination was discovered (Smith, Robins, Przybeck, Goldring, & Solomon, 1986). Thus, in this case, the actual onset of the exposure predated the objective personal impact of the event. By contrast, the accidents at Three Mile Island and Chernobyl were sudden, their immediate duration persisted over several days, but the duration of effects, both in terms of cleanup of the facilities and impact on health, may persist for many years. Furthermore, community residents continued to live with the knowledge that occasional radiation leaks from TMI occurred after the accident and that problems associated with the cleanup operations might become manifest.

As is true in other types of diasters, the level of toxicity and severity of each technological catastrophe will undoubtedly be the most important determinants of the extent of mental and physical health sequelae. In the case of Three Mile Island, an unactualized disaster, no tangible effects were reliably observed, and the mental health findings, although statistically significant in many studies, did not reveal serious psychological disability that resulted in impaired daily functioning. If the psychological aftermath of the Chernobyl incident were to be evaluated, on the other hand, it would be reasonable to predict that the levels of dysfunctional anxiety and depression would far exceed the levels observed in studies following TMI.

The issue of control over future events is a significant one. At first blush, it would appear that in technological disasters, people have the opportunity to prevent recurrences because human beings are often responsible for the initial events. However, although one segment of the population—workers involved in such situations—may perceive ability to control future occurrences, community residents often react to the potential for recurrence by promulgating the shutdown of the responsible facility or by attempting through legal channels to force the facility to remove the toxic exposure. The issue of control often becomes a focus in the aftermath of technological disasters, and this issue can serve as a source of continued stress.

Not only can disasters be distinguished from one another in terms of the characteristics of the disasters themselves, but the demographic and cultural characteristics of the populations affected by them also contribute to their uniqueness. Disasters are not random events that occur to randomly selected individuals. They often take place in populations which are demographically and culturally distinct. For example, the Buffalo Creek Flood occurred in remote Appalachian villages (Gleser, Green, & Winget, 1981), and its impact on these communities may or may not be generalizable to other small villages around the world. The unique demographic and cultural characteristics of the communities affected by a disaster will have implications for the cognitive appraisal of the event taking place, the appropriateness of certain forms of interventions for alleviating mental and physical suffering, and the effectiveness of communications surrounding these activities. Thus, in addition to considering the characteristics of each disaster, researchers need to take into account the unique characteristics of the communities affected by them.

Having acknowledged the unique characteristics of disasters and exposed populations, what implications should be drawn in designing and integrating research on their psychosocial effects? With respect to technological disasters, investigators designing studies of their effects must be cognizant of (1) the natural history of the disaster as it unfolds; (2) the timing of data collection points to coincide with secondary events ensuing from the disaster; (3) the identification of groups with higher and lower degrees of exposure; (4) the tracking of people who will have been removed from the area permanently as a result of the contamination (e.g., relocated residents of Love Canal or Times Beach); (5) the specific health hazards thought to be associated with the specific exposure; and (6) assessment of the residents' perceptions over time of the nature and magnitude of the event.

The special characteristics of the exposed population will have implications for (1) the choice of the exposed sample(s) and the means by which a representative sample will be drawn; (2) the selection of the control group(s) with similar sociodemographic, cultural, and social area characteristics; (3) the selection of mental health measures that meaningfully capture the clinical and subclinical problems likely to be observed in the particular population to be studied; (4) the identification of pertinent competing risk factors needed to ascertain the unique contribution of the disaster itself to the types of psychological impairment being studied; and (5) the choice of potential mediating variables that might influence the relationship between exposure and the mental health outcomes.

By their nature, technological disasters generally dictate that investigations into their health effects must be longitudinal. A necessary component of the investigator's responsibility, therefore, is a serious commitment to the communities involved, which includes providing feedback of results to groups of interested parties. The benefit to the research is twofold: First, it will ensure that new data collection during the unfolding of the disaster will tap the concerns of the community and thus will more precisely measure the perceptions that might indeed mediate the relationship between exposure and mental health among the survivors; and second, it will provide a background of trust between the community and mental health professionals that might facilitate the successful implementation of intervention activities.

Integrating the existing body of disaster research is a difficult task because of the array of differences in the types of disasters and methodologies of existing studies (Bromet & Schulberg, 1987). Technological disasters have been recent occurrences and have rarely been studied from a systematic perspective. The one exception is the psychological aftermath of the accident at Three Mile Island, which was studied by a number of investigators. The next section first presents an overview of the four major investigations of the psychological effects of the TMI accident to illustrate the conceptual and pragmatic contributions that technological disaster research can have for understanding of the stress process. An attempt to synthesize this body of research follows. However, the reader must keep in mind that "TMI's status as a community disaster is open to question" (Hartsough & Savitsky, 1984, p. 1113); thus as a nonactualized disaster, the mental health research findings may not be generalizable to other actualized technological disasters. During the next decade, the psychological effects of these other events may be evaluated, and comparisons with research on TMI will then be possible.

EFFECTS OF A TECHNOLOGICAL CATASTROPHE: THREE MILE ISLAND

On March 28, 1979, a malfunction occurred in the Unit 2 reactor at Three Mile Island. Conditions remained out of control for several days, and on March 30, the governor issued an advisory to pregnant women and preschool children to evacuate the 5-mile area surrounding the plant. In all, 144,000 residents evacuated temporarily, including mothers of young children within a 10-mile radius.

Prior to TMI, several research reports on effects of natural or other human-made disasters on both adults and children had been published but by and large had not employed epidemiologic strategies (for reviews of this literature, see Bromet, Hough, & Connell, 1984; Bromet, Parkinson, Schulberg, Dunn, & Gondek, 1982; Chamberlin, 1980; Cohen & Ahearn, 1980; Kinston & Rosser, 1974). Because TMI was a technological disaster and, as noted earlier, differed from previous events on several dimensions, pertinent research strategies had to be formulated for the first time. Specifically, the onset of the accident was prolonged; its duration was uncertain because problems at TMI persisted and unfolded over time; personal impact was objectively low, in that no lives or property were lost after the nuclear reactor failed, yet the fear of future health hazards persisted; and residents were so concerned about future similar events that community organizations were formed to attempt to prevent the restart of the undamaged reactor (Hartsough & Savitsky, 1984).

Several sets of investigations were conducted into the mental health effects of the accident. The most prominent among them were (1) the work of the Task Force on Behavioral Effects of the President's Commission on the Accident at Three Mile Island (Dohrenwend, Dohrenwend, Kasl, & Warheit, 1979; Kasl, Chisholm, & Eskenazi, 1981a, 1981b); (2) research sponsored by the Department of Health of the Commonwealth of Pennsylvania in collaboration with the Pennsylvania State University College of Medicine (Houts & Goldhaber, 1981); (3) research sponsored by the Nuclear Regulatory Commission (Baum, Fleming, & Singer, 1983; Baum, Gatchel, & Schaeffer, 1983; Collins, Baum, & Singer, 1983; Davidson, Baum, & Collins, 1982; Fleming, Baum, Gisriel, & Gatchel, 1982; Gatchel, Schaeffer,

& Baum, 1985; Schaeffer & Baum, 1984); and (4) epidemiologic research funded by the National Institute of Mental Health (Bromet & Dunn, 1981; Bromet, Hough, & Connell, 1984; Bromet, Parkinson, Schulberg, Dunn, & Gondek, 1982; Bromet & Schulberg, 1986; Bromet, Schulberg, & Dunn, 1982; Cornely & Bromet, 1986; Dew, Bromet, & Schulberg, 1987; Dew, Bromet, Schulberg, Dunn, & Parkinson, 1987; Fienberg, Bromet, Follmann, Lambert, & May, 1985; Parkinson & Bromet, 1983; Solomon & Bromet, 1982).

Task Force on Behavioral Effects Report

The first set of studies was included in the report submitted by the Task Force on Behavioral Effects to the President's Commission on the Accident at Three Mile Island (Dohrenwend et al., 1979). The Task Force report focused on effects observed during the first 5–6 months following the accident and was based on data collected by individuals at local universities as well as new data collected by the Task Force itself. The findings from this report, which formed the basis for the conclusions about mental health effects published in the Commission's report (Kemeny, 1979), were subsequently published in the *Annals of the New York Academy of Science* (Dohrenwend et al., 1981).

The Task Force report presented findings on five groups of residents in the TMI area: a general population sample of male and female heads of households living in a 20-mile radius; mothers of preschool children sampled from birth announcements (and compared to similarly sampled mothers from the Wilkes-Barre community); TMI workers (who were compared to workers at the Peach Bottom Plant of Philadelphia Electric Company located approximately 40 miles away); 7th-, 9th-, and 11th-grade students in a nearby county; and clients of community mental health centers in the TMI area. Each study was conducted on a shoestring budget, and therefore sampling and data collection strategies were not without their limitations. However, the data collection consistently focused on Dohrenwend's measure of demoralization, and the analysis for the report used cutoffs for determining severe distress based on the scores of male and female mental health clients from the local area.

The following are highlights of the major findings of the Task Force. First, in the general population and sample of mothers of young children, the highest level of demoralization was found in April, with the rates dropping precipitously in May and June. People living in the 5-mile radius were significantly more symptomatic than people living 5–10 miles away from the plant. The teenagers, studied at the end of May, reported retrospectively on their symptomatology at the time of the accident. Those most symptomatic tended to live within 5 miles, to have evacuated the area, and to have a preschool sibling. Levels of symptomatology appeared to have decreased over time in a pattern similar to that observed among the adults.

Finally, workers, particularly nonsupervisory employees, retrospectively reported significantly more distress following the accident when compared with their peers at Peach Bottom. Telephone interviews conducted 6 months after the accident with 324 TMI and 298 Peach Bottom workers also revealed that supervisory workers with a preschool child at home were more symptomatic at the time of the incident than were their peers without preschool children. Thus, the President's Commission Report came to the following conclusion: "The major health effect of the accident appears to have been on the mental health of the people living in the region of Three Mile Island and of the workers at TMI" (p. 35). Furthermore, the Commission concluded on the basis of evidence obtained during the summer after the accident, that the distress was "short-lived."

Pennsylvania Department of Health Research

Concurrent with the work being conducted by the Task Force, the Pennsylvania Department of Health funded a series of telephone surveys with a randomly selected population within the 5-mile radius, as well as a control group from 41 to 55 miles away. The surveys were conducted in July 1979 (focusing on concurrent information as well as retrospective symptom data for the period following the accident), January 1980, and October 1980. The interviews contained measures of respondents' worry and emotional upset about TMI, behavioral and somatic symptomatology, and the Langner 22-item distress index. Respondents in the 5-mile radius were significantly more symptomatic on the behavioral and somatic scales during July (and retrospectively April) and the following January than controls, but significant differences were not observed in October 1980. Furthermore, the Langner scale did not reliably distinguish between residents living near TMI and the ones living farther away. Thus, for the most part, these telephone surveys confirmed the findings of the President's Commission that psychological effects were acute and short-lived.

Nuclear Regulatory Commission (NRC) Research

By contrast to these two sets of studies, the two other major studies conducted to date used face-to-face interviews, collected data over a longer period of time, and have reached somewhat different conclusions about the mental health impact of the accident. The NRC-funded work of Baum and colleagues was initiated 15 months after the accident and continued over the ensuing 4 years. A small group of residents living within 5 miles of TMI ($N = 38$) were compared with controls living within 5 miles of another nuclear reactor ($N = 32$), within 5 miles of a fossil-fuel (coal-fired) power plant ($N = 24$), and living more than 5 miles from any power plant ($N = 27$). Subjects were evaluated twice yearly on a variety of measures, including a symptom checklist and neuropsychological tasks requiring concentration and motivation (a proofreading task and the embedded figures test); they also provided 15-hour urine samples that were assayed for stress-related hormones (norepinephrine, epinephrine, and cortisol). TMI subjects performed more poorly on all measures than controls across time, and the investigators have concluded that some residents experienced chronic stress as a result of the accident attributable to (1) the uncertainty of TMI residents about the long-term effects of the radiation exposure after the accident, (2) the possibility of future radiation leaks, and (3) their mistrust in officials and the media about the accuracy of the information conveyed. However, consistent with the inferences from the previous two sets of report, the distress levels described were in the subclinical range, albeit at the high end of the range.

National Institute of Mental Health (NIMH) Research

To the extent of present knowledge, the TMI research funded by NIMH was the first psychiatric epidemiologic investigation of a disaster, that is, the first quasi-experimental, longitudinal investigation to test a conceptual model of chronic stress employing representative, high-risk exposed and nonexposed samples, clinical as well as subclinical mental health measures, competing risk factors, and potential moderating variables. The initial goal of the study was to extend the findings of the Task Force on Behavioral Effects by similarly focusing on mothers of young children, workers employed at the plant, and psychiatric outpatients in the public mental health sector.

Home interviews were conducted from December 1979 through January 1980 and in April 1980 with 312 mothers of young children living within 10 miles of TMI and a comparison group of 124 similarly selected women living within 10 miles of the Beaver Valley–Shippingport nuclear reactor in western Pennsylvania; 161 employees of the TMI nuclear plant and 124 employees of the Beaver Valley facility; and 151 persons treated at community mental health centers serving the TMI area during the 6 months perceding the accident and living within 10 miles of the plant, along with 64 similarly selected western Pennsylvania controls. Subsequent NIMH funding provided for reinterviews with the mothers and workers in the fall of 1981 and 1982 to expand these samples and to add in samples of mothers of young children and employees living near or working at two fossil-fuel plants in western Pennsylvania. Funds obtained from the W. T. Grant Foundation made it possible also to interview 8–16-year-old children in the families of the TMI and Beaver Valley mothers and workers. In all, 150 TMI area children and 99 comparison site children were interviewed. Finally, after the restart of the undamaged Unit 1 reactor at TMI in October 1985 (occurring after an extended legal battle which eventually reached the U.S. Supreme Court), questionnaires were mailed to and returned from a representative subset of the mothers of young children living in the TMI area (199 of the 385 TMI women interviewed in the fall of 1981 and 1982).

The interviews were designed to collect data relevant to three hypotheses. The first hypothesis was that TMI subjects would be significantly more symptomatic and would exhibit higher rates of clinical depression and anxiety than comparison site subjects. Second, among TMI subjects, the ones with a prior psychiatric history, with less adequate social support, and with residences in closer proximity to TMI would exhibit more symptoms and more clinical disturbance than persons without these vulnerability factors. Finally, it was hypothesized that the rate of psychopathology would not abate over time, since the controversies surrounding the cleanup operations and reopening of the undamaged reactor ensured constant media attention to TMI's dangers. To test these hypotheses, the interviews contained a comprehensive symptom inventory (Symptom Checklist-90; Derogatis, 1977), the Schedule for Affective Disorders and Schizophrenia–Lifetime Version (SADS-L; Endicott & Spitzer, 1978), information on social support, and attitudinal questions about TMI (see Bromet & Schulberg, 1986, for a detailed review). The post-restart mailed questionnaire focused exclusively on symptomatology and attitudes toward the current situation at the plant. The four face-to-face interviews were conducted by mental health professionals with advanced academic degrees and at least 5 years of clinical experience; recruitment and screening focused not only on their clinical skills, but also on their attitudes toward nuclear energy and TMI's mental health impact in order to eliminate individuals with extreme views.

The group clearly most affected by TMI comprised the mothers of young children. Compared to their Beaver Valley counterparts, they had significantly higher (i.e., twofold greater) incidence and prevalence rates of affective disorder during the year after the accident and significantly higher symptom levels on a variety of dimensions such as depression, anxiety, hostility, and somatization. Among the TMI group, mothers living within 5 miles of TMI, reporting episodes of major depression or generalized anxiety predating the accident, and reporting less adequate social support and less intimacy with their husbands were the most distressed.

Immediately following the 1981 interviews, the comparison sites underwent massive layoffs and plant shutdowns due to a severe economic depression in the steel industry. During this time frame, covering the period of 2½ to 3½ years after the accident, the TMI mothers' levels of distress remained elevated, and interestingly, the comparison mothers' distress levels became elevated to similar degrees. Thus, while unemployment mitigated any differences between groups, the TMI mothers' symptom levels remained elevated throughout the follow-up period.

The data collected post-restart were the most startling. The TMI mothers' post-restart symptom levels were elevated over all previous levels, and their pre-restart attitudes toward nuclear power were for the first time significant and strong predictors of symptomatology. Furthermore, a history of major depression and/or generalized anxiety in the 18 months following the accident led to subsequently higher levels of pre-restart symptomatology and stronger beliefs of greater personal risk; these responses, in turn, were directly associated with elevated post-restart distress (Dew et al., 1987).

The mental health status of the 150 TMI school-aged children and 99 children from the Beaver Valley was determined 3½ years after the accident using standardized measures of social competence, behavior problems, fearfulness, and self-esteem (Bromet et al., 1984). No significant differences in current symptomatology were found between the TMI children and the comparison group. Children whose fathers worked at TMI were a special concern because of reports that they had been ostracized at school and by their neighbors during the year after the accident. It should be noted that the parent company for TMI established a counseling service for families of workers at the plant and conducted an independent evaluation to verify these anecdotal reports. They confirmed the fact that these children had been belittled by teachers and school staff and even failed in courses because of their fathers' employment at TMI. However, the NIMH study did not find current differences in the mental health status of the workers' children compared to the children of the mother cohort, nor were there retrospective differences in mental health for the period immediately following the accident.

Not unexpectedly, children who remembered being upset at the time of the accident tended to be more symptomatic currently than children who recalled the experience as being less stressful. This finding was mediated by family milieu. That is, in families perceived as highly supportive, there were no differences in mental health for children reporting high or low levels of stress, whereas in families with relatively less support, children experiencing higher levels of stress at the time of the accident were more symptomatic at the time of interview than children recalling less TMI-related stress.

The results of research into the determinants of mental health in the worker cohorts and determinants of symptomatology in the mental health clients tended to demonstrate no significant differences in post-TMI mental health between TMI area respondents and controls. TMI workers reported somewhat greater psychopathology after the accident, but these differences were also retrospectively reported for the period of time before the accident occurred. Even though the problems at TMI continued, their impact on workers at the plant was unremarkable 2½–3½ years after the accident (Parkinson & Bromet, 1983). It should be pointed out that although the longitudinal findings from the nuclear plant workers revealed little that was unique about TMI per se, the data did provide important information on the links between mental health and occupational stress, which tends to be highly prevalent in the work environments of nuclear power plants (Bromet, Dew, Parkinson & Schulberg, 1988).

With respect to the mental health outpatients in the TMI area, the variations in current symptom level were partially explained by negative perceptions of TMI. That is, patients who were the most symptomatic 1 year after the accident were significantly more likely to perceive TMI as dangerous and to believe that it was unsafe to live within 10 miles of a nuclear power plant. On the other hand, evacuation and distance of residence from the plant were unrelated to symptomatology. Although the findings do not permit a disentangling of the causal sequence, the conclusion from these data was that clinicians should inquire about patient's fears after a technological accident because this information might suggest the need for crisis counseling in some cases.

Integrating the TMI Research Findings

The most parsimonious conclusions to be reached from a careful inspection of the various sets of findings about the psychological impact of the TMI accident are that (1) contrary to the early findings of the President's Commission, long-term studies have revealed persistent elevations in psychological distress, but (2) the levels are by and large at the high end of the normal range, and the functioning of TMI residents appears not to have been impaired as a result of the stressors in the area. Moreover, there were differential effects with certain groups, particularly mothers of young children, exhibiting more symptomatology than other groups.

One source of evidence to support the conclusion that the effects observed did not reach the intensity associated with other severe traumatic events is that no reports of post-traumatic stress disorder have been described in any of the major TMI studies. By contrast, the Shore, Tatum, and Vollmer (1986) study of the Mount St. Helens volcanic eruption, in which 50 people died and extensive property damage occurred, found several cases of post-traumatic stress disorder. It also reported a *10-fold* difference in onset rates of depression, anxiety, and post-traumatic stress disorder combined in their high exposure group, compared to nonexposed controls. A second source of evidence was the archival research on effects of TMI by Mileti, Hartsough, Madson and Hufnagel (1984) which found no observable changes in rates of crime, psychiatric admissions, or suicide before and after the accident. Thus, the finding that the absolute levels of symptomatology in all four sets of investigations are within the normal range cannot be dismissed as unreliability in the measures, since no instances of functional impairment have been noted.

Another conclusion to be drawn is that although most people reestablish normal life patterns, for some groups, adaptation is a slower and more difficult process. Thus, there appear to be long-term sequelae as a result of the TMI accident, perhaps caused in part by the lack of resolution of the problems that ensued as a result of the damage that occurred at the plant in 1979. In the NIMH study data, subjects who were initially more symptomatic at the 9-month interview tended to maintain their elevated symptom levels throughout the data collection period. Whether the maintenance of high levels of symptomatology will eventuate in a clinical episode is unknown.

Initially, attitudes toward TMI were only weak predictors of symptomatology in the group of mothers of young children, whereas after the restart, their contribution was heightened.

The final issue that should be addressed in integrating findings from research on the psychological effects of the TMI accident is whether the unique characteristics of the TMI accident led to a qualitatively distinct pattern of psychological effects or predictors of such effects. Approaching this issue is particularly difficult, because most prior studies of natural and other human-induced disasters were cross-sectional, short-term, and/or based on different types of data often obtained from volunteer samples. The following comments should, therefore, be regarded as tentative and necessarily speculative.

First, with respect to absolute rates, the short-term prevalence findings from the TMI studies are perhaps lower than those reported in studies of extreme traumatic events or disasters with extensive overt damage, such as the Mount St. Helens eruption described earlier. For example, Terr (1981) found that 5–13 months after children on a school bus in California were kidnapped and buried alive, 100% exhibited moderate to severe posttraumatic emotional sequelae. Unfortunately, there are few long-term follow-up studies of acute events, such as airplane crashes or floods, with which to compare the effect of a chronic threatening situation like the one at TMI. It is noteworthy that Baum and colleagues are currently conducting longitudinal research in which short- and long-term psychological effects of chronic human-made disasters and acute natural disasters will be compared.

There also appear to be some similarities in the risk factors determining at least short-term psychological response to disasters. The most consistent finding has been that affective responses are experienced more intensively by individuals more directly touched by disasters. Individuals hospitalized as a result of a nightclub fire (Adler, 1943), directly affected by the Mount St. Helens Volcano (Shore et al., 1986) or directly affected by the floods caused by Hurricane Agnes (Logue, Hansen, & Struening, 1979) or by the flooding in Bristol, England (Bennet, 1970), and children whose parents were more upset by a disaster (Bloch, Silber, & Perry, 1956; Lacey, 1972) were more distressed than individuals exposed to these events but not directly suffering loss of life or property. Similarly, all of the TMI studies have found that people living closer to the plant were more symptomatic than people living farther away, even though as both the Pennsylvania Department of Health research and the NIMH research have shown, the people living farther away were often more concerned about the plant itself.

If enduring psychological sequelae are to be expected among significant proportions of the affected populations after a technological disaster, how should the community respond to meet such needs, given the human service system's finite resources? The next section describes the special difficulties in implementing disaster-related services in technological disasters as compared to other natural or human-induced situations.

INTERVENTION EFFORTS FOLLOWING TECHNOLOGICAL CATASTROPHES

In the immediate aftermath of a disaster, including a technological disaster, there typically is a consensus of values around the provision of care for victims, restoration and maintenance of community services, and the maintenance of public order (Dynes & Quarantelli, 1976). This value consensus facilitates the reallocation of resources toward restabilization of the natural ecology of community life that has been so dramatically and severely disrupted. In a classic paper published almost 4 decades ago, Tyhurst (1951) outlined three overlapping phases characterizing psychological response to disaster: (1) a period of impact; (2) a period of recoil; and (3) a posttraumatic period. These phases have since formed the structure for the design of disaster plans (e.g., Cohen & Ahearn, 1980; Hartsough, 1982). Cohen and Ahearn, for example, addressed the changing needs of disaster victims over time by suggesting the following specific elements:

a. *Period of Impact.*   Alleviate immediate cognitive disorganization and/or psychophysiologic reactions of the victims.
b. *Period of Recoil.*   Assess level of need and implement crisis counseling and therapy as needed.
c. *Posttraumatic Period.*   Assist those individuals with social and legal problems as well as those with vulnerable defenses who are unable to cope with new stressors or who are exhausted.

In technological disasters, these three periods have unique characteristics compared to other more acute catastrophes. First, the duration of the initial crisis period may be prolonged. For example, the accident at TMI unfolded over several days, not several hours. Furthermore, the original leakage triggered a series of concomitant events, including the disruptions caused by evacuation, fears associated with the hydrogen bubble, continued uncertainty about how and when the decontamination process would be carried out, subsequent revelations that the accident came within 30 to 60 minutes of a meltdown (Rogovin, 1980), the venting of krypton gas the following spring, and the uncertainty of whether the undamaged reactor would be started up again. Thus, crisis intervention models usually employed in acute crisis situations may not be entirely appropriate in a technological disaster. For example, the military model for dealing with psychiatric casualties has been espoused for natural disasters. The elements of this model contain four principles: immediacy or early intervention; expectancy or maintaining an attitude that the patient will soon return to duty; simplicity of treatments that emphasize normality and anticipated recovery; and centrality of treatment facilities. For a variety of reasons, this model would be difficult to implement during the early phase following a technological mishap.

There are several specific concerns that arise in considering how such an intervention scheme might be implemented in the immediate aftermath of a technological emergency. They include whether adequate staff will be available who have not been injured or killed, whose families have not been injured or killed, or who have not evacuated and then permanently relocated away from the area. When the TMI accident occurred, for example, health and mental health professionals by and large left the area for several days. A second issue is that mental health professionals may have preconceived ideas about how the disaster directly affected the population and thus may have inadequate distance from the patients to effectively treat them. A third issue is that the facilities themselves may have been contaminated in a technological incident, necessitating selection of alternate sites located miles from the area. Finally, a unique difficulty in implementing crisis services in a first phase of a technological disaster is that nonexposed trained mental health professionals may avoid exposed survivors because of their personal fear of contamination. For example, the survivors of Hiroshima were given the label *Hibakusha,* being regarded by others in their community as "pregnant with death" and having a total sense of contamination (Lifton, 1965). Consequently, the organization and implementation of mental health services during the immediate phases of extreme technological disasters may be fraught with difficulties.

In the recoil phase, crisis resolution is the fundamental goal. A general premise in the organization of such disaster relief efforts is that the human service system's resources are most efficiently utilized when directed to high risk cohorts rather than to all residents of an affected locale. Within this planning framework, Cohen and Ahearn (1980) emphasized the value of a needs assessment that surveys affected groups to determine the nature and extent of their problems. As they note, however, adequate time seldom exists during postdisaster field interviews for complete psychiatric history taking. Thus, in most disaster situations, it is vital for administrators and clinicians to have previously identified a community's psychiatrically vulnerable population so that limited resources are deployed in the most expeditious and effective manner possible (Schulberg, 1974).

The literature would suggest that two factors can be used to identify high risk survivors: level of involvement (i.e., death of family members, extensive property loss, prolonged disruption of life) and prior psychiatric status. In the absence of information on prior psychiatric status, should psychological status during the period of immediate impact serve as an indicator of vulnerability? Unfortunately, there is little longitudinal empirical evidence on the relationship between short- and long-term adjustment processes. Accordingly, a key dilemma exists for the identification of populations potentially vulnerable to the effects of technological catastrophes (Bromet & Schulberg, 1987). Are the individuals who experienced high levels of symptomatology in the immediate aftermath of a disaster likely to continue to demonstrate prolonged difficulties? In other words, does a pathological stress response develop only among persons exhibiting initial vulnerability, or are the risk factors for symptomatology in the immediate versus the recoil periods different?

An attempt was made to examine this issue with the data collected during the TMI research. Once again, the reader must keep in mind that the TMI accident has not yet had any tangible effects. Using data on subclinical symptomatology and clinically diagnosable depression and generalized anxiety, the NIMH study showed that a high level of pathology on either index in the accident's immediate aftermath was significantly related to poor adjustment during the "recoil" phase. Thus, at face value, the data suggest that mothers of young children who react to a disaster with acute maladjustment patterns be carefully monitored for the development of chronic pathology as well.

It should also be noted, however, that this method of identifying a targeted sample of vulnerable individuals contains numerous false positives, that is, individuals who are defined to be at high risk because of initial distress but who subsequently show little pathology. Thus, even among young mothers reporting significant pathology in the first 12 months after the TMI accident, two thirds of the SADS-diagnosable women and one third of the women classified in the top quintile with respect to symptomatology did not continue in these categories over time. It is therefore necessary to more precisely define the characteristics of vulnerable persons who warrant long-term observation.

Regardless of the precision with which vulnerable people in the recoil phase of a technological disaster can be identified, questions remain about the psychiatric sector's role in disaster intervention. One central concern in the provision of such care is that community residents do not ordinarily turn to mental health providers for help in coping with psychological difficulties. For example, Lindy and Lindy (1981) noted that after the Beverly Hills Supper Club fire in 1977, only 147 survivors (approximately 6%) responded to several different outreach methods. Similarly, the ECA study of utilization of health and mental health services by persons reporting recent DSM-III disorders found that only 16%–19% of persons with affective disorders visited a mental health specialist; the remainder visited a general medical or other type of human service provider (Shapiro et al., 1984). In the NIMH-funded study of TMI, among 96 mothers of young children meeting criteria for a depressive disorder during the 1-year period between fall 1981 and fall 1982, 39 (40.6%) sought professional help during the episode (Dew et al., 1988). Of these, 16 consulted a mental health professional, 17 went to a nonpsychiatric physician, and 6 exclusively consulted other human service professionals. In short, more than half of the diagnosable women did not seek professional treatment of any sort. Thus, the dilemma of identifying vulnerable populations is compounded by the need to develop mechanisms for facilitating help-seeking behavior.

Because the long-term aftermath of a technological disaster can be expected to be protracted, the third phase may not occur for some years after such a catastrophe. Nevertheless, a significant problem, as Hartsough (1982) succinctly stated, applies equally to technological as well as other disaster situations, namely: "A final barrier to long-range disaster planning is the absence of guidelines for such a plan." Hartsough outlined five elements necessary for addressing the long-term psychological effects of a disaster. These are anticipating or identifying what the psychological effects will be, maintaining awareness of disaster-related psychopathology in regular mental health services, designing outreach services, providing consultation to disaster relief and related agencies, and educating the public about disaster-related phenomena. Thus, the fundamental questions of what services should be provided in the posttraumatic phase, for whom, where, and how have not been adequately addressed in the disaster literature. It is timely that appropriate strategies for long-term interventions rather than just crisis intervention be developed, because the evidence suggests that technological events will have long-term psychological effects.

CONCLUDING REMARKS

In a world of increasing technological sophistication, the prospects for greater numbers of mishaps of varying magnitude are unfortunately rising. For example, there are now approximately 75 nuclear power plants in the United States. Each has made major contributions to the economic and community development of its respective region. However, many states containing nuclear power plants do not have adequate emergency plans, and among those with plans, few have tested their plans through the conduct of field drills involving actual community residents.

Janis (1962) postulated that perception of continuing threat profoundly influences coping style and adjustment. According to this postulation, persons able to deny the lingering danger of a situation such as TMI, or to compromise between a vigilant and reassured posture, would experience less distress; persons unable to deny the situation's severity or to engage in compromise formations would fare more poorly. At present, it is unclear in what manner and direction perception of danger and distress level are causally linked. Understanding this dynamic is vital, since a disaster may create major imbalances in a community's ecologic system.

Subsequent interventions in technological emergencies should potentially seek to meet the personal needs of vulnerable individuals, coordinate and link human service systems, and/or adopt appropriate public policy regarding information dissemination. Because technological disasters are likely to be protracted, it is critically important that implementation be maximally efficient and effective over a period of years. Planning for long-term care is admittedly difficult, because with a few exceptions (i.e., follow-up studies of concentration camp survivors), most stress research on extreme situations has examined short-term rather than long-term or persistent sequelae. Thus, it is hoped that current epidemiologic studies of technological disasters will provide new information on the dynamics and consequences of long-term stress, which will contribute on both a practical and theoretical level to knowledge of the natural history of psychological response to these catastrophes.

REFERENCES

Adler, A. (1943). Neuropsychiatric complications in victims of Boston's Cocoanut Grove disaster. *Journal of the American Medical Association, 123,* 1098–1101.

Bachrach, K. M., & Zautra, A. J. (1985). Coping with a community stressor: The threat of a hazardous waste facility. *Journal of Health and Social Behavior, 26,* 127–141.

Baum, A., Fleming, R., & Davidson, L. M. (1983). National disaster and technological catastrophe. *Environment and Behavior, 15,* 333–354.

Baum, A., Fleming, R., & Singer, J. E. (1983). Coping with victimization by technological disaster. *Journal of Social Issues, 39,* 117–138.

Baum, A., Gatchel, R. J., & Schaeffer, M. A. (1983). Emotional, behavioral, and physiological effects of chronic stress at Three Mile Island. *Journal of Consulting and Clinical Psychology, 51,* 565–572.

Bennet, G. (1970). Bristol floods 1968: Controlled survey of effects on health of local community disaster. *British Medical Journal, 3,* 454–458.

Berren, M. R., Beigel, A., & Ghertner, S. (1980). A typology for the classification of disasters. *Community Mental Health Journal, 16,* 103–111.

Bloch, D., Silber, E., & Perry, S. (1956). Some factors in the emotional reaction of children to disaster. *American Journal of Psychiatry, 113,* 416–422.

Bromet, E. J., Dew, M. A., Parkinson, D., & Schulberg, H. (1988). Predictive effects of occupational and marital stress on the mental health of a male workforce. *Journal of Organizational Behavior, 9,* 1–13.

Bromet, E. J., & Dunn, L. (1981). Mental health of mothers nine months after the Three Mile Island accident. *The Urban and Social Change Review, 14,* 12–15.

Bromet, E. J., Hough, L., & Connell, M. (1984). Mental health of children near the Three Mile Island reactor. *Journal of Preventive Psychiatry, 2,* 275–301.

Bromet, E. J., Parkinson, D., Schulberg, H., Dunn, L., & Gondek, P. (1982). Mental health of residents near the Three Mile Island reactor: a comparative study of selected groups. *Journal of Preventive Psychiatry, 1,* 225–276.

Bromet, E. J., & Schulberg, H. C. (1986). The TMI disaster: A search for high risk groups. In J. H. Shore (Ed.). *Disaster stress studies: New methods and findings* (pp. 1–19). Washington, DC: American Psychiatric Press.

Bromet, E. J., & Schulberg, H. C. (1987). Epidemiologic findings from disaster research. In R. Hales & A. Frances (Eds.), *American Psychiatric Association Annual Review* (Vol. 6, pp. 676–689). Washington, DC: American Psychiatric Press.

Bromet, E. J., Schulberg, H., & Dunn, L. (1982). Reactions of psychiatric patients to the Three Mile Island nuclear accident. *Archives of General Psychiatry, 39,* 725–730.

Chamberlin, B. (1980). MAYO Seminars in Psychiatry: The psychological aftermath of disaster. *Journal of Clinical Psychology, 41,* 238–244.

Cohen, R., & Ahearn, F. (1980). *Handbook for mental health care of disaster victims.* Baltimore: The Johns Hopkins University.

Collins, D. L., Baum, A., & Singer, J. E. (1983). Coping with chronic stress at Three Mile Island: Psychological and biochemical evidence. *Health Psychology, 2,* 149–166.

Cornely, P., & Bromet, E. (1986). Prevalence of behavior problems in three-year-old children living near Three Mile Island: a comparative analysis. *Journal of Child Psychology and Psychiatry, 27,* 489–498.

Davidson, L. M., Baum, A., & Collins, D. L. (1982). Stress and control-related problems at Three Mile Island. *Journal of Applied Social Psychology, 12,* 349–359.

Derogatis, L. (1977). *The SCL-90 Manual I: Scoring, administration and procedures for the SCL-90.* Baltimore: The Johns Hopkins University School of Medicine, Clinical Psychimetrics Unit.

Dew, M. A., Bromet, E., & Schulberg, H. C. (1987). A comparative analysis of two community stressors' long-term mental health effects. *American Journal of Community Psychology, 15,* 167–183.

Dew, M. A., Bromet, E., Schulberg, H. C., Dunn, L., & Parkinson, D. (1987). Mental health effects of the Three Mile Island nuclear reactor restart. *American Journal of Psychiatry, 144,* 1074–1077.

Dew, M. A., Dunn, L., Bromet, E. J., & Schulberg, H. C. (1988). Factors affecting help-seeking during depression in a community sample. *Journal of Affective Disorders, 14,* 223–234.

Dohrenwend, B. P., Dohrenwend, B. S., Kasl, S., & Warheit, G. (1979). Report of the public health and safety task force on behavioral effects to the President's Commission on the Accident at Three Mile Island (stock no. 052-003-00732). Washington, DC: U.S. Government Printing Office.

Dohrenwend, B. P., Dohrenwend, B. S., Warheit, G., Bartlett, G., Goldsteen, R., Goldsteen, K., & Martin, J. (1981). Stress in the community: a report to the President's Commission on the accident at Three Mile Island. *Annals of the New York Academy of Science, 365,* 159–174.

Dynes, R. R., & Quarantelli, E. (1976). The family and community reactions to disaster. In H. J. Parad, H. Resnik, & L. Parad, (Eds.), *Emergency and disaster management.* Bowie, MD: Charles Press.

Endicott, J., & Spitzer, R. (1978). A diagnostic interview: The Schedule for Affective Disorders and Schizophrenia. *Archives of General Psychiatry, 33,* 766–771.

Fienberg, S. E., Bromet, E. J., Follmann, D., Lambert, D., & May, S. M. (1985). Longitudinal analysis of categorical epidemiological data: A study of Three Mile Island. *Environmental Health Perspectives, 63,* 241–248.

Fleming, R., Baum, A., Gisriel, M. M., & Gatchel, R. J. (1982). Mediating influences of social support on stress at Three Mile Island. *Journal of Human Stress,* 14–22.

Gatchel, R. J., Schaeffer, M. A., & Baum, A. (1985). A psychophysiological field study of stress at Three Mile Island. *Psychophysiology, 22,* 175–181.

Gleser, G., Green B., & Winget, C. (1981). *Prolonged psychosocial effects of disaster: A study of Buffalo Creek.* New York: Academic Press.

Hartsough, D. M. (1982). Planning for disaster: A new community outreach program for mental health centers. *Journal of Community Psychology, 10,* 255–264.

Hartsough, D. M., & Savitsky, J. C. (1984). Three Mile Island: Psychology and environmental policy at a crossroads. *American Psychologist, 39,* 1113–1122.

Houts, P. S., & Goldhaber, M. K. (1981). Psychological and social effects on the population surrounding Three Mile Island after the nuclear accident on March 28, 1979. In S. Majumdar (Ed.), *Energy, environment and the economy* (pp. 152–164). Easton, PA: Pennsylvania Academy of Sciences.

Janis, I. (1962). The psychological effects of warning. In G. Baker & D. Chapman (Eds.), *Man and society of disaster* (pp. 55–92). New York: Basic Books.

Kasl, S. V., Chisholm, R. F., & Eskenazi, B. (1981a). The impact of the accident at the Three Mile Island on the behavior and well-being of nuclear workers. Part I: Perceptions and evaluations, behavioral responses, and work-related attitudes and feelings. *American Journal of Public Health, 71,* 472–483.

Kasl, S. V., Chisholm, R. F., & Eskenazi, B. (1981b). The impact of the accident at the Three Mile Island on the behavior and well-being of nuclear workers. Part II: Job tension, psychophysiological symptoms, and indices of distress. *American Journal of Public Health, 71,* 484–495.

Kemeny, J. (1979). *The President's Commission on the Accident at Three Mile Island.* Washington, DC: U.S. Government Printing Office.

Kinston, W., & Rosser, R. (1974). Disaster: Effects on mental and physical state. *Journal of Psychosomatic Research, 18,* 437–456.

Lacey, G. (1972). Observations on Aberfan. *Journal of Psychosomatic Research, 16,* 257–260.

Lechat, M. (1979). Disasters and public health. *Bulletin of the World Health Organization, 57,* 11–17.

Levine, A. (1982). *Love Canal: Science, politics and people.* Lexington, MA: Lexington Books.

Lifton, R. J. (1965). Psychological effects of the atomic bomb in Hiroshima: The theme of death. In R. Fulton (Ed.), *Death and identity* (pp. 8–42). New York: Wiley.

Lindy, J., & Lindy, J. (1981). Planning and delivery of mental health services in disaster: The Cincinnati experience. *The Urban and Social Change Review, 14,* 16–21.

Logue, J., Hansen, J., & Struening, E. (1979). Emotional and physical distress following Hurricane Agnes in Wyoming Valley of Pennsylvania. *Public Health Reports, 94,* 495–502.

Mileti, D., Hartsough, D., Madson, P., & Hufnagel, R. (1984). The Three Mile Island accident: A study of behavioral indicators of human stress. *International Journal of Mass Emergencies and Disasters, 2,* 89–113.

Parkinson, D., & Bromet, E. (1983). Correlates of mental health in nuclear and coal-fired power plant workers. *Scandinavian Journal of Work Environment and Health, 9,* 341–345.

Raphael, B. (1986). *When disaster strikes: How individuals and communities cope with catastrophe.* New York: Basic Books.

Rogovin, M. (1980). *Three Mile Island: A Report to the Commissioners and to the Public: Volume 1.* Nuclear Regulatory Commission Special Inquiry Group, Washington, DC. Unpublished report.

Schaeffer, M. A., & Baum, A. (1984). Adrenal cortical response to stress at Three Mile Island. *Psychosomatic Medicine, 46,* 227–237.

Schulberg, H. C. (1974). Disaster, crisis theory and intervention strategies. *Omega, 5,* 77–87.

Shapiro, S., Skinner, E., Kessler, L., Von Korff, M., German, P., Tischler, G., Leaf, P., Benham, L., Cottler, L., & Regier, D. (1984). Utilization of health and mental health services. Three epidemiologic catchment area sites. *Archives of General Psychiatry, 41,* 971–978.

Shore, J., Tatum, E., & Vollmer, W. (1986). The Mount St. Helens stress response syndrome. In J. Shore (Ed.), *Disaster stress studies: New methods and findings.* Washington, DC: American Psychiatric Press.

Smith, E., Robins, L., Przybeck, T., Goldring, E., & Solomon, S. (1986). Psychosocial consequences of a disaster. In J. Shore (Ed.), *Disaster stress studies: New methods and findings,* (pp. 49–76). Washington, DC: American Psychiatric Press.

Solomon, Z., & Bromet, E. (1982). The role of social factors in affective disorder: an assessment of the vulnerability model of Brown and his colleagues. *Psychological Medicine, 12,* 123–130.

Terr, L. (1981). Psychic trauma in children: Observations following the Chowchilla school-bus kidnapping. *American Journal of Psychiatry, 138,* 14–19.

Tyhurst, J. (1951). Individual reactions to community disaster. *American Journal of Psychiatry, 107,* 764–769.

CHAPTER 6

Crime, Violence, and Terrorism

MARLENE A. YOUNG

BACKGROUND: RESPONSES OF VICTIMS OF VIOLENCE

Although criminal violence has long afflicted United States far more than other western societies, only recently has serious attention been paid to the impact of that violence on its victims. This chapter addresses that impact as the human response to human cruelty. Such cruelty may be manifested through individual assaults, group riots, or acts of political terrorism. All of these behaviors will be referred to as criminal activity, even though some countries do not deem state-sponsored terrorism and torture as criminal.

Most literature on criminal victimization focuses on certain types of victims, for example, rape victims (Burgess & Holmstrom, 1974, 1976, 1979; Holmstrom and Burgess, 1983; Kilpatrick, Veronen, & Resick, 1979, 1982); victims of spouse abuse (Pagelow, 1984; Schechtz, 1982; Walker, 1984); victims of incest and child sexual abuse (Burgess, Groth, Holmstrom, & Sgroi, 1978; Finkelhor, 1979, 1984; Herman, 1981; MacFarlane, et al., 1987); marital rape victims (Russell, 1982) the survivors of homicide victims (Lord, 1987; NOVA, 1985), victims of terrorism (Ochberg, 1978; Ochberg & Soskis, 1982); victims of burglary (Clarke & Hope, 1986; Maguire, 1980; Waller & Okihiro, 1978); victims of robbery (Lejeune & Alex, 1973); and victims and survivors of the holocaust (Danieli, 1982; Eitinger, 1964/1972, 1980).

Despite all the different ways people do violence to one another, the literature on victimization displays similar psychological reactions across types of victims. Analysts who have addressed the more generic issues of victim reaction have developed similar descriptions grounded in general theories about crisis, stress, or trauma (Bard & Sangrey, 1979/1986; Figley, 1985; Figley & McCubbin, 1983; Symonds, 1975; Williams, 1987; Young, 1986; Young-Rifai, 1982).

The following is a description of those generic victim reactions.

The State of Human Equilibrium

The framework begins with the individual perceived as existing in a state of equilibrium within his or her natural and social environment. That rough equilibrium is defined by limits to the range of events that the individual can tolerate or cope with on an everyday basis. These events produce an endurable tension or stress that is a part of human life. The tension can be positive or negative but remains tolerable as long as it falls within the range of equilibrium.

When that rough equilibrium is disrupted by an event that is beyond the tolerable range, the event is perceived as traumatic to the individual and that person suffers a crisis. The crisis may be acute and short-lived, or if the event continues over time, it may become a state of chronic crisis.

Events that are traumatic to most individuals are those events that are unexpected, random, or arbitrary; are life- or health-threatening; take away all or most of the individual's autonomy or control; and cause a loss to the individual—whether that loss be of property, values, or self.

Criminal Victimization as Crisis

Violent victimization is usually a traumatic event. And victims of human violence generally suffer a crisis. Reactions to that crisis are both physiological and psychological, moving through stages that include shock and disbelief, the fight-or-flight reaction, and regression.

Instinctive Responses

Physiological shock is usually manifested through numbing sensations, immobility, or fainting. The phrase *frozen fright* has been used to describe that reaction in victims of violence (Symonds, 1975). The psychological response of shock often involves a sense of disbelief. The victim does not believe what is happening or has just happened. It is not within the normal range of his or her reality, and the mind rejects much of the frightening messages the senses are trying to tell it.

But when that fright thaws—in milliseconds or minutes—the individual seeks to react with what has been called the *fight-or-flight* response (Selye, 1974, 1976). Physiologically, the individual's body prepares itself to take action. Adrenalin begins to flow. The heart begins to beat faster. One of the senses becomes more acute at the expense of other senses. The victim becomes ready to respond in an instant. That instinctual response may be to run from or to attack the source of the threat. Neither response seems related to a logical assessment of any one situation. In the days following the reaction, the victim may not be able to understand his or her behavior at the time of the event.

The fear inherent in the crisis seems to precipitate a regression to a childlike state in victims. A victim recollected crawling away from a shooting scene "like a baby." Another remembered "wanting Mommy or Daddy." A third—a person in her 50s—finally safe after others had died, went outdoors and, walking in a small circle, intoned, "Ring around the rosie."

Emotional Turmoil

The stage of instinctive responses is often followed by a period of extreme emotional turmoil. Victims may go through, virtually simultaneously, a range of emotions such as anger that rises to rage, fear that rises to terror, confusion that rises to feelings of chaos, self-blame that evolves to profound guilt, sorrow that evolves into grief, relief that is experienced as euphoria. These and other such emotions, so beyond normal ranges of experience, are in fact reasonable, given the crisis endured and the postcrisis struggle of survival.

Anger may be directed at others, at the world, or even at oneself. Anger is most common in victims who have suffered an acute act of violence. Enduring chronic violence may also cause anger, but because the source of the anger is, or must be, endured, that anger is repressed. One often finds victims of spouse abuse, child abuse (particularly child physical abuse as opposed to sexual abuse), and hostage taking who, even after the chronic violence is over, are reluctant to feel or express anger at either the aggressor or the situation.

Fear is often the result of being incapable of defending or protecting oneself, one's loved ones, or one's valuables. The victim has been made acutely aware of his or her vulnerability to harm or death. The stronger feelings of terror are often directly related to whether the victim believed that he or she was actually going to die. The more strongly the victim perceived that the act of violence would cause death, the more desperately afraid the victim is likely to be afterwards.

The crisis of criminal violence throws the victim's world into disorder. There is no expectation of criminal attack in most people's lives, and when it does happen, there is, at least for most victims, no adequate explanation of cause. Victims are often plagued with a "Why me?" response, leaving them confused and frustrated as they search for a reason for the destruction.

It is the search for reason that often evolves into feelings of guilt and self-blame. Victims who cannot find a reason for the attack in any other way may decide that they were to blame. Something they did precipitated the violence. Perhaps they were in the wrong place at the wrong time; perhaps they did something wrong. Whatever the reason, it is perceived by many as their own fault.

Some observers have suggested that these feelings of self-blame are actually therapeutic, since they provide victims with a method of gaining control over criminal events and may yield ways to ward off that danger in the future. However, most practitioners feel that it is important for victims to understand that it was not their fault and that no one has a right to do violence to anyone else.

The harm that crime does may be calculated in terms of losses. Those losses may be tangible, such as financial loss, property loss, disabilities associated with physical injuries, or the murder of a loved one. Other losses may be intangible. Criminal attack takes away control from the victim, causes the victim to lose trust in other people, precipitates the loss of a sense of justice, often brings the loss of one's conception of human values, and for some, generates a loss of identity or sense of a future. Whatever the losses, victims grieve over them. That grief may be a deep sorrow or a more minor sense of the void created by the loss, but the sadness is distressing.

One loss—that of a sense of justice—should be particularly underscored. Most people are raised to believe in the concept of a just society. A common formulation of that justice is the statement, "Good things happen to good people; bad things happen to bad people." This is, after all, the precept by which childrearing is conducted in most cultures of the world, and it certainly describes the regimens of rewards and punishments by which most adults in the West were socialized.

But in the aftermath of crime, the victim confronts an unwelcome truth: "Bad things happen to good people." The impact of that truth is compounded when the perpetrator of the crime is not apprehended or brought to account, when there is a failure to punish wrongdoing. That failure, whatever its cause, can shatter the victim's concept of a just society. It is for this reason that victims of violence often become so active within the criminal justice system, both in their own cases and in those of other victims. They seek a restoration of the justice that has been destroyed.

Finally, some victims experience feelings of relief or euphoria. They have survived a terrible ordeal. They confronted death and were victorious. Not all victims experience such relief. Survivors of homicide victims feel a bitter triumph at best. However, the fact that many victims do respond with a renewed sense of well-being should not be overlooked, particularly since those positive feelings are often masked by simultaneous feelings of fear, grief, or anger.

The very fact that victims often experience a multitude of emotions simultaneously causes many victims to feel they are going crazy. The struggle to survive this turmoil can be particularly complex. This stage of emotional stress may last for days or even years. Victims find themselves vacillating between good periods and bad as they try to reestablish a sense of equilibrium. Their feelings remain beyond the range of precrisis equilibrium, and the effort to bring them within a tolerable level of tension is often overwhelming. It is, however, important to work toward that goal, for victims who exist in a state of excessive tension for long periods of time are prone to physical and mental exhaustion with the attendant biological consequences.

The New Equilibrium

If victims successfully work their way through the stage of emotional turmoil, they are usually able to reestablish a sense of equilibrium. However, it will be a new equilibrium. They will have new limits and new perspectives on what they can do and what they can endure. For some, the new equilibrium may be more restrictive than the one in which they existed prior to the crisis. For others, the new equilibrium may be far more expansive. In either case, the new equilibrium may be defined in part by symptoms of post-traumatic stress disorder.

The Aftermath of Criminal Victimization: Post-Traumatic Stress Disorder

In the American Psychiatric Association's *Diagnostic and Statistical Manual* (DSM III-R; APA, 1987), post-traumatic stress disorder (PTSD) is described clinically. Salient features include reexperiencing the event through intrusive recollections and nightmares, numbing of affect, and physical arousal. It should be emphasized that this catalog of symptoms describes natural responses; they are not generally considered pathological. However, when they are intrusive enough to meet the PTSD criteria—and so prevent an individual from functioning as before—the symptoms become problematic. In such cases, intervention or treatment may be needed to reduce the frequency, duration, or intensity of the symptoms.

There is mixed opinion as to the nature and outcome of such treatment or intervention. Some authorities seem to believe that appropriate treatment can be defined and that PTSD can be cured. Others argue that there is not enough known about the effectiveness of various interventions to define appropriate treatment in all cases and that PTSD can be ameliorated but probably never completely cured.

No matter which view is taken of PTSD, ongoing manifestation of symptoms can be observed in many crime victims. In particular kinds of victims for example, victims of chronic child sexual assault, survivors of homicide victims, victims of terrorist attack—there is some evidence that the symptoms never desist completely. And, in virtually all who have suffered PTSD-type symptoms, future life crises or other events may trigger the return of the symptoms even after they seem to have disappeared.

The Aftermath of Criminal Victimization: The Impact of the Second Assault

The individual's reconstructing of an equilibrium is often complicated by the effects of a "second assault." This second assault is brought on by the actions or reactions of other people or institutions in response to the individual's victimization. These reactions are termed an assault because they often create additional emotional turmoil and other losses. Some examples of such actions or reactions by others to the original victimization follow.

Criminal Justice Response

One of the most commonly cited sources of the second assault comes from the responses of the criminal justice system. Two components stand out as particularly problematic.

First, the reactions of victims to the violence perpetrated through human cruelty include the loss of a sense of justice, as explained earlier. Hence, the criminal justice system becomes the arena for restoring justice, and the failure to achieve such restoration is often a source of profound disillusionment.

Second, the criminal justice process has traditionally failed to include the victim, unless the victim is also a witness. The victim is given no more legitimate status than any other carrier of evidence and hence feels ignored. Thus, the very institution that the victim automatically approaches to restore justice seems to turn away. The victim is left without a personal sense of recourse or remedy, and one can see this sense of betrayal even among other victims whose cases resulted in an arrest, prosecution, conviction, and a just sentence relative to other sanctions for like crimes.

In many jurisidictions, the system continues to respond in this manner. The victim often receives no information about the case; the victim may be barred from attending the trial except to testify; the victim is not consulted about plea bargains (whereby over 80% of convictions are obtained in the U.S. justice system); the victim is not routinely told what happened at the trial, at the sentencing, or on appeal. Because the victim's sense of justice was seriously damaged as a result of the original attack, this second assault— indifference to the victim's personal interest in the legal proceedings—causes additional anger, confusion, and grief. In some cases, the defense is predicated on impugning the victim's credibility, and this action may add to the existing feelings of self-blame—even when the defense allegations are baseless—or to an impotent sense of outrage at the process of justice.

If the process of bringing the case to trial or the appeal process continue over a period of years, the victim's work at establishing a new equilibrium is often severely impeded. Every time the victim thinks he or she has begun to get things under control, a new hearing date or a new stage of the proceedings may again trigger the negative feelings of being in the control of others.

Media Response

If the individual has been a victim of a sensational act of violence—for example, terrorist attack, hostage taking, rioting, or a particularly brutal sexual assault or homicide—the event will likely receive intense media attention, often of a dramatic and intrusive nature. Media exposure can cause loss of privacy and changes in life style for the victim. Names, addresses, and family life may be dissected in public. The victim may become recognized on the street, subjected to interviews, and provoked into anger or tears in front of cameras or audiences.

Misrepresentations in the media may cause additional anger. Many victims are made more afraid because they are now known to a wider number of people and feel even more vulnerable to future attack. And, as new sensations and debates are dramatized in the media, they may trigger recollections and thoughts of the past crisis.

Traditional Helping Agencies

Traditional helping agencies such as social service organizations, hospitals, mental health clinics, and the like may also inflict second assaults, as may private service organizations like insurance companies. Victims may find it maddeningly difficult to replace stolen documents such as a driver's license, a Social Security card, or credit cards. Hospitals have been known to turn victims of criminal violence away because their physicians don't want to become involved in a criminal justice proceeding. Mental health professionals are often not trained to deal with the crisis reaction of victims of violence and hence fail to understand their turmoil and sense of loss. Victims often feel that the people who are there to help do not understand and thus cannot provide aid. There are many instances of what may be called misguided compassion from counselors, clergy, and others seeking, ineptly, to act in altruistic ways.

Families and Friends

Perhaps the most painful reactions of others come from the ones who are closest to the victims. Often families and friends are upset as well, but they direct their own anger, fear, and frustration at the victims. They may ignore or isolate the victims because they do not want to hear about what happened and certainly do not want to hear it repeated again and again. They may also join in blaming the victims for their plight and consequently make them feel even worse. Any of these second assaults may add to the victims' turmoil and complicate their long-term reactions to the violence.

Criminal Victimization as a Community Crisis

Just as an individual victimized by crime faces a crisis, criminal violence may affect an entire community or city. Such violence may consist of rioting, terrorist bombings, or mass killings. In some cases, however, the violence may involve a single criminal act such as the abduction, torture, and slaying of a small child or the assassination of a major public figure. Although less has been written about the effects of such vicarious victimization, there has been documentation that such crises go far beyond one or two individuals.

The type of violence with the greatest potential to affect entire communities exhibits one or more of the following nonexclusive characteristics:

1. Causes death or realistic threat of death to all members of a community
2. Occurs within communities in which people are strongly affiliated with each other
3. Is witnessed by community members
4. Involves individuals who have a special symbolic significance to the community affected, such as a random child, or a targeted political leader

5. Causes the community to be exposed to extraordinary carnage or misery
6. Calls for numerous rescue workers or helpers
7. Attracts a great deal of media attention

Interestingly, the crisis confronting community members following a violent criminal attack is strikingly similar to the crisis faced by an individual. The community often responds as a singular entity. Disbelief may be expressed and reinforced by community bonding. Emotional turmoil is often made more difficult, both because different community members may exhibit different reactions at different times and because such responses reaffirm the perception of crisis and grate on others in turmoil. Indeed, symptoms of long-term stress disorder may be even found in communities as a whole if they continue to be composed primarily of the same individuals over a period of time.

More often, however, it is not a nation or a city that is the community most affected in terms of degree or duration. It is rather a subcommunity of the ones who are closest to the event that often show the most acute symptoms—close physically, as with the police and paramedics who respond to a murderous shooting spree, or close in terms of identity with the primary victims, as with the students, parents, and teachers in a school where someone was brutalized.

Victims of violence, whether individuals or whole communities, seem to react to violence in a similar manner. The pattern of that response gives prospective helpers the ability to design and test possible intervention techniques. Although there has been little research concerning the effectiveness of different types of intervention, there has been a proliferation of programs offering victim assistance that, in practice, has developed into a basic model for service. Reports of various agencies indicate that this general model seems to be effective in individual cases. It is examined in more detail in the following sections.

INTERVENTION TECHNIQUES FOR INDIVIDUAL AND COMMUNITY VICTIMS OF VIOLENCE

The general model of intervention is based on an understanding of the crisis reaction and tends to follow rather precisely the stages of that reaction. It also seeks to respond to specific losses that the victim may suffer. This section will examine intervention techniques, first with regard to individual victims of violence and then in relationship to communities in crisis.

Intervention Techniques for Individual Victims of Violence

Ideally, intervention services should be available for victims of violence immediately after the event. Practitioners in the victim service field generally support the idea that crisis services should be provided on a 24-hour basis. The minimum recommended level of service availability is telephone crisis response. A trained crisis intervenor is contacted by an answering service and pager system as soon as a victim or an intermediary–for example, a law enforcement officer or an emergency room nurse—calls for help, and that counselor responds to the victim by telephone within 15 minutes. If there are resources to support a more comprehensive response, a trained crisis intervenor may be dispatched to the victim's location. Once a crisis intervenor responds to a call, standard patterns of intervention may be implemented.

Safety and Security

Because the individual's first reaction to the crisis of violence is typically one of helplessness, shock, and regression, it is natural that one of the primary needs of the victim may be a need for safety. The fight-or-flight response may have pushed the person's body into a state of extraordinary tension. The victim needs to feel that he or she has been removed from harm's way and can now relax.

The first mandate for a crisis intervenor is therefore to provide the victim with a sense of safety and security. That sense will, in part, be based on the actual physical safety of the victim. Often victims do not know whether they are physically injured, because they remain numb to physical sensation. A victim of a burglary who remains at home when the front door and window have been broken, may not be objectively safe from further attack and, in any event, is unlikely to feel safe. The intervenor should always act based on a subjective test of whether the victim is in a safe situation. Even if the victim is indeed physically safe, he or she may not feel safe without receiving some reassurance or being removed from the actual scene of the violence.

A retired police officer told this story:

> A woman and her husband were walking to their car after closing their retail store for the night when three young men robbed them of the shop's receipts. In the course of the robbery, they shot and killed the woman's husband and ran from the scene.

> Police officers arrived within seconds of the shooting. They chased and caught the robbers. They then returned to the scene with the assailants and lined them in the headlights of several police cars so that the woman, standing with officers behind the headlights, could identify them. She denied that she had ever seen them before.

> After the police officers released the offenders, she approached one of the officers and told them that, indeed, the men were the ones who had shot and killed her husband. The officer, in frustrated anger, asked her why she had refused to identify them. Despite the large numbers of police officers protecting her at the scene, she said simply, "I was still afraid." (The criminals were ultimately caught and convicted of armed robbery and murder.)[1]

---

[1]James Ahrens, Retired Lieutenant, Metropolitan Police Department, Washington, DC, related this anecdote in a private conversation with the author, June 1981.

Sometimes it is difficult to help a victim feel safe because the fear is so overwhelming. The intervenor should focus on what the victim thinks would increase feelings of safety at that particular moment. For instance, in one case a victim who had been assaulted was talking to a crisis intervenor in his own living room but couldn't concentrate because of fear. When the intervenor asked what the victim thought would help him feel safe, the victim said that if the curtains on the windows were closed, he would feel better. It was a simple but important issue.[2]

In the case of survivors of homicide victims, the crisis reaction is usually triggered by the death notification. Safety may have little relevance to their concerns in the immediate aftermath of that notification. The homicide rarely places their own lives in threat, so their response is somewhat different than other victims of violence. Shock may be so intense that it lasts for days, weeks, or months. Disbelief is usually very strong as well. In reaction to the notification homicide victims may regress to a childlike state, even to the point of assuming the fetal position or crying out for Mommy or Daddy.

One of the primary methods of assisting at this critical stage is to provide care that may be needed by victims who are in shock. While all victims may need an opportunity to regain a measure of control over their environments, victims in severe shock and trauma may simply need an opportunity to rest, physically or mentally, in the aftermath. Helpers can alleviate some of the distress by providing needed tangible services such as calling a funeral home, helping with insurance claims, and the like.

Ventilation and Validation

After helping victims feel a bit safer or more secure, it is important to allow them to talk about the event. What happened? How does it feel? This is often referred to as the ventilation and validation phase of intervention, one that may span hours or days or even months.

Victims may need to express anger, fears, self-doubt, confusion, or frustration, all of which may grow over time and any one of which may be the source of particular turmoil at a given moment. They need to be reassured that such feelings are normal and natural. Victims sometimes feel as if they are going crazy because they are not used to experiencing such a range or intensity of reactions. Even victims who "feel nothing" are in fact feeling a void or an unaccustomed numbness. The intervenor should let victims know that he or she is "sorry it happened."

The intervenor should also remind victims that they are not to blame for the violence. Victims will often blame themselves for what happened, no matter how remote their self-identified complicity was. Burglary victims say how stupid they were for failing to lock a door; robbery victims will talk about how they should not have been walking alone at night. One such victim, a homicide survivor, blamed herself for the murder of her four boys because she had stopped working at the window overlooking her driveway

---

[2]Confidential case files, National Organization for Victim Assistance, Washington, DC.

to get a glass of iced tea in her kitchen. At that moment the four killers drove up, got out the their car, and walked into her home—an action they would have never taken had they first seen her in the window, or so she told herself for years.[3]

Although it is natural for victims to feel it is their fault, it is important for intervenors to emphasize that in such situations the assailant has committed a crime, and no matter who the victim is or what the victim's actions may have been, he or she was a victim of a criminal, on whose shoulders— not those of the victim—rests the blame.

Prediction and Preparation

After victims have talked about their feelings and thoughts concerning the attack, the intervenor should begin to tell them what they can expect in the coming days, weeks, months, or years. This stage of intervention is referred to as prediction and preparation. The prediction may deal with what the victims can expect from the criminal justice system, the media, social services, health and mental health professionals, their employers or the like. But, more importantly, the prediction and preparation need to address the emotional reactions that victims may continue to feel.

Some victims may feel fine within a few hours of the attack and just want to forget it ever happened. However, they should be told that events in the future may cause them to relive their feelings or to be reminded vividly of the crime. Such renewal of feelings, if unexpected, can be very distressing.

Other victims may have a fairly severe crisis reaction at the time of the violence, but they still may not be prepared for the days or weeks ahead. They may find themselves modifying their behavior in ways that are difficult to explain to themselves or their loved ones.

A sexual assault victim who had been raped in an elevator was unprepared for her terrifying physical reaction to boarding an elevator several weeks later. She became nauseous and very faint. She went to a doctor who could find nothing physically wrong with her. It was only after talking with a victim service counselor that she realized that any elevator could trigger a severe phsyical or mental reaction because of its association with the attack.[4]

If victims are told that this type of reaction is natural and may occur for a considerable time into the future, as well as being given some ways to prepare for such a reaction, they can more easily endure each triggering event. One victim of rape in her home has used her knowledge of her own reactions to the anniversary of the assault to schedule time off from work and a short vacation in a nearby hotel.

---

[3]Betty Jane Spencer talked about this feeling of self-blame in a private conversation with the author, April 1984 (for more information on the case, see Magee, 1983).

[4]Confidential case files, National Organization for Victim Assistance, Washington, DC.

Losses

In addition to providing safety and security, ventilation and validation, and prediction and preparation for victims of trauma, intervenors should also help them to deal with their losses. Although there may be little the intervenor can do to assist with tangible losses, there are several techniques that may be used to address the intangible losses.

First, intervenors can help victims begin to regain some control over their lives and their world by giving them choices to make. These choices do not have to be difficult or have major implications, but they provide a symbolic way for victims to put some order back into their lives. Problem solving with victims is another initiator of restored control. Some intervenors ask victims to define the three most immediately pressing problems in their lives in the aftermath of the crime and then assist them in reviewing options for dealing with those problems. Often the problems would have been easily dealt with if the victims had not been in a state of crisis.

One assault victim defined her problems as letting her employer know that she would not be at work the following day (she felt she could not face the questions he would ask); arranging for transportation to day care for her child (she was injured and could not drive); and finding a temporary place to stay (she no longer felt safe in her apartment, where the assault had taken place). After the victim had defined those problems, the intervenor was able to help her develop a plan—one the victim herself worked up—to deal with each problem in a satisfactory way. The victim felt much better because the process helped her believe she could function again.[5]

Second, intervenors can help victims restore a sense of trust in others again. Victims may never regain the level of trust in others that they had prior to attack, but they will renew their trust. Initially it is useful for victims to identify the people whom they would like to have contacted or told about the trauma. And, where possible, those people should be encouraged to be available if the victim needs them, either in person or by telephone. Victims with strong personal support systems are more likely to have less long-term trauma.

In addition, intervenors should establish a concrete basis for trust between the victim and the intervenor. Such a basis is developed if the intervenor assures the victim of absolute confidentiality of communication, provides honest and accurate information for the victim, makes no promises that cannot be kept, and defines a plan of action for continued contact or communication in the days to come.

Not all losses can be restored, hence most victims will grieve over their loss. This sorrow is real, even though it may not relate to anything tangible. It is therefore important for intervenors to be familiar with the process of

[5]Confidential case files, National Organization for Victim Assistance, Washington, DC.

grief and grief counseling (see Osterweis, Solomon & Green, 1984; Rando, 1984; Schiff, 1986).

Some victims of violence find that their lives have been changed so radically that they have virtually lost their original identity or their sense of any future. These victims often face a much longer period of grieving and reconstruction. Often, they are survivors of homicide victims or are victims of massive physical injuries, incest, or catastrophes.

It may take months or years of ventilation and validation before such individuals even want to start to think of redefinition of life. Others may rush into tremendous activity in an effort to find or establish new meaning that might give them a reason to live or give reason to a loved one's death. Either way, the eventual redesign of a new future and self-concept may seem to be a slow process.

Candy Lightner founded Mothers Against Drunk Driving (MADD) shortly after her daughter, Cari, was killed by a drunk driver. In retrospect, she says she put off grieving for several years, working ceaselessly to get MADD launched. It was only after she retired from MADD, she says, that her grief work began (C. Lightner, personal communication, March 1987). Interestingly, she was an instigator of the generally sensible rule requiring MADD chapter leaders to be at least a year distant from the crime and its loss. Her example is a reminder that even those who fail to confront their loss in some ways or display denial may nonetheless be working at reconstructing their lives in ways that they and their helpers can applaud.

Appropriate interventions should include both peer support groups and support from nonpeer helpers. Mutual support groups seem to be particularly effective in assisting victims to work through overwhelming life changes. They offer unique opportunities for ventilation and validation, and they provide a source of new trust that may not be found elsewhere.

However, such groups may prolong the crisis reaction and the grieving process for some victims. Nonpeer helpers may provide an impetus to talk about some other concerns in life and help avoid getting stuck at any particularly stage of crisis or grief. In addition, many victims find that nonpeer helpers are an especially effective source of validation. Other victims may confirm that the victimization experience is universal, but nonvictim helpers confirm that the victimization experience is natural and acceptable.

One victim of spouse abuse commented that she was gratified to hear her counselor explain the stages of crisis and the symptoms of long-term stress, even though she had discussed such issues in her support group. She felt that the confirmation of her feelings by a nonvictim removed some of the shame and stigma of her victimization.[6]

It should be emphasized that the underlying problem being discussed here—a kind of dependency on the intervention or treatment process without making significant progress—is not confined to self-help modalities. Indeed, the hallmark of untrained crisis intervenors is the formation of dependency

[6]Confidential case files, National Organization for Victim Assistance, Washington, DC.

relationships between victim and helper, with neither party understanding that a prime goal is restoring control (decision making being the lead example) in the victim. And sometimes, it seems to be peers alone who can shake a victim out of a state of sad dependency. It is therefore desirable to make available both peer-support and supportive counseling services and to carefully monitor client progress.

Other Interventions

In addition to the interventions that may help victims deal with trauma and its emotional aftermath, concrete practical interventions may assist in restoring control to the victims' lives and in dealing with potential second assaults from the society as a whole. First, there should be assistance to help victims regain or replace tangible resources that were lost or destroyed as a result of the violence. Such assistance should include monetary compensation, a system of "insurance of last resort" now found in most states to cover medical and counseling bills, time off from work, physical therapy, vocational rehabilitation, and the like.

Second, victims who become involved in the criminal justice process because of arrest of one or more suspects, may need even more support. Most victims will want to know if the defendant has been released, and in many cases—especially when the victim had a prior relationship with the accused—victims will want to have their concerns voiced at each stage of the judicial process. One of the most common ongoing needs of victims of violence is simply the "need to know." Though not an official party to the judicial action they feel personally involved. They want to know about motions, pleas, dismissals, possible diversions, evidentiary hearings, continuances, and any other procedure that affects the process. And they want to know why things happen the way they happen.

The desire to understand seems to be more intense in victims of violence than in others involved in the justice system because it is so directly related to the irrationality of the criminal attack. Just as the victim seeks to restore a sense of justice through the criminal justice process, there seems to be a need to restore a sense of order. Hence, although victims do not always agree with the way the system works, if they understand why the system works the way it does, it seems to help them in dealing with the consequences.

Experienced victim service providers have learned that a great many victims cannot or do not begin to begin the process of reconstructing their lives until the various legal proceedings are completed. Hence, crisis intervention services may once again be needed at this stage, as well as assistance with the effects of long-term trauma.

Intervention Techniques for Communities in Crisis

The trauma faced by communities as a result of catastrophic violence is often parallel to that faced by individuals, but it is magnified by the sheer number of concurrent and disparate responses that are involved. One community crisis response team from the National Organization for Victim Assistance (NOVA) went to Mt. Pleasant, Iowa, after the point-blank slaying of the mayor and the wounding of two other City Council members during a city meeting. The NOVA team members found a town in which the entire visible population was moving in a daze (NOVA, 1986b).

Few in Mt. Pleasant seemed to know what to do or what was going to happen next. Their feelings of helplessness were underscored by the manifest helplessness of their leaders during the shooting itself. The Chief of Police had witnessed the shooting but was unable to intervene, as he had left his gun in his car. Other city council members who were present had felt immobilized or afraid (NOVA, 1986b).

This kind of community-wide shock is one reason that it seems important to have outside crisis intervenors available to visit communities in crisis, even if such communities have local mental health personnel or other responders available. The local responders may be capable and competent in dealing with the physical injuries or the deaths occasioned by the violence but at first may be ineffective in dealing with the scope of the emotional injury. For in the first 24 to 72 hours after the catastrophe, the natural helpers may themselves be immobilized in the community's traumatic shock.

Community Intervention

Intervention techniques for communities in crisis are similar to the ones used with individuals, but there are some unique features. A first step in community intervention is to identify particular groups likely to need some assistance. In most community disasters, such subgroups include rescue workers, law enforcement officers, fire fighters, emergency room and other hospital personnel, the clergy, mental health workers, schoolchildren, and neighborhood groups. Also, in most disasters, the subgroups include the direct victims—those individuals who were injured or were targets of attack during the disaster and their families, and the families of individuals who were killed.

For instance, in the massacre in which a U.S. Post Office employee in Edmond, Oklahoma, killed 14 co-workers and himself, the postal employees who had been injured or almost injured and the families of the ones who were killed, along with the families of the injured employees, were a special community in trauma in the aftermath (NOVA, 1986a). In contrast, the survivor communities that were present at the San Ysidro restaurant massacre or the shopping mall shootings in Palm Bay, Florida, in 1987, were people bound together only by the chance occasion of being at the wrong neighborhood establishment at the wrong time (NOVA, 1987).

The reason for identifying the subgroups is threefold. First, each one has a particular perspective on the event and its aftermath that is likely to differ from other subgroups and hence to create a feeling of isolation and identity within itself. Second, each group member will find a special sense of validation from others because they saw or heard similar things. Third, it is impossible in most cases to provide rapid, individual intervention to the many people affected by a widespread disaster. Making a virtue of necessity by reaching the individuals through group meetings both solidifies the group as a source of mutual support and helps to screen individuals who may need additional help later on.

Once the subgroups have been identified, the second concern for the outside intervenors is to identify the most appropriate helpers for each group. In some cases, those helpers may be community mental health workers, and in other groups it may be their own critical incident debriefing teams (such may exist in local fire departments or law enforcement agencies). Other natural helpers to recruit are the clergy, teachers, victim service providers, and the like.

Because many mental health professionals and their allies may lack adequate background in crisis intervention and trauma-specific interventions, a basic training session is both appropriate and necessary in most circumstances. Such training sessions should include an outline of crisis reaction, intervention techniques, a review of grief reaction, a review of long-term trauma or stress reaction, and suggestions for coping with such reactions in everyday life. In addition, the training sessions should provide a general primer on active listening, the techniques of validation, and examples of possible questions or problems that might arise from individuals or the community at large.

After completion of the 3-to-5-hour training sessions, community meetings may be organized with various subgroups. The purpose of these meetings will be to conduct initial debriefings of the participants and to model debriefing techniques for the natural helpers (unless the helpers feel up to running the meetings themselves, using the outsiders as resources and as post-debriefing critics). The essence of a debriefing session is to give the participants a sense of security within their own group; to allow them to ventilate and share their feelings with each other; to provide them with group validation for the feelings; and to predict for them the common feelings and events that may occur in the future.

In many cases, the group may want to reconvene within a few days, weeks, or months, and the facilitator should raise this idea with the participants. Indeed, one reason for ensuring that a local helper is a part of each group is so that such a helper may become the lead facilitator in future meetings if he or she has not already assumed such a role.

Children

One particular point of concern for most communities is the potential response of their children. The reaction of children to disaster can be quite distressing for parents and other adults. Children often act out their responses in ways that may seem inappropriate to adults but in reality are natural to a child. It is important to spend some time with teachers and parents in order to discuss the various developmental stages that children normally go through, and what the impact of crisis may be at any specific stage.

Teachers and parents should also be given some suggestions on how to respond to children's distress. One critical aspect of children's reactions—particularly young children—is that they experience the disaster as two losses. They survive the destruction of the disaster itself but then often face the fact that their parents have changed as a result of the disaster. Children lose the stability of their parents and, in some cases, even lose the security of their parents' former personalities as they construct new futures. The fundamental survival question of all dependent creatures—Who will take care of me?—no longer has a confident answer.

For most children, the most important of these two losses is the loss of their parents. Hence, reassurance that their parents are still there for them, still love them, and will still care for them is essential—if it is true. If, on the other hand, their parents are incapable of such reassurance, it may be necessary for others to assist in parenting duties.

Long-term Planning

Even with immediate intervention and debriefing, it is not unusual for a community and its members to continue to have problems as the result of the trauma many months or years after the catastrophe. In order to address and acknowledge the acute change in the community's life, it is advisable for the community to maintain some types of crisis response service for individual community members for a while.

The community mental health center in Edmond, Oklahoma, opened a private office across the street from the building where 14 postal workers were killed so that postal employees could drop in at any time. It is a well-used service. The community of Mt. Pleasant installed a telephone hot line to answer calls of people having ongoing disturbances. Other communities may simply identify some local helpers who are willing to be available at any time for assistance, offering both individual and group counseling services.[7]

Another service that communities can provide to their members is the establishment of an annual memorial or anniversary of the event. Anniversaries of catastrophes are often very difficult to endure. Whether someone has been a victim of an individual criminal attack or has survived a large-scale catastrophe, the date of the event may become a triggering factor for recurring crisis. A community-wide memorial service or other symbolic gathering can help community members again stand together in their memories, as they did in the immediate aftermath of the disaster.

[7]Community crisis case file, National Organization for Victim Assistance, February 1987.

CONCLUSIONS

For both individuals and communities, violence is endured as an unjust, terrifying, enraging victimization, one that creates an immediate crisis and often a long-term traumatic reaction. When the violence is perpetrated by human cruelty, the normal crisis reaction and ensuing trauma are complicated by a loss of a sense of justice and order in the world. And when the violence causes physical maiming or the death of loved ones, the crisis and trauma may be exacerbated by a loss of identity and a sense of future.

Because of the intensity of the emotional turmoil following violent victimization, communities are advised to establish crisis intervention services that can provide basic emotional first aid to individuals and to the community at large. Such intervention seems to assist victims in regaining a sense of order and control over the event and to help them cope with predictable trauma reactions. To ensure comprehensiveness, the intervention service should be supplemented with specialized assistance in agencies of the criminal justice system and other social institutions. Often, victims of violence find that the isolation, stigma, and injustice perpetrated on them in the aftermath of the event are more painful than the immediate injuries. An array of services designed to assist them in replacing tangible resources, provide support through the criminal justice process, and serve their long-term mental health needs will be useful in ameliorating the destructive impact of the victimization and its aftermath.

REFERENCES

American Psychiatric Assocation. (1987). *Diagnostic and statistical manual of mental disorders* (DSM-III-R; 3rd ed.–Rev.) Washington, DC: Author.

Bard, M., & Sangrey, D. (1986). *The crime victim's book*. New York: Brunner/Mazel. (Originally published 1979.)

Burgess, A., Groth, A. N., Holmstrom, L. L., & Sgroi, S. M. (1978). *Sexual assault of children and adolescents*. Lexington, MA: D. C. Heath.

Burgess, A., & Holmstrom, L. L. (1974). Rape trauma syndrome. *American Journal of Psychiatry, 131*, 981–985.

Burgess, A., & Holmstrom L. L. (1976). Coping behavior of the rape victim. *American Journal of Psychiatry, 133*, 413–417.

Burgess, A., & Holmstrom, L. L. (1979). Adaptive strategies and recovery from rape. *American Journal of Psychiatry, 136*, 1278–1282.

Clarke, R., & Hope, T. (Eds.), (1986). *Coping with burglary*. Boston: Kluwer-Nijhoff.

Danieli, Y. (1982). *Group project for holocaust survivors and their children*. Paper prepared for the National Institute of Mental Health, Washington, DC.

Eitinger, L. (1972). *Concentration camp survivors in Norway and Israel*. The Hague: Nijhoff. (Originally published 1964; Oslo: Universitetsforlaget.)

Eitinger, L. (1980). Jewish concentration camp survivors in the post-war world. *Danish Medical Bulletin, 27*(5), 232–235.

Figley, C. R. (1985). *Trauma and its wake.* New York: Brunner/Mazel.

Figley, C. R., & McCubbin, H. I. (Eds.). (1983). *Stress and the family: Vol. II. Coping with catastrophe.* New York: Brunner/Mazel.

Finkelhor, D. (1979). *Sexually victimized children.* New York: Free Press.

Finkelhor, D. (1984). *Child sexual abuse.* New York: Free Press.

Herman, J. L. (1981). *Father-daughter incest.* Cambridge, MA: Harvard University Press.

Holmstrom, L. L., & Burgess, A. (1983). *The victim of rape.* New Brunswick: Transaction Books.

Kilpatrick, D. B., Veronen, L. J., & Resick, P. A. (1979). The aftermath of rape: Recent empirical findings. *American Journal of Orthopsychiatry, 40*(4), 658–669.

Kilpatrick, D. G., Veronen, L. J., & Resick, P. A., (1982). Psychological sequelae to rape: Assessment and treatment strategies. In D. M. Doleys, R. L. Meredith, & A. R. Ciminero (Eds.), *Behavioral medicine: Assessment and treatment strategies* (pp. 473–497). New York: Plenum.

Lejeune, R., & Alex, N. (1973). On being mugged: The event and its aftermath. *Urban Life and Culture 2*(3), 259–287.

Lord, J. H. (1987). *No time for goodbyes.* Ventura, CA: Pathfinder.

MacFarlane, K., & Waterman, J., with Conerly, S., Damon, L. Durfee, M. & Long, S. (1987). *Sexual abuse of young children: Evaluation and treatment.* New York: Guilford.

Magee, D. (1983). *What murder leaves behind: The victim's family.* New York: Dodd, Mead.

Maguire, M. (1980). The impact of burglary on victims. *British Journal of Criminology, 20*(3), 261–275.

National Organization for Victim Assistance (NOVA). (1985, October). *Survivors of Homicide Victims,* Washington, DC: Author.

National Organization for Victim Assistance (NOVA). (1986a, August). *Community crisis report.* Washington, DC: Author. Unpublished report.

National Organization for Victim Assistance (NOVA). (1986b, December). *Community crisis report.* Washington, DC: Author. Unpublished report.

National Organization for Victim Assistance (NOVA). (1987, March). *Community crisis report.* Washington, DC: Author. Unpublished report.

Ochberg, F. M. (1978). The victim of terrorism: Psychiatric considerations. *Terrorism, An International Journal 1*(2), 151.

Ochberg, F. M., & Soskis, D. A. (1982). *Victims of terrorism.* Boulder, CO: Westview.

Osterweis, F. S., & Green, M. (Eds.). (1984). *Bereavement, reactions, consequences and care.* Washington, DC: National Academy Press.

Pagelow, M. D. (1984). *Family violence.* New York: Praeger

Rando, T. (1984), *Grief, dying and death.* Champaign, IL: Research Press.

Russell, D. E. (1982). *Rape in marriage.* New York: Macmillan.

Schechter, S. (1982). *Women and male violence.* Boston: Southend Press.

Schiff, H. S. (1986). *Living through mourning*. New York: Viking.

Selye, Hans. (1974). *Stress without distress*. New York: New American Library.

Selye, Hans. (1976). *The stress of life* (Rev. ed.). New York: McGraw-Hill.

Symonds, M. (1975). Victims of violence: Psychological effects and aftereffects. *American Journal of Psychoanalysis, 35,* 19–26.

Walker, L. (1984). *The battered woman syndrome*. New York: Springer.

Waller, I., & Okihiro, N. (1978). *Burglary: The victim and the public*. Toronto, Ont.: University of Toronto Press.

Williams, T. (Ed.). (1987). *Post-traumatic stress disorders; A handbook for clinicians*. Cincinnati, OH: Disabled American Veterans.

Young, M. A. (1986). Stress, trauma, crisis: The theoretical framework of victimization revisited. In K. Miyazawa & M. Ohya (Eds.), *Victimology in comparative perspective* (pp. 188–198). Tokyo: Seibundo Publishing.

Young-Rifai, M. A. (1982). Victimology: A theoretical framework. In H. Schneider (Ed.), *The victim in international perspective* (pp. 65–79). Berlin: Walter de Gruyter.

PART 3

Approaches to Intervention

The major concern of human service personnel confronted with a disaster situation obviously revolves around intervention. Much of the discussion in the preceding section demonstrated such a focus with respect to each of the major types examined. Yet each discussion made specific note that any given situation will present a set of unique features that must be addressed before successful intervention is possible. Intervention must therefore be approached from the framework of general models that are at the same time specific enough to provide structure and guidance but flexible enough to allow broad adaptation.

Yates, Axsom, Bickman, and Howe begin this section with a significant conceptual piece regarding help seeking among disaster victims. Their work is of particular consequence in the context of mental health interventions with disaster victims, in that the schemata involved in seeking assistance for mental health problems tend to involve dispositional attributions, whereas the attributions of disaster victims tend to be (usually quite rightfully) situational. Interventions likely to be utilized by such persons must therefore be designed to offer help in ways that will prove congruent with the perceived needs of their intended constituents, and the services must be delivered in fashions that reflect accepted patterns of behavior among their target groups.

Myers discusses in some detail the application of what have traditionally been called *preventive* approaches to a variety of disaster scenarios. She describes interactive and collaborative approaches designed to mitigate, manage, and minimize inevitable stressors that accompany each stage of disaster response.

No matter how effective the preventive activity, some clinical fallout is likely inevitable. The clinical assessment and management of these cases is addressed by Wilkinson and Vera, who also present contemporary medical and psychiatric viewpoints on such key issues as treatment of post-traumatic stress disorder and the medical management of disaster-induced decompensation in previously impaired clients.

Lebedun and Wilson, mental health administrators with a wealth of practical experience in responding to major disasters, conclude this section with a discussion of the sometimes subtle issues surrounding the planning and execution of disaster responses. Their major points concern the need for advance effort to establish the interpersonal and interorganizational relationships that will allow appropriate responses to emerge when disaster strikes.

Too often, although detailed disaster plans are developed, including such minutia as the names and titles of individuals responsible for radio batteries, there is a failure to establish the critical but more global issues of access, legitimacy, and funding. Both formal and informal mechanisms are suggested to help ensure that the best laid plans of an organization can ultimately be put to effective use in the field.

CHAPTER 7

Factors Influencing Help Seeking for Mental Health Problems after Disasters

SUZANNE YATES, DANNY AXSOM, LEONARD BICKMAN, AND GEORGE HOWE

In natural disasters lives may be lost, people seriously injured, property destroyed, and communities left in havoc. The psychological consequences of such events can be severe. Common reactions in the immediate aftermath of a disaster can include shock, anxiety, sleep disturbances, and impaired interpersonal relationships (Boyd, 1981; Crabbs & Heffron, 1981; Hartsough, 1982). Although longer term deleterious effects will only rarely be seen at more aggregate (i.e., community) levels of analysis, individual and family recovery is not so easily assured (Wright, Rossi, Wright, & Weber-Burdin, 1979). Problems such as depression, alcoholism, child and spouse abuse, somatization, and severe anxiety have been reported 2 to 4 years following disasters (Chamberlin, 1980; Cohen, 1983). Although there is controversy over the duration and extensiveness of such symptoms (Cook & Bickman, 1987; Quarantelli & Dynes, 1977; Rubonis & Bickman, 1986; Smith, Robins, Przybeck, Goldring, & Solomon, 1986), few researchers question the existence of such reactions in at least a subset of victims. Furthermore, there is some evidence for a stress reaction following disaster that is less severe but more widespread than full-blown psychopathology (Adams & Adams, 1984; Logue, Hansen, & Struening, 1981).

To meet the mental health needs of victims, an array of federal, state, and local intervention programs are often brought to bear. Although these programs have not been the focus of systematic evaluations, anecdotal evidence suggests that mental health interventions may help alleviate short-term emotional distress and prevent the development of long-term problems (Blaufarb & Levine, 1972; Butcher, 1980; Gist & Stolz, 1982; Grossman, 1973; Schanche, 1974). However, evidence also suggests that these programs

Suzanne Yates and Danny Axsom contributed equally to the writing of this chapter. Preparation was made possible primarily by a National Institute of Mental Health Grant (No. I RO1MH4139-01) awarded to Leonard Bickman. Additional support was also provided by a PCS-CUNY Faculty Research Award (No. 6-65366) awarded to Suzanne Yates.

are commonly underutilized (Bromet & Dunn, 1981; Lindy, Grace, & Green, 1981; Taylor, Ross, & Quarantelli, 1976).

In the absence of seeking formal aid, how do people cope with the emotional sequelae of disasters? When victims do not seek professional psychological help, do they rely on other professionals (e.g., medical doctors, clergy), informal helpers (e.g., family, friends), themselves, or simply do nothing? Do preferred coping modes change over time and, if so, why? How effective are these alternative forms of coping in reducing victims' distress? Unfortunately, very little research exists that provides answers to these and other questions. The phenomenon of help seeking for mental health problems after disasters is not well understood.

This chapter provides a framework for understanding this type of help seeking. It draws upon theories, models, and research in nondisaster settings to suggest a general, descriptive model of mental health help seeking after disasters. Factors likely to be important at each stage of the model will be specified. It is the specification of these factors that constitutes the main focus of the chapter. In addition, there is a brief description of a project currently underway to examine several questions raised in the chapter.

HELP SEEKING IN NONDISASTER SETTINGS

Until recently, research in psychology tended to focus more on understanding help giving then help seeking (Fisher, Nadler, & Whitcher-Alagna, 1982; Gross & McMullen, 1983). In part, this was attributable to the publicity created in the 1960s by dramatic incidents, such as the Kitty Genovese murder, that highlighted the reluctance of bystanders to intervene in emergencies. An implicit assumption created by these events was that the primary problem facing victims was the nonavailability of help. A second assumption, related to the first, was that if the proper resources were made available, people who needed them would use them. Thus, the topic of help seeking was relatively ignored.

More recent research has shown that help seeking is not nearly so straightforward. Several studies have documented the reluctance of people to ask for help, even when it is needed and readily available (DePaulo & Fisher, 1980; Nadler & Porat, 1978; Tessler & Schwartz, 1972). Because much of this research is laboratory based and involves achievement settings, one might question its relevance for understanding help seeking in natural settings for more severe problems related to mental health. In contrast to seeking help for minor problems in these laboratory studies, it might be assumed that when the problem is more severe and intractable, people would more readily seek help from professionals. A comparison of estimates of the prevalence of psychological impairment in the general population with data on the actual utilization of mental health services, however, suggests that professional help is often not sought. Estimates are that up to 75% of persons with mild disabilities and 20% with severe disabilities do not obtain services (Goldsmith, Jackson, & Hough, in press). Moreover, because people without diagnosable difficulties sometimes seek and receive mental health services, utilization estimates may be slightly overstated. Similarly, studies of college students have found that there are many more people reporting high levels of psychological distress who choose not to seek help than who seek help (Bosmajian & Mattson, 1980; Greenley & Mechanic, 1976). The conclusion, from both laboratory and field studies in nondisaster settings, is that people are generally reluctant to seek help. At several points in the chapter there is discussion of why this might be so.

Several models have been proposed to explain help seeking, both in general (see Gross & McMullen, 1983, for a review) and with regard to mental health (Goldsmith et al., in press). They provide a useful starting point from which to consider mental health help seeking after disasters and share many features with the model detailed in this chapter. For example, several models, as well as the one described here, separate symptom experience from symptom interpretation (e.g., Ostrove & Baum, 1983), which is to say that symptoms are not necessarily labeled as problems, or at least problems for which psychological help is needed.

Despite the usefulness of these models, it has proved necessary to construct a new model for two reasons. First, other models generally lack the level of detail necessary to understand the myriad of factors likely to influence help seeking; they point to major nodes in the decision-making process (i.e., problem awareness, decision to seek help) but seldom detail systematically the factors operating at each node (for an exception, see Goldsmith et al.'s model of help seeking in nondisaster settings, in press). Second, other models are not designed with the unique aspects of disaster settings in mind.

UNIQUE ASPECTS OF DISASTER SETTINGS

Disasters have several features that are important for understanding mental health help seeking. First, they are rare, sudden events for which people are usually unprepared and with which they have little experience. This heightens people's *uncertainty:* Which reactions are normative and which are aberrant? Which problems are temporary and which are more long lasting? What is the exact nature of the problem? Are there competent people who might be able to help? For physical ills, people may have a regular source of professional medical help, even to the extent of visiting the source periodically for preventative checkups. In contrast, most people do not have a professional source for help with emotional distress. Fischer, Winer, & Abramowitz (1983) have proposed that, compared to general help seeking, help seeking for psychological distress is more fraught with uncertainty. This uncertainty appears to be even greater after disasters.

One consequence is that people will be actively involved in attempts to make sense of the situation—what they are experiencing, why, and what to do about it. Thus, the model emphasizes the importance of attributions people make about their distress and possible solutions (Brickman et al., 1982). Attributions, in turn, are likely to be influenced by social comparisons made with others affected by the disaster (Taylor, Wood, & Lichtman, 1983; Wills, 1983; Wortman & Dunkel-Schetter, 1979). Another consequence of uncertainty is that people are likely to be more susceptible to social influence because they look to others for help in interpreting the situation. Because of this, the model emphasizes the role that external information (from family, friends, co-workers, the media, mental health outreach programs, etc.) plays in influencing help seeking.

A second aspect of disasters is that they typically *affect many people,* indeed, entire communities.[1] This fact may affect help seeking in several ways. First, social comparison with other victims may be easier and therefore play a more prominent role in the interpretation of distress and consideration of coping alternatives. Second, strong norms may arise within the community about how people should be adjusting. In contrast to individual misfortunes (e.g., criminal victimization), after disasters any one person's plight may be shared by many. Thus, a collective definition of reality may emerge (for example, that distress will only be transient) that influences individual help seeking. This is yet another reason external information is emphasized in the model.

Third, the large number of victims creates frequent opportunities for help giving. Concerns about reciprocity and equity can discourage help seeking (Fisher, Nadler, & Whitcher-Alagna, 1982). Therefore, *giving* help may make help easier to receive. For this reason, the model described here emphasizes opportunities for help giving. Fourth, because others are affected, a person's normal social support network may be disrupted. This means that perceived social support is important to assess, as well as whether multiple help-seeking strategies and changes in strategy are employed to adjust to the situation. Finally, the large number of victims means that offers of help, because of outreach mobilization, may be more frequent than in nondisaster settings. This includes offers of help for psychological distress that come when one seeks nonpsychological assistance. Because victims are often in need of material and/or medical help, psychological help may be offered when it is not sought in the usual sense.

With these unique aspects of disaster settings in mind, discussion now turns to the model of mental health help seeking.

---

[1]The reference here is mainly to disasters that affect many people in the community in which they live rather than to events, sometimes called centrifugal disasters (e.g., an airplane accident), that affect people who have come together temporarily. In centrifugal disasters, survivors are usually dispersed into communities where most other people have not been directly affected. The differences in help seeking that follow these two types of disasters form an interesting topic for future research.

A CONCEPTUAL OVERVIEW

The decision to seek help, rely on oneself, or do nothing about a problem is a complicated one. Before discussion of the many specific factors that influence help seeking, it seems helpful to provide the reader with an overview of the major stages at which the more specific factors operate. The framework, depicted in Figure 7.1, divides the help-seeking process into four stages. The first stage focuses on one's awareness of distress. The presence of symptoms does not guarantee that a person will be aware of distress, and a host of factors determine whether a person concludes he or she has a problem. If one does conclude that a problem exists, the next stage involves an attempt to interpret the problem. Again, many factors are likely to influence how a problem is defined. Once the problem has been defined, the person turns to a consideration of coping alternatives. The solution(s) chosen will depend on a variety of factors detailed later in the chapter. During the fourth stage, the person attempts to enact the chosen coping alternative(s).

The model depicts help seeking as an iterative process. As coping attempts are made, changes in level of distress are assessed to determine the success of the strategy. If the distress persists, a reassessment of the nature of the problem and/or of possible coping alternatives is likely. Thus, the post-disaster coping process is an ongoing cycle of coping attempts, assessments, and revised strategies. The process ends when the person concludes either that the distress is no longer a problem or that the distress has no real solution.

At each of the first three stages of the model—the awareness of distress, the interpretation of the problem, and the consideration of coping alternatives—the many factors that affect help seeking are organized from the standpoint of a person's schema. Because this concept is central to the analysis being discussed, it will be addressed here at a general level. Schemata are organized knowledge structures that guide a person's perception, organization, and recall of information (Bartlett, 1932; Fiske & Taylor, 1984; Markus & Zajonc, 1985). Schemata may concern people (including the self), objects, events, social roles, or other such conceptual entities. They develop directly from experience and indirectly as a product of socialization. Schemata serve an important function because they help organize and simplify the world. By abstracting the essential features of some person or event, schemata assist in the development of expectations and inferences about the person or event in question. Because a schema is an organized knowledge structure, memory is also enhanced for schema-relevant information.

The model posits that people possess three different schemata that influence the help-seeking process: a distress awareness schema that contains information about emotional and behavioral functioning, a problem schema that contains information about the essential characteristics of distress, and a solution schema that contains information about a range of coping alter-

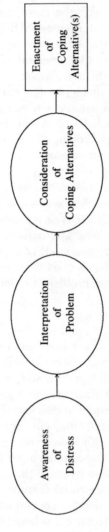

Figure 7.1. Model overview of the help-seeking process.

natives. The person's distress awareness schema determines whether symptoms occurring after a disaster are seen as indicators of distress; the problem schema determines how the distress is interpreted; and the solution schema determines the appropriate coping alternative(s).[2] The many specific factors thought to affect help seeking are included in the model either as components of a schema (e.g., perceived efficacy of a potential coping option as a component of the solution schema) or as variables that influence the content of a schema (e.g., information received from others).

Several assumptions about the organization of the framework should be made explicit. First, the model is psychological in nature and individual based. It is true that other perspectives (e.g., sociological) and other levels of analysis (e.g., family, community) are important. To the extent that variables such as the structure of community outreach efforts and family problem-solving style affect help seeking, they are represented in the model in terms of their impact on an individual's *perceptions* of resource alternatives. It is hoped that the single level of analysis employed here will make exposition of the help-seeking process more clear.

Second, a strong social-cognitive perspective underlies the exposition of the stages. This fact is reflected most clearly in the reliance on the concept of schema. More generally, each of the three stages (awareness of distress, interpretation of problem, and consideration of coping alternatives) leading to the enactment of a coping alternative is most concerend with the individual's *interpretation* of relevant inputs. The awareness of distress, for example, is not viewed simply as a function of the objective loss from the disaster and the resulting number of dysfunctional behaviors. Rather, the awareness of distress presupposes that a person possesses a schema for interpreting behavioral or emotional changes as indicators of distress.

Third, other models of help seeking usually assume that people will first attempt to solve a problem themselves and then turn to informal sources, before seeking professional help. Although this is generally a reasonable assumption, there are a number of reasons it is not appropriate for mental health problems in postdisaster settings. To begin with, choice of coping alternative depends on one's interpretation of the distress. For certain kinds of distress, a person may feel that self-help or aid from family or friends will be ineffective or inappropriate. Additionally, as noted earlier, because of the widespread impact of disasters, the person's social network may be disrupted or severely strained. Those from whom support is normally sought may be in need of aid themselves and unable to meet the person's needs. Further, offers of help from formal sources should be more common after disasters than when a single individual experiences distress. Finally, professional sources may be a last resort in other situations because they cost

---

[2]Although these schemata are conceptually distinct, in reality they are likely to overlap or even to exist as one general "psychological functioning" schema. Certain distinctions have been drawn to parallel the stages of the help-seeking process outlined earlier.

money. But after disasters, mental health services are frequently provided at little or no charge. This fact may remove a large barrier so that, in some cases, formal sources are sought before informal ones.[3]

Finally, in considering this overview, it is important to keep in mind, as others have noted about similar models (Gross & McMullen, 1983), that although the stages of help seeking depicted in Figure 7.1 are conceptually distinct, the help-seeking process is, in practice, more complex. In particular, it may not, as suggested by Figure 7.1, always be linear or unidirectional. Processes identified as occurring later in the help-seeking sequence may affect processes that, conceptually, occur earlier. For example, the interpretation of distress may be influenced on occasion by considerations about coping alternatives (such as their perceived availability). The general model is meant as a heuristic aid for organizing the many factors that influence help seeking. A more detailed consideration of these factors follows.

The Awareness of Distress

The help-seeking process begins with the awareness that one is experiencing distress. As noted earlier, the presence of symptoms is not necessarily synonymous with the level of distress one is experiencing. Rather, the person's awareness and interpretation of emotional and behavioral disruptions are key. A person who has become withdrawn may not be aware, for example, of being unresponsive to the needs of family members. Similarly, a person may report drinking at least a six-pack of beer a night without concluding that such behavior indicates any degree of alcohol abuse. If a person does not view feelings or behaviors as dysfunctional, that individual will not interpret them as problematic or consider various coping alternatives.

Recognition of distress depends largely on what individuals believe constitutes acceptable emotional and behavioral functioning. As Figure 7.2 indicates, such information is organized into a distress awareness schema. The content of this schema includes information about both emotional and behavioral functioning.

Concerning the latter, expectations about role obligations (e.g., as a worker, spouse, parent) are especially important. Not everyone, of course, has clearly formed expectations about all areas of functioning; domains considered most important to the person are the ones most likely to carry well-articulated expectations. For example, a man who values his role as father should be more likely to notice (and treat as problematic) lapses in his parenting be-

---

[3]Although help seeking has been discussed as though different coping alternatives are mutually exclusive, there is no reason to assume this. Just as people with colds may try several remedies— getting more sleep, taking nonprescription medications, eating chicken soup, seeing a doctor— so might people experiencing emotional distress enlist the help of sources at several levels simultaneously.

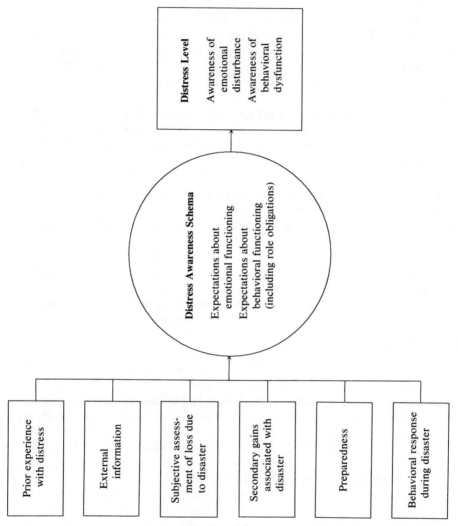

Figure 7.2. Awareness of distress.

171

havior than a father who is less concerned with child rearing. Emotional and behavioral functioning are closely interwoven.

Severe shifts in emotional functioning are, in part, likely to be manifest in behavioral changes. A common illustration is the person who, because of stress experienced at work, responds by dealing harshly with family members. At the same time, the ability to maintain consistent functioning in one area of one's life may mask or compensate for difficulties in other areas. People who are able to meet all of their role obligations, for example, are better able "to maintain self identity during periods of extreme stress and thus not feel the need for informal or formal help" (Veroff, Kulka, & Douvan, 1981, p. 17).

There are many factors that influence the content of a person's distress awareness schema (see Figure 7.2). First, a person's prior experience with distress is likely to play a large role in determining whether current behavioral or emotional reactions are experienced as distress. Prior experience establishes expectations about functioning. These expectations, in turn, help determine whether current symptoms are noticed and how they are interpreted. Individuals with histories of distress may develop self-schemata that sensitize them to the presence of disruptions in functioning. Alternatively, if past experience includes failed coping attempts, people may develop self-schemata that allow them to selectively attend to nonproblematic behaviors in an effort to deny or ignore distress cues until functioning is severely disrupted.

In addition to influencing a person's distress awareness schema, prior symptoms are likely to affect postdisaster symptoms in at least two ways. First, there is often continuity of functioning before and after a disaster; in general, individuals and families with prior histories of poor coping skills continue to experience similar difficulties during the postdisaster period (Birnbaum, Coplon, & Scharff, 1973). Secondly, predisaster emotional distress may affect one's preparedness before and behavioral response during the disaster. A person whose functioning is only marginal, for example, is not likely to have engaged in many preparedness activities and may be unable to respond in a prompt, flexible, and appropriate manner during the height of a crisis. As a result, both the traumas and the tangible and intangible losses suffered by such persons may be greater.

External information (e.g., from family, friends, the media, mental health outreach efforts) may also play a critical role in determining one's distress awareness schema. Awareness that one's emotions or behaviors have changed or become dysfunctional sometimes does not occur until questions or comments from family, friends, or co-workers prompt self-reflection. Until someone else observes, "You seem distracted lately," a person may not realize that she or he has indeed been feeling anxious or depressed or been having more trouble concentrating or sleeping than normal. Of course, external information can serve to decrease as well as increase awareness of distress. Sometimes, a person initiates conversations with others in an attempt to determine whether symptoms are present. If listeners dismiss the described behavior by saying they haven't noticed the person acting any differently, then the individual may deny or disregard internal cues of distress as unimportant.

Another factor to consider is the person's subjective assessment of loss caused by the disaster. In a straightforward way, the assessment of loss is probably related to symptoms such that the greater the subjective sense of loss, the greater the likelihood of symptomatology. But the assessment of loss may also affect the help-seeking process by influencing the person's distress awareness schema. Expectations about functioning based on prior experience may be altered in light of losses suffered from the disaster. For example, the disaster may serve as a salient event that sensitizes the person to the possibility of distress arising.

The sense of loss from the disaster may stem from several sources. Tangible losses might include the death of a loved one, a debilitating injury, property loss, or sudden unemployment, whereas intangible losses refer to events such as the breakup of the neighborhood, loss of free time, or witnessing horrifying events.[4] In each case, important dimensions to consider are the severity, extent, and permanence of the loss. Photographs and other memorabilia are often upsetting to lose, for instance, not because of their great monetary value, but because they cannot be replaced. Individuals who can more easily repair damage to dwellings because of insurance coverage are likely to judge home damage as less devastating than those without such coverage.

Concerning the experience of life-threatening trauma during the disaster, research has indicated that, regardless of the actual physical impact of the disaster, the greater the experience of trauma, the greater the likelihood of subsequent impairment (Lindy, Grace, & Green, 1981). The subjective impact of the disaster should be considered at two separate but interrelated levels, emotional (e.g., feelings of shock and anxiety) and cognitive. Concerning the latter, evidence suggests that the maintenance of a positive self-image and sense of self-efficacy, along with an ability to find meaning in what has happened, all contribute to adjustment after misfortunes (Taylor, 1983).

An important and sometimes overlooked influence on distress awareness is, in addition to subjective loss, whether there are secondary gains associated with having gone through the disaster. A person may make new friends, be freed from oppressive obligations, have the neighborhood draw closer together, become more spiritual, and so forth. If so, even when the

---

[4]It should be noted that the tangible and intangible impact of a disaster need not be closely related. For example, rescue workers not directly harmed by the disaster may still suffer from grief reactions, survivor guilt, anxiety, and depression (Palmer, 1980; Raphael, Singh, & Bradburg, 1980). Similarly, individuals in households spared physical damage may grieve over the breakup of their neighborhood when others move away.

disaster has led to negative consequences, there may be little distress afterwards. This is consistent with the theorizing of Shontz (1965, 1975), who, based largely on observations in nondisaster health care and rehabilitative settings, cautions against automatically assuming that misfortunes will lead to crisis and distress (see also Silver & Wortman, 1980).

Finally, two other factors should be mentioned that, in addition to influencing the objective and subjective impact of the disaster, may influence expectations about postdisaster functioning, and thus, the content of one's distress awareness schema. The first is a person's predisaster preparedness. Preparedness actions may lead people to expect less disruption in their postdisaster functioning. Also, early work by Drayer (1957) and McGonagle (1964) as well as more recent work by Hargreaves (1980) stresses the importance of preparedness for eliminating panic and extreme fear responses in life-threatening situations. Preparedness, therefore, may enable effective coping during the disaster that should help mitigate the actual physical and psychological harm suffered.

Preparedness relates to the second factor: behavioral response during the disaster. Such considerations as whether the person had an opportunity to intervene during the disaster and, if so, the appropriateness and effectiveness of the intervention may be important. For example, individuals who respond effectively may expect that postdisaster distress will be lessened.

The Interpretation of the Problem

How distress is interpreted determines to a large extent the range of coping options one considers. Very different strategies may be pursued for distress that is viewed as economic or physical versus distress construed as psychological in nature, or for distress ascribed to an individual as opposed to the family unit. Mental health professionals and disaster researchers, as noted earlier, have observed that victims tend to underutilize the psychological services available to them. The belief that services are underutilized probably reflects fundamental differences between professionals and lay persons in their willingness to attribute disruptions in functioning to psychological causes. Although the physical loss of home and possessions is likely to be accompanied by psychological suffering, many victims focus on the visible loss and identify postdisaster difficulties as being solely economic in nature (Feld, 1973; Poulshock & Cohen, 1975). In other cases, symptoms generally attributed to psychological concerns by professionals are labeled as physical ailments by victims (Abrahams, Price, Whitlock, & Williams, 1976; Killian, 1954; Menninger, 1952).

Factors likely to influence a person's interpretation of the problem are depicted in Figure 7.3. This interpretative process provides information on any of the aspects of distress noted in Figure 7.3 under Problem Definition: Labels for the distress, expectations about associated symptoms, and beliefs about the likely course, duration, and controllability of the distress.

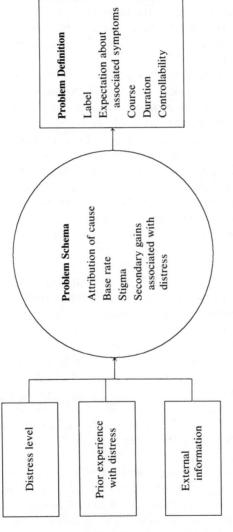

Figure 7.3. Interpretation of the problem.

Distress level is the first factor likely to influence the content of a person's problem schema. A person's prior experience with distress is likely to have led the person to develop a schema for interpreting distress. Thus, it plays a large role in how current distress is interpreted. In addition, distress level plays an important role in activating the problem schema. In general, the higher a person's distress level, the more likely the person will be to see the distress as a problem that must be diagnosed. However, the exact nature of the problem from the person's point of view is dependent on a number of other considerations.

As Figure 7.3 indicates, another determinant of one's problem schema is information received from others. External information may come from family, friends, co-workers, the media, a local community mental health center, or any number of sources. It can be solicited or unsolicited. In the aftermath of a disaster, the desire for information is high (Takuma, 1978).

According to social comparison theory (Festinger, 1954; Taylor, 1983; Wills, 1983), uncertainty leads people to compare their own situation with that of others. Comparisons usually provide at least two different types of information: normative and comparative. Normative information concerns guidelines about modal standards of conduct and belief, while comparative information allows individuals to assess how they stand (relative to other people) with reference to these group norms. Comparative information may alter one's problem schema and thus alter one's interpretation of the distress.

Several examples are relevant. During the postdisaster phase, Moore (1958) observed that strong norms of self-reliance in one community hindered residents from admitting emotional difficulties that might imply a need for outside help. In another community, residents acknowledged experiencing psychological symptoms such as interpersonal strain and nervousness but dismissed them as nonproblems because such reactions were commonly viewed as natural and temporary (Penick, Powell, & Sieck, 1976). Finally, Taylor and her colleagues have suggested that one way people who have encountered such misfortunes as breast cancer cope with their plight is by actively seeking "downward" social comparisons with others whose plight is worse, thereby lessening their own distress (Taylor, Lichtman, & Wood, 1984; Taylor, Wood, & Lichtman, 1983).

Up to this point, factors hypothesized as influencing a person's problem schema have been described. An examination of the content of such a schema reveals that one important component of a problem schema is the attributions made about the likely cause(s) of distress. Attribution theory is largely concerned with the rules lay people use to understand the world, especially in terms of causality (Heider, 1958; Kelley, 1967). Important dimensions of causality include locus (internal-external to the person), stability (stable-unstable), and globality (global-specific).

In general, victims who perceive the distress as being due to unstable external factors are less likely to seek formal help. Some disaster victims may assume that the distress will disappear shortly because the precipitating cause (the disaster) has come and gone. If these people see their distress as being due solely to the temporary impact of the disaster and not related to anything about themselves, they will probably engage in less help seeking. In contrast, individuals who make stable and internal attributions about the cause of distress are most likely to enter psychotherpay (Robbins, 1981). Unfortunately, seeking help for distress that has been caused by internal rather than external factors is more stigmatizing (Calhoun, Pierce, Walters, & Dawes, 1974; Yuen & Yates, 1987). The high psychological cost associated with stigma can discourage individuals from making internal attributions about the cause of their problems until dysfunctioning becomes extreme. Conveying an internal attribution about the distress while keeping the stigma attached to seeking help low is a difficult balance that outreach efforts must manage with care.

Another part of the problem schema, one especially likely to affect attributions of cause, is the base rate information a person holds about the occurrence of distress. How many others are thought to be experiencing similar distress? If the estimate is high, the distress may be considered normal and thus not a problem. For example, Robbins (1981) reports that individuals who judge their unique emotional distress as similar to the everyday suffering of their peers tend to conclude that their own symptoms are not indicative of problems. Unfortunately, base rate estimates made in the aftermath of disasters, when the everyday suffering of peers is extreme, may lead individuals to conclude that living with unusually high levels of emotional distress is natural. Base rate estimates are likely to depend on a person's prior experience with distress as well as information from others.

The stigma attached to certain kinds of distress may influence a person's interpretation of the distress (Archer, 1985; Katz, 1981; Mechanic, 1972). People may shy away from concluding that their distress is caused by something that would make them feel embarrassed or ashamed and may instead interpret distress in more socially acceptable terms. If a stigmatizing label is attached to the distress, subsequent help seeking may be affected (for example, choosing a professional source in part because of the privacy afforded or refusing professional help because doing so would confirm personal fears that one is "crazy").

The final component of a person's problem schema is whether there are secondary gains associated with the distress. As noted earlier, secondary gains from the disaster may attenuate the distress one experiences. In a similar vein (but different direction), secondary gains associated with the distress itself (such as increased attention from others) may influence how the distress is interpreted. If the potential gains are high, a person may conclude a problem exists irrespective of his or her level of distress. This may account in part for why people without diagnosable disabilities sometimes seek and receive professional mental health services.

The Consideration of Coping Alternatives

Once it is decided that a problem exists, one then turns to a consideration of various coping alternatives. This phase is depicted in Figure 7.4. Earlier, when discussing the concept of a problem schema, it was emphasized that such a schema would guide one's interpretation of distress. It is now important to add that a problem schema would also likely contain information about various ways of dealing with the distress. In fact, information about various coping alternatives is probably organized into a solution schema, the content of which overlaps partially with one's problem schema. Figure 7.4 depicts the crucial elements of a solution schema.

Knowledge of coping alternatives is obviously a *sine qua non* for their utilization. This includes an awareness not only of their existence, but of what they have to offer. The Veterans Administration, for example, may offer mental health assistance, but if the VA is mainly viewed in terms of medical and financial aid, help will not be sought there for emotional distress.

A closely related factor is the perceived availability of different sources of help. Sometimes one may be aware of an option (such as visiting a mental health professional) but feel the option is not really available. The literature on barriers to seeking mental health services (Goldsmith et al., in press; McKinlay, 1975; Mechanic, 1982) has identified several variables such as inconvenience, expense, and lack of insurance, that may discourage utilization. In the model, these variables influence help seeking by changing the perceived availability of an option.

The perceived efficacy of an option is also important. This refers to how likely an option will be to reduce distress, in other words, to its effectiveness. The greater the perceived efficacy of an option, *ceteris paribus,* the more likely it will be utilized.

In addition to tangible costs such as time and money associated with the use of a coping option, perceived psychological costs are important too. Indeed, they are probably more important in postdisaster settings, where mental health services are frequently available for little or no financial cost. One psychological cost to consider is the extent to which a helping option threatens one's self-esteem (Fisher, Nadler, & Whitcher-Alagna, 1982). Some options, particularly seeing a mental health professional, may have a great deal of stigma attached to them. Furthermore, seeking help from others may be taken as a sign that one is helpless. In each case, one's self-esteem is threatened.

There are other psychological costs as well. Receiving help may create an onerous sense of indebtedness to the helper, particularly if the source is an informal one (family, friends), where no fee-for-service transaction takes place. Social psychological studies based on equity theory (Clark, Gotay, & Mills, 1974; Greenberg & Shapiro, 1971) have shown that people are sometimes reluctant to accept even necessary aid when they lack the ability to reciprocate. The sense of indebtedness is aversive (Greenberg, 1980).

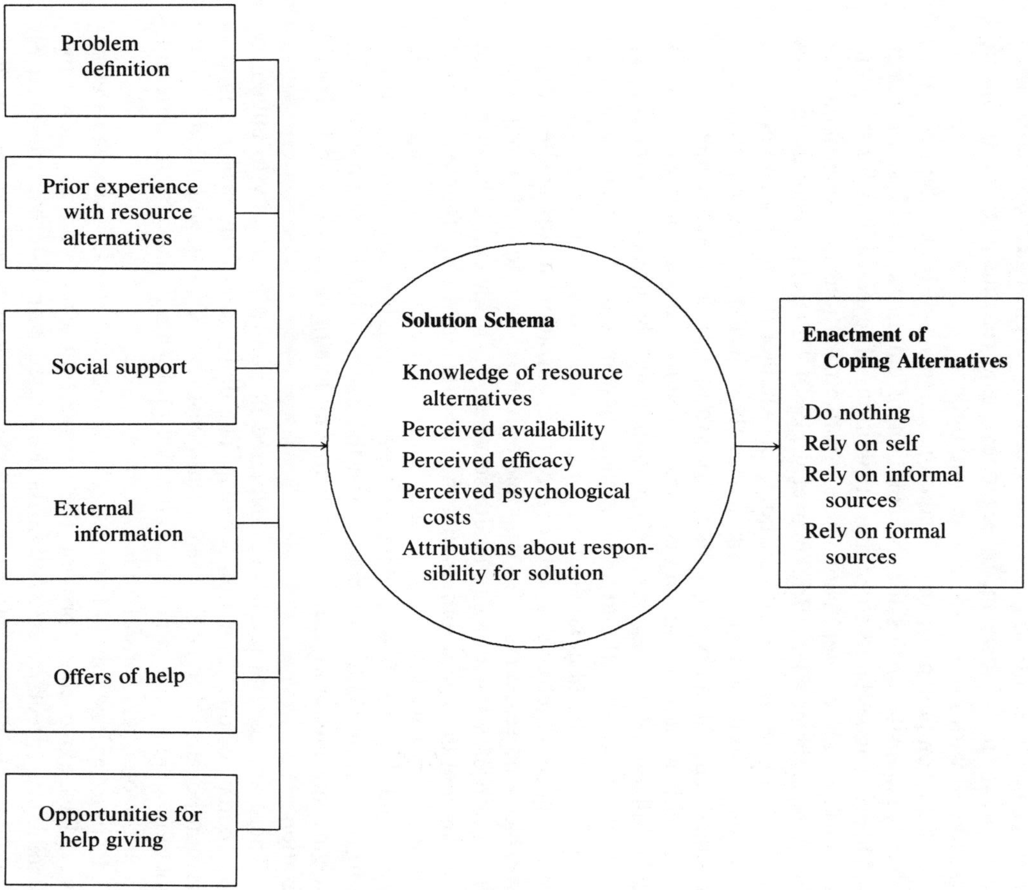
Problem definition
Prior experience with resource alternatives
Social support
External information
Offers of help
Opportunities for help giving
Solution Schema
Knowledge of resource alternatives
Perceived availability
Perceived efficacy
Perceived psychological costs
Attributions about responsibility for solution
Enactment of Coping Alternatives
Do nothing
Rely on self
Rely on informal sources
Rely on formal sources

Figure 7.4. Consideration of coping alternatives.

Moreover, when one cannot fully reciprocate, what is given back to the helper is often acknowledgment of status and power (Blau, 1964). Conceding status and power to a helper then allows that person a degree of control over one's life. Within social psychology, the theory of psychological reactance (Brehm, 1966; Brehm & Brehm, 1981) postulates that when a person's freedom is constrained, a negative arousal state called reactance ensues, leading to efforts to restore that freedom. Psychological costs associated with threats to self-esteem, indebtedness, and reactance, then, should be considered with respect to each coping option.

A final component of one's solution schema will be attributions about where responsibility lies for the solution of emotional distress. Brickman and his colleagues have noted that attributions of responsibility for solutions to a problem are conceptually distinct from attributions of responsibility for the cause of the problem (Brickman et al., 1982). Different coping alternatives are likely to be considered depending on whether one makes an internal or external attribution of responsibility for the solution; in the latter case, for instance, one would be more likely to turn to a professional helper.

As with attributions about distress, attributions about solutions are likely to be influenced by base rate information about the use of different coping strategies by others. If certain strategies such as self-reliance are thought to be prevalent, the likelihood of an internal attribution of responsibility will be enhanced. Of course, it is the *perceived* utilization of coping alternatives to which one responds. This may have little relation to actual utilization. Users of professional mental health services, for instance, may, for privacy reasons, not divulge to others that they are seeking help. If the use of such services is not well publicized, people may make erroneous base rate estimates and shy away from seeking professional help. For this reason, outreach efforts such as media compaigns and the use of models are important for heightening public awareness about mental health resources and their utilization.

There are several factors (as depicted in Figure 7.4) likely to influence the content of one's solution schema. The definition of the problem is important because it answers the crucial question, "Coping with what?" The solution schema one holds for economic problems is likely to be different from the one held for emotional distress.

Prior experience should affect one's solution schema in a straightforward way. Past experiences provide the person with a basis for estimating the availability, effectiveness, and costs associated with different solutions. A potential solution may not be considered seriously if past attempts to implement it indicated it was unavailable, costly, or ineffective. For example, an easily accessible help source such as a parent may be avoided because, in the past, the resulting threat to the person's sense of autonomy was too high. An unproductive previous encounter with a mental health professional may discourage the person from pursuing this option with another counselor. Coping attempts judged effective in the past, on the other hand, will receive more serious consideration. Because the model assumes a longitudinal perspective, it should be noted that as strategies are implemented, new information about efficacy, psychological costs, and so forth, are integrated into the preexisting schema.

Social support is important at several levels. It is likely to influence knowledge of coping alternatives as well as their perceived availability, efficacy, and psychological costs. Research indicates that people use a variety of social supports in dealing with emotional distress, although the patterns of such use are by no means simple (Cohen & McKay, 1984). It is hypothesized in this model that, in general, the greater one's perceived social support from informal sources, the greater the likelihood those sources will be utilized to help with emotional distress. Of course, there are different kinds of social support (e.g., tangible, such as money or goods, vs. appraisal, as in having someone with whom to talk about problems; Cohen & McKay). Only if the appropriate kind of social support is available will it be utilized.

Finally, information from family, friends, the media, or similar sources, as well as actual offers of help, are likely to influence any of the aforementioned variables that make up one's solution schema. As was the case with the interpretation of distress, information about "comparison others," or those in the community who have had similar experiences, may have strong effects on choice of coping strategy. If comparison others maintain that only the totally destitute accept financial aid or that well-adjusted people can adapt to any stressful situation, then individuals should be more likely to favor self-reliance than the use of formal helpers.

Evidence does indicate that disaster victims resist seeking financial aid because it is associated with the stigma of welfare—they feel it implies a loss of status in the community (Feld, 1973; Huerta & Horton, 1978). Individuals in the rural town of Buchanan, Virginia, have turned down outside flood assistance so often and so completely in the past few decades that the *Washington Post* was moved to write about "The Buchanan Syndrome" (Allen, 1985). In other cases, vigorous outreach programs legitimizing formal help for postdisaster psychological symptoms have increased victims' willingness to obtain professional mental health services (Heffron, 1977; Okura, 1975). Outreach programs using testimonials from community members (who are potential comparison others) may be particularly effective (Gist & Stolz, 1982). Such outreach programs should prove effective for at least three reasons. First, testimonials should increase the perceived efficacy of an option. Second, knowing that relevant peers have sought help should decrease perceived psychological costs by reducing stigma. Third, such efforts may cause attributions concerning who is responsible for solving the problem to shift away from the individual to the outreach organization.

Because of the potential psychological costs associated with help seeking (i.e., stigma, indebtedness, loss of status and power), opportunities for help *giving* may allow one to receive help more easily. The help given to others may be in a different form (e.g., material, labor) and may even be given to a different source (e.g., a community volunteer organization). Regardless, such efforts tend to make one feel more deserving of help and less indebted if it is received (see Austin & Walster, 1975, regarding "equity with the world").

Enactment of the Coping Alternative

Based on the consideration of the coping alternatives, a person will select what he or she perceives to be the most desirable option(s). The decision as to which coping alternative(s) to choose will likely be a combined function of the value placed on reducing the distress, the expectancy that a given coping alternative will be successful at reducing the distress, and the expected costs for employing the given alternative. It is possible that a person will conclude, after considering his or her distress and various coping alternatives, that (at least for the moment) nothing can or should be done. Otherwise, the person will actively attempt to ease the distress and/or enlist the aid of others. Outside help may come from informal sources such as family and friends or formal sources such as mental health professionals or others (e.g., medical doctors). As noted earlier, help may be sought from several sources simultaneously. As each coping strategy is enacted, the person will reassess the level of distress. If distress still exists, then the person can be expected to reconsider her or his interpretation of the problem or assessment of coping alternatives to determine whether the current mode of coping should be continued or changed.

Demographic and Personality Variables

The model contains no explicit mention of demographic or personality variables. This is not because these variables are considered trivial. Quite the contrary, a person's sex, age, socioeconomic standing, or self-esteem, to cite only a few examples, may be highly related to help seeking. However, demographic and personality variables are important only to the extent they influence variables already specified by the model. For example, demographic factors such as age may affect help seeking because of differences in behavorial response during the disaster, in the perceived stigma attached to acknowledging emotional distress, in the perceived efficacy of coping options, and so forth. As one example, the elderly are less likely to evacuate endangered areas (Friedsam, 1960, 1962). In contrast, families with pre-school-aged children are more likely to take protective measures and to respond to evacuation notices (Lechat, 1979). These differences may lead to differences in amount of distress experienced, thereby affecting the help-seeking process. Beyond such indirect effects, demographic and personality variables are hypothesized to have little influence on help seeking.

A LONGITUDINAL FIELD STUDY

In an effort to test many of the hypotheses advanced in this chapter, a longitudinal field study is currently being conducted with flood victims in the Roanoke Valley of Virginia. Several features distinguish the design and implementation of this research project from previous efforts. First, a problem that typically plagues disaster studies was avoided: slow start-up time. When initial data are collected 6 months (Lindy et al., 1981) or even 1 year (Bolin, 1982) after a disaster, valuable information—critical to an analysis of processes expected to change over time—is lost. Slow start-up time also forces the researcher to rely more exclusively on retrospective, self-report data that is likely to be less reliable (Ostrove & Baum, 1983). In this study, all the initial interviews were completed within 2½ to 4 months after the flood. Second, in contrast to most research in this area, it has utilized a longitudinal design. Such designs have not often been used because they are expensive and more difficult to implement. A longitudinal perspective, however, is crucial for understanding processes like help seeking that may change over time. Data collection at multiple points in time also allows causal inferences to be drawn more easily from correlational data.

In November 1985, flash flooding in the greater Roanoke area caused an estimated 300 million dollars in property damage and claimed 10 lives. According to Red Cross records, approximately 350 homes were destroyed, 519 suffered major damage, and nearly 1,100 experienced minor damage. The cooperation of the American Red Cross and local religious and business leaders made possible the compilation of a master list of close to 1,400 households affected by the flood during the first few weeks following the disaster. Within 3½ months after the flood 593 individuals had been contacted by telephone. Most victims agreed to take part in a telephone screening. Of these participants, 306 reported symptoms associated with anxiety, depression, somatization, family conflict, or alcohol abuse.

Of the 306, 190 completed an in-person interview during which individuals described their help-seeking activities in regard to a postflood global episode of distress as well as for a variety of specific individual symptoms. In addition to help seeking that had taken place to that point, data were also collected on symptomatology, beliefs about distress and possible solutions, behavior prior to and during the flood, damage suffered, and so forth. Self-reports of using mental health professionals, as well as Red Cross home damage estimates, were verified where possible as an accuracy check. A follow-up was conducted with 181 of the original 190 victims 6 to 8 months later.

In addition to the previously mentioned factors, the follow-up procedure assessed help seeking that had occurred in the intervening period. The follow-up included the addition of 44 control participants who initially reported levels of distress above threshold but who were not interviewed during the first wave of data collection. This was done to determine if the initial interviews, by asking about help-seeking attitudes and behavior, had a reactive effect on subsequent help seeking. In addition, a random subsample of 73 individuals whose distress levels fell below threshold when first contacted were rescreened by telephone to determine if there was evidence for a delayed stress reaction. This group was also asked to report the incidence of any help sought since the flood from a list of formal and informal sources.

A second follow-up is planned with all participants 7–9 months after the second wave (or 17–18 months after the flood). Data from the three panels should help determine the role of external information on all phases of the help-seeking process, examine the relationship of help giving to help seeking, assess how responsibility for the origin and solution of a problem is assigned, and document the perceived costs and benefits associated with a variety of coping alternatives. In sum, the data should allow documentation of not only where victims turn for help and how help-seeking strategies change over time, but also why these decisions are made.

CONCLUSION

Earlier in the chapter it was noted that mental health services offered after disasters are frequently underutilized. Reasons for this are not clear, but the model presented here suggests several possibilities. First, the argument that psychological distress after disasters is neither widespread nor long-lasting may be correct; for many, emotional distress may be relatively mild. For others, the distress may not be interpreted as a problem or may not be seen as primarily psychological in nature; a host of factors, ranging from base rate occurrence estimates to perceived stigma, have been identified as likely to influence the interpretation of distress. Even if the distress is identified as a psychological problem, there remain many roadblocks in the consideration of coping alternatives that would discourage use of mental health services (e.g., poor knowledge of resource alternatives, low perceived efficacy, high threat to self-esteem). The decision to use mental health services, then, is the by-product of several prior decisions, any of which could result in other (or no) sources being sought (Gross & McMullen, 1983, reach a similar conclusion in their review of models of general help seeking).

It is hoped that, by delineating the many factors that may influence mental health help seeking after disasters, this model can serve as a guide for future research. Given the meager empirical work on the topic, much research is needed. Finally, this research may provide answers that will benefit practitioners and policy makers. The more effective and efficient the planning and delivery of services, the less likely that emotional distress will prolong the suffering of disaster victims.

REFERENCES

Abrahams, M. J., Price, J., Whitlock, F. A., & Williams, G. (1976). The Brisbane Floods, January 1974: The impact on health. *The Medical Journal of Australia, 2*, 936–939.

Adams, P. R., & Adams, G. R. (1984). Mount St. Helen's ashfall: Evidence for a disaster stress reaction. *American Psychologist, 39,* 252–260.

Allen, H. (1985, December 1). The Buchanan syndrome. *The Washington Post,* p. C5.

Archer, D. (1985). Social deviance. In G. Lindzey & E. Aronson (Eds.), *The handbook of social psychology* (Vol. II, pp. 743–804). New York: Random House.

Austin, W., & Walster, E. (1975). Equity with the world: An investigation of the trans-relational effects of equity and inequity. *Sociometry, 38,* 474–496.

Bartlett, F. (1932). *A study in experimental and social psychology.* New York: Cambridge University Press.

Birnbaum, F., Coplon, J., & Scharff, I. (1973). Crisis intervention after a natural disaster. *Social Casework, 54,* 545–551.

Blau, P. M. (1964). *Exchange and power in social life.* New York: Wiley.

Blaufarb, H., & Levine, J. (1972). Crisis intervention in an earthquake. *Social Work, 17,* 16–19.

Bolin, R. C. (1982). *Long-term family recovery from disaster.* Boulder: University of Colorado, Institute of Behavioral Science.

Bosmajian, C. P., & Mattson, R. E. (1980). A controlled study of variables related to counseling center use. *Journal of Counseling Psychology, 27,* 510–519.

Boyd, S. T. (1981). Psychological reactions of disaster victims. *South African Medical Journal, 60,* 744–748.

Brehm, J. W. (1966). *A theory of psychological reactance.* New York: Academic Press.

Brehm, S. S., & Brehm, J. W. (1981). *Psychological reactance: The psychology of freedom and control.* New York: Academic Press.

Brickman, P., Rabinowitz, V. C., Karuza, J., Jr., Coates, D., Cohn, E., & Kidder, L. (1982). Models of coping and helping. *American Psychologist, 37,* 368–384.

Bromet, E., & Dunn, L. (1981). Mental health of mothers nine months after the Three Mile Island accident. *The Urban and Social Change Review, 14,* 12–15.

Butcher, J. N. (1980). The role of crisis intervention in an airport disaster plan. *Aviation, Space and Environmental Medicine, 51,* 1260–1262.

Calhoun, L., Pierce, J. R., Walters, S., & Dawes, A. (1974). Determinants of social rejection for help seeking: Locus of casual attribution, help source, and the mental illness label. *Journal of Consulting and Clinical Psychology, 42,* 618–627.

Chamberlin, B. C. (1980). Mayo seminars in psychiatry: The psychological aftermath of disaster. *Journal of Clinical Psychiatry, 4,* 238–244.

Clark, M. S., Gotay, C., Mills, J. (1974). Interpersonal attraction in exchange and communal relationships. *Journal of Personality and Social Psychology, 37,* 12–24.

Cohen, R. (1983, June 27). Natural disaster: Hidden legacy of pain. *The New York Times,* p. B5.

Cohen, S., & McKay, G. (1984). Social support, stress and the buffering hypothesis: A theoretical analysis. In A. Baum, J. E. Singer, & S. E. Taylor (Eds.), *Handbook of psychology and health:* (Vol. 4, pp. 253–267). Hillsdale, NJ: Erlbaum.

Cook, J., & Bickman, L. (1987). *Social support and psychological symptomatology following a natural disaster.* Unpublished manuscript. Program Evaluation Laboratory, Peabody College, Vanderbilt University, Nashville, TN.

Crabbs, M. A., & Heffron, E. (1981). Loss associated with a natural disaster. *The Personnel and Guidance Journal, 59*, 378–382.

DePaulo, B. M., & Fisher, J. D. (1980). The costs of asking for help. *Basic and Applied Social Psychology, 1*, 23–35.

Drayer, C. S. (1957). Psychological factors and problems, emergency and long-term. *The Annals of the American Academy, 309*, 151–159.

Feld, A. (1973). Reflections on the Agnes Flood. *Social Work, 18*, 46–51.

Festinger, L. (1954). A theory of social comparison processes. *Human Relations, 7*, 117–140.

Fischer, E. H., Winer, D., & Abramowitz, S. I. (1983). In J. D. Fisher, A. Nadler, & B. M. DePaulo (Eds.), *New directions in helping: Applied perspectives on help-seeking and -receiving*. (Vol. 3, pp. 163–185). New York: Academic Press.

Fisher, J. D., Nadler, A., & Whitcher-Alagna, S. (1982). Recipient reactions to aid. *Psychological Bulletin, 91*, 27–54.

Fiske, S. T., & Taylor, S. E. (1984). *Social cognition*. Reading, MA: Addison-Wesley.

Friedsam, H. J. (1960). Older persons as disaster casualties. *Journal of Health and Human Behavior, 1*, 269–273.

Friedsam, H. J. (1962). Older persons in disaster. In W. G. Baker & D. H. Chapman (Eds.), *Man and society in disaster* (pp. 151–182). New York: Basic Books.

Gist, R., & Stolz, S. B. (1982). Mental health promotion and the media: Community response to the Kansas City hotel disaster. *American Psychologist, 37*, 1136–1139.

Goldsmith, H. F., Jackson, D. J., & Hough, R. (in press). A process model of seeking mental health services: A proposed framework for organizing the research literature on help seeking. In H. F. Goldsmith, E. Lin, R. Bell (Eds.), *Need assessments: Its future*. (Series BN: Needs Assessments and Evaluation). Washington, DC: U.S. Government Printing Office.

Greenberg, M. S. (1980). A theory of indebtedness. In K. Gergen, M. S. Greenberg, & R. Willis (Eds.), *Social exchange: Advances in theory and research* (pp. 3–26). New York: Plenum.

Greenberg, M. S. & Shapiro, S. P. (1971). Indebtedness: An adverse aspect of asking for and receiving help. *Sociometry, 34*, 290–301.

Greenley, J. R., & Mechanic, D. (1976). Social selection in seeking help for psychological problems. *Journal of Health and Social Behavior, 17*, 249–262.

Gross, A. E., & McMullen, P. A. (1983). Models of the help-seeking process. In J. D. Fisher, A. Nadler, & B. M. DePaulo (Eds.), *New directions in helping: Help-seeking*. (Vol 2, pp. 47–70). New York: Academic Press, 47–70.

Grossman, L. (1973). Train crash: Social work and disaster services. *Social Work, 18*, 38–44.

Hargreaves, A. G. (1980). Coping with disaster. *American Journal of Nursing, 80*, 683.

Hartsough, D. M. (1982). Planning for disasters: A new community outreach program for mental health centers. *Journal of Community Psychology, 10*, 255–264.

Heffron, E. F. (1977). Project Outreach: Crisis intervention following natural disaster. *Journal of Community Psychology, 5*, 103–111.

Heider, F. (1958). *The psychology of interpersonal relations*. New York: Wiley.

Huerta, F., & Horton, R. (1978). Coping behavior of elderly flood victims. *The Gerontologist, 18,* 541–546.

Katz, I. (1981). *Stigma: A social psychological analysis.* Hillsdale, NJ: Erlbaum.

Kelley, H. H. (1967). Attribution theory in social psychology. In D. Levine (Ed.), *Nebraska Symposium on Motivation* (Vol. 15, pp. 192–240). Lincoln: University of Nebraska Press.

Killian, L. M. (1954). Some accomplishments and some needs in disaster study. *Journal of Social Issues, 10,* 66–72.

Lechat, M. F. (1979). Disasters and public health. *Bulletin of the World Health Organization, 57,* 11–17.

Lindy, J. D., Grace, M. C., & Green, B. L. (1981). Survivors: Outreach to a reluctant population. *American Journal of Orthopsychiatry, 51,* 468–478.

Logue, J. N., Hansen, H., Struening, E. (1981). Some indications of the long-term health effects of a natural disaster. *Public Health Reports, 96,* 67–79.

Markus, H., & Zajonc, R. B. (1985). The cognitive perspective in social psychology. In G. Lindzey & E. Aronson (Eds.), *Handbook of social psychology* (Vol. 1, pp. 137–230). New York: Random House.

McGonagle, L. C. (1964). Psychological aspects of disaster. *American Journal of Public Health, 54,* 638–643.

McKinlay, J. B. (1975). The help-seeking behavior of the poor. In J. Kosa & I. K. Zola (Eds.), *Poverty and health: A sociological analysis* (Rev. Ed., pp. 224–273). Cambridge, MA: Harvard University Press.

Mechanic, D. (1972). Social psychological factors affecting the presentation of bodily complaints. *The New England Journal of Medicine, 286,* 1132–1139.

Mechanic, D. (1982). The epidemiology of illness behavior and its relationship to physical and psychological distress. In D. Mechanic (Ed.), *Symptoms, illness behavior and help-seeking* (Vol. 3, pp. 1–24). New Brunswick: Rutgers University Press.

Menninger, W. C. (1952). Psychological reactions in an emergency. *American Journal of Psychiatry, 109,* 128–130.

Moore, H. E. (1958). Some emotional concomitant of disaster. *Mental Hygiene, 42,* 45–50.

Nadler, A., & Porat, I. (1978). When names do not help: Effects of anonymity and locus of need attribution on help-seeking behavior. *Personality and Social Psychology Bulletin, 4,* 624–626.

Okura, K. P. (1975). Mobilizing in response to a major disaster. *Community Mental Health Journal, 11,* 136–144.

Ostrove, N. M., & Baum, A. (1983). Factors influencing medical help-seeking. In J. D. Fisher, A. Nadler, & B. M. DePaulo (Eds.) *New directions in helping: Applied perspectives on help-seeking and -receiving* (Vol. 3, pp. 107–129). New York: Academic Press.

Palmer, E. L. (1980). Student reactions to disaster. *American Journal of Nursing, 80,* 680–682.

Penick, E. C., Powell, B. J., & Sieck, W. A. (1976). Mental health problems and natural disasters: Tornado victims. *Journal of Community Psychology, 4,* 64–67.

Poulshock, S. W., & Cohen, E. S. (1975). The elderly in the aftermath of a disaster. *The Gerontologist, 15,* 357–361.

Quarantelli, E., & Dynes, R. (1977). Response to social crisis and disaster. *Annual Review of Sociology, 3,* 23–49.

Raphael, B., Singh, B., & Bradbury, L. (1980). Disaster: The helper's perspective. *The Medical Journal of Australia, 2,* 445–447.

Robbins, J. M. (1981). Lay attributions of personal problems and psychological help-seeking. *Social Psychiatry, 16,* 1–9.

Rubonis, A., & Bickman, L. (1986). *A meta-analytic review of psychological impairment in the wake of disaster.* Unpublished manuscript. Program Evaluation Laboratory, Peabody College, Vanderbilt University, Nashville, TN.

Schanche, D. A. (1974). The emotional aftermath of "the largest tornado ever." *Today's Health, 52,* 16–19.

Shontz, F. C. (1965). Reactions to crisis. *Volta Review, 67,* 364–370.

Shontz, F. C. (1975). *The psychological aspects of physical illness and disability.* New York: Macmillan.

Silver, R. L., & Wortman, C. B. (1980). Coping with undesirable life events. In J. Garber & M. E. P. Seligman (Eds.), *Human helplessness: Theory and applications* (pp. 297–340). New York: Academic Press.

Smith, E. M., Robins, L. N., Przybeck, T. R., Goldring, E., & Solomon, S. (1986). Psychosocial consequences of a disaster. In J. H. Shore (Ed.), *Disaster stress studies: New methods and findings* (pp. 49–76). Washington, DC: American Psychiatric Press.

Takuma, T. (1978). Human behavior in the event of earthquakes. In E. L. Quarantelli (Ed.), *Disasters: Theory and research* (pp. 159–172). Beverly Hills, CA.: Sage Publications.

Taylor, S. E. (1983). Adjustment to threatening events: A theory of cognitive adaptation. *American Psychologist, 38,* 1161–1173.

Taylor, S. E., Lichtman, R. R., & Wood, J. V. (1984). Attributions, beliefs about control, and adjustment to breast cancer. *Journal of Personality and Social Psychology, 46,* 489–502.

Taylor, S. E., Wood, J. V., & Lichtman, R. R. (1983). It could be worse: Selective evaluation as a response to victimization. *Journal of Social Issues, 39,* 19–40.

Taylor, V. A., Ross, G. A., & Quarantelli, E. L. (1976). *Delivery of mental health services in disasters: The Xenia Tornado and some implications.* Columbus Disaster Research Center, Ohio State University.

Tessler, R. C., & Schwartz, S. H. (1972). Help-seeking, self-esteem, and achievement motivation: An attributional analysis. *Journal of Personality and Social Psychology, 21,* 318–326.

Veroff, J., Kulka, R. A., & Douvan, E. (1981). *Mental health in America: Patterns of help-seeking from 1957–1976.* New York: Basic Books.

Wills, T. A. (1983). Social comparison in coping and help-seeking. In J. D. Fisher, A. Nadler, & B. M. DePaulo (Eds.) *New directions in helping: Help-seeking* (Vol. 2, pp. 109–141). New York: Academic Press.

Wortman, C. B., & Dunkel-Schetter, C. (1979). Interpersonal relationships and cancer: A theoretical analysis. *Journal of Social Issues, 39,* 120–155.

Wright, J. D., Rossi, P. H., Wright, S. R., & Weber-Burdin, W. (1979). *After the clean-up: Long-range effects of natural disasters.* Beverly Hills, CA: Sage Publications.

Yuen, M., & Yates, S. (1987). *Problem cause as a determinant of help seeking among male and female teenagers.* Unpublished manuscript. Lehman College, CUNY, New York.

CHAPTER 8

Mental Health and Disaster

Preventive Approaches to Intervention

DIANE GARAVENTA MYERS

Prevention in the context of *disaster* might seem a paradoxical concept. Indeed, although extensive strides have been made in mitigating certain hazards and effects of disaster, the strength of nature and the limitations of human beings are evidenced continually in disasters around the globe. And what of the psychological aftermath of disaster? *The American Heritage Dictionary of the English Language* (Morris, 1981) defines disaster as "an occurrence inflicting widespread . . . distress." The American Red Cross defines disaster as "an occurrence . . . that causes human suffering or creates human needs that the victims cannot alleviate without assistance" (American Red Cross, 1978).

Human distress and suffering are then, by definition, integral parts of disaster. It would seem unlikely that mental health professionals could prevent the painful emotions that are normal reactions to a catastrophic event. One could argue, in fact, that it would be countertherapeutic to circumvent or postpone the intense emotional reactions that must be worked through in order to recover.

What, then, is meant by prevention in the context of mental health and disaster? What do people seek to prevent? What is it possible to prevent? What approaches and techniques are applicable? Can their effectiveness be evaluated? This chapter will explore the answers to these questions.

BASIC PRINCIPLES OF PRIMARY PREVENTION IN MENTAL HEALTH

Gerald Caplan (1964) was the first to apply the public health concepts of prevention to the field of mental health. By his well-accepted definition, primary prevention involves lowering the rate of new cases of mental disorder in a population over a certain period by counteracting harmful circumstances *before they have a chance to produce illness.* Caplan points out that, in observing a whole population exposed to harmful influences, some individuals become sick while some remain healthy. Following a disaster, for example, some individuals cope well and move fairly smoothly through their recovery; others have difficulty coping and may suffer a variety of emotional or psychological sequelae that may be indicative of maladjustment.

This observation suggests it is useful to study not only the harmful circumstances that may befall a population, but also those circumstances that modify the vulnerability or resistance of persons exposed to them. These *host factors,* or qualities of members of a population that determine their vulnerability or resistance to stress, are made up of two groups of attributes: those such as age, sex, and ethnic group, which cannot be changed; and those such as general ego strength, problem-solving skills, and capacity to tolerate anxiety and frustration, which can be altered by experience. Caplan's model of a program of primary prevention, then, would focus on identifying harmful influences and attempting to mitigate them, as well as identifying environmental forces that support individuals in the resistance of harmful influences. It is hoped that the equilibrium of forces can be changed so that, by reducing harmful pressures and helping to strengthen people in their ways of dealing with them, a healthy adaptation and adjustment is possible, thus lowering the incidence of mental disorder.

This chapter organizes the discussion of primary prevention in disaster according to Caplan's two-pronged paradigm of *social action* and *interpersonal action.* Although a quarter century has passed since Caplan first developed this model, it continues to be a valid and useful framework for organizing and describing current preventive mental health activities. Several recent works present paradigms remarkably similar to Caplan's earlier conceptualizations (Catalano & Dooley, 1980; Jason, 1980; Ketterer, Bader, & Levy, 1980). These and other recent approaches are presented here, using Caplan's model not as the last word of preventive theory, but simply as a framework within which to organize the theories and approaches discussed here.

Primary prevention in mental health is based on two assumptions. First, there must be a provision of continual *supplies* if an individual is to grow and develop. These supplies are physical, psychosocial, and sociocultural. The second assumption is that, in each individual's life, accidental and developmental *crises* arise with which he or she must cope. Besides internal coping mechanisms that each individual possesses, the sociocultural environment affects ability to cope (Caplan, 1964; Taillie, 1969).

Most of the literature on primary prevention focuses on the organization of prevention efforts around life crises. A life crisis is defined as a stressful event that exceeds an individual's usual coping resources and that can produce both vulnerability to development of enduring maladaptation as well as the potential for rapid psychological growth (Caplan, 1964; Felner, Farber, & Primavera, 1980; Goldston, 1978; Lindemann, 1956). The ability to predict life crises is mixed. Certain life transitions (e.g., marriage, birth of a child, or job change) are easily predicted, and the development of a crisis can often be prevented. Other events, such as a sudden death or disaster, cannot usually be anticipated. It is possible, however, to anticipate how people will react to various types of crises. Once a population or individual is identified as being affected by a stressful event, a number of approaches can be used to prevent maladaptation and to promote growth (Hoff, 1984).

In the context of crisis theory, then, primary prevention has as its goal the reduction of mental disability and the promotion of people's capacities for dealing with crisis (Goldston, 1977; Hoff, 1984). Bloom (1979) sets forth a paradigm for organizing primary prevention efforts under this crisis perspective. This involves (1) identification of the stressful event (in this case, the disaster) and the persons undergoing the stress (i.e., the population affected by the disaster); (2) research and study into the consequences of the event, with hypotheses regarding how to reduce harmful outcomes; and (3) research and evaluation of interventions aimed at reducing the harmful consequences.

Catalano and Dooley (1980) made a distinction between *proactive* and *reactive* primary prevention approaches. A proactive approach assumes that the causal agent is controllable or preventable and seeks to eliminate the causal agent or modify the hazardous situation (Hoff, 1984). In the field of public health, this includes such efforts as removal of mosquito breeding grounds, thus eliminating an agent which spreads disease. In the field of disaster, such proactive approaches might include flood control projects to eliminate dangers of flooding in areas prone to heavy rains or tides or community zoning to prevent building on soil subject to landslides or earthquake movement.

A reactive approach assumes that the causal agent, if unavoidable, is at least resistable. Such an approach, which can be applied before or after a stressor occurs, aims at reducing the person's exposure to the hazardous situation (Hoff, 1984) or preparing one to react effectively (Catalano & Dooley, 1980). In the public health field, such an approach might include strengthening individuals' resistance to disease by vaccination. In disaster, such approaches might include early warnings (as in a hurricane or tornado-prone area) to allow people to take cover. Disaster-preparedness training, fire drills, and the like can further prepare people to take safety precautions to minimize exposure.

A reactive approach would also seek to reduce a person's vulnerability by helping him to increase his coping abilities (Hoff, 1984). Caplan (1964) pointed out that an individual's tools for coping with crisis include *personal factors* (such as perception of the event, prior crisis resolution skills, and the like) and *sociocultural factors* (such as family; social support network; and such key members of the community as authority figures, agencies, and helping persons). This leads to Caplan's conceptualization of prevention activities in two modes: (1) *social action,* or environmental interventions (Jason, 1980), which seek to modify policy or action on a community or widespread scale in order to attenuate hazardous circumstances; to improve provision of basic physical, psychosocial, and sociocultural supplies; and to improve helping resources to foster healthy crisis coping; and (2) *interpersonal action,* or a person-centered approach (Jason), which focuses on direct intervention with individuals and caregivers in order to help these individuals improve coping skills and therefore eliminate the need to use regressive, nonreality based, or socially unacceptable ways of dealing with their predicaments (Caplan). Catalano and Dooley (1980) describe these approaches as taking place at the *macrolevel* (community-wide approach) or at the *microlevel* (psychobiological, one-to-one, or family approaches).

An interesting sidelight is that the Prevention Task Panel of the President's Commission on Mental Health (1978), while recognizing societal stress as "capable of producing profound emotional distress in individuals," also pointed out that the Commission had no magical power to eliminate such sources of stress and suggested, moreover, that societal conditions were possibly not "part of mental health's purview." Thus, microlevel primary preventive approaches were identified as being of more interest for research and development, whereas macrolevel approaches were seen as being beyond the province of mental health workers (Catalano & Dooley, 1980). To some extent, this perspective may have developed because the traditional training of mental health professionals has taken the psychological perspective that focuses on the individual or family as the unit of intervention. The mental health profession has far less experience with or methodological equipment for aggregate-level analysis (Bronfenbrenner, 1977; Katona, 1979). Historically lacking skills in macrolevel interventions, mental health workers have naturally sought interventions that are within their realm of competence (Catalano & Dooley). Increasingly, however, mental health professionals are moving into the field of community organization and other macrolevel social action interventions in an attempt to influence stressors and risk factors at a wider level.

Ketterer, Bader, and Levy (1980) attested that, despite attention given to prevention in mental health, relatively little is known about prevention strategies or about the knowledge and skills required by prevention practitioners. They pointed out that this problem exists largely because the whole field of prevention is still in a formative stage, and few studies have either defined precisely the nature and range of prevention services or identified strategies and techniques to be used in service delivery. They also cited the scarcity of opportunities for training and skill development in prevention. Evaluation of the effectiveness of prevention programs has also proven difficult (Heller, Price, & Sher, 1980; Plaut, 1980; Swift, 1980).

Ketterer et al. (1980) contended that the premise underlying the traditional public health framework of prevention is that disorders can be prevented by identifying and then eliminating the specific factors causing the disorders. Bloom (1979) pointed out that this premise is more useful in the field of communicable or nutritional diseases than in the prevention of mental and behavioral disorders, which are generally recognized as being a consequence of multiple precipitating events. He further stated that all persons are variously vulnerable to stressful life events that might play such precipitating roles in mental disorder. Cassel (1976) expressed similar doubt that any given psychosocial process or stressor will prove etiologically specific for any mental disease. Rather, psychosocial stressors are believed to increase susceptibility to disease without leading to a specific, universally predictable disorder.

Although such stressful life events as disaster cannot be shown to have specific adverse outcomes, they are assumed to have pervasive though nonspecific adverse effects (Ketterer et al., 1980). This leads Bloom (1979) and Ryan (1971) to argue that it is necessary to move away from the idea of *prevention* in mental health, and shift toward the concept of mental health *promotion*. According to Ketterer et al., promoting mental health means enhancing the competencies and well-being of individuals and communities through the application of system-change efforts and person-centered efforts. In their model, mental health promotion strategies would include (1) modifying social policies, social systems, and environmental factors that impede the mental health and well-being of groups in the community, and (2) improving the well-being and strengths of normal and at-risk populations through competency training. Strategies for promoting these ends fall into the previously mentioned two-pronged typology of social action and interpersonal action and will be discussed in this chapter under the general category of prevention.

SPECIAL RISK FACTORS

Tableman (1980) contended that the crucial issue in prevention programming is not methodology, however important that may be, but is rather the definition and recruitment of high-risk populations. How one defines and accesses the population to be served will, in effect, determine whether efforts are targeted or diffuse, and whether those reached are actually at risk or merely willing participants. Generally, too little attention is paid to identification of the relevant characteristics of the population at risk (Tableman, 1980).

Heller et al. (1980) noted that the concept of a population or a group at risk is well accepted in the prevention literature. They defined a risk group as any group that, based on epidemiological evidence, shows a higher probability of developing psychological distress or disorder compared with the general population. Price, Bader, and Ketterer (1980) noted that a model of preventive programming targeting groups at risk is quite useful where specific diseases or other causal factors are easily identifiable. However, in the field of mental health, precise definitions and specific disease entities with known etiologies are the exception rather than the rule. Partly in response to these conceptual difficulties, new directions are being explored in the mental health arena.

Bloom (1979) described a shift of interest from *predisposing* factors to *precipitating* factors as causal agents in the development of psychological disorders. In other words, instead of attempting to identify an underlying precondition associated with a pattern of maladaptive behavior, researchers are beginning to focus more directly on stressful life events which appear capable of triggering patterns of maladaptive behavior in a proportion of the population that experiences those events (Bloom). Thus, a shift of attention from high-risk populations to high-risk situations has started (Dohrenwend & Dohrenwend, 1974; Price, 1974). Tableman (1980) expanded this concept by defining populations at risk as those people in situations that generate stress and deficits in physical and/or emotional resources over an extended period of time. The population at risk, therefore, is not one that is subjected to a single critical event, but is one that is likely to experience continuing stress or deprivation (Birch, 1974), as in a long recovery period following a disaster.

This section lists factors that research and practice have identified as placing individuals or groups at risk for severe or prolonged stress reactions or maladapative coping following a disaster. The factors include ones related to the *individual* and others related to the *situation*. It is hoped that an understanding of these factors can assist the mental health practitioner to identify those groups likely to be at risk in his or her own community.

Factors Related to the Individual

Myers (Hartsough & Myers, 1985), Cohen and Ahearn (1980), and Hoff (1984) suggest evaluating the following factors to determine whether an individual or group may be at risk.

Age and Developmental Phase. Skill level and life experience may be a risk factor, as in the case of children, who do not have the capacity to understand and rationalize what has happened and may not have the verbal ability to describe their experiences; or older adults, who might be physically or mentally impeded in their ability to reach out and use available resources.

Health. Poor health or recent ill health may place one at risk because of physical limitations, cumulative stress, or inability to obtain needed treatment or medications. Mentally ill persons, for example, may be at risk for decompensation if they fail to obtain needed medicine.

Disability. Impairment of mobility, sight, hearing, or speech may place one at risk of injury or at risk of not obtaining needed supplies for recovery.

Preexisting Stresses. Recent job change, financial worries, relocation, family problems, divorce, and so forth may place an individual at risk because of such factors as cumulative stress and impaired social support systems.

Previous Traumatic Life Events.   Successful outcomes may have helped individuals to develop coping strengths and survival skills. However, unsuccessful outcomes or emotional reactions that have not been worked through may leave individuals vulnerable to maladaptive coping and strong emotional reactions to the current stressors.

Strength of Social Support System.   Absence or loss of social and psychological support systems can place individuals at risk.

Coping Skills.   Poor coping skills or maladaptive coping efforts (such as excessive drinking) indicate an individual may be at risk.

Expectations of Self and Others.   Family members needing care, such as small children or relatives with health problems or disabilities, may add to a victim's stress. In addition, high self-expectations, as in the case of rescue workers, can put an individual at risk for a sense of failure and loss should efforts prove unsuccessful.

Status of Family Members.   If family members are separated at the time of disaster and an individual is unsure of their well-being, that individual may be at risk of severe stress and possible injury in attempts to locate them.

Ethnic and Cultural Milieu.   Language barriers may endanger individuals if they cannot understand evacuation orders, as well as interfere with their ability to obtain or use services or supplies. Recent immigration may leave an individual without family or social support.

Perception and Interpretation of the Event.   How an individual perceives an event will affect the level of stress experienced and the effectiveness of coping. For example, an individual who believes he or she was at fault in a situation may suffer from severe guilt and depression.

Factors Related to the Event

Certain characteristics of an event or disaster may make the situation highly stressful for the individuals experiencing it. Hartsough and Myers (1985) and Mitchell (1983) have cited the following factors as among the ones that might precipitate more severe anxiety or problems in recovery for survivors.

Lack of Warning.   With sufficient warning, individuals can prepare for a situation both physically and psychologically, and traumatic effects may be reduced. A disaster that strikes without warning produces the maximum social and psychological impact.

Abrupt Contrast of Scene.   An abrupt change of reality that is difficult to comprehend (for example, airplane debris and bodies raining down on a sunny, peaceful neighborhood) increases the trauma for persons experiencing it.

Type of Disaster. Technological disasters are often more stressful for victims and workers than natural disasters because of the belief that the event should have been prevented. Feelings of anger and blame are often difficult to work through and may increase, rather than decrease, over time.

Nature of the Destructive Agent. If the cause of the disaster is clearly perceived and well known (such as a river that floods every year), it is less psychologically disturbing than an agent that is invisible and whose effects are unknown or delayed (such as chemicals or radiation).

Degree of Uncertainty and Duration of Threat. Those disasters with a high degree of uncertainty regarding recurrence, additional damages, or outcome of rescue attempts are more traumatic than disasters with fairly predictable outcomes. For example, aftershocks following an earthquake make it difficult for survivors to define when the danger is over and often cause increasing anxiety over time.

Time of Occurrence. Disasters occurring at night may be more psychologically disturbing than ones occurring during the day, due to the inability to orient oneself to the scope and danger of the situation in the darkness.

Scope of the Event. The more damage, injuries, and deaths there are, the greater is the intensity of psychological impact.

Personal Loss or Injury. The *degree* of loss, such as injury to self; injury or death of loved ones; loss of a home, job, or items of meaning; and the *duration* of loss (whether short, long, or irreversible) are important factors.

Traumatic Stimuli. Such stimuli might include prolonged or extensive contact with dead or injured; loss of life following extraordinary or prolonged rescue efforts; death of babies or children; unusual or distressing sights, sounds, or smells; or a situation that presents serious physical or psychological threats to an individual, such as a hostage or terrorist situation.

Human Error. A situation that seemingly could have been prevented can generate emotional reactions making it difficult for victims to recover.

Lack of Opportunity for Effective Action. Such a situation (e.g., an event in which there are no survivors) may leave the ones affected by it with unrealistic but entrenched ideas and emotions that interfere with recovery ("If only I could have . . ."). *Survival guilt* is a common manifestation of this type of event.

Properties of the Postdisaster Environment. *Weather conditions* (such as exposure to heat, sunburn, cold, frostbite, rain); *hazards* (such as toxic substances; insect, animal, and snake bites; poison ivy or poison oak; communicable diseases; accidents; wounds; burns), *poor living conditions* (poor food, poor sleeping accommodations; lack of water for drinking, bathing, and sanitation; lack of privacy); and *frustrations* (lack of supplies and equipment; transportation and communication disruptions, etc.) add intense, prolonged, and cumulative stresses to victims trying to recovery.

Programming Issues Related to Risk Factors

The social action and interpersonal action approaches described in this chapter provide the mental health practitioner with the techniques necessary to work with various special risk groups. The *choice* of technique should be governed by the characteristics of the target group. For example, if targeting a group whose mobility is impaired (as with the frail elderly or persons with disabilities), aggressive outreach would be important both to assess needs and to provide services in the home. If targeting young children, the mental health practitioner could maximize scope and effectiveness by giving training and consultation to day-care providers and teachers. Providing them with techniques to assist young children in recovery and helping them to develop observation and referral skills would allow for early identification and treatment of problems. If targeting specific cultural or ethnic groups, techniques should be tailored to the appropriate cultural milieu and value system, and services should be made available in the individual's own language, preferably by workers of that cultural group. If targeting individuals particularly traumatized by the disaster or event, the practitioner might use outreach approaches such as letters, phone calls, or home visits to individuals identified through damage reports, newspaper or television accounts of the event, or lists of persons applying for assistance. Education and anticipatory guidance could help those traumatized individuals to prepare for what they might encounter in the postdisaster period; support groups might assist them in their recovery; and training and consultation to care givers might expand the scope of available assistance.

Tableman (1980) emphasized the importance, whenever possible, of attempting to access high-risk populations by systematically connecting with an established, ongoing service team—in the case of disaster, through the Red Cross shelter or service center, the Federal Emergency Management Agency (FEMA) Disaster Application Center, the school system, and so forth. This ensures that mental health prevention becomes an integral part of the ongoing service process to all disaster victims. Several available texts (e.g., American Red Cross, 1985; Farberow & Gordon, 1981; Hartsough & Myers, 1985; Lystad, 1985) provide detailed approaches for a variety of groups and situations.

SOCIAL ACTION APPROACHES TO PRIMARY PREVENTION

This section begins by expanding somewhat on the definition of social action presented earlier. Also called *environmental* interventions, these approaches are aimed at organizational, community, and societal target points (Jason, 1980). These macrolevel, system-change efforts seek to influence such things as policy, regulations, legislation, organization of services, community attitudes and behavior, and environmental factors which impede the mental and emotional well-being of groups in the community (Caplan, 1964; Jason; Ketterer et al., 1980). In other words, the mental health professional attempts, through techniques such as consultation and education, to influence the community and its leaders in such a way as to enlarge their view of the mental health aspects of the issues and problems with which they deal so that their decisions will be made with an increased awareness of consequences for the mental health of the population (Caplan), and with increased knowledge of appropriate mental health approaches to the problems.

The goals of social action approaches to primary prevention in disaster, based upon a modification of Caplan's (1964) typology include: (1) attenuation of hazardous circumstances; (2) provision of basic physical, psychosocial, and sociocultural supplies; and (3) fostering of healthy crisis coping.

Social Action to Influence Attentuation of Hazardous Circumstances

By Caplan's (1964) definition, a *hazard* constitutes a situation of challenge in which there may be a loss of basic supplies. Such hazards may occur predictably, in the form of life cycle developmental crises, or accidentally, as in the form of an emergency or disaster. In the context of disaster, a hazard might be an actual physical danger, such as flooding or mudslides, or it might be a situation in the aftermath of disaster that could cause a crisis or the victimization of an individual (such as loss of employment due to postdisaster conditions).

The goal of the mental health practitioner in attenuation of hazardous circumstances is to identify commonly occurring hazards in the community and modify them so that their impact on individuals is less severe. Atlhough such hazards cannot always be eliminated, persons at risk may be helped to develop healthy, adaptive ways of handling them. The practitioner seeks to examine the circumstances that precipitated the crises and to determine whether certain elements in the situation can be modified to prevent the crises or to make them easier for people to master (Caplan, 1964). For example, a practitioner concerned about the isolation of recently widowed elderly persons might work with churches, funeral parlors, and the coroner's office to establish an outreach program for contacting the bereaved, providing information about the grief process, offering counseling or support groups, establishing a foster grandparents program to combat isolation, and so forth.

Mitigation of Physical Hazards

In the arena of prevention in disaster, attenuation of hazardous circumstances should logically begin with the mitigation of phsyical hazards to the health of the community. This might involve legislation, community planning, public education, and the like to protect life and property. Examples might include ordinances requiring smoke detectors and sprinkler systems to prevent loss of life and property from fire, or laws such as California's Field Act requiring schools to be built to certain structural standards for earthquake safety. Although such mitigation policies are ordinarily in the jurisidiction of elected representatives, building and fire officials, city planners, and the like, involvement in such social action efforts can be a cathartic and adaptive way for survivors to work through some of their feelings of loss and helplessness following a disaster, while at the same time contributing to the rebuilding and improvement of the community. Such planning and social action efforts are logically of interest to mental health practitioners who wish to contribute to community safety and the recovery of victims. The role of a mental health practitioner in such activities might include encouragement of survivors' participation in community efforts, testimony at hearings on proposed ordinances or legislation, or provision of consultation to community officials on the mental health aspects of disaster recovery.

Such preventive actions are of particular importance in the realm of human-caused disasters. Studies of communities such as Buffalo Creek (Erikson, 1977; Hoff, 1984; Lifton & Olson, 1976; Stern, 1976) and Love Canal (Gibbs, 1982; Hoff), which were virtually destroyed by events of human origin have shown that the psychological effects on survivors are tremendously different from those occurring in a natural disaster. Similar effects have been observed among survivors of Hiroshima and the Nazi Holocaust (Lifton, 1967). Even though the mining company responsible for the Buffalo Creek dam collapse and flood was forced to pay 13.5 million dollars in a psychic damage suit, Buffalo Creek residents seemed to feel that they and their community would never be healed (Hoff). In Love Canal, considering the genetic, health, and material damage suffered by residents, monetary compensation became practically meaningless (Hoff). Nothing can repair such losses. *Prevention* and *learning* from such tragic error and neglect seem the only reasonable response (Hoff).

Prevention of Victimization

Also falling under the category of attenuation of hazardous circumstances is the identification of groups of individuals who may have survived a disaster unharmed but who might become victimized by postdisaster conditions or situations. For example, several researchers have suggested that, during the recovery phase of disaster, the elderly tend to be slower in responding to the full extent of their losses (Dynes, 1970; Friedsam, 1962; Kiljanek & Drabek, 1979; Lang & Lang, 1964; Moore, 1958). Evans (personal interview, 1975) and Bell (1976) have documented that insurance and reconstruction problems may be dealt with later by older victims than by younger victims. Such delay on the part of older victims has, in numerous instances, caused them unknowingly to miss deadlines in applying for financial assistance. Indeed, research has shown that, as a group, the elderly are frequently reluctant to utilize disaster relief and insurance resources, even in cases of obvious need, based on a strong value of independence or a desire to avoid utilization of what they may perceive as welfare (Bell; Bolin, 1975; Huerta & Horton, 1979; Poulshock & Cohen, 1975). Such underutilization of financial resources could well serve to undermine the health, self-sufficiency, and independent living of an elderly person who, because of limited funds and physical incapabilities, might be unable to restore his or her home to a habitable condition.

Mental health professionals, aware of such practices on the part of the elderly following a disaster, could help to prevent possible deterioration of older citizens' conditions by providing training and consultation to disaster relief agencies, insurance companies, and other personnel who come in contact with the elderly, encouraging them to develop policies and practices to combat this underutilization of benefits (for example, by making thorough explanations of benefits, both verbally and in writing, and by explaining benefits in such a way that the elderly clearly understand that these are not welfare, but have been purchased by their tax dollars or insurance premiums over the years).

In the northern California winter storms of 1982, a similar dynamic was found to exist among the elderly (Grooh, personal communication, July, 1982). Public health nurses and gerontological mental health nurses found that elderly persons frequently underreported physical health problems or concerns following the disaster, for fear of hospitalization or admission to a convalescent facility. This underreporting of health problems frequently resulted in a worsening of such problems under the stresses of the disaster situation, with some elderly persons actually coming to require the hospitalization they so feared. Armed with an understanding of this dynamic, several communities instituted door-to-door outreach programs to seek out the elderly and to assess and assist them with their needs.

Disaster Planning

Mental health staff have an important role to play in the attenuation of hazardous situations by educating emergency planners and public officials about the reality of human response to emergency situations. A tremendous mythology exists regarding human behavior in disaster. For example, a common misperception is that panic and looting are common occurrences following a disaster. *Accurate* information, in this case, that panic and looting are extremely rare in natural disasters, can help planners and responders to base their action plans for deployment of staff and materials on a more realistic prediction of what may be needed.

A difficult issue for prevention personnel respecting disaster is confronting a community's *denial* that disaster could affect them. Because disaster is so dreaded, people deny its likelihood even when living in high-risk areas. However, confronting this denial is central to preventing victimization by natural disaster (Hoff, 1984). Mental health practitioners can be helpful to disaster planners and officials by providing consultation on how to deal with such issues.

For example, denial may significantly contribute to citizens' reluctance to evacuate an area, even in the face of imminent danger. People tend to normalize a frightening situation in order to minimize its terror and make it seem manageable, as in the case of individuals hearing a tornado but thinking it to be a train, even though the neighborhood has no train tracks (Farberow & Gordon, 1979). Knowledge of these phenomena can assist emergency officials in giving warnings that will be effective. Warnings must be clear, consistent, specific, and given by a person with authority and credibility, leaving no loopholes for disbelief. They must be given repeatedly and must be followed by instructions of what to *do,* as warnings followed by long silences and no action plan can heighten anxiety and lead to further denial (Hoff, 1984). If such actions still do not mobilize individuals, emergency officials may need to escalate tactics to combat denial, for example, by asking residents refusing to evacuate for the names and addresses of their next of kin.

Public Education for Disaster Preparedness

Educating the public to be prepared for disaster is a difficult task. It is impossible to plan for disaster as one would for transition states such as marriage, parenthood, or retirement. In addition, the previously discussed mechanism of denial may be at play. However, preparation on a community-wide scale before disaster strikes may reduce the impact of disaster trauma and equip people with personal tools for living through the experience with less physical, social, and emotional damage than they might otherwise suffer (Hoff, 1984). Mental health practitioners can be helpful to disaster educators in developing approaches to overcome such denial.

Mental health staff working with preparedness educators in Marin County, California, have found the following approaches to be useful in combating the denial and disinterest about disaster preparedness prevalent in the general population.

1. *Timing of Preparedness Education.* Ideally, preparedness training should occur *before* an emergency happens. Frequently, however, citizens are most eager for information of this type *following* an incident or disaster. Public service announcements, talk shows on radio and television, newspaper articles, informational fliers in public places, classes and workshops should take advantage of incidents which heighten public interest in preparedness. Certain seasons of the year may heighten public interest, such as the return of the tornado or hurricane season after a previous year of severe storms.

2. *Frequency and Consistency of Preparedness Messages.* As discussed in the previous section on warnings, public education messages must be frequent and consistent, must be given by people with credibility and authority, and must provide specific information about what to do in a given situation. The more simple and straightforward they are, the more likely it is that they will be remembered in time of need.

3. *Relevance of Preparedness Messages.* Messages are more likely to get through to people if they have some significance for daily life, rather

than focusing on highly unlikely circumstances. For example, single family fires are one of the most common disasters in the United States. Public service announcements on making a family escape plan are relevant to every family, while at the same time teaching principles of escape that might also be used in a more unusual situation.

4. *Impact of Preparedness Messages.* Mental health staff working with volunteer neighborhood organizers for disaster preparedness have found that certain approaches cut through denial and motivate people to prepare. Volunteers report that one must find out what things are most important to people and use those things to motivate them. Things that seem to motivate people most include concern for the safety of loved ones, especially children; concern for protecting their homes; concern for pets; and concern for protecting family keepsakes, mementos, photographs, and other irreplaceable objects.

In a community that has had prior disaster experience, *fear* is often listed as a primary motivation for people to attend preparedness workshops—fear of recurrence of the disaster and of not knowing what to do to protect oneself and loved ones. A balance must be struck, however, in using fear as a motivational factor. Raising some anxiety will get people's attention; too much may tip the scale into denial. Neighborhoods who developed disaster preparedness networks as part of the San Anselmo, California, Disaster Preparedness Project often adopted such slogans as "Preparedness Prevents Panic" and "Prepare, Not Scare," thus addressing people's fear and suggesting preparedness as the logical antidote (Stawowy, personal communication, January, 1983).

Mental health staff have important knowledge about human responses to disaster that can help disaster educators make their material factual and effective. For example, mental health staff involved in counseling disaster victims know the grief that victims experience over losses. Loss of life and property are the obvious targets of disaster preparedness programs. Mental health counselors, however, also know the grief that victims experience with the loss of such things as pets, photos, and mementos. As a result of mental health consultation, many preparedness classes now include such topics as safety plans for pets and protection of irreplaceable items, in an attempt to prevent such emotionally significant losses.

Preparedness curricula that include factual information on human reactions in disaster can be important in helping citizens to have realistic expectations of themselves and others should disaster occur, providing a form of emotional inoculation. Mental health staff can provide this input by consultation to trainers or by teaching this part of disaster preparedness curricula themselves. Topics might include myths and realities of human behavior in disaster; common emotional reactions to disaster; phases of emotional reactions; simple techniques of psychological first aid or crisis intervention, including when and how to refer to mental health professionals; and helpful and unhelpful styles of relating to victims. Such information can actually contribute to the safety and well-being of individuals following a disaster. It is important, for example, to know that one's concentration, perceptions, and cognitive abilities may be impaired immediately following impact. Such knowledge can assist one in slowing down and taking special care to avoid hazards and prevent injury. Citizens have reported that it is useful and reassuring to know that certain behaviors, such as panic and looting, are not common occurrences after disaster and that people generally respond in adaptive, helpful, and creative ways.

Mental health staff can advise preparedness educators to stress the importance of *practicing* home-preparedness plans in the form of drills. The importance of this practice is based upon the psychological knowledge that people operate in certain consistent patterns, and when faced with situations calling for immediate problem-solving and minimal delay, they will revert to habitual mechanisms and reactions (Caplan, 1964). The more ingrained survival behavior becomes, the more effectively it will be used in time of emergency.

Studies indicate that living under the fear of recurrence is a major stressor to disaster victims (Leik, 1982). In addition to reducing anxiety and increasing individuals' confidence in dealing with future emergencies (Garaventa, 1983b), education regarding actions to be taken in an emergency can directly contribute to more effective and appropriate actions by individuals, helping them to protect their safety and prevent victimization. Knowing what to expect and what to do in time of emergency can alleviate apprehension and help individuals to think more clearly and channel energy in more constructive directions, thus increasing the likelihood of their taking correct actions to help themselves and others (Moir, 1980).

Community Organization

Community organization is a method of social action in which individuals and groups in the community are brought together to function as an integrated unit. The community or neighborhood becomes involved in identifying its needs or objectives, finding resources to deal with them, and taking action to bring about desired changes (Ross, 1967; Taillie, 1969). The process can bring together unaffiliated people and increase a sense of community and environmental mastery (Taillie). Thus, both the *product,* or outcome, and the *process* of community organization take on importance with respect to mental health (Dumont, 1968).

As a method of predisaster planning to mitigate hazardous circumstances, community organization can be used to develop neighborhood disaster-preparedness teams. Such teams are being extensively developed in California as an approach to preparing for earthquakes. Based upon a model similar to neighborhood watch programs for crime prevention, such disaster networks bring neighbors together in an attempt to identify and mitigate actual hazards in the neighborhood. In addition, neighbors get to know one another and their respective skills, becoming in that process a support system and potential action team that can lead to more effective action and that can help to reduce injury, loss of property, and further victimization of citizens following an emergency (Garaventa, Martin, & Scremin, 1984).

Such a program is based upon the belief that there is generally a host of resources (tools, equipment, etc.) and skills (first aid, carpentry, fire fighting, etc.) in most neighborhoods to meet the immediate needs of individuals during the first few hours or days of an emergency. A predetermined inventory of those resources can prepare people to help each other in the confusion of an emergency situation. Such a neighborhood organization can also provide a way to identify children or homebound citizens who may need assistance in time of emergency, as well as people in the area who could care for them. Such a neighborhood plan can identify where residents would obtain food, water, and shelter if they had to evacuate. It can also identify alternative methods of communicating important information to emergency personnel if phones are inoperative and roads are impassable (e.g., runners, horseback riders, bicycles). Some neighborhood groups have shared maps of each house's utility turnoffs so that neighbors can turn off utilities, if needed, to protect the neighborhood from fire.

Groups that have organized around emergency preparedness have reported a marked increase in individuals' sense of well-being, confidence in their ability to perform effectively in an emergency, and sense of support and teamwork among neighbors. Many groups reported having used their neighborhood networks successfully in minor emergencies. Groups have consistently reported their satisfaction in getting to know their neighbors and have often expanded their scope to work together on a variety of other neighborhood concerns (Garaventa et al., 1984).

In addition to the trauma sustained by *individuals, communities* themselves are traumatized by disaster. Erikson (1977) describes collective trauma as a "blow to the tissues of social life that damages the bonds linking people together and impairs the prevailing sense of community." The degree of social disorganization and its duration following a disaster are major stressors that affect individuals' recovery. An equally important factor in the recovery process is the presence and strength of an individual's support network (Cohen & Ahearn, 1980). Neighborhood disaster preparedness networks can potentially prevent some of the postdisaster social disorganization described by Erikson, or at least decrease its extent and duration. In addition, such groups, postdisaster, can provide some of the ongoing social support essential to the emotional/psychological recovery of individuals and the community (Garaventa, 1983b).

The role of the mental health professional in such community organization efforts may range from providing consultation to disaster-preparedness groups (such as the Red Cross, or the local Office of Emergency Services) to actually becoming involved in the community organization process, helping citizens to set up meetings, facilitating group process, providing technical information, and participating in related activities. In Marin and San Mateo counties in California, mental health staff have utilized community organization for disaster preparedness as a specific mental health social action intervention to assist disaster-affected communities in their recovery (Garaventa, 1983a; O'Callahan, 1983a).

Social Action to Influence Provision of Basic Supplies

Caplan's (1964) conceptual model of primary prevention bases itself on the assumption that, in order not to become mentally disordered, a person needs continual supplies commensurate with his or her current stage of growth and development. These supplies are roughly classified into three groups: *physical, psychosocial,* and *sociocultural.* The categorization of these conditions of mental health is somewhat arbitrary, and the three sets of factors are inextricably woven together. The goal of the mental health specialist is to influence the policies of organizations, agencies, and the like to foster the provision of these supplies and counteract influences that interfere with their adequate delivery.

Physical Supplies

These include food, shelter, opportunity for exercise, sensory stimulation, and the like, that are necessary for bodily growth and development and for the maintenance of health and protection from bodily damage. Referring to the American Red Cross (1978) definition, disaster creates human needs that the victims cannot alleviate without assistance. Such things as food, clothing, shelter, utilities, and medical supplies and equipment may be damaged or lost through destruction of homes, stores, warehouses, hospitals, utility lines, and transportation routes. In addition, families may be without money to purchase what is needed. Such physical needs are also important on psychological, emotional, and symbolic levels. Dry clothes, safe shelter, and a hot drink or meal can provide an important sense of comfort and safety to someone coming in from a storm, immediately beginning to restore a sense of security and order to an environment that has been shattered.

The provision of physical supplies in time of disaster is accomplished by a variety of disaster relief organizations, both formal and informal, including the Red Cross, Salvation Army, church groups, and voluntary organizations that exist in the community or may develop in time of disaster. Mental health staff may assist in provision of supplies in a variety of ways. First, local mental health professionals have a knowledge of the community that disaster relief agencies, who often come from outside the area, may not have. Mental health staff can provide valuable orientation and consultation to such agencies regarding where to set up operations and how to overcome barriers or resistance to using services. In addition, mental health professionals can work directly with citizen groups who might need assistance but be reluctant to seek it, as with the elderly who traditionally underutilize disaster relief and insurance.

In addition, mental health specialists can provide program-centered consultation to disaster relief agencies regarding certain health and mental health aspects of physical supplies. For example, stress and the physical strain of disaster place added demands on the body, thus increasing the importance of good nutrition. While an ideal diet may not be available in the early days of a disaster operation, it will be important in the long run, and mental health staff with a background in nutrition can assist food providers in disaster to provide a diet that will assist victims and workers alike to withstand the stresses and demands of the situation. Examples might include substitution of fruit and high-protein snacks for doughnuts and cookies; or the substitution of decaffeinated coffee, tea, and other beverages for coffee and caffeinated soft drinks, which can increase anxiety and interfere with sleep (Hartsough & Myers, 1985). Exercise can help to ameliorate some of the psychological stresses involved in disaster and can help to maintain the good physical condition necessary to meet the physical demands and endurance required for recovery. Mental health staff can work with relief officials to ensure some physical exercise programs for victims in shelters, as well as for disaster workers.

The physical layout and ambience of shelter accommodations are also important aspects of physical supplies. Temporary mass care shelters are usually chaotic at best, due to the large numbers of distraught people brought together in such large places as school auditoriums and recreation halls. However, mental health staff can consult with relief staff to assure that families are not separated, that areas are established to allow privacy as well as interaction, and that noise, lighting, and temperature are controlled in such ways as to increase comfort. The physical properties of both the work and living environments of disaster workers are equally important.

Psychosocial Supplies

Psychosocial supplies include the stimulation of a person's cognitive and affective development through personal interaction with significant others in the family and with other persons in school, church, work, and other places of interchange. In other words, this area of supplies entails "satisfaction of interpersonal needs" (Caplan, 1964). For the purpose of this discussion, psychosocial supplies will also include those activities or opportunities that assist individuals in working through the psychological aspects of their recovery. A working list of psychosocial supplies might include three main areas: (1) needs for exchange of love and affection, (2) needs for limitation and control, and (3) needs for participation in joint activity. According to Caplan, resistance to mental disorder is dependent on the continuity and health of relationships. He also emphasizes that the most important psychosocial supplies are provided through relationships in the family, and a major aim of primary prevention is the safeguarding of family integrity.

With regard to psychosocial supplies, mental health staff may seek to influence a number of policies related to disaster response and recovery. For example, during severe flooding in Holland, child psychiatrists persuaded the government to refuse the hospitable offers of surrounding countries to provide sanctuary for children whose homes had been destroyed, because this would have separated them from their families during a period of major stress (Caplan, 1964).

Mental health staff can also assist those organizations and agencies that work with survivors. The importance of keeping families together in shelters has already been noted as one example. When families must be separated during the day, as when adults must go about the business of applying for financial aid or cleaning up damaged property, care for children is important so that children have a secure and predictable environment and interaction with caring adults. Mental health staff can assist or consult in the development of child-care services in shelters or at other sites. As a matter of policy, child-care staff and parents can be provided with information on dealing with children's separation anxieties when parents leave (for example, reassuring children about their parents' return).

An important psychosocial need for disaster victims in the early postdisaster phase is to obtain news about what has happened to people they know and to the community. This phase is often called *inventory* (Farberow & Gordon, 1979) and is the beginning of reorientation after a tremendously disruptive event. Mental health staff can encourage disaster personnel to help victims in this process by providing such things as clocks, television and radio, newspapers, bulletin boards, and maps (detailing damages, road conditions, and medical and disaster relief sites) in shelters or other sites where victims congregate. Such items assist victims in obtaining needed information, reestablishing a sense of orientation, and establishing contact with friends, neighbors, and needed resources.

Mental health professionals can also seek to influence shelter staff to provide victims with items and opportunities to help them begin to work through their feelings from the disaster. For young children, this means the opportunity for play reenactment of their experiences (Lystad, 1985). Elaborate toys are not necessary. Crayons and paper can allow children to draw pictures, and adults can encourage children with adequate verbal skills to tell stories about their experiences. A sandbox, shovels, and water can allow children to play out their experiences from a flood. Children can be encouraged to make up disaster games in which they set the rules and develop outcomes that can allow them to develop feelings of mastery over events.

Adults begin to deal with their feelings by talking about them. Mental health staff can work with disaster personnel to assure that opportunities exist for such conversations. Adults can be provided with a social corner for snacks and conversation with other victims or with volunteers. Mental health professionals may provide training for volunteers to assist them in their interactions with victims. Mental health workers can help to establish recreation activities, such as skits, which can be therapeutic to people of all ages, victims and workers alike. In one crowded shelter, following a flood and mudslide, survivors had not bathed for several days due to destruction of the town's water system. They were tired, irritable, and dirty. During the day, while adults were at work digging out homes and clearing debris, shelter workers suggested that children and teens prepare a skit for evening entertainment. The young people presented an "evening news program" with accurate but satirical reporting of events that had occurred in the disaster. A commercial parodying a popular shampoo advertisement brought out three pert but grungy teenage girls, attempting to fluff up their dirty hair and saying, "We used to have bouncin' and behavin' hair. . . ." The laughter of the group was one of the most therapeutic events of the day.

Mental health professionals can seek to influence disaster relief agencies to establish policies for relocation and housing of victims that assure basic psychosocial supplies are being met. A particularly traumatic relocation occurred following the Buffalo Creek Flood when survivors from previously close-knit hollows were relocated in newly built temporary housing among people from other hollows and families with whom they had nothing in common. Social networks were disregarded, and people found themselves without the social support systems that could have been so important to their recovery (Erikson, 1977). Such neighborhood and family ties, should, whenever possible, be considered in relocation of survivors. In addition, people can be assisted in recovery from their trauma if they are not relocated to an area that is reminiscent of the disaster scenario (e.g., not housing people on a creekbank following a flood, nor on a windy hilltop following a tornado). Mental health consultation can help disaster relief agencies to make their relocations with understanding and sensitivity to the psychological needs of victims.

Mental health staff can also consult with and seek to influence policies of disaster agencies with regard to disaster workers' psychosocial needs. As already mentioned, nutrition, opportunity for exercise, recreation, and rest are important. So are reasonably adequate living arrangements that allow workers the opportunity for privacy as well as for letting down their hair and relaxing with co-workers.

The atmosphere of the working sites is also important to workers' relationships with both co-workers and clients. For example, one Red Cross supervisor visited a disaster site in which an extremely small room held approximately 15 staff members. He learned from the family service officer that she had to work beneath a table, taking her phone there so that she could hear what the person on the other end of the line was saying. Although this is amusing at one level, it is an example of a situation that can lead not only to stress for the worker, but also to difficulty in relationships with co-workers and clients (Eby, 1985).

Mental health staff can remind disaster workers of the importance of maintaining and using their social support networks, both during and after the disaster operation. For example, disaster workers can be reminded of the importance of maintaining contact with family while they are away on a disaster assignment. Taking along family photographs, calling home often, and, if possible, having family members visit or volunteer at the disaster site can help to maintain family ties to bridge the gap between the disaster assignment and home (Hartsough & Myers, 1985; O'Callahan, 1983b). In addition, mental health staff can encourage the establishment of routine debriefing sessions for workers following a traumatic event or disaster operation. Debriefings are possibly one of the most helpful preventive interventions for personnel, helping them to work through their experiences and to prevent deleterious, stress-related aftereffects. The debriefing of a group of workers can further strengthen the peer support system among the group. Mental health staff can assist agencies to set up debriefing programs for their workers and may in fact perform the actual debriefing services (Hartsough & Myers; Mitchell, 1983).

As the community recovers, mental health staff can seek to influence school policies and practices to ensure provision of basic psychosocial supplies for children. Consultation, training of school personnel, and provision of brochures and manuals can assist school personnel in recognizing and providing for needs of school-age children and adolescents. Such educational materials for school personnel were prepared and disseminated by mental health personnel in the Marin, San Mateo, and Santa Cruz counties of California following the northern California winter storms of 1982. Handouts included "Reactions of Children to Disaster"; "Classroom Activities," to help children work through their experiences; "Taking Care of Yourselves and Each Other," to help teachers avoid burnout; and "When to Refer to Mental Health Professionals" (Garaventa, 1983a; Lystad, 1985; O'Callahan, 1983a; Peuler, 1983). School staff reported the activities to be extremely helpful in assisting children with their disaster recovery.

Similar outreach and education materials can be developed by mental health staff and disseminated to the general community. Such public information efforts are helpful in provision of psychosocial supplies by emphasizing the importance of maintaining and using social support systems. Such outreach materials emphasize family and friendships, problems that occur in relationships, and other things that might prove helpful (Lystad, 1985).

Sociocultural Supplies

Sociocultural supplies include those influences on personality development and functioning that are exerted by the customs and values of the culture and social structure. The culture of one's group, as embodied in language, values, and traditions, establishes an individual's place in society and influences one's path in life. The more stable the society, the more likely it is to provide an individual with perceptual tools, problem-solving skills, and a set of values to deal with life's difficulties. Societies in transition, on the other hand, may not provide the individual with well-developed ways of handling new problems, and individuals may be compelled to rely solely on individual resources (Caplan, 1964).

A community affected by a disaster is, in itself, a society in transition, and community members may not have prior history with such an event to guide them through their recovery. Mental health staff, equipped with knowledge of the values and problem-solving approaches that have assisted other communities to survive and rebuild, may be in a position to share those traditions and techniques for survival with agencies and groups helping the community to recover. In Santa Cruz County, California, following devastating mudslides in 1982, mental health staff worked with community recovery groups to create rituals to help deal with losses and to celebrate accomplishments. Seven months after a mudslide took the life of her husband, one recovery group member held a memorial service for him attended by group members and mental health facilitators. There was a reading, the scattering of the ashes, and a picnic. It was a moving experience for all who were present. Groups also established farewell rites for homes and animals lost. There was a homecoming party for the first family able to return to their home, and a potluck dinner was held on the first anniversary of the storm. All of these activities were reported as helpful to victims in achieving some closeure on their disaster experiences and helping them to prepare to take the next steps in getting on with their lives (Peuler, 1983).

The existing customs and values of a community experiencing disaster must be understood in order to assure provision of sociocultural supplies. Mental health professionals seeking to prevent deleterious mental health consequences following disaster may be in an important position to affect legislation, policies, and community attitudes by promoting an understanding of the importance of these customs and values to disaster recovery. This is of vital consequence in dealing with a community with a multiethnic population. In determining policies and practices toward disaster recovery, it is useful to consider the following issues about the population groups one is seeking to serve, and to evaluate whether disaster assistance approaches fit with the cultural customs and values (Garaventa, 1984; Romero, 1983).

1. Acculturation level of the group within the community (i.e., recent immigrants, 1st, 2nd, or 3rd generation?)
2. Immigration experience (i.e., Was it traumatic? Did it entail losses? Did family and friends immigrate? Are they nearby?)
3. Relationship/experience of population group with respect to agencies or government (i.e., legal immigration status, trust, fear)
4. Language fluency
5. Social class
6. Economic status before and after disaster
7. Importance of family and family roles (i.e., father, mother, children, grandparents, extended family)

8. Concrete and symbolic meaning of role disruption (e.g., father's loss of job and status as breadwinner)
9. Customs and values relating to age
10. Importance of work
11. Importance of education/school
12. Orientation to time, daily schedules and habits
13. Role of religion or belief system, including:
    a. Fate, causality, responsibility, guilt, punishment, forgiveness
    b. Importance of symbols of faith, mementos
    c. Importance of rituals
    d. Traditions of death and mourning
14. Definition and importance of community, social networks
15. Definition and role of helpers (i.e., religious personnel, folk healers, agencies)
16. Concept of boundaries (e.g., keeping of problems within the family)

In multicultural communities, it can be most useful to have representation from various ethnic groups on citizens' advisory boards for agencies assisting in disaster relief. In addition, cultural awareness training for workers providing services is essential. Mental health staff, knowing the importance of such cultural understanding, should seek to influence practices in this direction.

Social Action to Foster Healthy Crisis Coping

Caplan (1964) contends that the outcome of a crisis is influenced by the help or hindrance an individual receives from a variety of sources, including family, friends, and both informal and professional care givers. Primary prevention programs seek to influence these care givers positively in a direction toward assisting individuals with crisis coping. In order for professional workers to help a person in crisis, it is necessary for them to understand the nature of crisis reactions and to have the skills to help the individual. In addition, the agency or care giver must be able to respond to the crisis in a timely and appropriate manner.

The provision of professional services can be considered in four categories: (1) *education and training of workers* and (2) *organization and delivery of services*. In seeking to influence informal care givers or the individual in crisis, the mental health professional will use techniques of (3) *public education* and (4) *assistance to natural support systems*. The mental health professional concerned with primary prevention in disaster will find all four approaches helpful in influencing systems to provide better assistance for disaster victims in their recovery.

Education and Training of Workers

Mental health staff may encourage helping groups and agencies such as the Red Cross, Salvation Army, local social services, public health agencies, or police, fire, and emergency medical departments to train their staffs in understanding reactions of disaster victims and in providing effective approaches for dealing with victims within the scope of their organizational responsibilities. Mental health professionals may actually develop and provide such training to professional groups. The format might include workshops or seminars, professional papers, or brochures sent to groups of individuals such as physicians or clergy. Topics might include myths and realities of behavior in disaster; human response in various phases of disaster; major stressors and basic themes of recovery; stress symptoms; appropriate ways of relating to victims; crisis intervention techniques; when and how to refer to mental health professionals; and specific issues of particular groups, such as older adults, children, and specific ethnic groups. The National Institute of Mental Health has developed the *Training Manual for Human Service Workers in Major Disasters* (Farberow & Gordon, 1979), which provides an excellent format for training helpers.

Organization and Delivery of Services

In addition to having the understanding and skills to assist disaster victims, the worker must be available and able to respond in a helpful way to persons who need assistance. Mental health staff can assist this process by providing consultation and system-change interventions to care-giving agencies in an effort to create more responsive organizations (Ketterer et al., 1980). The mental health professional may serve as a *process* consultant, to help the organization become aware of organizational processes that may help or hinder service delivery (Schein, 1969), or may serve as a *program* consultant (Ketterer et al.), providing technical assistance on issues such as administrative structure; policies and procedures; methods of service delivery; recruitment, training, and utilization of staff; and establishment of linkages with other agencies.

The mental health professional who attempts to influence community agencies to provide help for people in crisis cannot be content with stimulating existing agencies to change their policies. He or she must also survey the community to see whether any major categories of crisis recovery fall outside the sphere of current agency operations (Caplan, 1964). In other words, the mental health professional may become involved in program development. In some locales, for example, mental health services may be insufficient to provide the needed services following a disaster. Staff may need to seek additional funding to establish a disaster crisis counseling program to provide the scope and depth of mental health services necessary to assist the community with recovery. Immediate emergency funds are available in the form of 2-month grants funded and administered by the Federal

Emergency Management Agency (FEMA). More long-term funding for mental health disaster recovery projects is available in the form of 9-month grants, funded by FEMA and reviewed and administered by the National Institute of Mental Health (Lystad, personal communication, Feb. 9, 1988). In addition, mental health staff may bring together mental health practitioners in private practice to form a coalition of service providers who, after special training in disaster counseling techniques, could provide services to disaster victims.

Public Education

Social action aimed at improving the help offered to persons in crisis by family members, friends, and informal care givers of the community is more difficult to plan than that which focuses on professional workers, in part because the former are not organized into structured groups that can be located and influenced easily. By and large, the most effective way open to community-wide effect is by public education through the mass media and by group education conducted by mental health specialists (Caplan, 1964). Topics of such public education efforts might include such things as normal psychological reactions to disaster; techniques for helping individuals to cope with disaster; causes for concern; and the availability of professional mental health assistance in case of need. Effective methods of dissemination include the mass media—newspapers, radio, and television—using such approaches as Public Service Announcements (PSAs), interviews with disaster victims or professionals, or talk shows; fliers or brochures posted on bulletin boards in laundromats, post offices, medical centers, relief centers, and so forth; articles in church bulletins; fliers inserted in bags in food or liquor stores; letters sent home with schoolchildren; inserts included in utility bills; or a speakers' bureau to address school classes, service organizations, and the like.

Programs of public education to help with crisis coping can also focus directly on the individual victims themselves, by preparing them ahead of time to develop healthy approaches to problem solving (Caplan, 1964). Such education could include disaster-preparedness content already discussed. Public education may also include the information developed for informal caretakers on such topics as normal reactions to disaster, things that may help the individual to cope, and methods of seeking professional assistance.

Assistance to Natural Support Systems

Mental health staff can, as previously noted, assist in the development of natural support systems within the community through the process of community organization. The goals of these community groups may be concrete (such as physically rebuilding the neighborhood after disaster) or emotional (such as assisting victims in emotional aspects of recovery). Mental health staff may also provide consultation to existing support systems, such as extended families, neighborhood groups, homeowners' associations, church organizations, and social clubs. These natural support systems can assist victims by passing along information, offering material help, or providing emotional support (Hartsough & Myers, 1985).

The health implications of these exchanges are especially important during crises, as more and more evidence demonstrates that people's relationships with spouses, family, friends, colleagues, co-workers, and neighbors can buffer stress and have a positive effect on crisis outcome (California Department of Mental Health, 1981). Research with disaster victims shows the importance of social support systems to their recovery, and health education literature for victims emphasizes the importance of maintaining and using these supportive relationships (Hartsough & Myers, 1985).

INTERPERSONAL ACTION APPROACHES TO PRIMARY PREVENTION

Interpersonal action approaches to primary prevention entail face-to-face interaction between a mental health professional and an individual or small group. Although the focus of the specific intervention is the individual, the overall strategy is directed toward a community-wide problem. This strategy is manifested by the choice of the individuals who are made the targets of intervention (Caplan, 1964). In the case of a mental health prevention program for disaster, such targets may be individuals at risk for deleterious effects of disaster or key members of the community, who in turn affect the mental health of many others. Targeting key community members will maximize the range of the mental health specialist's reach, especially in time of high demand for mental health services (e.g., postdisaster).

Interpersonal action aimed at individuals or key community leaders undoubtedly holds the potential to alter community attitudes and behaviors. In this respect, interpersonal action overlaps into the category of social action. Likewise, social action will undoubtedly involve the mental health specialist in face-to-face interventions with individuals and small groups, overlapping into interpersonal action. Thus, the two categories are not mutually exclusive; often the two categories may simply be different ways of looking at the same situation or process (Caplan, 1964). The goals of interpersonal action are therefore much the same as those of social action: (1) attenuation of hazardous circumstances, (2) provision of basic supplies, and (3) fostering of healthy coping in time of crisis.

Interpersonal Action to Influence Attenuation of Hazardous Circumstances

Hazards to be attenuated might be either physical hazards or situations in the aftermath of disaster that could cause a crisis or the victimization of an individual.

With regard to physical hazards, disaster victims will frequently express a wide range of anxieties related to recurrences of the disaster or to future emergencies. Such anxieties frequently revolve around feelings of lack of control and inability to protect oneself and one's family. Thus, mental health staff counseling disaster victims have frequently found that helping families to develop emergency plans becomes a specific technique in individual or group counseling (Garaventa, 1983a; O'Callahan, 1983a; Peuler, 1983).

In the same light, individual or group counseling may incorporate techniques of anticipatory guidance to help victims prepare for or deal with situations that could cause further victimization. For example, families may find it helpful to be forewarned about the emotional stages through which they may pass during the aftermath of disaster. Advanced warning about fatigue, irritability, and family stress, with suggestions for approaches to mitigating those stressors, can help to prevent a breakdown in communication or a rupture in family relationships. Handouts for families covering these topics may also be useful (Lystad, 1985).

Such guidance may also be part of face-to-face or telephone counseling. For example, in one postdisaster crisis counseling program, a young woman called the project director in tears, reporting that she was fearful that her marriage was on the verge of dissolving. She reported that for 6 months her husband had worked relentlessly, every night after work and every weekend, on rebuilding their mudslide-damaged home. They rarely had a conversation anymore, their sexual relationship had become nonexistent, they argued continuously, and they had not gotten away from the scene of their half-destroyed home once to go to a movie or out to dinner. This couple was clearly in a hazardous circumstance with regard to the future of their marriage. Such relationship problems were among the most commonly reported difficulties in this project (Garaventa, 1983a).

The intervention consisted of talking with the wife regarding common postdisaster reactions and providing suggestions of strategies that could help. For example, the husband's intense involvement in rebuilding the home was both a concrete and symbolic attempt to restore order and safety to the family's environment. This reaction, it was pointed out, was extremely common among men in the disaster-struck community, as was the man's difficulty in talking about his feelings related to the disaster. The wife, too, had remained silent about her feelings of abandonment, lest her husband feel she did not appreciate his efforts to rebuild their home. The counselor pointed out the normalcy of their reactions, but also the inherent hazard.

It was suggested to the couple that the relationship needed rebuilding as well as the house. A plan was developed in which the couple made arrangements to spend specific times together each week in nondisaster-related activities. In a follow-up phone call 1 month later, the woman reported a marked improvement in the situation and expressed extreme gratitude for having what later seemed like the obvious pointed out to her. Such education, feedback, and guidance on the part of mental health professionals can be important in identifying to victims the roadblocks they may encounter and in suggesting alternate, less hazardous routes.

Interpersonal Action to Influence Provision of Basic Supplies

There is little to be added to the concept of provision of supplies that has not already been covered under social action. Undoubtedly, in the course of working with individual disaster victims and their families, the mental health professional will identify situations where basic physical, psychosocial, or sociocultural supplies are lacking. The following examples highlight interpersonal action approaches to such situations.

Regarding physical supplies, after the northern California floods and mudslides of 1982, elderly individuals and couples were found to be isolated in their homes, suffering from lack of heat, food, drinking water, medicines, and, in the case of one man, the oxygen necessary because of his emphysema. In some cases, individuals had not sought assistance for their conditions because they did not know it was available. In other cases, frail persons were unable to walk through the debris and mud to the disaster center to obtain supplies. In such cases, the services of the worker varied from provision of information about available assistance, counseling to help individuals to overcome their reluctance to accept aid, or advocacy on a case-by-case basis to encourage disaster relief organizations to bring needed physical supplies to individuals' homes.

Regarding psychosocial supplies, the mental health worker will undoubtedly identify situations where there are disturbances in key relationships, as in the previous example of the stress between husband and wife. Education and counseling can offer approaches to help individuals and families to more effectively meet their psychosocial needs.

The mental health worker may also identify specific cases in which sociocultural supplies are lacking. For example, in one Hispanic community devastated by a flood, a mother with six children was referred to the mental health center by a concerned neighbor. The mother was suffering anxiety, depression, and inability to sleep since the flood. In talking to the mental health worker, she revealed that the family's statue of the Virgin of Guadalupe had been shattered during the flood. It was the mother's belief that the statue, blessed by the bishop, protected her family and provided for their well-being. Without it, she felt totally vulnerable. Searching religious supply stores, the mental health worker found a replica of the statue, and, working with the local priest, had it blessed by the bishop. The woman's anxiety subsided significantly through this concrete intervention to assure that her sociocultural needs were met (Romero, personal communication, 1983).

Interpersonal Action to Foster Healthy Crisis Coping

This aspect of a primary prevention program deals with individually focused methods to ensure that persons in crisis choose effective, reality-based ways of handling their crisis tasks and emerge from the period of upset without an increased vulnerability to mental disorder. This goal may be achieved by the mental health worker (1) intervening directly in the lives of individuals and their families during crisis or (2) establishing personal contact with caregiving professionals who may in turn intervene in the crisis situation (Caplan, 1964).

Direct Intervention with Individuals and Families

Caplan's (1964) description of this activity envisions the mental health specialist gaining access to a population of individuals in crisis and screening this population to identify the ones who may be having difficulty dealing with the crisis or who show such maladaptive coping responses as evasion of crisis tasks, lack of activity in exploring the crisis situation, inability to express and to master negative feelings, or difficulty in obtaining help from others. Such screening underscores the importance of mental health workers having access to disaster victims. This means that mental health staff must not wait in their offices for referrals but must pursue an approach of aggressive outreach. They must get out into the field to the places where victims may be found—in shelters, first aid stations, hospital emergency rooms, food halls, disaster assistance centers, community halls, and the like. In some communities, mental health staff have gone door-to-door in severely affected areas (Hoff, 1984).

The most effective outreach seems to be done by staff who are not bound to an office-based counseling role. Workers must feel comfortable approaching people in a wide variety of settings and simply asking them how they are feeling and what happened to them during the disaster (Peuler, 1985). Experience has shown that the best disaster outreach workers are usually the ones with prior mental health outreach experience, such as case managers, public health nurses, and crisis intervention workers.

Staff need to remember that, in postdisaster recovery, they are working with a normal population in an abnormal situation, and that disaster victims cannot be viewed in fashions similar to clients treated in case loads of the mental health system (Peuler, 1985). There is a need to avoid psychological terminology and diagnostic categories. Any conditions that create barriers to intereaction with the victims—distance, transportation problems, bureaucratic forms or regulations, culturally insensitive approaches, and the like—will diminish the chances of success for the mental health worker (Cohen & Ahearn, 1980). The major goal of outreach is to identify victims, assess their problems and coping, and link victims with needed assistance. Cohen and Ahearn report that outreach activities can help to achieve the following objectives toward assisting disaster victims:

1. Education and information about resources available to help reorganize their lives

2. Help in identifying ambivalent feelings, acknowledging needs, asking for help, and accepting support

3. Help in interacting on a cognitive level, assigning priorities to needs, obtaining resources, and increasing individual capacity to cope with specific priorities identified

4. Opportunities to become engaged and affiliated

5. A structured method of perceiving specific problems, self-observations, behavior patterns, and powerful emotions through help in understanding, defining, and ordering events in the larger world

Once these objectives have been accomplished, specific problems can be singled out and worked on. If maladaptive coping is observed, the outreach activities may have established a basis of trust with the mental health worker from which further work can be done (Cohen & Ahearn, 1980).

After outreach activities have taken place and victims have been identified who may need assistance, a major objective of the mental health intervention is to restore the capacity of the victims to handle the stressful situations in which they find themselves (Cohen & Ahearn, 1980). It is then that classical, well-established techniques of crisis intervention may be called into play (see, for example, Aguilera & Messick, 1982; Cohen & Ahearn; or Hoff, 1984, for detailed discussions of these techniques). A number of person-centered strategies aimed at promoting and enhancing healthy adaptation may be of particular utility in disaster situations.

The first of these strategies is education about stress reactions in general, and disaster reactions specifically. Caplan (1964) has labeled this technique *anticipatory guidance*. Such education might include information about *losses* that have occurred, including losses that are less tangible than loss of life and property (e.g., loss of health; loss of income and status as a wage earner; loss of sense of safety and security; or loss of family history through destruction of mementos and photographs). The individual might be informed of the potential for additional stressful life events consequential to other losses or in adaptation to them (Catalano & Dooley, 1980); for example, how the demands inherent in taking a second job to provide supplemental income needed to rebuild destroyed property might place stresses on health and family life. Education would also include the *phases* of adjustment to be expected and their symptom patterns (Catalano & Dooley). Such information may provide a type of *emotional inoculation* by evoking ahead of time an anticipation of the experience, with its associated feelings of anxiety, tension, depression, and the like (Caplan).

The mental health specialist can assist the individual to envision possible ways for solving problems, including mastery of negative feelings (Caplan, 1964), thereby allowing for psychological preparation and a heightened sense of control (Catalano & Dooley, 1980). Such techniques might use the preventive model based on classical conditioning proposed by Poser (1970) and termed *antecedent systematic desensitization*. Individuals are given gradu-ated preexposure to anxiety-arousing situations to prevent the establishment of conditioned-avoidant responses (Jason, 1980). This approach might in-clude, for example, gradually reintroducing children to environments that recall a traumatic disaster experience. When the experience itself arrives, the hazards have been made familiar by being anticipated, and the individuals will have been set on the path of healthy coping responses (Caplan).

Catalano and Dooley (1980) expand upon the stress inoculation approach with *behavioral training* in the form of teaching relaxation in the face of stressful stimuli. The client is taught to monitor mental and physical reactions and to control them through deep breathing, systematic muscular relaxation, and cognitive strategies such as distraction or mental imagery.

A final technique to strengthen individual's coping capacity is *cognitive restructuring*. This technique involves modifying the internal statements that people make to themselves (Jason, 1980). It assists the individual to identify negative self-statements or attributions and to replace them with more pos-itive ones. For example, if the self-talk in which an individual engages is realistic and accurate, the person generally functions well. If it is irrational or untrue, the person will likely experience additional stress, emotional disturbance, and poor coping (Davis, Eshelman, & McKay, 1982; Hartsough & Myers, 1985).

A main target of this intervention is self-esteem (Catalano & Dooley, 1980). Goldfried and Merbaum (1973) have successfully applied these tech-niques to a wide range of clinical problems. Meichenbaum and Turk (1976), have developed a model that enables clients to apply cognitive restructuring techniques to deal effectively with present as well as future stressful situ-ations. By shifting the emphasis from clinical to normal populations, the approach has limitless possibilities for primary prevention (Jason, 1980). Myers (Hartsough and Myers, 1985) has reported that emergency service workers frequently use positive self-talk as a way to get through stressful or tragic situations. In talking themselves through such events, workers may use self-enhancing monologues to deal with stress reactions, saying for ex-ample, "It's normal to feel queasy. It will go away in a minute." She suggests training techniques for emergency and disaster workers that help them to identify negative self-talk and replace it with positive, encouraging statements.

Training, Consultation, and Support for Care Givers

Caplan (1964) points out that however effective the above approaches with individuals and families may be, they require a great deal of mental health time and effort, and their community effect is therefore necessarily re-stricted. He suggests that a preventive program aiming at a broader base of coverage would therefore place considerable emphasis on efforts with profes-sional care givers, who can vastly expand the scope and impact of the mental health interventions. The first step includes training for community profes-sionals, discussed previously under social action approaches. Such training would include specific information about human response to disaster, crisis intervention skills appropriate to the worker's scope of responsibility, and referral resources and procedures.

The final, often crucial, step of a primary preventive program of interpersonal action, then, is to support or backstop the care-giving professionals through consultation when they run into difficulties from time to time in carrying out their work. The continued success of the preventive program may well depend on how adequately the care-giving professionals are supported when they encounter inevitable difficulties in their work with clients in crisis (Caplan, 1964).

Cohen and Ahearn (1980) point out that victim-centered case consultation is the service most often needed in a disaster recovery program. A wide variety of community professionals and disaster workers may have difficulty dealing with mental health problems presented by victims and can use the assistance and advice of mental health staff. Usually the disaster worker will present the problem to the mental health professional for advice, but at times the latter can also examine the victim, reach a diagnostic impression, and make recommendations, which can then be translated into a plan that is feasible in the given setting. If necessary, referral to mental health specialists for treatment of specific problems can be made.

RESEARCH AND PROGRAM CONSIDERATIONS

Heller et al. (1980) point out that, despite the logic and appeal of programs of prevention, there is a conceptual inadequacy that makes prevention research extremely difficult. One reason is that prevention goals statements do not specify how those goals can be operationalized. Knowledge about the etiology of mental disorders is still in such a rudimentary state that prevention programs keyed to etiological factors are fraught with uncertainty and lack of precision (Heller et al.). Another issue is the importance of adopting multifactorial causation models in conceptualizing prevention activities. As Price (1974) suggests, identifying risk factors is a more realistic way of viewing the etiology of mental disorder than seeking simple cause-and-effect relationships. The effect of interventions seeking to minimize risk factors is, however, difficult to evaluate.

Cooper (1980) cites a lack of specificity as a problem in most prevention programs. Better mental health or improved coping skills are too global and too undifferentiated to be measured. To examine the effectiveness of a preventive intervention, one needs to spell out *specific* outcomes expected and then develop precise, *specific* measures of targeted behavior (Heller & Monahan, 1977; Plaut, 1980). The complexity is increased when one is required to measure outcome for the beneficiary of service, who is not necessarily the person to whom the service was given. For example, the target of a consultation might be a group of teachers, but the outcome must be evaluated in terms of behavior of the *students,* who are expected to benefit from changes in the teachers' approaches.

Plaut (1980) and Heller et al. (1980) raise the question of whether the *assumptions* behind prevention goals are valid. For example, prevention projects to increase competency in problem-solving and coping skills seek to build adaptive strengths with the assumption that a strengthened individual will be better able to deal with a variety of stresses that might eventually lead to disability. The issue is whether the basic assumption of such projects is correct, that is, whether those individuals whose competencies are increased are truly less vulnerable to disability later on (Heller et al., 1980). One can assume, for example, that disaster preparedness education may lead citizens to more effective handling of emergency situations, increased safety, more realistic expectations of themselves, and inoculation regarding what to expect on an emotional level. Whether, in fact, such preparedness actually decreases serious mental health sequelae such as anxiety or depression following disaster has yet to be proven.

Evaluation of preventive programs is further complicated by the clinical, political, and fiscal aspects of the settings in which they are usually undertaken—community-based mental health centers. For one thing, local programs may not have staff experienced in research design (Plaut, 1980). Clinical services often take priority (Swift, 1980), and in many local community mental health settings, prevention and community services have been curtailed or eliminated as funding has dwindled. When preventive programs are attempted, it is difficult to establish and maintain control groups (Tableman, 1980). A public service delivery system often requires that staff provide services to all who seek help (Cooper, 1980), and as subjects in a control group exhibit pathology, staff may be ethically or legally required to provide treatment. Long-term follow-up is difficult, with changes in staff and funding making it difficult to evaluate programs over a number of years (Swift).

Swift (1980) further points out the difficulties of evaluation in a field setting rather than the laboratory, with political, economic, and environmental events disrupting data collection and analysis. Cowen (1978) underscores this point, adding that the vulnerability of findings from any single evaluation study dictates that greater evidence be placed on converging sources of evidence. He points to the importance both of replication and of tolerance for a slow, accretive process in which small pieces in a puzzle gradually culminate in weight-of-evidence conclusions about new programming approaches.

Tableman (1980) contends that prevention projects are often held to a high level of accountability, which is unrealistic where existing standardized measures do not adequately tap the relevant dimensions, and measures to document clinical judgments are still being formulated. Some prevention advocates say that there is a double standard in which more evidence about effectiveness seems to be required before preventive programs receive support than is required for treatment endeavors. They argue that prevention programs are accepted in principle, but when hard resource allocations are made, the decision is generally in the direction of treatment (Plaut, 1980).

This leads, then, to a look at realistic programming and research expectations regarding primary prevention in the arena of disaster mental health. Clearly, local mental health programs, with their current levels of funding and high demands for service, are decreasing their preventive efforts. Planning for what most people see as the unlikely event of a disaster usually is not a local mental health priority until such an event has actually occurred. In addition, local prevention programs have not been expected (at least historically) to generate revenues, thus making local fiscal support for such programs a problem (Swift, 1980; Cooper, 1980). For these reasons, the federal government has recognized the need for categorical funding for post-disaster mental health programs, providing fiscal support for local mental health disaster response in presidentially declared disaster areas. Funding for these crisis counseling programs comes from the Federal Emergency Management Agency (FEMA), with programs administered through the Center for the Mental Health Studies of Emergencies of the National Institute of Mental Health (NIMH). In addition to crisis counseling services for victims, these projects typically include substantial preventive programming, utilizing many of the techniques described in this chapter.

Despite the aforementioned problems in research and evaluation of community-based preventive programs, most professionals would stipulate the importance of continued research efforts. The Task Panel on Prevention of the President's Commission on Mental Health (1978) cited a large body of research documenting the effectiveness of prevention programs; however, minimal evaluation standards for programs need to go beyond what is currently available (Swift, 1980). In this light, the Center for the Mental Health Studies of Emergencies has supported research programs on the psychosocial responses to natural disasters and technological emergencies (Lystad, 1985). One of the categories of research supported by the Center has been *research on prevention of mental health sequelae and on intervention in mental health problems related to emergencies,* including:

Evaluation studies of dissemination techniques and programs to promote community awareness of specific roles that individuals may play in helping themselves, their families, and their significant others to avoid some/most of the deleterious effects of emergencies

Studies of community interventions for reducing or ameliorating emotional trauma and long-term consequences of emergencies and

Studies evaluating the mental health implications of emergency plans in such institutions as hospitals, schools, and custodial care facilities. (Lystad, 1985, p. 5)

The Center has also funded research on methodologies and/or techniques required to advance research in these areas. The service delivery and research programs of the NIMH have been mutually reinforcing, with service programs providing questions for research, and research forming the basis for more effective service and planning activities (Lystad, personal communication, Feb. 9, 1988).

This is not to imply that *all* planning and programming for mental health services in time of disaster should be left to programs funded by the federal government. At the very least, every local mental health center should have in place a *plan* for mobilization and delivery of services in time of emergency. Such a plan should outline services to be provided, likely sites to be covered, mobilization and deployment of staff, and relationships with emergency and disaster relief agencies. Mental health staff should be trained and updated annually on principles of human behavior in disaster and effective interventions to assist victims. It is most helpful if outreach materials are assembled and available ahead of time, to be duplicated for distribution in time of need.

Ideally, collaborative relationships should be developed between the local mental health and emergency service agencies before disaster strikes. Such collaboration should include familiarization with agency disaster plans, cross-training of workers, and a referral process for victims of day-to-day traumatic events (such as transportation accidents or single family fires) as well as for major disasters. Approaches to developing such collaborative relationships between mental health and emergency services are detailed in Hartsough and Myers (1985), and elsewhere in this text. Mental health staff should participate wherever possible in all local disaster drills.

It is hoped that, with these local mechanisms and relationships in place, and with the aid of external sources of program and research support, local mental health staff can move swiftly and effectively to prevent some of the serious, long-range effects should disaster occur in their communities.

REFERENCES

Aguilera, D. C., & Messick, J. M. (1982). *Crisis intervention* (4th ed.). St. Louis: Mosby.

American Red Cross and National Funeral Directors Association. (1978). *Statement of understanding between the National Funeral Directors Association and the American National Red Cross with respect to disaster services.* (Red Cross Form No. ARC 2257).

American Red Cross. (1985). *Disaster preparedness for disabled and elderly people.* Los Angeles: Author.

Bell, W. D. (1976). Service priorities for the elderly in national disasters—a research report. *Gerontology Programs.* Omaha: University of Nebraska.

Birch, H. G. (1974). Methodological issues in the longitudinal study of malnutrition. In D. F. Ricks, A. Thomas, & M. Roffs (Eds.), *Life history research in psychopathology* (Vol. 3,). Minneapolis: University of Minnesota Press.

Bloom, B. L. (1979). Prevention of mental disorders: Recent advances in theory and practice. *Community Mental Health Journal, 15,* 179–191.

Bolin, R. (1975). Research on reconstruction following disaster: Working paper No. 1. Second Annual Invitational Conference on National Hazards, Boulder, CO.

Bronfenbrenner, V. (1977). Toward an experimental ecology of human development. *American Psychologist, 32,* 513–531.

California Department of Mental Health. (1981). *Friends can be good medicine.* San Franciso: Pacificon Publications.

Caplan, G. (1964). *Principles of preventive psychiatry.* New York: Basic Books.

Cassel, J. (1976). The contribution of the social environment to host resistance. *American Journal of Epidemiology, 104,* 107–123.

Catalano, R., & Dooley, D. (1980). Economic change in primary prevention. In R. H. Price, R. F. Ketterer, B. C. Bader, and J. Monahan (Eds.), *Prevention in mental health: Research, policy, and practice* (pp. 21–40). Beverly Hills, CA: Sage Publications.

Cohen, R. E., & Ahearn, F. L. (1980). *Handbook for mental health care of disaster victims.* Baltimore: The Johns Hopkins University Press.

Cooper, S. (1980). Implementing prevention programs: A community mental health center director's point of view. In R. H. Price, R. F. Ketterer, B. C. Bader, & J. Monahan (Eds.), *Prevention in mental health: Research, policy, and practice* (pp. 253–261). Beverly Hills, CA: Sage Publications.

Cowen, E. L. (1978). Some problems in community program evaluation research. *Journal of Consulting and Clinical Psychology, 46,* 792–805.

Davis, M., Eshelman, E. R., & McKay, M. (1982). *The relaxation and stress reduction workbook.* Oakland, CA: New Harbinger Publications.

Dohrenwend, B. S., & Dohrenwend, B. P. (Eds.). (1974). *Stressful life events: Their nature and effects.* New York: Wiley.

Dumont, M. (1968). *The absurd healer.* New York: Science House.

Dynes, R. R. (1970). *Organized behavior in disaster.* Lexington, MA: D. C. Heath.

Eby, D. L. (1985). Healing the helper: A disaster worker's response. In *Role stressors and supports for emergency workers* (pp. 119–125). Rockville, MD: National Institute of Mental Health.

Erikson, K. T. (1977). *Everything in its path.* New York: Simon & Schuster.

Farberow, N. L., & Gordon, N. S. (1979). *Training manual for human service workers in natural disasters.* Rockville, MD: National Institute of Mental Health.

Farberow, N. L., & Gordon, N. S. (1981). *Manual for child health workers in major disasters.* Rockville, MD: National Institute of Mental Health.

Felner, R. D., Farber, S. S., & Primavera, J. (1980). Children of divorce, stressful life events, and transitions. In R. H. Price, R. F. Ketterer, B. C. Bader, & J. Monahan (Eds.), *Prevention in mental health: Research, policy, and practice* (pp. 81–108). Beverly Hills, CA: Sage Publications.

Friedsam, H. J. (1962). Older persons in disaster. In G. W. Baker & D. W. Chapman (Eds.), *Man and society in disaster.* New York: Basic Books.

Garaventa, D. (1983a). *Marin County crisis counseling project: Final report.* Marin County, CA: Community Mental Health Services.

Garaventa, D. (1983b). [A study of community education and community organization techniques as interventions to prevent victimization of individuals and to prevent social disorganization of communities in emergencies or disasters]. Unpublished research idea statement, Community Mental Health Services, Marin County, CA.

Garaventa, D. (1984). *Factors to keep in mind in working with various ethnic groups.* Unpublished training guide, Community Mental Health Services, Marin County, CA.

Garaventa, D., Martin, P., & Scremin, D. (1984). Surviving the flood: Implications for small town disaster planning. *Small Town, 14,* 11–18.

Gibbs, L. (1982). *Love Canal—My story.* Albany: State University of New York Press.

Goldfried, M. R., & Merbaum, M. (Eds.) (1973). *Behavior change through self-control.* New York: Holt, Rinehart, & Winston.

Goldston, S. E. (1977). Defining primary prevention. In G. W. Albee and J. M. Joffee (Eds.), *Primary prevention of psychopathology: Vol. I. The issues.* Hanover, NH: University Press of New England.

Goldston, S. E. (1978). A national perspective. In D. G. Forgays (Ed.), *Primary Prevention of Psychopathology. Volume II. Environmental Influences.* Hanover, NH: University Press of New England.

Hartsough, D. M., & Myers, D. G. (1985). *Disaster work and mental health: Prevention and control of stress among workers.* Rockville, MD: National Institute of Mental Health.

Heller, K., & Monahan, J. (1977). *Psychology and community change.* Homewood, IL: Dorsey Press.

Heller, K., Price, R. H., & Sher, K. J. (1980). Research and evaluation in primary prevention: Issues and guidelines. In R. H. Price, R. F. Ketterer, B. C. Bader, & J. Monahan (Eds.), *Prevention in mental health: Research, policy and practice* (pp. 285–313). Beverly Hills, CA: Sage Publications.

Hoff, L. A. (1984). *People in crisis: Understanding and helping* (2nd ed.). Menlo Park, CA: Addison-Wesley.

Huerta, F., & Horton, R. (1978). Coping behavior of elderly flood victims. *The Gerontologist, 18,* 541–545.

Jason, L. A. (1980). Prevention in the schools: Behavioral approaches. In R. H. Price, R. F. Ketterer, B. C. Bader, & J. Monahan (Eds.), *Prevention in mental health: Research, policy and practice* (pp. 109–134). Beverly Hills, CA: Sage Publications.

Katona, G. (1979). Toward a macropsychology. *American Psychologist, 34,* 118–126.

Ketterer, R. F., Bader, B. C., & Levy, M. R. (1980). Strategies and skills for promoting mental health. In R. H. Price, R. F. Ketterer, B. C. Bader, & J. Monahan (Eds.), *Prevention in mental health: Research, policy, and practice* (pp. 263–283). Beverly Hills, CA: Sage Publications.

Kilijanek, T. S., & Drabek, T. E. (1979). Assessing the long-term impacts of a natural disaster: A focus on the elderly. *The Gerontologist, 19,* 555–566.

Lang, K., & Lang, G. E. (1964). Collective responses to the threat of disaster. In G. Grosser et al. (Eds.), *The threat of impending disasters: Contributions to the psychology of stress.* Cambridge, MA: M.I.T. Press.

Leik, R. K. (1982). *Under the threat of Mt. St. Helens: A study of chronic family stress.* Unpublished manuscript. Federal Emergency Management Agency, Washington, DC.

Lifton, R. J. (1967). *Life in death.* New York: Simon & Schuster.

Lifton, R. J., & Olson, E. (1976). The human meaning of total disaster: The Buffalo Creek experience. *Psychiatry, 39,* 1–18.

Lindemann, E. (1956). The meaning of crisis in individual and family living. *Teachers' College Record, 57,* 310–315.

Lystad, M. (Ed.). (1985). *Innovations in mental health services to disaster victims.* Rockville, MD: National Institute of Mental Health.

Meichenbaum, D. H., & Turk, D. (1976). The cognitive-behavioral management of anxiety, anger, and pain. In P. O. Davidson (Ed.), *The behavioral management of pain.* New York: Brunner/Mazel.

Mitchell, J. T. (1983). When disaster strikes . . . the critical incident stress debriefing process. *Journal of Emergency Medical Services, 8,* 36–39.

Moir, J. (1980). *Just in case.* San Francisco: Chronicle Books.

Moore, H. E. (1958). *Tornadoes over Texas.* Austin: University of Texas Press.

Morris, W. (Ed.) (1981). *The American heritage dictionary of the English language.* Boston: Houghton Mifflin.

O'Callahan, W. T. (1983a). *Pacifica emergency preparedness: Final report.* San Mateo County, CA: Community Mental Health Services.

O'Callahan, W. T. (1983b). *Psychological implications of disaster for disaster workers.* Unpublished pamphlet. San Francisco: American Red Cross, Golden Gate Chapter.

Peuler, J. (1983). *Project COPE: A community-based mental health response to disaster. Final report.* Santa Cruz County, CA: Community Mental Health Services.

Peuler, J. (1985). Family and community outreach in times of disaster: The Santa Cruz experience. In M. Lystad (Ed.), *Innovations in mental health services for disaster victims* (pp. 18–23). Rockville, MD: National Institute of Mental Health.

Plaut, T. F. A. (1980). Prevention policy: The federal perspective. In R. H. Price, R. F. Ketterer, B. C. Bader, & J. Monahan (Eds.), *Prevention in mental health: Research, policy, and practice* (pp. 195–205). Beverly Hills, CA: Sage Publications.

Poser, E. G. (1970). Toward a theory of behavioral prophylaxis. *Journal of Behavior Therapy and Experimental Psychiatry, 1,* 39–45.

Poulshock, S. W., & Cohen, E. S. (1975). The elderly in the aftermath of a disaster. *The Gerontologist, 15,* 357–361.

President's Commission on Mental Health. (1978). *Report to the President's Commission on Mental Health* (Vols. 1, 4). Washington, DC: U.S. Government Printing Office.

Price, R. H. (1974). Etiology, the social environment, and the prevention of social dysfunction. In P. Insel & R. H. Moos (Eds.), *Health and the social environment.* Lexington, MA: D. C. Heath.

Price, R. H., Bader, B. C., & Ketterer, R. F. (1980). Prevention in community mental health: The state of the art. In R. H. Price, B. F. Ketterer, B. C. Bader, & J. Monahan (Eds.), *Prevention in mental health: Research, policy, and practice* (pp. 9–20). Beverly Hills, CA: Sage Publications.

Romero, J. (1983). *Needs of mono-lingual and bi-lingual Spanish-speaking community*. Unpublished training guide. Santa Clara County, CA: Community Mental Health Services.

Ross, M. (1967). *Community organization: Theory, principles, and practice*. New York: Harper & Row.

Ryan, W. (1971). *Blaming the victim*. New York: Random House.

Schein, E. H. (1979). *Process consultation: Its role in organization development*. Reading, MA: Addison-Wesley.

Stern, G. M. (1976). *The Buffalo Creek disaster*. New York: Vintage Books.

Swift, C. F. (1980). Primary prevention: Policy and practice. In R. H. Price, R. F. Ketterer, B. C. Bader, & J. Monahan (Eds.), *Prevention in mental health: Research, policy, and pratice* (pp. 207–236). Beverly Hills, CA: Sage Publications.

Tableman, B. (1980). Prevention activities at the state level. In R. H. Price, R. F. Ketterer, B. C. Bader & J. Monahan (Eds.), *Prevention in mental health: Research, policy, and practice* (pp. 237–252). Beverly Hills, CA: Sage Publications.

Taillie, D. (1969). *The role of the psychiatric nurse in community organization*. Unpublished master's thesis, Yale University, New Haven, CT.

CHAPTER 9

Clinical Responses to Disaster

Assessment, Management, and Treatment

CHARLES B. WILKINSON AND ENRIQUE VERA

Throughout history human beings and disasters have coexisted, and over centuries, surviving disasters has become a natural experience for all species in existence today. The human species adapts in a slow but consistent evolutionary fashion and in so doing has become resilient in body and adroit of mind. A view across cultures reveals that most rituals and beliefs have developed to help people protect their own vulnerability and to accept with bearable pain that which they do not want but cannot control. The accumulation of genetic, biological, psychological, social, cultural, and religious systems of protection provides for people's needs most of the time.

It is only when these protective systems are threatened or break down that persons become symptomatic beyond consensual standards. Such a system failure as a result of the psyche being overwhelmed is now known as post-traumatic stress disorder (PTSD).

Disasters are one among the phenomena that can overwhelm the psyche. They, however, attract the attention of a large audience and understandably earn the concern of a sympathetic proportion of the population. This is perhaps because the ones who are affected are generally innocent victims of a catastrophe of which all other persons, under certain circumstances could, also be victims. This maxim holds whether a disaster is natural, the result of human error (accidental or planned), or the product of structural failures. Although there are a number of symptomatic commonalities, the content of the symptomatic expression will vary according to the specific disaster. The variations relate not only to whether the disaster is natural or human-induced, but also to duration of exposure, the extent of destruction and injury, the underlying personal characterology, the ages of persons affected, degree of loss, and strength of the systems of support.

In recent years disasters have attracted a growing scientific following, reflected in the increase in published articles relating to various aspects of these phenomena. It is perhaps not coincidental that this increase in published reports has followed the codification of symptoms that result from psychologically overwhelming incidents into a diagnostic category in the Third Edition of the American Psychiatric Association's *Diagnostic and Statistical Manual* (DSM-III) under the rubric, *post-traumatic stress disorder* (PTSD) (APA, 1980). Disasters, of course, are not the only causative agent of PTSD, as stress in combat situations, vehicular accidents, rape, concentration camp experiences, or other intense stressors can all produce this disorder.

As is often the case, the first recorded findings attributable to severe stress were the descriptions of disabling reactions during military combat situations. One of the earliest reports is that of a French officer in 1766 who suffered head and neck injuries when thrown against the wall of a carriage while returning to his duty post. He nevertheless engaged in a campaign, but within 6 months developed a weakness of one arm and an impediment in his speech (Trimble, 1981).

DaCosta (1871) described findings in soldiers of the American Civil War, but not having a psychological orientation, he considered them to be cardiac in nature. Similarly Lewis (1919) described casualties in World War I who experienced nightmares, fear, trembling, and the inability to carry out their duties. He also believed the problems to be organic in nature, labeling his findings "Soldier's Heart and Effort Syndrome." Exploding shells were postulated as another contributing factor, causing rupture of blood vessels and cerebral concussion. This belief is reputed to be the origin of the term *shell shock* (Horowitz, 1986).

Somewhat earlier, at about the turn of the century, the label of *traumatic neurosis* had been assigned to victims of train wrecks (Trimble, 1981). However, their findings were attributed not to psychological trauma but to spinal cord injury. In World War I, physicians in all armies were increasingly confronted with shell-shocked casualties. The belief in organic etiology was interrupted by Simmel's report that German soldiers obtained relief through hypnosis (Ferenczi, Abraham, Simmel, & Jones, 1921).

As is frequently the case, the lessons of war are forgotten over time, only to be relearned with the next military occurrence. It was not until World War II that a psychological basis was utilized from the outset to explain this war-bound symptomatology and to apply a psychiatric treatment methodology. Grinker and Spiegel (1945) in their studies of soldiers removed from combat listed, in order of frequency, 19 symptoms that continued to persist in the soldiers under study. Although these symptoms are similar to the ones categorized under PTSD, ill-defined diagnoses continued to exist, for example, war neurosis, combat neurosis, and combat fatigue.

Virtually everyone reacts to a life-threatening event with alarm or fear. Those initial reactions common for everyone are recognized as the natural physiological accompaniments of anxiety or fear, for example, tremulousness, tachycardia, palpitations, and sometimes nausea and vomiting. Reflexive responses such as bewilderment, confusion, and an incomprehensible daze are commonly noted at the onset of a disaster. Afterwards there may be a stunned expression of disbelief at what has happened.

In a disaster, three discrete phases have been described by Tyhurst (1951). These include the *impact* phase, a period of *recoil*, and the *posttraumatic* phase. The first, the *impact* phase, occurs at the beginning of the disaster and continues for as long as the phenomenon is in force. It is estimated that the majority of persons affected (75%) show the physiological responses cited earlier and are bewildered, stunned, and behave automatically. Afterwards they report a lack of feeling for the entire incident. From 12% to 25% of the victims remain calm during the disaster interval and are even able to function quickly and in an appropriate fashion. It is often this group of surviving victims who mount rescue efforts for the severely injured. The remaining 10% to 25% demonstrate highly inappropriate responses, e.g., confusion, anxiety, or panic reactions, crying hysterically, screaming, and sometimes experiencing a break with reality.

The second phase begins when the initial stress has ended and is no longer a threat. In this phase, the period of *recoil*, awareness and recall return, along with emotional expression and concern for others. Many show a child-like type of dependency and are very responsive to anyone who assumes a leadership role. This may account for the cooperativeness that has been described in survivors, who frequently leave the scene of a disaster in a quiet and orderly manner.

The final phase is the *posttraumatic* period in which an array of symptoms may appear. These may begin within a few days or several months following the trauma. A delay in the appearance of disturbing symptoms may be misleading to the survivors and to those concerned with their welfare, in that the lateness in onset evokes a tendency to attribute their presence to some factor other than the disaster.

In response to the phenomenon, the self-preserving functions of the organism set into motion a group of reactions geared toward restoring an equilibrium between the organism and its surrounding environment. In this reparative activity, two seemingly diametrically opposed processes are operative. These are in the form of a pair of alternating phases, that of *intrusion* and that of *denial*. The intrusive phase is marked by the involuntary, repetitious appearance of phenomena such as images, sleep disturbances, and sensations and symptoms of arousal. In the denial phase the intrusions are warded off, but a blunting of affect and constriction of thinking is the price paid for the overuse of this defense. The massive denial of an event, accompanied by emotional numbness has been called "supersuppression" by Menninger (1954).

The dynamic basis for the understanding of the repetitious nature of the unwanted intrusions has its historical roots in the work of Freud and Breuer (1957). They observed that psychological trauma could produce a variety of hysterical symptoms. They also noted that, not infrequently, a latency period existed between the occurrence of the stressful precipitating event and the onset of symptomatology. Once this conflation was established, there was a tendency for it to persist long after the event had ended. Further, a bland denial of any meaning attached to the symptoms was apparent and was labeled by them as "la belle indifference."

Horowitz's (1986) englightening discussion of Freud's (1920/1958) postulation of the *stimulus barrier* sheds further light on the antecedents of responses to severe stress as in a disaster. This barrier, proposed as a theoretical construct, was said to serve to regulate the perceptual entry into the psychic apparatus of information and energy from sources external to the organism. Emotional threats such as fear and anxiety would be sampled by an initial perception. If such threats were to increase, the stimulus barrier would be raised, thus reducing input.

The model also called for a feedback loop. That permitted continuous sampling and allowed the processing of this information to be regulated. (Horowitz substitutes the term *modulation of stimulus* for stimulus barrier as a means of maintaining the metaphorical nature of the concept.) The degree of modulation (or plasticity of the barrier) is dependent upon the magnitude of the aroused emotions. Excessive anxiety increases defensive inhibitions and decreases information processing. The converse is also true. Low levels of emotion can have a motivational effect, which influences the ego's controls. These controls, in turn, can modify the cognitive process, serving as a stimulus to learning. High levels of anxiety, however, activate inhibitory controls, resulting in a constriction of the ability to associate and inhibition of thought processing. Although many revisions in the theory of hysteria were made by Freud, this signal discovery still remains the hallmark not only of this neurosis but also of psychological trauma.

A complementary concept is offered by Lindy (1985); he proposes the presence of a *trauma membrane* that blankets disaster victims. The membrane is likened to the outer surface of a cell, formed to guard or ward off deleterious outside forces. This protective covering allows the reparative process to be carried out without interference or disturbance of the healing process.

In individuals, assistance is often provided to enhance this protection, for example, through a spouse or relative. When a number of victims have experienced like difficulties during and following a disaster, a common trauma membrane is formed. Access is granted only to individuals seen as being helpful, for example, highly respected persons and/or those deliverers of specific short-term services to aid the victims. Even then, sanction may have to be granted by community leaders. Because of this generalized exclusion of outsiders, only a small percentage of survivors of the Beverly Hills Supper Club disaster consented to a long-term follow-up by the University of Cincinnati's Department of Psychiatry, despite the latter's involvement in the catastrophe shortly after its occurrence. Interestingly, members of the Department who had accompanied families to the morgue to identify victims and who subsequently developed close relationships, kept other Department members interested in research and therapy away from "their families" (Lindy, Grace, & Green 1981). The workers apparently identified with these families so strongly that they excluded any outsiders, even their own Department members, lest they rupture or disturb the membrane.

The trauma membrane can be viewed as an artifact. Further it is enhanced and strengthened by a collectivity of like victims and by the admission of individuals who are viewed as helpful.

SYMPTOMS AND SIGNS

Generally, everyone involved in a disaster will immediately experience some symptoms and behavior related to stress. This is a normal response. Scrignor (1984) has tabulated 28 symptoms that can occur in situations or events perceived as an immediate threat to life, and which he describes as comprising Stage I of Responses to Trauma (See Table 9.1). Any combination of these symptoms can be observed in survivors of disasters.

TABLE 9.1.   Responses to Trauma

Helplessness
Increased heart rate
Dyspnea
Hyperventilation
Nausea
Vomiting
Extreme trembling or shaking
Excessive sweating
Dizziness
Feeling faint (light-headedness and unsteadiness)
Blurry vision
Hot flashes or flushing
Tingling sensations in the arms or hands (parasthesias)
Diarrhea
Urinary or fecal incontinence
Nervousness
Ringing in the ears
Outbursts of anger
Inability to remember recent events
Headaches
Pain
Restlessness
Hypersensitivity to sudden or rapidly changing stimuli (noise, light)
Sleep disturbances
Nightmares
Irritability
Difficulties in concentration
Feelings that familiar things are strange or unreal

Note. Adapted from Scrignor, 1984.

Because all of the special senses are impacted upon, symptoms referable to the organs of perception are apparent. In addition there is an overresponse of the autonomic nervous system resulting from its sudden stimulation. A brief break with reality can occur (brief reactive psychosis), and as a result of physical trauma some persons experience an amnesia for the event. Because there is no recollection of the disaster, they are spared many of the symptoms noted in Table 9.1. This situation may be particularly true for persons rendered unconscious at the very outset of the trauma.

Not every victim will develop PTSD or dwell for any length of time on the consequences of the catastrophe. Others may experience PTSD symptoms briefly. Persons who respond to the scene after impact, for example, may be subject to an intrusive phase and not experience or have only limited exposure to a phase of denial. They may experience uncomfortable and sometimes alarming emotions such as anxiety, depression, and anger. They may also experience sleep disturbances, with or without upsetting dreams. These symptoms subside over a period of several weeks and in time the event remains only as an affectless memory.

The following case excerpt demonstrates such a response.

CASE 1

F.W., a 38-year-old married male and father of two, worked in a managerial capacity with a heavy equipment company. Although he held principally a desk job, he was called on to oversee the use of some of the equipment used to remove heavy objects and debris that had fallen and crushed a number of guests when the skywalks gave way in the Hyatt Regency Hotel disaster (Kansas City, Missouri, July 1981).

He stated that he worked through the night and into the early morning hours. He recalled that, while taking a break, he had accepted and eaten a sandwich provided by a waitress from one of the hotel restaurants. At the same time, he had felt it odd to be able to be hungry and eat, considering the circumstances that had brought him to the scene.

F.W. had no problems over the remainder of the weekend that followed and was able to sleep without difficulty. Two days into the following work week, however, he noticed restlessness and difficulty keeping focused on his work. Ordinarily he enjoyed his work and could not understand his sudden diminished interest in it. He nevertheless persevered and was able to complete his tasks each day but left work so fatigued that he had to retire shortly after the evening meal.

Although he did not have disturbing dreams, his sleep was fitful and restless. At home he had become irritable and short-tempered with his children. He and his wife were concerned about his apparent personality change, but he did not associate it with the disaster until 2½ weeks after it had occurred.

The association was abruptly and dramatically brought to his attention when, in need of a minor repair on his car, he had taken it to an auto shop that regularly handled such work for him. When told that the part required to complete the repairs had not arrived, he exploded in a rage, broke into tears, and angrily drove away. Once home, he realized that he had grossly overreacted and called the shop to apologize to the manager. His apology was graciously accepted. In the conversation he stated, "I guess you thought I was some kind of nut." He recalled the manager to have replied, "Yes, we did until one of the men pointed out that he had seen your name in the newspaper as having been very much involved in that hotel disaster." He had priorly made no connection between his symptoms and the disaster. His symptoms began to subside over the next 7-day period, and he subsequently remained symptom-free.

It is apparent that after F.W. experienced a short phase of denial, the phase of intrusion made its appearance. His difficulty in concentrating and his fatigue resulted from the enormous expenditure of mental energy required to carry out his work and at the same time ward off complete disruption of his daily activities. F.W.'s awareness of not functioning adequately contributed to the intensification of the other intrusive elements he was experiencing—irritability, anger, and sleep disturbance.

Fortunately, he did not have to deal with grossly disturbing intrusive images and excessive emotions, probably because of the fact that he had been less involved in the removal of mangled bodies and severely injured people than were other rescuers, as well as the strength of his own ego. Although he experienced predominantly the intrusive phase, aspects of denial are also apparent in his working-through process.

In most instances, the denial phase occurs shortly after the disaster. When it lasts for several months, victims may believe that they have not reacted to the catastrophe and may even appear surprised that they have handled it so well. They may then be amazed upon experiencing intrusive images that they do not associate (or do not choose to associate) with the disaster. Unable to account for these images, they may feel they are losing their minds or "going crazy." After the Hyatt disaster, several persons made contact with mental health centers 2 to 4 months later, often with "What's wrong with me, am I going crazy?" being their first question (Wilkinson, 1983). On occasion, symptomatology may be delayed and appear 6 or more months following the event.

There is evidence that not only are those disaster victims who suffer injury and loss subject to psychological sequelae but so too are virtually all people who have had intimate or prolonged contact with the catastrophe. These include persons who narrowly miss injury or severe injury, as well as onlookers and rescuers (Wilkinson, 1983; Jones, 1985). The signs and symptoms of PTSD may appear in any exposed persons and reflect the intrusive and denial phases of their response.

SYMPTOMS: PHASE OF DENIAL

The phase of denial most frequently begins shortly after the disaster. At this time, mental processes work overtime in warding off painful and frightening feelings and images. There is diminished responsiveness to the external world, and complaints of estrangement or detachment from others are not uncommon. This diminished responsiveness or psychic numbing can become pervasive. Things previously enjoyed may no longer hold an interest, appetite may decrease, and emotions, particularly ones associated with intimacy and sex, may be blunted.

Denial and numbing can be especially dramatic in children. A 6-year-old child who witnessed her mother being killed no more than 6 feet away from her denied that her mother was dead, stating that she was just away on a trip. Several days later when her pet canary, of which she was very fond, was killed and eaten by the family cat, she told her father about what had happened in a bland and unemotional way.

Blunting, Numbness, Feelings of Unreality, Withdrawal from Activity, and Depression

Feelings of bewilderment and of being in a daze may appear as products of denial. Because any reminder of the event may cause flooding of the ego, external stimuli may be shut off so that appreciation of things outside of oneself may be lacking. Similarly, internally generated feelings as warmth and tenderness may be blocked such that interpersonal relationships suffer. Withdrawal from relatives and friends, feelings of unreality, and estrangement may exist.

Depression is not infrequently a secondary manifestation when the disorder becomes chronic. These individuals not only look unhappy, anhedonia permeates their existence. They suffer pessimistic preoccupation, may feel worthless, have a low energy level, experience sleep disturbances, and can have thoughts of death or suicide.

Constriction of Thinking, Overactivity, Excessive Fantasies

The overuse of denial may produce constriction of the mental apparatus. The degree of this limitation varies with the extensiveness of the use of this defense. Constriction of thought, together with selective inattention to avoid images and other sensations of the trauma, can affect practical consideration of daily activities and concentration. Overactivity, particularly busying oneself with purposeless or unnecessary activities, is also a defense against thoughts and emotions of the event. Likewise the excessive use of fantasy is another way of trying to avoid reality.

Amnesia

Anterograde amnesia can occur, erasing events from the beginning of the disaster. If rendered unconscious by injury at the onset of the disaster, there may also be retrograde amnesia for a short period preceding the event.

Sleep Disturbances

Disturbances in sleep can occur during the denial phase as well as in the intrusive phase. Hypersomnia in order to avoid images of the trauma, as well as insomnia for the same purpose, may be observed.

SYMPTOMS: PHASE OF INTRUSION

Intrusive Repetitive Thoughts and Emotions

An *intrusive thought* is defined as any thought that enters consciousness against one's will, is hard to dispel, and/or requires suppressive efforts. Such thoughts are persistent and are experienced as something to be avoided (Horowitz, 1986). Thoughts of the disaster may be consciously reviewed, but they may shortly develop a life of their own and advance to a point at which they are beyond control.

These thoughts may unceremoniously break through and flood consciousness with visual or other sensations experienced during the disaster. On occasion, emotions may inundate consciousness, reach a crescendo, and then subside. Physiological responses such as tremor, nausea, vomiting, or diarrhea, in preparations for fight or flight that occur with stimulation of the autonomic nervous system may accompany the breakthrough. The images and accompanying emotions related to the disaster intrude particularly in sleep, resulting in disturbing dreams and nightmares.

Sleep Disturbances, Dreams, Nightmares

Difficulty in falling asleep may occur because of recollections of the event, vivid repetitive images, or emotions. If depression is present, a depressive sleep pattern of early morning awakening may be noted. Sleep can be interrupted by disturbing dreams that may replay some sequence of the disaster. Dreams can also assume nightmarish proportions; they may, however, not necessarily be a replay of the disaster but can be of some other equally disturbing threats to one's safety or life. Because of the fear of dreams or nightmares, bedtime can be a dreaded part of the day.

The pathological defense of undoing may occasionally be utilized in an effort to deal with intrusion in dreams (Titchener & Kapp, 1976). By reliving the past experience (the disaster) in dreams and giving it a different outcome, the undoing may function as an attempt to change the past. It is as if the repetitious compulsion (the intrusion) can be replaced, and one then will not have to deal with the anxiety associated with the trauma. Rather than being helpful, however, undoing can be an obstacle that interferes with or prevents dealing with the experience, a necessary step in readapting.

Illusions, Hallucinations, Pseudohallucinations

Mental images involving one or more of the sensory organs may occur. These may appear in the form of hallucinatory, pseudohallucinatory, or illusionary experiences. They may involve images of persons injured or killed or of sounds, sights, and odors associated with the disaster.

These unwanted occurrences generally take place when the individual is relaxed, at the beginning of sleep (hypnogogic hallucinations), or upon awakening from sleep (hypnopompic hallucinations). Despite the awareness of their unreality, these reactions are felt as real. They are frightening episodes and can lead to anticipatory anxiety or concern about one's sanity (Horowitz, 1986).

Startle Reactions

Flinching, grimacing, jumping, or even an outcry may take place when stimuli simulate aspects of the disaster. The response is an overreaction; it is spontaneous and can be embarrassing to the person. In the Hyatt disaster, for example, noises that brought to mind the skywalks tearing away from their attachment and crashing to the floor produced such reactions in many victims (Wilkinson, 1983). One professional, a hotel guest turned rescuer, was attending a stage play several weeks later. During an intermission, he reacted to a scraping noise of scenery being moved backstage by jumping across three people and into the aisle.

Hypervigilance

Hypervigilance is characterized by excessive alertness and preparation for flight or other forms of self-protection when confronted with a situation perceived as a threat to survival. The situation itself may be innocuous, but it is nevertheless viewed as dangerous.

A number of persons involved in the Hyatt Regency Hotel disaster avoided balconies; others were uncomfortable in rooms with high arched ceilings. Several were also uncomfortable in walking under overhead bridges, walkways, or other suspended structures. They were observed to peer up at them anxiously and to go out of their way rather than pass underneath (Wilkinson, 1983).

Occasionally, hypervigilance appears to approach the bizarre. After the Buffalo Creek Flood in West Virginia, the entire community manifested "obsessions and phobias about water, rain, and any other reminder that the disaster could recur" (Titchener & Kapp, 1976, p. 297). The community leader and his wife never slept at the same time so that at least one of them could always remain alert. On rainy nights, he would be deluged with phone call rumors that another dam might break. He would then spend the night sitting on the dam with a rifle. Other community members stayed on shore nearby in order to protect him from attack.

Difficulties in Memory and Concentration

Preoccupation or rumination in which images, sensations, and sounds related to the disaster occupy large segments of the waking hours, may almost exclude all other associations. Inattentiveness to what is currently transpiring in the immediate environment may result, concentration may become difficult or impossible, and recall may be affected.

ASSOCIATED SYMPTOMS

Guilt

When there have been injuries and death resulting from a disaster, persons who have survived without harm are obviously relieved. It is, however, a strained relief, as they may question why they rather than others were picked to survive. If someone lives, does not someone else have to die? Surviving, at what appears to be the expense of someone else, conflicts with moral attitudes of unselfishness and sharing the pain of others (Frederick, 1981). Since people constantly seek solutions to unexplainable problems, magical thinking provides an uneasy answer, that is, perhaps destiny has a quota for a designated number of victims at such times.

On the other hand, some survivors appear to savor their guilt, expressing the feeling that they deserve to feel the way they do as punishment for past sins. Guilt is even more poignant when a survivor assumes responsibility for the death of a friend or relative, as, for example, when the deceased is at the place of the disaster at the invitation or insistence of the survivor.

Although it may be generally believed that injured persons have less reason to feel guilty because through injury penance has already been paid, this is not necessarily true. Survivor guilt can be present, because in being alive such individuals still are more fortunate than others who are not. Rescue workers, health professionals, and paramedics may also express guilt feelings because of a belief that they did not do enough or did not act rapidly enough to save lives.

Anger

Anger or rage is a frequent response to helplessness and frustration. Helplessness is experienced by disaster victims who feel they had no control over the occurrence of the event and were impotent in preventing it. Rage may then develop from a need to determine who is responsible and to attach blame. In disasters resulting from human failings, the anger tends to be focused and is sometimes more intense. Blame is less easily placed with natural disasters and the anger is instead displaced, not infrequently toward the people who are attempting to provide assistance.

Rage can extend to anyone directly or symbolically connected with the incident. After the Hyatt disaster, 36 of the subjects responding to a questionnaire openly admitted anger, with 15 (42%) showing generalized anger, 8 (22%) expressing anger toward the builder, and four (11%) reacting with anger toward the hotel corporation. Three respondents felt anger toward lawyers, and 2 each indicated anger toward doctors and other rescuers, the news media, and the engineers or designers of the building (Wilkinson, 1983).

There are occasions in which relatives or close friends of someone who has died during a disaster feel rage toward another or others who were more fortunate and were not killed or injured. Despite an intellectual awareness of the irrationality of their anger, hatred and death wishes may dominate their thinking. In a manner similar to situations when death is due to natural causes, anger toward a deceased spouse for having left the survivor can also be a source of guilt.

OTHER FACTORS THAT RELATE TO DISASTERS

In addition to the attack on the self from effects of trauma, there are other factors that bear upon the severity of outcome and the ability to readapt. These factors may be external to the victim and can contribute either to the development or the minimization of psychiatric sequelae. Such factors may also be internal and may play a key role in the permanency of symptoms or the deflection of stress into other channels. The results of such deflections may be more or less debilitating, depending upon the nature of the alternative channels employed.

Duration of the Disaster

The time factor is an important variable in the psychological responses to a disaster. Disasters that occur over a period of days or weeks, for example, floods and hurricanes, appear to exact a greater psychological toll than the ones that end quickly (Frederick, 1977).

Human-Induced Disasters versus Natural Disasters

If the experiences of Vietnam veterans are extrapolated to those of disaster victims, PTSD may be more severe after a deliberate human-induced disaster than an accidental disaster. Pearce (1985), in a study of 90 veterans, divided her subjects into three groups, based on involvement in (1) a war-related event; (2) a non-war-related event; and (3) one in which there was no trauma. Those veterans experiencing a war-related event reported more problems than those experiencing a non-war-related trauma and those who experienced no trauma.

Loss

The loss of objects of importance can be devastating to individuals who survive a disaster. The type of loss may vary, for example: a loved one, prized possessions, or even a community. In addition to those responses noted under guilt and anger, bereavement becomes a part of the symptomatic picture. Loss of a prized possession such as a home may also be mourned to the extent to which the owner attached value.

A community can be viewed as more than a collection of structures and the people who live and work in them. It is made up of a series of subsystems with a set of intertwined and integrated functions, including economic, religious, educational, and political activities. Disorganization occurs when one or several of these systems fail to effectively function (Bernard, 1968). When a community is wiped out, as by floods, hurricanes, or destruction, a way of life is lost.

Fritz (1968), however, believes that disasters may produce therapeutic effects on social systems. The sharing of a common threat to life by the survivors can result, he holds, in social solidarity and a breakdown of preexisting social boundaries and economic distinctions. Although it may not always be the case, this kind of solidarity is a factor of vital significance if a community is to recuperate after its destruction.

Cultural Factors

Little information is available on the role of cultural factors in disaster. It can be assumed, however, that culturally bound beliefs affect how an individual interprets the cause of the disaster, accounts for its aftermath, and views his or her need for assistance. In the Beverly Hills Supper Club tragedy, Lindy et al. (1981) reported that many of the survivors saw their psychological impairment as evidence of weakness and felt they would have to adjust without outside help. The researchers also described the reaction of several fundamentalist ministers who would not recognize survivors as members of their respective congregations, contending that the fire was God's means of punishing the wicked behavior that takes place in a supper club.

Age

Children are often the forgotten victims of disasters (Wilkinson, 1985). Research in this area has been spotty, some of the more pertinent of which involved children in concentration camps and homeless orphans who wandered about Europe during the closing days of World War II. During the bombing of London, for example, it was found that small children who remained with their mothers or mother substitutes rather than being removed from home and taken to the safer countryside did not appear to be adversely affected. Children tended to reflect the concerns of their parents, making parental responses a critical factor in the development of pathology (Benadek, 1985).

Terr (1979) conducted extensive interviews of 26 children, ages 5–14, who were kidnapped in Chowchilla, California, in 1976 and buried alive in a truck trailer. All of the children appeared to suffer from PTSD. Observable effects 5–13 months following this stressful phenomenon included misidentification of perpetrators and/or hallucinations; absent vegetative nervous effects; fear of death, separation, or further trauma; and mild to minimal denial. It is apparent then, that children are quite vulnerable in disaster situations and that any attempts at providing relief must also involve parents.

Influence of Preexisting Psychopathology

Despite the possible roles of preexisting conflicts, functional deficits, or possible genetic relationships, it should not be assumed that the development of symptoms following a disaster signals a more impaired member of the population than others who have been exposed.

Controversy exists over the degree to which preexisting personality characteristics play a part in the psychological sequelae of disasters. The early symptomatology of PTSD will not necessarily differ in persons with underlying conflictual situations from others whose psychological picture is healthier. The importance of preexisting pathology may, however, lie in the severity and permanency of the symptoms.

Krystal (1978, p. 101) defines trauma as "the overwhelming of the normal self-preserving functions in the face of inevitable danger. The recognition of the existence of unavoidable danger and the surrender to it marks the onset of the traumatic state." Psychogenic death is the result if the traumatic process is allowed to continue uninterrupted. He states further, "What is frequently referred to as psychic trauma actually refers to the nearly traumatic situations which did not progress to a traumatic state, but which in the process of prevention precipitated neurotic or other syndromes."

Considered from this point of view, the nature and severity of already present impairment would affect the outcome of exposure to trauma. Horowitz (1986) lists six preexisting characteristics that may interfere with adaptive responses after a disaster has ended:

1. The magical belief that bad thoughts could bring about the present harm

2. The presence of an active conflict that has a theme similar to that of the disaster

3. Long-standing habitual tendencies to utilize pathological defenses (e.g., extreme projections) that externalize one's own undesirable wishes and beliefs, leading to memory distortions of the catastrophe

4. Habitual use of fantasies as a means of reparation for injuries or losses, hindering the realistic appraisal of the personal implications of the disaster

5. The presence of latent self-concepts of incompetence that can be activated as a result of the disaster

6. Fatigue of biological substrates from acute and chronic stress, leading to a repetition of depressions and/or previous somatic reactions as a consequence of the activation of emergency response systems. (Not only will these somatic responses create additional stress, but they may hinder the ability to cope with the stress of the disaster.)

A recent study by Davidson, Swartz, Storck, Krishnan, and Hammett (1985) adds another dimension to causative factors in PTSD. Family history studies of 36 veterans of Vietnam (26) and of World War II and Korea (10) revealed a family history of psychopathology in 66% of the veterans. Alcoholism, depression, and anxiety disorders were the ailments found with greatest frequency. These same patients had a higher prevalence of siblings who were alcoholic than did a retrospectively derived control group of anxious and depressed patients, at least suggesting the possibility of a genetic vulnerability to PTSD.

PTSD, CHRONIC TYPE

Personality disturbances and difficulties in interpersonal relationships are frequent concomitant findings in chronic PTSD. Job loss, marital discord with separations and divorce, increased consumption of alcohol or other chemical substances, and suicide attempts all can occur. Psychosomatic problems such as stomach ulcers, headaches, and hypertension may be prevalent, representing what Frederick (1977) calls "the psychological equivalents of self-destructive behavior." Kolb (1984) mentions one particular symptom, pain, that generally goes unmentioned in chronic cases. This symptom, particularly in the form of backache, he reports to have been prevalent also in acute PTSD during World War II.

Prominent symptoms appearing 1 or 2 years after a disaster were observed in children exposed to a tornado in Xenia, Ohio, an earthquake in San Fernando, California, and the Buffalo Creek Flood. Phobias concerning natural elements, sleep disturbances, and fear of future disasters were present, as were a loss of interest in school and an unwillingness to assume responsibility. These did not abate after the disaster, but continued 1 to 2 years afterwards. Three fourths of all of the youngsters in the community were affected (Frederick, 1977). Later effects of trauma observed by Terr (1981) in the children of Chowchilla included personality changes or chronic anxiety, fear of further trauma, traumatic play, reenactment, somatic dreams, cognitive errors, and daydreams at will.

When the disorder reaches chronicity, it can ultimately offer some diagnostic problems. In time, coexisting mental conditions can also become a part of the diagnostic picture. Assessment is necessary to differentiate other conditions such as anxiety disorder, alcohol and/or drug abuse, depression, and organic brain syndrome. Not infrequently, however, one or more disorders can also be present.

Sierles, Chen, McFarland, and Taylor (1983), utilizing a tight methodological approach, studied 25 veterans (24 of whom were Vietnam veterans), all diagnosed as having PTSD and all also having one or more additional diagnoses. Fourteen had one other diagnosis, 5 had two additional diagnoses and 2 had three additional diagnoses. Specifically, 16 were alcoholic, 5 were drug dependent, 3 had antisocial personalities, 3 displayed somatization disorders, 2 were diagnosed as having endogenous depression, and 1 presented an organic brain syndrome.

When there are several concomitant disorders, thorough medical and psychiatric history can lead to clues that the patient has experienced severe psychological trauma, allowing further inquiry to take place. Because of the associated discomfort, thinking about the event may bring about denial and conscious avoidance. Historical voids or lacunae will need to be subjected to closer scrutiny, using knowledgeable informants when available. Behaviorally and physiologically, the one symptom cluster that appears to be persistent and invariant over the years is comprised of reactions associated with arousal. Thus a startle response when exposed to stimuli specific to the stressful phenomenon, followed by active or passive efforts at shutting out this disruption, will be evident. These efforts will generally be accompanied by physiological responses consistent with excitation of the autonomic system.

Loss is the common persistent fear of disasters. The loss of life, function, and appearance due to injury, or of valued possessions all exact a toll on the surviving victim. To this is added an immediate overwhelming stress that exceeds personal coping capacities. The result can be a series of reactions that may leave the victim vulnerable to the development of additional neurotic disorders.

Specific preexisting conditions may also influence outcome. The task incumbent upon the victim involves facing the stress and all of its meanings to past and present psychical representations. This is made difficult, since the disaster will have produced a change in one's personal reality and the inner models of the world to which adaptation has to be made in order to continue life comfortably. How professionals can assist in this task is presented in the material to follow on treatment.

THEORETICAL FRAMEWORK FOR DISASTER HELP

In considering the possible interventions, one finds a spectrum of available psychotherapeutic tools and community strategies. This is a mixed blessing, in that frequently the distress of the person coupled with alterations in his or her self-regulatory mechanisms and the stress in the community tend to lead the inexperienced therapist and the rescue workers to develop complex and often confusing plans. In discussing the different models, the focus will be on conceptual clarity.

Contemporary attempts to recognize the psychological roots of the reactions in victims of disasters can be traced back to Simmel, who used hypnosis with soldiers of the German Army during World War I (Ferenczi et al., 1921). Grinker and Spiegel (1945) developed this notion further when they developed a method of treatment that included Sodium Amytal and hypnosis to facilitate remembering and emoting. The observations of Cobb and Lindemann (1943) and Lindemann (1944) of disaster victims following the Cocoanut Grove fire provided a systematic study of loss and grief reactions, stimulating in the process the work of many authors into what has come to be loosely known today as Crisis Theory. This body of knowledge has profited further from advances in community psychiatry, military medicine, and psychoanalysis. Wilkinson and Vera (1985) explored these theories and integrated different approaches to the assessment, management, and treatment of disaster victims and PTSD with knowledge gained from the Kansas City Hyatt Regency Hotel disaster.

The victims of a disaster represent a normally distributed population and therefore include persons with levels of adjustment ranging from normal to high risk in proportion to the population at large. An exception would be a disaster in a setting that selects its population, such as a fire in a mental hospital. All persons involved in a disaster respond in a qualitatively similar manner. This includes the victims, the observers, the helpers, and the community.

There is a predictable succession of phases through which a person will proceed following the impact of a disaster. The first phase consists of numbing and denial, followed by repetition and intrusion, leading to resolution or healing. The exact duration of these phases is neither predictable nor universal but in normal resolution they blend with each other in the given order and not infrequently overlap and are intertwined.

The quantitative response varies greatly for all the groups mentioned earlier and seems to be influenced by several variables, including the type of disaster, the anticipation time, the duration of the event, the availability and nature of the help provided, and individual parameters such as sociocultural and genetic backgrounds, preexisting psychopathology, life circumstances and many others. The specific roles and influences of these variables are not yet known.

MANAGEMENT OF DISASTER VICTIMS

Following a disaster, immediate solutions to practical problems are the first priority. The danger must be contained, the injured need extrication and medical care, the dead must be buried, and food and shelter must be provided for the survivors. Police, firemen, the Red Cross, physicians, and emergency medical technicians have difficult duties to perform under less than ideal circumstances. These activities should be carried out by the persons trained to do so without compounding an already crowded situation with willing but untrained helpers. Mental health professionals, although well-meaning, are unlikely to be helpful for these functions. It then follows that the emergency-preparedness plan of any community should include basic disaster assistance training for emergency physicians, nurses, policemen, fire fighters and emergency fieldworkers. The National Institute of Mental Health and the Public Health Service publish and maintain a number of books and field manuals on the subject, which are easily available from the U.S. Government Printing Office.

During the early phases of a disaster, mental health workers are best utilized away from the immediate site, in aid stations, hospital emergency rooms, and so forth. The victims are bewildered, frightened, and in a state of helplessness. It is helpful for the provider to convey genuine regard, interest, and respect. Within the framework of a flexible structure, empathic listening should occur, as well as locating loved ones, reassuring relatives, and answering questions. To be perceived as helpful the provider must assist the victims to face the reality of the moment, which is also the beginning of working through feelings of helplessness engendered by the disaster.

Mental health professionals with formal training in diagnostic and assessment skills, besides providing supervision and consultation for such efforts, are needed to help identify high-risk victims. There is some consensual agreement that the severely injured with anticipated loss of function, victims entrapped for an extended period, any person with preexisting psychopathology, the young, the elderly, and persons undergoing a life crisis are high-risk groups deserving special follow-up.

Generally, assistance for disaster victims centers around three basic areas of intervention, namely education, support, and crisis intervention.

Education

Victims and relatives need to be told that they will experience unusual reactions that are normal following a disaster, what those reactions will be, and how to deal with them. They should also receive information regarding the resources to contact should they feel the need for expert help. Encouragement should be given to access those resources without hesitation, but only in the case of high-risk victims should this encouragement become advice. The main purpose of education is to give disaster victims the tools with which to take charge of their lives again.

Education can be enhanced by the cooperation of the mental health community with radio and television stations broadcasting to the afflicted area. During the Hyatt disaster, mental health and media representatives met and developed a general education series to be aired repeatedly. If at all possible, the audience can be greatly helped if the information addresses the phase-specific experiences of the survivors, the timing of which may be based on when most practitioners see persons with a given cluster of responses during their clinical contact. In the absence of a predictable timetable, but knowing that for most people the different phases are experienced in a predictable sequence, this self-regulating feedback loop appears the best way to maintain relevancy. Persons in a denial phase are not likely to find information about startle responses very relevant if they are not experiencing them, and victims who are having repetitive nightmares of the disaster may actually wish they could forget that it ever happened. Because normally there is a period in which almost all affected persons avoid any sensory input that reminds them of the disaster, radio and television stations should avoid pictures and background sounds that are likely to make uncomfortable the very same public that they are trying to reach.

Support

Offering education, support, and crisis intervention in group settings provides many advantages in disaster help. It is economical in the use of the already taxed time of mental health professionals and provides a setting in which victims can realize the commonality of their experience.

The sense of a group working together toward a common goal is reassuring to people who have experienced helplessness and loss, perhaps to a degree never before encountered in their lives. It should be clear that the reference here is a working group and not to a psychotherapy group; the participants are by definition normal people learning to deal with a very unusual experience. The themes of normalcy of the response, temporary emotional turmoil, and the need for time to settle things down cannot be emphasized enough, especially to mental health professionals accustomed to conceptualizing in terms of psychopathology. The general attitude should be, ''We are here to help you, and you must tell us what is or is not helpful to you. We do not know exactly what this is like for you, but we have a general idea of what most people go through. Don't be afraid, you are not alone.'' For disaster victims who have already experienced being out of control and confused, it is even more confusing to be told by "experts" that they are not feeling or reacting appropriately.

In order to help the victims maintain a clear separation between these responses and psychopathological ones, it is useful, if possible, to conduct the groups in places other than mental health centers and hospitals. Churches and community centers, shopping centers, and town halls are better choices. Knowing the natural tendency for disaster victims to avoid physical reminders of the trauma, if choices are available, it is better to avoid closeness to the disaster site or access routes that require seeing the area again. For instance, after the Hyatt disaster, some persons avoided the support groups offered by one mental health center two blocks away and in direct view of the hotel.

One area often overlooked in group support for disaster victims is the uniqueness of the individual within the commonality of the experience. Whereas the need to tend to large groups without prior warning calls for generic planning, overlooking ethnic and sociocultural backgrounds, religious beliefs, individual value systems, and personal cognitive styles diminishes the relevancy of the help offered and in some cases could even be counterproductive. For instance, a quiet and introspective working-class Protestant, who has resolved a prior crisis drawing from inner resources and guidance from the Bible and who perceives a disaster as a test of faith in God, may not find angry emoting in a cathartic group a very coherent way to deal with inner pain. Similarly a Catholic spouse of Italian extraction with an extended family may not find much help in the explanation that his wife's withdrawal from church and family is a temporary phenomenon and that she needs to be given time to herself.

In regard to ethnicity, sociocultural differences, religious beliefs, value systems, and personal style, the most astute approach is to recognize that because most mental health personnel are not experts in these areas, it is essential to learn about such values from "inside the person." Not only would it increase the likelihood of helpfulness, it would, in addition, provide the opportunity for learning quite a bit.

Crisis Intervention

The basic concepts of crisis intervention are that (1) the coping skills of normal persons are temporarily overwhelmed, (2) rapid and specific help from others can restore the person to the precrisis level of functioning, (3) only those functions that the persons cannot handle should be handled by others, (4) the help offered must be congruent with the usual coping style of the person, (5) help should be discontinued as soon as possible.

Crisis intervention is the accepted first line of approach for disaster victims. The attempt is to resolve an immediate crisis situation. The goals are symptom relief and restoration to a precrisis level of functioning. The areas of emphasis are the manifest complaints of the victim and the alteration in the present level of functioning. The interactions between the crisis helper and the victim are confined to the conscious experiences and problems in the here and now, in a time-limited manner. The intervention of the helper is active and direct, and the technical process may include support, reassurance, guidance, clarification, environmental manipulation, and group support. The following example describes such an intervention.

CASE 2

A middle-aged man brought his wife to the emergency room of a mental health center in the early hours of the morning approximately 10 days following the Hyatt Regency Hotel disaster. He felt that she needed admission for depression and exhaustion. In the initial interview he provided information while she sat despondently in a chair, looking down and making occasional comments to indicate disagreement and frustration. According to him, she had not gone to work for 4 days, was not eating, refused to go to bed at night, and instead just sat in the family room crying. He could not sleep knowing that she was alone and crying, but she would send him back to bed asking to be left alone. She would take cat naps during the day while he was at work. He had taken her to the family doctor about 6 days earlier, and the doctor had advised that she should eat and sleep and had prescribed an antidepressant. She had refused to take it after the first few doses because it made her mouth dry and because, she stated, she was not crazy. The interviewer asked everyone else to leave the room and said to the woman that perhaps she had not had a chance to tell her side of the story and that he would like to hear it (removing her from the passive role of a woman who was going crazy). She said that a co-worker with whom she shared an office had died in the disaster. She, with a group from her department, had gone to the hotel for the Friday happy hour. She left the hotel early and heard the news at home while watching TV with her husband. She spent most of that evening and the next morning contacting co-workers, and by early Saturday afternoon she learned that her friend was in critical condition at a hospital near the Hyatt. On Sunday morning she did not go to church with her husband, their usual custom, so that she could visit her friend. Twice she got into the car and started on her way but turned around each time and returned home. She stated she could not bring herself to drive by the Hyatt or return to the general area. Her friend died late Sunday evening. When she returned to work on Monday morning, she gave a donation for the family of the deceased and learned that the family had requested a closed casket funeral as there were massive injuries. She could not tolerate the empty office and went home shortly before noon. Since then she had been as her husband had described her, but he did not know that she avoided going to sleep because she had bad dreams in which she saw images from the TV newscast and her friend trying to talk to her. The husband had been trying to take her out to help her get her mind off of the catastrophe, but although she knew better, she felt irritated with him and felt he was insensitive. She could not refrain from acting angry at him and was afraid that she was losing her mind. The interviewer stated that there was no evidence that she was losing her mind but that she was responding to the loss of her friend and feeling guilty at not having seen her before her death (the interviewer here was providing expert information and giving some sense to her experience). In the joint interview that followed, the couple was told that the wife did not need hospitalization but that they needed to deal with the way that the disaster had affected their life (defining the problem as a workable one and taking into account the distress of the husband). The family needed to rest and sleep better as they were both exhausted (focusing on a common problem). She had bad dreams at bedtime, but could take naps during the day. He worried about her at night but had to go to work during the day. They were asked if they knew how each felt about it (no longer mental illness or insensitivity but a lack of communication). As is usually the case, they began to talk to each other and with some help reached the following compromises. She would stay in bed and not try to sleep if she did not feel comfortable, a light would be left on, and she would wake him up if she needed him. The next Sunday he would drive her to the cemetery and be with her while she paid her respects to her friend (a constructive act for her that involved both). As soon as she felt like it, she would call the family of her friend and find out if she could help by watching the children after her working hours. Her husband would drive her and help also (again a way for her to constructively deal with her guilt within her value system). One or two evenings per week they both would attend a support group for disaster victims to learn how to deal with these normal reactions (focusing on normal, and giving the couple an active role in learning how to deal with this problem). She had enough sick leave for the remainder of the week but would start to work the following Monday (indicating without pressing that life had to go on). The interviewer would call the family doctor and explain why the antidepressant was not needed any more (removing a source of friction and taking responsibility for something that the couple could not be expected to handle at that point). On leaving, they were told that in case of need, they should not hesitate to call, but the interviewer expected them to handle this together as they had most things for the last 20 years (giving the couple responsibility back for their life together). A phone call from the husband several days later indicated that she was back at work and had occasional nightmares but was feeling much better.

Mental health professionals working with disaster victims need to remember that although the expectation is that most people receiving assistance will be fairly normal people reacting to the events, occasionally a person may feel suicidal or be deeply disturbed and this possibility must not be overlooked in the midst of focusing on normal responses and normal reactions. Ideally, anyone working in this area should be able to do a quick assessment of the mental state and suicidal potential of disaster victims, both in the initial contact and on an ongoing basis. Realistically, following a disaster, more mental health workers will be needed than are available. Many will be pressed into action who do not, as part of their regular work, have the opportunity to practice and maintain the skills needed for dealing with the kind of emergency caused by the disaster. On these occasions it is reassuring and helpful to know that consultation is available, and this service should be arranged as a part of the overall approach.

Since suicidal potential is frequently an issue whether one is providing education for victims, offering individual or group support, or conducting crisis intervention, it merits detailed consideration. The mental health worker making the first contact with the victims is in the most strategic position to identify vulnerable persons and initiate the line of referral that could prevent unnecessary loss of life.

Evaluation of Suicidal Potential

The major concern in evaluating suicide potential is not whether a person will engage in suicidal behavior, but rather whether the person exhibits a state of mind in which suicide may appear as a possible alternative. Other than in the most general sense, prediction of specific behavior is not yet within the reach of mental health professionals. It is possible to hypothesize under what conditions a patient may feel very despondent, but there is no way of knowing what a given person will specifically do after he leaves the presence of the mental health worker.

In assessing suicidal potential it is helpful to remember that victims tend to become frightened by their suicidal ideation, may fear to be labeled crazy, and may not volunteer information in this regard. Along the same line some will project this apprehension on the worker and will then fear rejection or involuntary hospitalization. It is reassuring for the victim to hear the worker approach these issues in the same calm, professional, and matter-of-fact manner in which other issues are discussed, using the words of the patient but avoiding euphemisms.

In a systematic manner the following areas should be explored, deepening the exploration on cue from the responses of the victim:

1. Is the person thinking about suicide?
2. Has the person contemplated or acted on suicidal thoughts before?
3. Are suicidal thoughts occasional and mildly disturbing, frequent and frightening, or intrusive and not resisted?
4. Has the person made specific suicidal plans?

Even if one of these statements is positive it can indicate a serious suicidal risk. One would then want to know if the means to carry out the act is easily available or if the person has considered how to effect the means and has a point of reference to act on the suicidal plans; for example, "If I continue having these nightmares, I am going to jump off a bridge" (an actual case).

Further exploration should also be given to the following known parameters that influence suicidal potential:

1. Is there a history of suicide by family members?
2. Is this a religious person, a believer rather than simply a member? What is the position of his or her faith regarding suicide?
3. What are the attitudes of the person's sociocultural group in regard to suicide?
4. Is the person disenfranchised or a member of a group?

If suicidal potential cannot be ruled out, arrangements must be made for safe referral. If the conclusion has been reached that the person represents an unacceptable suicidal risk, the most frequent mistake is to revise one's decision to obtain further evaluation in response to the person's denial of intent.

Effects on Disaster Workers

Disaster assistance must also be considered in regard to the impact that this exposure has for disaster workers. Wilkinson (1983) finds that the workers are affected qualitatively in a manner that cannot be distinguished from the responses of the victims. The issues confronted by emergency care providers involve the awareness of their own personal vulnerability, which is no different from that for the rest of the community. They are also made aware of their own professional limitations at a time when normally professional identity is a source of internal support. Guilt related to the idea of profiting from the pain of others is another issue that confronts them. Besides protecting workers from personal pain, understanding of these responses facilitates coherent functioning of trained emergency personnel under the trying pressure of disaster work. Vera (1982) describes role- and function-specific responses and suggests some preventive strategies that could be incorporated in emergency-preparedness planning.

To protect themselves from threats to their own sense of personal and professional omnipotence, denial and hypomanic defenses are frequently used. To ward off the massive sensory assault caused by blood, pain, and dismemberment, intellectual defenses and isolation of the affect appear to be favored mechanisms. Guilt regarding professional or monetary gains tends to cause a narcissistic wound that develops and heals slowly and seems compensated by intensified identification with the peer group and compensatory altruism. A few examples will make these problems of disaster workers clear.

The Monday following the Hyatt Regency Hotel disaster, mental health professionals from all the neighboring mental health centers met to coordinate crisis support efforts. It was clearly too early to know the full impact on the community, and even the state-of-the-art knowledge regarding disaster victims could not provide clear information as to what would be needed. A single-page memorandum was circulated that was no more than a speculation as to who might be at risk. It was treated by all as a scientific document. It provided enough reassurance to allow the group to get on with the work without too much anxiety, but for it to work the memo had to be treated as meaningful, and a great deal of time was spent reviewing it in detail. It was only recognized for what it was many months later.

A group of mental health professionals met with media representatives to plan a series of general education bulletins to be aired by a local TV station. The meeting began by considering the different high-risk groups to be covered, but it soon became a highly unrealistic enterprise in which the general mental health of the population and the cause of community mental health were about to be drastically improved. It was only after someone commented that the meeting was being held because a lot of people could be in trouble and no one knew how else to reach them that the task got underway.

A group of nurses who were working the emergency room of a hospital two blocks away from the Hyatt Regency Hotel were given occasional breaks from their work with the most seriously wounded. Later they stated that they preferred to work until exhausted and leave the area permanently, as those short interruptions caused them to have to shift emotional gears and that was more distressing. They found dealing with relatives who were their social and cultural peers the most painful part of the experience.

A support group for emergency room personnel was mainly attended by medical students who had not been present at the time of the disaster. It was later learned that the senior residents and other physicians responsible for arranging the meeting, who had actually been in the emergency room the evening of the disaster, felt that they did not need it but that the medical students could learn something from it.

After the completion of the taping for a TV interview, the reporter and a mental health professional engaged in informal talk. The reporter stated that he had been in Vietnam but nothing had prepared him for what he saw at the Hyatt. He went on to say that for several days he had been aware of a repetitive thought, namely that his career could benefit from good professional work in covering the events but he wished that this did not have to come about by the loss of so many lives. He noticed that he had volunteered to man an aid station after hours and he wondered about his reasons since he was in general working double shifts and exhausted.

The area of disaster workers' personal and group responses is in need of formal exploration as it has important implications for the military and for communities in peacetime disasters.

TREATMENT OF POST-TRAUMATIC STRESS DISORDERS

Helping and Treating

It is important to separate clearly the action of helping disaster victims from that of treating patients suffering from incapacitating symptoms. This separation is particularly important in a condition in which it is often impossible to predict from the initial responses who will go on with life and who will become a psychological casualty.

Those victims of a disaster whose responses exceed the consensual norm and who are therefore diagnosed as suffering from PTSD prompt consideration of preexisting conflict, deficits in adjustment, or already taxed coping skills. Such considerations must be kept in mind, because those persons in need of treatment after disaster are the ones with post-traumatic stress disorder, that is, individuals who have not been able to reconstitute or heal spontaneously or in a sufficient manner utilizing the available resources. They are therefore not likely to derive benefit from more of the same.

Diagnostic Assessment

For most mental health professionals, diagnosis refers to labeling and may bring to mind the official diagnostic manual of the American Psychiatric Association, DSM-III-R. Other than as a starting point, the use of a descriptive diagnosis is inadequate. Assessment for treatment involves many areas of inquiry that are impossible to consider in a descriptive diagnosis. An added problem with all descriptive diagnostic codifications is that they cannot provide a conceptual framework to separate the universal stress experienced by all persons exposed to a traumatic experience from the enduring experience of the ones who will require treatment for it. In defense of DSM-III-R, however, it must be said that as a system of labeling, developed principally from symptom counting (as is the case of all medical diagnoses), it provides more objectivity than previous descriptive diagnoses.

Assessment begins with the initial contact, which frequently is made by phone.

The First Contact

It is important to notice who is requesting the appointment. If other than the patient, that is, family member, lawyer, minister, physician, or other mental health provider, the contact person can provide early clues about the current functioning of the patient. Such clues may pertain to interpersonal relationships, legal complications, moral issues, somatic manifestations, or psychological conflicts. A note should be made about the nature of the observations for future comparison with the patient's perception of the catastrophe.

If the patient is available to come to the phone, this should always be requested in order to establish early with whom one is working and to set clearly the lines of confidentiality. Whenever possible, an appointment should be set for the next day or no more than 2 days from the time of the call. If the patient is in distress, he or she should be seen the same day or offered a referral to a colleague who can arrange an immediate appointment.

Unless there is sufficient data to determine such things as suicidal intent, gross psychotic symptoms, or organic confusion, the patient must be involved and have the last say in these preliminary arrangements. The treatment of PTSD involves people who are in trouble because of events that were out of their control. Nothing could be more therapeutic than to put them back in charge of their affairs as soon as possible.

The First Interview

The first assessment session, as well as all future sessions, should provide an environment that is predictable and structured, yet flexible, so as to allow the patient to tell his or her story and explore its meaning without feeling restricted. An analogy that is useful compares the therapist to a set of training wheels, allowing the patient to pedal away in safety.

If someone has accompanied the patient, that person should be greeted and recognized as someone important to the patient but should not follow the patient into the interview room. It should be stated in gentle but clear terms that one wants to hear about the situation from the patient and that others can be seen later, in the presence of the patient, if it is jointly decided that this is indicated.

The patient should be told that the interview is likely to last 45 minutes (or whatever may be the therapist's custom) and that at the end a joint decision will be made as to how future contacts will proceed.

The therapist must provide structure from the beginning without restricting content. A question such as "What brought you to me?" or "How can I help you?" should suffice. The patient must not be left wandering and not knowing what to do or made to feel that events are out of his or her hands and under control of the therapist.

As the patient's narrative unfolds, the role of the therapist is to file away information for further exploration and to note the level of anxiety. If the patient becomes uncomfortable, anxious, silent, or circumstantial, the therapist should refocus without contaminating, mainly by rephrasing the patient's last relevant statement or by stating that there will be time to go over things again and directing the patient back to the main theme.

This first exposure to the patient's spontaneous thoughts should be utilized to obtain a general idea of the patient's overall level of functioning and main areas of pain. As one is listening, a gross differential diagnosis to rule out organic, psychotic, or suicidal content must be performed. Exploration of any of these areas as they occur is probably the only valid reason to interrupt the patient at this time.

Following the patient's recount, one can embark on the exploration of significant material following the patient's clues. On behalf of clarity both for the patient and the therapist, it is best to keep the early exploration centered around the chief complaint and the history of the present illness. Although the reminder for flexible order and structure may appear repetitive, it is only to stress the therapeutic importance of role modeling for the patient. Approaching a problem in an organized manner, proceeding from the general to the specific, establishing levels of priorities and breaking down large areas into small manageable ones tends to decrease the anxiety of the patient. It also creates a sense of predictability and appeals to integrative ego functions without unnecessary distractions.

It is important for the therapist to have a definite interview model from which to proceed. The following is offered as a guide for organizing one's approach.

1. The chief complaint
2. The history of the present illness
3. Developmental history including psychiatric history and substance abuse
4. Medical sequelae and past medical history
5. Sociocultural and educational background and work history
6. The support system

Also, it is necessary to have a clear frame of reference with which to organize data regarding the mental status.

1. General observations
2. Orientation to time, place, person, and situation
3. Memory of recent and remote events and immediate retention and recall
4. Intellectual functions
5. Level of abstraction
6. Thought format
7. Thought content
8. Mood
9 Affect
10. Insight and judgment

Having clear protocols like the ones presented here will help the therapist follow the patient without jumping back and forth and confusing the patient or missing important data in the midst of the patient's affective intensity.

It should be clearly understood that the format presented here is for the written record and not for interrogating the patient.

If suicide potential, psychosis, or organicity is found, it would be addressed in the standard manner, otherwise arrangements can be made for a second interview soon to follow. It is likely that the patient or the family, with understandable concern, will request a statement regarding what to expect next. For the sake of trust and credibility it is important to relay only what is thus far known. "You are uncomfortable, and it seems related to the events that you experienced. There is help for this, but now I need to think about what you told me, and together we can explore what else in your life is making things difficult for you."

If the patient has been able to provide a fair amount of information, one should be able to construct a general theory regarding the diagnosis and overall level of functioning. Information about the basic personality structure will give not only a descriptive personality type but also a perspective of enduring patterns of behavior, feeling, and thinking. It provides a psychological blueprint of the person beyond the present disruption of balance. The technique for personality assessment is beyond the scope of this chapter, but it should be familiar to professionals involved in psychotherpay.

Evaluation of Ego Functions

It is important to evaluate ego functions as thoroughly as possible. A structured review of ego functions as presently displayed by the patient, compared with a reconstruction of the habitual and stable level of pretrauma functioning, can offer a clear picture of traumatic alterations versus the overall level of organization. This can be very helpful in establishing achievable treatment goals and measurable progress. (See Bellack, 1973; Wilkinson and Vera, 1985.)

The Developmental History

A systematic exploration of age-specific developmental milestones is needed to learn areas of successful resolution or of potential vulnerability. This is significant because a similarity exists between mastery of developmental stages and resources to master crises. Erickson's (1963) model of eight developmental phases might provide insight into the nature of the anxiety, the perception of the experience, and likely perceptions of the therapy and the therapist.

It is helpful in general, and specifically with disaster victims, to train oneself to listen to the patient for persecutory or depressive anxieties and for the intensity of their content. This allows the therapist to make contact with the patient in a supportive manner while making interpretative comments. The following case excerpt demonstrates this technique.

CASE 3

Approximately 5 months following the Hyatt Regency Hotel disaster, a middle-aged man was brought to the emergency room by his wife, apparently much against his will, because of concern over his drinking and his stated expression of wanting to get a divorce. Both his behavior and his open statement about divorce were out of character for him.

From the wife it was learned that the patient had invited a good friend for a drink in the bar in the main lobby of the hotel but had arrived late. His friend suffered severe trauma, loss of a limb, and permanent brain damage. The patient was instrumental, after the disaster, in helping the family of his friend and seemed normal until he was invited to a block party given to celebrate his good luck. Shortly afterward he began to act as described by the wife.

When seen in the emergency room he was restless and angry, stating his sarcastic disbelief in shrinks and other charlatans. He felt that he needed no help and that his wife was uptight because finally she would have to take care of herself without having anyone on whom to depend. After a moment of silence the interviewer made the following comment, "Perhaps to accept that you need help and that something can be done for you makes you feel more guilty." The man became quite moved by this and after a cathartic discharge settled down to the business of the interview.

Following the disaster, this man had entered a denial phase rather abruptly, perhaps precipitated by his need to avoid thoughts of how lucky he was (compared with his friend). The party upset this shaky balance, and he entered the intrusion phase. With denial no longer available, he attempted to escalate his defenses to protect against guilt.

As the therapist identified the conflict (getting or receiving something increases guilt) the patient was able to give up the hypomanic defenses of omnipotence and devaluation (I do not need anything, my wife does; you are charlatans) that were defenses against his depressive anxiety (I am bad and deserve no help), thus allowing him to feel his distress (a cathartic discharge followed) and to accept assistance.

In order to complete the assessment of a patient it is necessary to know what type of disaster assistance was available and his or her overall opinion of its helpfulness. Cultural and individual variables may be identified that might otherwise go unnoticed. The major purpose of the assessment includes identification of what is healthy and working and therefore needs no tampering. It also tries to establish what type of intervention is likely to be most helpful to a patient.

As one listens to the patient, data can be organized as belonging to the past, the present, and/or the interaction with the therapist. It matters little in what area a clue is first noticed, its significance can be ascertained by looking for parallels in any of the other areas. The formulation of its meaning can be tested by exploring the anticipated answer in the area in which the problem exists. The following case example demonstrates this principle.

CASE 4

A Hyatt disaster victim who had in his first interview discussed at length his frustration regarding legal delays in the settlement of his claim for medical bills suddenly shifted to his childhood years and began to talk about an uncle whom he considered quite knowledgeable in mathematics. This was a subject that the patient had struggled with but believed could have been made much easier had his uncle volunteered to help. The comment that perhaps he wondered if help from the therapist would be forthcoming or withheld brought about a confirmatory response, and he went on to say that he had postponed calling his lawyer for help with the Hyatt attorneys because he did not expect much help there. He commented that this had not been typical of him prior to the disaster as he was considered quite effective and assertive.

The diagnostic assessment should not be considered complete until the therapist feels confident of understanding the data sufficiently to formulate the problem. The formulation should take into account the known developmental history, the nature of the disaster, the present reality of the patient, the defensive meaning of the symptoms, and the anticipated complications, including the transferential and countertransferential reactions. The following case excerpt demonstrates such an assessment.

CASE 5

The patient, a 28-year-old female, a college graduate with a master's degree in business administration grew up feeling insecure and rejected as the older daughter of alcoholic parents. Competition with her younger sister based on the family's tendency to polarize the siblings, had caused confusion and guilt during the teen years and an avoidance of her femininity. Insecure and longing for parental acceptance, she accepted the parental stereotype as "the ugly one" and avoided dating to confirm the role of her sister as "the good-looking one." With the independence gained by her years at college and success in her chosen field, she began to feel somewhat confident and became engaged. To celebrate her promising future and to set aside their earlier conflicts, she invited her sister to join her on the fateful night of the Hyatt disaster. Her sister was severely injured in the holocaust that followed.

The sister's injuries reawakened old hostilities and concomitant guilt. Her devotion to helping her sister recover, setting aside her wedding plans and career aspirations, was both a demonstration of her capacity for caring and of the unresolved masochistic guilt. The transference of this patient was likely to be ambivalent, with strong wishes for nurturance and rejection of help to avoid guilt. Countertransferentially, insistence on emoting the disaster experience could represent the therapist's identification with critical parental attitudes. At the same time granting the patient unlimited time to explore her pain might reinforce the feeling that she was not likely to achieve very much. The correct therapeutic stance was to help her explore the painful memories of the event while remaining available to protect her from too much pain (like a competent and sober parent), encouraging her to try to explore as much as she could without selling herself short (as did her parents whose attitude and behavior polarized her to feel as if she were the ugly and incompetent child at war with her sister).

The treatment plan consisted of dynamically oriented psychotherapy, bi-weekly, for approximately 6 months. The suicidal potential was minimal but required watching. There was no anticipated need for psychotropic medication.

The most frequently found problems in the treatment of patients with post-traumatic stress disorders are early avoidance of affect and the expectation that the therapist can heal without their having to face the painful memories, images, sensations, and so forth. There may be a reluctance to consider prior conflict by finding sufficient explanation in the disaster itself, as well as ambivalence between getting better and collecting compensation. Unconsciously there can be the refusal to reengage with life because it is too unpredictable and/or fear of the reactivation of guilt on getting better. Finally there may be reluctance to leave the safety of psychotherapy and to face life on one's own.

In the course of evaluation or treatment one often encounters deeply seated conflicts sufficient to warrant psychotherapy even if the PTSD were absent. The appropriate course is to highlight the need for definitive work in that area but to stick with the business at hand. The patient can be advised to seek elective psychotherapy some time after regaining the level of functioning existing prior to the disaster and subsequent PTSD. To do otherwise is to take the risk that neither the PTSD nor the preexisting pathology will be properly resolved.

The purpose of this chapter is not to cover techniques of psychotherapy. However, in addition to being skilled in techniques deriving from a variety of theoretical orientations, it would also be useful for the therapist working with victims of PTSD to be competent in dynamic psychotherapy and to have a reasonable understanding of his or her own countertransferential responses. When the concepts presented are ignored, the results can be disastrous for the patient. The following case excerpt is not an atypical course for patients with PTSD. It is included here to emphasize the need for order and conceptual clarity in the assessment and treatment of these patients.

CASE 6

W.H., a 30-year-old man, was born to an upper middle-class family. His father, whom he ambivalently loved and respected, appeared quite concerned with his own physical symptoms during W.H.'s growing-up years.

He presently is dying of a debilitating disease. The mother was highly idealized by W.H. and a source of both affection and guilt.

Following severe economical loss mainly caused by the father's neglect of his business because of preoccupation with his health, the family disbanded when W.H. was 5 years old, and shelter was sought with relatives in different nations.

W.H. and his siblings went to live with the mother at the home of her relatives in the United States while the father tried to reorganize his finances in another country. During these years, the patient was sexually molested and overstimulated by close relatives. He did not want to have this fact known because he feared it would further burden his family and also because he felt quite worried about and afraid of his distant father.

The family finally came together during W.H.'s teen years, and shortly after, he became very active sexually, in a casual and promiscuous manner. There was also the sporadic use of alcohol and occasionally, marijuana. By this time the patient felt quite unhappy, anxious, and guilty, and although he was active heterosexually, there were sexual identity doubts. Externally, he was doing very well in school, was popular with the peer group, and had many athletic and cultural interests. He had also maintained close contact with a few long-term friends in spite of the frequent moves.

When political tensions in the country intensified, W.H. was inducted into the military where he received paramedical training. On active duty, many of W.H.'s peers were maimed and killed. Once while awaiting evacuation at the end of patrol duty, 16 survivors died as a military air transport was hit by enemy fire during takeoff. W.H., who was waiting in line for the next airvac, had to push aside body parts and debris to clear the runway. Shortly after his removal from the combat zone, he became ill with fever and experienced nightmares. W.H. was evacuated to a field hospital and experienced a period of depersonalization; this episode, however, was attributed to smoking marijuana. A sporadic and fluctuating clinical picture, including an increase in anxiety, nightmares, startle responses, lassitude, muscle weakness, and vague somatic complaints, has existed since that time.

Following discharge from the military, he completed paramedical studies and has had continual employment as an emergency medical technician with one significant exception. On the evening of the Hyatt disaster in Kansas City, he was part of one of the rescue crews charged with removing bodies from the lobby of the hotel. He felt calm and competent and functioned until relieved by a fresh crew. He quit his job 2 weeks later, terminated his engagement 2 months before the wedding date, and roamed the country for several months. Upon return he was reemployed and to this date is considered a good and dependable worker.

However, W.H. cannot fly in an airplane because of anxiety. He avoids airports, cannot tolerate war or disaster movies, and will not talk about his military experience or the events at the Hyatt. He is afraid to go out because of an impending fear of bodily collapse, broods over the past in constant anxiety, and is unable to pursue relationships for fear of repeating a, by now, familiar cycle of initial enthusiasm followed by disenchantment. Heterosexual experiences, which are now infrequent, are tainted with the fear of not being able to perform and a wish to be free of the partner once the encounter is over. He does not now abuse drugs or use alcohol. W.H. has been receiving psychotherapy or some form of mental health services for several years.

Shortly after discharge from the military, a diagnosis of traumatic neurosis was made and W.H. attended a service-sponsored support group, which he found helpful in that it provided a sense of camaraderie but little more.

In response to a request for help with anxiety, W.H. was started on minor tranquilizers, which provided some relief, but after some months of use they were discontinued, as he became concerned with the increasing dosage and lessened relief.

Lack of any substantial progress led to another evaluation in which a diagnosis of schizophrenia was made. He was instructed about his "new illness," told what areas of conflict to avoid, and began a treatment regime consisting of a psychotropic medication and monthly visits of reality-oriented counseling. This evaluation took place after his return to Kansas City following the Hyatt disaster, but he was not asked and did not volunteer information about this experience. Initially W.H. felt hopeful in that even with the seriousness of the diagnosis, a promising course of action was offered. He found the reality sessions a bit demeaning as they seemed to reiterate the obvious but decided to stick it out. It was when the side effects of the psychotropic medication threatened to impair the clarity of mind needed for his line of work that he discontinued the therapy.

By now, W.H. had decided to seek help independently. However, he continued attending the veteran's support group and kept clinic appointments, prescriptions included, so as to not jeopardize the service-connected benefits. He began weekly sessions with a nonservice-connected therapist and began to feel better. After roughly 1 year this therapy was interrupted due to a serious illness on the part of the therapist.

W.H. felt that there was sufficient symptom relief and that a very limited lifestyle was possible at the price of phobic seclusion and avoidance of dating. Social activities were reduced to the workplace and weekly phone calls to members of the family. After some time, a budding sense of confidence led him to consider a serious relationship but after several months of romantic enjoyment, a disappointment precipitated the old symptoms again.

W.H. entered a psychiatric institution and was started on tricyclic antidepressants. When, after several weeks of increasing dosage, the patient showed no improvement and complained of increased muscle weakness, a neurological consultation was requested. His work-up included a muscle biopsy but failed to yield any significant findings.

W.H. was then offered the opportunity of participating in a new drug research trial. He accepted, experienced moderate side effects, but continued to maintain a faint ray of hope. At the same time, in rapid succession he consulted several clinics and independent practitioners who suggested and/or actually administered the following: an assertiveness group, transcendental meditation, an encounter group, hypnosis, autogenic training, an anger control group, crisis intervention, and short term anxiety-producing therapy.

The review of W.H.'s clinical records, by now quite massive, did not contain a longitudinal psychosocial history, formal diagnostic work-up, records of structured interveiws, or systematic personality assessment. The only formal review of the data was in connection with a summation for continued benefits and seemed more suited for a legal brief than for a clinical case summary.

Despite earning several diagnoses (marijuana use or abuse, schizophrenia, depression) and undergoing a myriad of treatment approaches, this patient fulfills the criteria for a DSM-III diagnosis of chronic post-traumatic stress disorder. The major problem is not necessarily one of wrong diagnosis but of incomplete diagnosis and incomplete assessment. The diagnosis of PTSD is clearly superimposed on long-term neurotic conflicts and maladaptive character traits, and chronicity has been enhanced by the overall mismanagement. Most of the operational decisions were made in response to a given symptom without a conceptual integration of all of the clinical data so necessary before embarking on a therapeutic intervention.

A retrospective view of the underlying psychopathology reveals a host of conflicts that singly or collectively would likely have culminated in an emotional illness even without the experience of an overwhelming trauma. Considering his conflicts from the standpoint of the ailment that would have to be the first considered for treatment—PTSD—it is apparent that for the most part he has been subject to the intrusive phase with all of its attendant symptoms. He has, despite the marked discomfort, continued working and tenaciously holds to the belief that he can eventually be relieved of his frightening and troublesome symptoms. Considering the fact that his work as a paramedic places him in the untenable position of having to unexpectantly confront from time to time the very things he would like to avoid, for example, maimed and mutilated bodies or even another disaster, one wonders if counterphobic mechanisms were operative in the selection of his choice of a career. In the periods in which he was relatively calm and in the instance in which he became romantically involved, the phase of denial was prominent.

Given the above factors, what does W.H. have to accomplish therapeutically in order to finally establish an acceptable level of adaptation? Ordinarily, a PTSD patient would have to correctly perceive the event and its true meanings and relate these meanings experientially to the representations of his or her own cognitive system. The individual would then be able to revise the memory, belief systems, and attitudes and decide on appropriate actions to promote assimilation of this new experience (Horowitz, 1986). However, the therapeutic work with W.H. will have to facilitate the mourning of early losses before the working-through process can begin.

This of course is easier said than done. If phase-oriented therapy, as proposed by Horowitz (1986) and utilized in the approach to treatment described in this chapter, is followed, the therapist must be cognizant of the phase of response being endured by the patient. During the denial–numbing phase, the therapist attempts to reduce controls and encourage memory of the event, catharsis, and a reproduction of images, affect, and other sensations associated with the event. If the patient is in the intrusive phase, structure becomes important in an effort to dampen the repetitious stimuli. Reality must be differentiated from fantasy, demands on the patient reduced, and support provided. Rest and permission for temporary dependency is allowed. The intrusive interruption has to be dealt with by titrating the amount that can be handled at a given time and at other times by helping the patient turn away from stress-laden material. Through all of this as much working through as can be tolerated should occur.

Individual psychotherapy is not the only treatment advanced for chronic PTSD; group therapy, group counseling, psychopharmaceutics, hypnosis, relaxation, and biofeedback all have been or are being used. Kolb (1984) feels that none of the current therapies alleviate the constant symptoms of PTSD. Although such treatments may reduce some of the intensity of the symptoms, he contends that the disordered process persists and may be aggravated when accosted by new social or physical stress. He supports Kardiner's contention (1941) after examining combat victims, that the constant symptoms are due to conditioning. The disorder was denoted by Kardiner as a physioneurosis, an unstable somatic condition. Kolb's interpretation of the origin of these chronic symptoms . . .

> is that there has occurred a conditioned stimulus attachment of overwhelming or long continued fear, inducing combat stimuli to the infantile startle reflex existent in all. It is known . . . that this infantile reflex may be conditioned. The latter arousal of the fear in social situations alone may induce the conditioned response. The conditioned response consists of not only the initial startle but may also be expressed in behavioral, cognitive, affective and somatic change (p. 238).

Other symptoms, such as guilt, rage, and other neurotic behavior are viewed as secondary symptoms aroused by the repetitious intrusion of images, dreams, and memories of the stress. These intrusions have their origin in the persistent conditioned emotional response. The existence of the fear-conditioned response with its inherent drive powers, Kolb further states, is not apt to be altered by the relearning process that takes place in the psychotherapies. Yet therapeutically the results from deconditioning through desensitization to sounds related to the stress in one study and to images in another have been pronounced as a failure and as inconclusive respectively.

Kolb, with several of his associates, has attempted to block the adrenergic system in two groups of Vietnam veterans, one with alpha and the other with beta blockers (chloridine and propanolol). Although preliminary results are viewed as favorable, to be considered conclusive they will have to withstand the test of time.

REFERENCES

American Psychiatric Association. (1980). *Diagnostic and statistical manual of mental disorders*. (3rd ed.). Washington, DC: Author.

American Psychiatric Association (1987). *Diagnostic and statistical manual of mental disorders* (3rd ed.—Rev.). Washington, DC: Author.

Bellack, L. (1973). *Ego functions in schizophrenics, neurotics, and normals*. New York: Wiley.

Benedek, E. D. (1985). Children and disaster: Emerging issues. *Psychiatric Annals, 15*(3), 168–172.

Bernard, J. (1968). Community disorganization. In *The international encyclopedia of the social sciences* (Vol. 3, pp. 163–168). New York: Macmillan and Free Press.

Cobb, S., & Lindemann, E. (1943). Neuropsychiatric observations after the Cocoanut Grove fire. *Annals of Surgery, 117*, 814–824.

DaCosta, J. M. (1871). On irritable heart: A clinical study forum of functional cardiac disorder and its consequences. *American Journal of Medical Sciences, 61*, 17–52.

Davidson, J., Swartz, M., Storck, M., Krishnan, R., & Hammett, E. (1985). A diagnostic and family study of post-traumatic stress disorder. *American Journal of Psychiatry, 142*(1), 90–93.

Erickson, E. H. (1963). *Childhood and society* (2nd ed.). Washington, DC.: Norton.

Ferenczi, S., Abraham, K., Simmel, E., & Jones, E. (1921). *Psychoanalysis and the war neurosis*. New York: International Psychoanalytic Press.

Frederick, C. J. (1977). *Current thinking about crisis or psychological equivalents of destructive behavior in mass emergencies* (Vol. 2, pp. 5–11) Washington, DC: U.S. Department of Health and Human Services.

Frederick, C. J. (1981). Overview of psychological sequelae in aircraft disasters. In C. J. Frederick (Ed.), *Aircraft accidents: Emergency mental health problems* (Monograph No. 2, pp. 5–11). Washington, DC: U.S. Department of Health and Human Services, NIMH.

Freud, S. (1958). Beyond the pleasure principle. In J. Strachey (Ed.), *Standard edition of the complete psychological works of Sigmund Freud*. London: Hogarth Press. (Original work published 1920)

Freud, S., & Breuer, J. (1957). Studies in hysteria. In J. Strachey (Ed.), *Standard edition of the complete psychological works of Sigmund Freud*. London: Hogarth Press.

Fritz, C. E. (1968). Disasters. In *The international encyclopedia of the social sciences* (Vol. 4, pp. 202–206). New York: Macmillan and Free Press.

Grinker, K., & Spiegel, S. (1945). *Men under stress*. Philadelphia: Blakeston.

Horowitz, M. J. (1974). Stress response syndromes. *Archives of General Psychiatry, 31,* 768–781.

Horowitz, M. J. (1986). *Stress response syndromes*. New York: Jason Aronson.

Jones, D. (1985). Secondary disaster victims: Emotional effects of recovering and identifying remains. *American Journal of Psychiatry, 142,* 305–308.

Kardiner, A. (1941). *The traumatic neuroses of war*. Psychosomatic Medicine Monograph. New York: Paul Hoeber.

Kolb, L. C. (1984). The post-traumatic stress disorders of combat: A subgroup with a conditioned emotional response. *Military Medicine, 149*(3), 237–239.

Krystal, H. (1978). Trauma and affects. *Psychoanalytic Study of the Child, 33,* 81–115.

Lewis, T. (1919). *The soldier's heart and the effort syndrome*. New York: Horber.

Lindemann, E. (1944). *Symptomatology and management of acute grief. American Journal of Psychiatry, 101,* 141–148.

Lindy, J. (1985). The trauma membrane and other clinical concepts derived from psychotherapeutic work with survivors of natural disasters. *Psychiatric Annals, 14*(3), 153–160.

Lindy J. D., Grace, M. C., & Green, B. L. (1981). Survivors: Outreach to a reluctant population. *American Orthopsychiatric Association, 51*(3), 468–478.

Menninger, K. (1954). Regulatory devices of the ego under major stress. *International Journal of Psychoanalysis, 35,* 412–420.

Pearce, K. A. (1985). A study of PTSD in Vietnam veterans. *Journal of Clinical Psychology, 41*(1), 9–14.

Scrignor, C. B. (1984). *Post traumatic stress disorder: Diagnosis, treatment and legal issues*. New York: Praeger.

Sierles, F. A., Chen, J. J., McFarland, R. E., & Taylor, M. A. (1983). Post-traumatic stress disorder and concurrent psychiatric illness: A preliminary report. *American Journal of Psychiatry, 140*(9), 1177–1179.

Terr, L. (1979). Children of Chowchilla. *Psychoanalytic Study of the Child, 34,* 552–623.

Terr, L. (1981). Psychic trauma in children: Observations following the Chowchilla school-bus kidnapping. *American Journal of Psychiatry, 138*(1), 14–19.

Titchener, J., & Kapp, F. (1976). Family and character change at Buffalo Creek. *American Journal of Psychiatry, 133,* 295–299.

Trimble, M. R. (1981). *Post traumatic neuroses*. New York: Wiley.

Tyhurst, J. (1951). Individual reactions to a community disaster: The natural history of a psychiatric phenomenon. *American Journal of Psychiatry, 107,* 764–769.

Vera, E. (1982). *Effects of disaster on emergency care providers*. Third National Symposium on Psychosocial Factors in Emergency Medicine, Chicago.

Wilkinson, C. B. (1983). Aftermath of a disaster: The collapse of the Hyatt Regency Hotel skywalks. *American Journal of Psychiatry, 140*(9), 1134–1139.

Wilkinson, C. B. (1985). Introduction: The psychological consequences of disasters. *Psychiatric Annals, 15*(3), 135–139.

Wilkinson, C. B., & Vera, E. (1985). The management and treatment of disaster victims. *Psychiatric Annals, 15*(3), 174–184.

SUGGESTED READINGS

Cohen, L., Claiborn, W., & Specter, G. (1983). *Crisis intervention.* New York: Human Sciences Press.

Guggenheim, F., & Weiner, M. (1984). *Manual of psychiatric consultation and emergency care.* New York: Jason Aronson.

Lindemann, E. (1979). *Beyond grief: Studies in crisis intervention.* New York: Jason Aronson.

Viorst, J. (1986). *Necessary losses.* New York: Simon & Schuster.

CHAPTER 10

Planning and Integrating
Disaster Response

MORTY LEBEDUN AND KARL E. WILSON

During the past several years, disaster response agencies have become increasingly aware of the mental health consequences of disasters. It is clear that people suffering the major trauma of natural and human-induced disasters experience emotional distress both during and for long periods after the event (e.g., Cohen & Ahearn, 1980; Farberow & Frederick, 1978). Substantial data also show effects felt by the disaster relief workers assigned to help the victims. Psychological first aid is a key ingredient in minimizing the long-term disabling effects of a disaster experience.

Most discussions of community mental health center (CMHC) responses to disasters assume that intervention is needed and that this need is widely recognized by all concerned. Clearly, the later assumption is often not correct. In describing the Wilkes-Barre, Pennsylvania, flooding of 1972, Okura (1975) notes that a psychiatrist serving as chief of staff at a Veterans Administration (VA) hospital publicly denounced the counseling efforts of Project Outreach, stating that it was "money down the drain." Ten years later, Wilson and Lebedun (1983) experienced similar resistance at the federal level in their efforts to secure a disaster counseling grant through the Federal Emergency Management Agency (FEMA).

This more recent experience involved the double trauma of flooding and dioxin contamination in 15 eastern Missouri counties. Nearly 85,000 people were evacuated and/or suffered property damage. Many of these people lived in high-risk, low-income areas, and up to 25,000 were estimated to need some level of mental health intervention. In spite of widespread and impressive losses, more than 100 days passed before funds were made available to create "Project Resurgence," a relief program that fielded eight mental health workers for 6 months. Resistance from leadership at the Regional Office of FEMA centered on the expressed belief that mental health concerns of flood victims either did not exist or were insignificant.

For a different set of reasons, it is not always fruitful to expect the local CMHC to serve as the primary care giver when disaster strikes. Any response by the CMHC will necessarily depend on its invited status in relation to the Red Cross, police, Disaster Assistance Center (DAC), and other agencies with legitimatized traditional roles. Even with that invitation readily forthcoming, the mental health agency will often find itself short on staff resources and long on funding crises. Outreach efforts of the type needed when a disaster strikes are no longer part of the routine array of care strategies in most CMHCs. Funding mechanisms in most states do not encourage the expensive outreach and case-finding approaches. As a result, many local centers operate with the following set of implicit expectations:

1. Clients are mobile and will transport themselves when they need help.
2. People who need help will, perhaps reluctantly, identify themselves as mentally ill in order to obtain service.
3. Services provided must be reimbursed (this is a necessary assumption because the CMHC cannot carry the excess service capacity needed for crisis response).
4. Motivation to solve a problem, or at least insight into its causes, will be needed to effect a cure.

Clearly, there exists a poor fit between these characteristics and those of the typical disaster victim because in disasters the following situations are likely:

1. Property, including cars, is often lost, thereby limiting the mobility of victims.
2. Victims may view themselves as needing help but usually do not consider emotional disability to be their problem at the moment.
3. Victims often suffer property losses that limit their ability to make payment for services or their interest in doing so.
4. Insights of victims are likely oriented to the notion that a recovery of lost property or lost physical function is all that is needed to be normal.

It would appear agencies with the greatest technical awareness of mental health needs (the CMHCs) are, at least on a structural basis, the least well equipped to mobilize a substantial therapeutic response in a disaster setting. It might be easy to believe that this lack of responsiveness or awareness of the mental health needs of disaster victims exists only as an artifact of large bureaucratic structures such as FEMA, or as a result of subsistence funding at the CMHC level. Actually, however, it appears to exist within the general population as well as to receive support from actions of disaster victims themselves.

The classic psychological phases of response to disaster—(1) Initial Impact, (2) Heroism, (3) Honeymoon, (4) Disillusionment, and (5) Reconstruction (Bard & Sangrey, 1980; Cohen & Ahearn, 1980)—are characterized first by emotional numbness and then by a mobilization of resources to deal with the immediate problems of food, clothing, shelter, and the like. Initially, this is also a time when victims are energized and do not perceive the impending long-term effects of property loss and emotional upheaval. This orientation is noteworthy and supports the idea of creating a service system that has a low mental health profile (Lindy, 1985). According to Lindy, this survivor health system must have broad community backing and arise soley in response to disaster needs.

This chapter is informed by the preceding issues and presents a plan for implementing an action strategy to establish mental health services when and where they are needed. It discusses a model of intervention based upon the assumption (and observation) that existing mental health agency structures are not intended for, or directly capable of, the rapid and efficient address of the needs of disaster victims. The model depends on successful use of natural helping networks of service that have a historical involvement with the target population and on a substantial commitment to assist persons in need, independent of any prospect of payment.

PLANNING A MENTAL HEALTH SERVICE

Klein (1968) and McGee (1974) have described community action procedures needed to establish a successful human services program. They include the following steps: (1) convergence of ideas or interests, (2) initiation of activity, (3) legitimization and sponsorship, (4) development of a plan, (5) development of an organizational structure, (6) implementation, and (7) evaluation. Each step proves important in implementing a disaster intervention program.

Because disaster intervention programs are dependent on gatekeepers and established response networks, they have little chance of coming into being or helping victims unless sanctioned by primary intervention agents. A sense of mutuality and support is needed first at the conceptual level of programming. Klein (1968) lists problems which can occur at the "convergence of ideas or interests" planning stage. The first one, which has already been discussed, deals with the false belief that the existence of a problem (the disaster) will automatically produce support for any attempt to give aid. In fact, the ones who will encourage the mental health effort are typically care givers with complementary, noncompetitive agency agendas.

Opposition occurs when an agency feels its turf is being threatened, either by dilution of funds or depletion of personnel. As an example, private practice psychologists and psychiatrists have traditionally resisted community mental health programs but may not consider a disaster intervention effort to be competitive. Local Red Cross and Salvation Army programs may be either neutral or supportive of community mental health in general but ambivalent about disaster intervention by a mental health center. However, if such agencies have a cooperative relationship with the center, these issues can be adequately resolved. This level of support is essential to the creation of a functional program of assistance.

Recent flooding in eastern Missouri offered an opportunity for mental health workers to assist victims (Wilson & Lebedun, 1983). The CMHC director enthusiastically approached the director of the local Red Cross office, offering field workers who had helped out in a similar situation a year earlier. This proposal was denied. The Red Cross director made it clear that she was in charge, and because existing agency agreements were lacking, she did not feel she had the time to consider a new program. She deprecated crisis counseling, stating there was little need. Her first concerns, she contended, were the physical problems of victims.

Klein's second and third stages, "initiation of activity" and "legitimization and sponsorship," are efforts to mobilize political and financial support in the affected community. Errors in this stage occur when steps are taken too hastily or with too much autonomy. By their nature, however, disaster programs must start quickly; program development will therefore prove most effective when fast tracked (i.e., when parallel steps are taken on a number of fronts). Still, an effort must be made to include, coordinate with, and cooperate with the efforts of other agencies.

Not recognizing the legitimizers of programs in the community is a common mistake. These are rarely experts or consultants, but rather are usually leaders from service clubs, business, the clergy, the schools, or other local constituencies, who often serve on a number of agency boards. Because mental health personnel must accomplish their goals through gatekeeper organizations, these persons can greatly enhance necessary cooperation. In the case just cited, a mental health director erred in bypassing the local Red Cross. Learning from his mistake, the CMHC director approached the Red Cross before the next disaster hit and instructed his board members to contact friends who served on the Red Cross board. This process produced a climate of reconciliation between the agencies.

The next steps, "development of a plan," refer to the setting of timelines and the development of interorganizational relationship agreements. Participants, who may represent a variety of organizations, must decide whether to become members of a consortium or part of the referral network. Within the mental health agency, this step signals a decision point regarding application for federal support (assuming the disaster site is federally "declared"). Demonstrated capacity to work with key gatekeepers and the ability to obtain state support for the application are essential to a successful venture. Commitment by these parties cannot be assumed; it must be secured in an open discussion where reservations and fears can be expressed. Critical discussion items include involvement, control, resource identification, goals, policies, and the actual program plan.

The final stages in this community action approach are "implementation" and "evaluation." If implementation occurs before the preceding steps, friction can develop within the organization or between the organization and gatekeepers. When this happens, the program misses a beat and may show limited effectiveness. Avoiding these pitfalls can be accomplished through the more structured approach described next. The balance of this chapter directs the reader toward a proactive style of intervention that applies the community approach. This method is not intended to supplant more traditional counseling-oriented designs but should instead be seen as a complementary model, designed to consider the ecological context of the particular event and community.

CREATING A RESPONSE

Mental health involvement in disaster situations ideally includes three response modes. Taken in their most useful order of progression, they are

1. *Consultation and education,* including predisaster planning events
2. *Facilitation,* offering on-site support, data collection, and relationship building with disaster assistance staff
3. *Direct care service delivery,* with emphasis placed on group intervention strategies

These efforts may be usefully interwoven with concepts of psychological stages affecting victims (discussed earlier) and intrusiveness of intervention programs. "Intrusiveness" can be arrayed on a continuum from *least,* as typified by consultation or primary prevention strategies, to *most,* that is, degrees of direct intervention from individual counseling to inpatient care. Figure 10.1 presents a continuum of program types as a balanced services model.

Programs at the top of the pyramid are the most intrusive and expensive; they reach the fewest people at the greatest cost. Conversely, at the base of the model are broadly targeted programs aimed at the community as a whole, usually utilizing mass media. These can be labeled preparedness or promotion programs. Between the two extremes are crisis counseling programs, ideally using natural groups such as church affiliates and service organizations.

The programs referenced in Figure 10.1 will also take different forms depending on the psychological phase relevant to the disaster victims when the effort is implemented. Figure 10.2 expresses these relationships.

For example, during the Heroism and Honeymoon phases, crisis counseling programs through gatekeeper relief organizations would be emphasized, along with press releases on emotional responses to disaster. Public information in later phases would be designed to prop up the sense of community, spur mutual support, and sensitize the community to the needs of target groups like children, the unemployed, or the elderly.

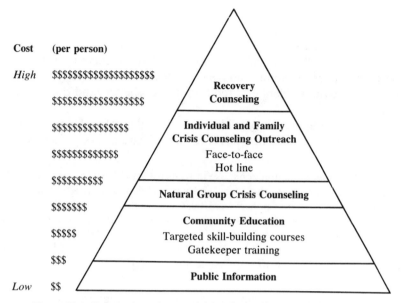

Cost   (per person)

High $$$$$$$$$$$$$$$$$$$$$

        $$$$$$$$$$$$$$$$$$$$

        $$$$$$$$$$$$$$$$

        $$$$$$$$$$$$$$

        $$$$$$$$$$$

        $$$$$$$$

        $$$$$

        $$$

Low $$

Recovery Counseling

Individual and Family
Crisis Counseling Outreach
Face-to-face
Hot line

Natural Group Crisis Counseling

Community Education
Targeted skill-building courses
Gatekeeper training

Public Information

Figure 10.1. Balanced services model for disaster intervention programs.

A Consultation Approach

Consultation was a major theme in the development of the community mental health movement late in the 1950s (Wagenfeld, Lemkau, & Jushie, 1982). It was an important cornerstone of the movement because it focused on the belief that a few well-trained mental health professionals could enhance the knowledge base of many direct care givers and thereby show an impact on very large numbers of citizens needing care. Unfortunately, funding philosophies shifted toward promotion of direct care, minimal involvement of paraprofessionals, and a networking approach to service delivery. As a result, most mental health systems now employ clinical staff as the primary service providers and can offer fewer alternative approaches to intervention. Such a model, however, is ill suited to disaster relief efforts.

Phases	Public Information	Community Education	Crisis Counseling	Recovery Counseling
Predisaster	*	*		
Impact/Heroism	*	*	*	
Honeymoon	*	*	*	
Disillusionment	*	*	*	*
Reconstruction	*	*		*

Figure 10.2. Disaster intervention program strategies for the phases of disaster response.

The role of mental health consultation is, therefore, critical in disaster planning. It works to establish the base of ideas and sponsorships discussed earlier. Its importance cannot be overstated in situations where direct care strategies are usually not well understood or well received by designated disaster assistance personnel and mental health is seen as secondary or ancillary to providing blankets, food, clothing, shelter, and other physical supplies.

A consultative approach provides a useful vehicle for the mental health worker to gain acceptance in a world of natural care givers. As an example:

> Within a few hours of a hotel collapse in Kansas City, Missouri, mental health professionals approached the scene and were denied access. Relief workers including firefighters and police were busy clearing debris, removing the injured, and controlling the crowds. Understandably, their involvement was focused on the physical needs of victims. After the fact, staff recognized the potential assistance to friends and relatives of victims that could have been given by mental health workers (Gist & Stolz, 1982).

Entry into an agency system is obviously an essential first step necessary to supporting or enhancing that system. However, successful consultation requires an invitation to get involved. This invited status cannot exist if the recipient agency is not aware of the available service or does not perceive the need for same. Where the local Red Cross or the Emergency Preparedness Office (EPO) is concerned, an educational/marketing approach is usually necessary.

Mental health agencies must initiate development of an ongoing working relationship with local Red Cross personnel in order to create immediate response structures that include a counseling component. Although this statement makes common sense, it is seldom put into practice. Most often, mental health staff spend time meeting with "their own kind," a social norm not unusual for most service organizations. It takes a special effort to establish a contact and "take a Red Cross director to lunch."

Many CMHCs create a disaster plan in accord with Civil Defense and Red Cross guidelines, but often these plans are historical documents with little applied value. They may sit on the shelf waiting for accreditation surveys but seldom lead to or advocate for an actual working relationship with disaster relief agencies. This relationship should be structured around training activities that allow staff of both agencies to share their respective knowledge bases in relation to serving disaster victims

Mental health strategies that assist victims to regain a lost sense of safety and a sense of control over their lives are an important part of a disaster response (Fraser & Spicka, 1981). A professional response to these needs should be immediate and can be provided by trained workers. The skills to deliver this service provide a central core to a multiagency consultative/educational approach. The focus here is to create the service under the auspices of the local EPO or the Red Cross, rather than to view it as being provided only by a team of mental health crisis workers (which may never materialize for any of the reasons cited earlier).

Immediacy of response, in this case, is critical to preventing a latent decompensation among victims. The response, if it is to succeed, cannot wait for grants to be submitted, workers to be trained, or systems to be planned.

The need for ongoing rapport with local primary response agencies is essential. It is the price of admission if mental health agencies expect to be truly participative in disaster relief efforts. Commitment to this process can determine the difference between a functional mental health disaster plan and a nominal document.

Facilitation of Existing Efforts

A history of useful program consultation with a local disaster agency can greatly enhance the capacity of mental health staff to obtain sanction to participate in federally sponsored DACs when tragedy strikes. Early involvement should focus on developing supportive relationships with DAC staff and meeting other community leaders who will participate in planning the interventions. These individuals generally represent government–funded services and goods such as police and fire protection, housing, food, and clothing. Many charitable organizations, including interfaith councils, the Salvation Army, and a variety of service clubs, may also assist, depending on the type and duration of the event. It is important that mental health agencies relate closely to this developing organizational structure.

Initial activities may not necessarily tie directly to deploying a team of crisis counselors. Instead, the mental health facilitator might spend time helping to hand out blankets, clothing, or other needed supplies. Besides becoming immediately useful, this time in the field is needed to establish a history of participation and begin an on-site process of needs assessment. Participant-observer data collected in these first few days at the disaster scene can pay important dividends in later planning efforts aimed at creating both immediate and long-term goals for intervention.

Collection of observational data at the site(s) enhances the workers' awareness of the number of people affected by the disaster and the meaning of the event in their personal lives, a dimension not reflected in the statistical data usually obtained in disaster situations. Sociocultural values held among the victims impact on the coping mechanisms available to them. The importance of those values can be observed firsthand through a studied involvement at relief centers. Techniques of participant observation are well described in social research literature (Glazer, 1972, provides a good compendium of field research approaches), so will not be discussed here, but the importance of on-site observation is easily shown:

In December 1982, major flooding in eastern Missouri found the community of Times Beach to be completely inundated with river water known to be tainted with dioxin. Besides the physical loss of property and lives, a tremendous emotional reaction on the part of residents was apparent. Many of the affected families earned marginal incomes and lived in modest trailer homes. One elderly man, whose uninsured trailer was swept down the river, stood in a far corner at the Disaster Assistance Center. A volunteer approached and asked the man if he needed help. Frightened and tearful, he told the story of losing his home and the contents. It was all he could do to save a mason jar full of pennies from the flood. In some detail he described holding the jar up to examine it while he was standing outside in the rain. He said, "The jar slipped out of my hand and broke—now I have nothing."[1]

Witnessing the type of event just described is invaluable to anyone assessing the impact of the disaster. This brief observation alerted the worker to the social and economic meaning of the flood to one victim. More importantly, it dramatically expressed the desperation and loss of control over the environment felt by the elderly man.

On-site facilitation also gives mental health staff a chance to intervene directly with relief workers who may show signs of severe fatigue and burnout. These interventions are important, not only because they help support the disaster worker, but also because they afford the mental health worker a chance to teach and model useful intervention skills that can later see application to identified victims of the disaster.

It should be noted that this level of intervention will not occur if mental health staff present themselves in their traditional role as therapist. Fraser and Spicka (1981) reported that mental health workers who established themselves at a table waiting for clients to appear spent the day with little business. Many people feared the stigma of approaching the table. Again, the participant model is needed to gain access to those needing help. Given that trust is an essential part of any therapeutic endeavor and cannot be created at a distance, participation on a volunteer level affords one way of promoting closeness.

Direct Care Methods

The concept of *direct care,* or direct services, was an early part of the language of community mental health. The term was often used to distinguish between consultation/education (C&E) services (termed "indirect") and case-by-case clinical service. To avoid confusion, this chapter maintains that terminological distinction but offers to broaden what might be appropriately called direct care.

Allowing that victims of disaster may be conceptualized as the target

[1]Anecdotal account from staff of Four County Mental Health Center, St. Charles, Missouri, following flooding of December 1982.

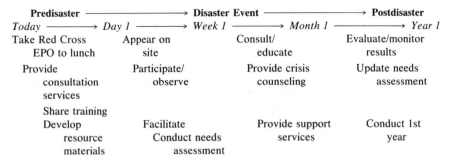

Figure 10.3. Timetable for mental health intervention.

population (clients), then an array of direct service involvements can be considered. The range of possibilities seen in Figure 10.1 constructs a continuum of sorts, which varies from a broad, generalized therapeutic impact to a limited, highly focused one. The continuum can be seen as largely educational/informational at one extreme and psychotherapeutically oriented toward individual coping mechanisms at the other. Similarly, the direct care methods may reach a few selected victims or an entire population, including surrounding communities not directly involved in the disaster. When best applied, this balanced service model may be operationalized on a time dimension. Figure 10.3 presents such a scheme, beginning with predisaster interagency training exercises, continuing with involvement of mental health personnel in immediate responses, and moving toward direct care approaches as specific needs emerge and are identified.

Application of these various strategies is usually needed in disasters that affect large numbers of people over a wide geographic area (flooding, hurricane, earthquake). These require the broadest approaches to direct care. This type of response was demonstrated in flooded areas around Times Beach in 1983.

Following an early planning effort with federal, state, and local personnel, mental health workers hired through federal funds authorized under Section 413 were trained by a CMHC in the area. Once in the field, they developed informational brochures on coping with stress brought on by the flood and dioxin conditions. They also obtained copies of a flood coloring book to be distributed through area schools to youngsters who lived in the disaster region. These materials assisted victims in verbalizing their problems to volunteer and paid workers who offered assistance. In addition, staff of the mental health project set up large weekly meetings, including casual events such as picnics and dances. On one occasion they even coordinated a play about the flood. All these events allowed victims a chance to ventilate, receive support, and obtain information about their situation. Case finding was an added role of these functions, as the public was informed about available counseling services. A follow-up meeting was held 1 year after the impact date (Wilson & Lebedun, 1983).

SUMMARY

A large proportion of the disaster literature dealing with mental health issues describes treatment techniques involving a crisis intervention orientation. Many references are made to the grief process common to the substantial losses felt when disaster hits and to the resultant need for counseling services. In spite of general agreement on this point, primary response agencies such as local offices of FEMA, Red Cross, and EPOs may question the mental health role in disasters and may still feel uncertain about what needs to be done and by whom.

Mental health workers themselves may share these uncertainties and are usually not confronted with these questions because the nature of their work most often approximates a clinical practice in an office setting. These situations screen the client in a controlled structure that dictates how and when treatment is provided. This inherent structure is absent when workers enter the field and assume multiple roles, including planning and implementation.

The typology described by Berren and Beigel (1982) presents the range of approaches available and suggests their application depending on the type and duration of the event. They clearly point out that multiple responses, including prevention and direct treatment, are needed in most situations. The question is not whether experiential or didactic services are to be offered; it is rather a question of who will deliver them and how much of both are needed and feasible.

The emphasis on consultative and facilitative approaches suggests a variety of vehicles through which to create opportunities for useful mental health interventions. These approaches may be an excellent starting point when direct care is being planned. Several observations support this strategy.

1. Clinical personnel needed for a large-scale effort providing individual therapy are usually not available.
2. Victims do not see themselves as mentally ill and often struggle with the need to maintain a sense of self-reliance.
3. Networks of natural helpers indigenous to the affected community will remain on the scene long after mental health crisis workers are forced to move on.

These issues augur well for a low profile, high-contact effort that evolves as a function of intervention receptivity displayed by victims and disaster team personnel. That is, when mental health staff enter the disaster circumstance, early efforts focus on building rapport through a consultative model. Insights gained through this approach are used to guide further educational and clinical intervention techniques. The entire process is represented as dynamic and interactive, not necessarily proceeding in a linear fashion, but taking advantage of opportunistic events as they occur in vivo. Predisaster involvement with primary response agencies is presented as a vital component of this method.

REFERENCES

Bard, M., & Sangrey, D. (1980). Things fall apart: Victims in crisis [Special Issue]. *Evaluation & Change,* 28–35.

Berren, M., & Beigel, A. (1982). A typology for the classification of disasters: Implications for intervention. *Community Mental Health Journal, 18,* 120–134.

Cohen, R., & Ahearn, F. (1980). *Handbook for mental health care of disaster victims.* Baltimore: Johns Hopkins University Press.

Farberow, N., & Frederick, C. (1978). *Field manual for human services workers in disasters.* Rockville, MD: National Insititute of Mental Health.

Fraser, J., & Spicka, D. (1981). Handling the emotional response to disaster: The case for American Red Cross/community mental health collaboration. *Community Mental Health Journal, 17,* 255–264.

Gist, R., & Stolz, S. B. (1982). Mental health promotion and the media: Community response to the Kansas City hotel disaster. *American Psychologist, 37,* 1136–1139.

Glazer, M. (1972). *The research adventure.* New York: Random House.

Klein, D. (1968). *Community dynamics and mental health.* New York: Wiley.

Lindy, J. (1985). The trauma membrane. *Psychiatric Annals, 15,* 153–160.

McGee, R. (1974). *Crisis intervention in the community.* Baltimore: University Park Press.

Okura, K. (1975). Mobilizing in response to a major disaster. *Community Mental Health Journal, 11,* 136–144.

Wagenfeld, M. O., Lemkau, P. V., & Justice, B. (1982). *Public mental health.* New York: Russel Sage Foundation.

Wilson, K., & Lebedun, M. (1983). *Project Resurgence.* Unpublished technical report, National Institute of Mental Health.

PART 4

Emerging Issues in Intervention and Investigation

Growth in knowledge of the mental health sequalae of disasters has led to increased roles in intervention and reconstruction. It has also opened a new area of litigation. Where the responsibility for a disaster can be fixed in an act of omission or commission by some culpable party, or where some set of effects might have been mediated or prevented by appropriate action of such a party, damages have been sought that have included compensation for psychological harm.

Hartsough provides an overview of this emerging area, supported by case studies illustrating a number of the complexities involved in attempts to unite the rather disparate viewpoints and goals of scientific inquiry and legal advocacy. He also discusses emerging public policy issues, such as environmental impact statements that include an assessment of disaster risk and its possible psychological consequences.

Disaster research, once the stepchild of intervention, has emerged as a pursuit in its own right. A significant body of information has evolved, much of it over the last decade, and a variety of productive research is currently underway.

Solomon provides an extensive integrative overview of contemporary research, including discussions of current trends, ongoing projects, and emergent issues. She also provides a critical review of methodological and theoretical concerns in the conduct of disaster studies, and she contributes an enlightening set of insights into current imperatives in the organization and support of disaster research programs.

The volume concludes with a few thoughts concerning the implications of disaster intervention for the future of community psychology and related disciplines. As some of the most salient examples of this developing niche, these endeavors offer a great deal that is instructive about both the strengths and the weaknesses of traditional models, as well as much that is enlightening concerning future directions.

CHAPTER 11

Legal Issues and Public Policy in the Psychology of Disasters

DON M. HARTSOUGH

This chapter focuses on two domains in which psychology, disasters, and the law interact. These domains are civil law concerned with personal injury (tort law) and the area of public policy. Psychologists can add substantially to the understanding of disaster victims and can assist in seeking their fair treatment under the law, but psychology is also limited in its potential contributions. The psychologist who plans to engage in forensic psychology associated with disasters must be aware of both sides of this coin.

The type of work described in the chapter overlaps with forensic psychological assessment (Grisso, 1987; Maloney, 1985; Weiner & Hess, 1987), but it also includes research into the basic nature of the psychological effects of disasters. First, it is necessary to review the differences between psychology and the law that will confront the investigator. Then each of the domains will be described separately as follows: (1) legal concepts; (2) psychological concepts; (3) measurement issues; (4) a case study; and (5) the role of the psychologist.

BASIC DIFFERENCES BETWEEN PSYCHOLOGY AND THE LAW

Psychologists in the legal system as consultants or expert witnesses will quickly discover basic differences between their usual mode of thinking and working and the requirements of the legal system. If the differences are understood, they need not impede a good working relationship with attorneys. However lack of appreciation of these differences may produce confusion, embarrassment, and possible incompetent performance by one or both parties.

Melton, Petrila, Poythress, and Slobogin (1987) provide a clear and forthright discussion of the uneasy alliance between the law and mental health professions. The authors argue that the most fundamental difference is found in the philosophies of each profession regarding behavioral causation. Although psychology as a science is deterministic and sees multiple internal or personality determinants as well as external or situational ones, the law endorses a philosophy that each individual's behavior stems from free choice. The authors note exceptions within both psychology and the law. An overpowering stimulus is seen to override individual choice in both disciplines, and in addition the perspective on free choice versus determinism may depend on which side of the legal argument one is arguing.

A second major difference lies in the conceptualization of what is considered a fact. Melton et al. comment, "Although the sciences are inherently probabilistic in their understanding of truth, the law demands at least the appearance of certainty, perhaps because of the magnitude and irrevocability of decisions that must be reached in law." (Melton et al., 1987, p. 9). Perhaps because of the pressures to produce credible evidence for the court, attorneys may exhort professional witnesses to overstate their evidence, thus creating as facts what are at best probability statements of uncertain strength. For example, conclusions drawn about an individual case that are derived from the results of grouped data are not a legal fact, but only a statement of probabilities about the behavior of the individual.

Melton et al. (1987) suggest that behavioral scientists who give expert testimony refrain from stating as a certain fact that which they know to be a probabilistic conclusion. In this way the limits of behavioral science are recognized and the responsibility for determining whether or not sufficient evidence has been presented to establish a legal fact remains with key players in the legal system, for example, judges and juries.

The third point of fundamental conflict between the law and psychology lies in the paucity of scientific data about human behavior. Melton et al. (1987) point out that there is often little knowledge that will apply directly to a legal question, and even knowledge that does exist may be unreliable. This point of conflict seems to relate to the general case in which the social need for behaviorally relevant knowledge has far outstripped the capacity of scientists to produce it. This is certainly the case in relation to the area of psychological effects of disasters and other stressful events, which is only now establishing its scientific base.

Another difference between the two disciplines is the way in which each attempts to discover truth and to test its validity. Although both the law and psychology rely on an accumulation of evidence that forms a consistent and logical pattern, the procedures for deriving this pattern of knowledge differ. Mental health professionals stress cooperation and harmony in relationships with clients and other professionals. Trust and objectivity are ideals. This has the effect of leveling conflict in the interests of personal well-being and accurate reality testing. On the other hand, the legal system is based on an adversary process that purposely sharpens conflict, the assumption being that if differing sides of the issue are presented competently, the truth will emerge in the process. Clinicians unfamiliar with adversarial professional relationships may find themselves especially uncomfortable or dismayed by the latter process. Melton et al. (1987) encourage behavioral scientists not to stray from their goal of objective presentation of the truth, but not to be put off when they find attorneys interested in presenting only a biased picture. This approach, they point out, is the task of the attorney.

Finally, Melton et al. (1987) point out that there are language and attitude differences between psychology and the law. Often, these are the differences dwelt upon by the participants in a psychology-law interface, and they may be blamed for conflicts or misunderstandings that arise. Vocabulary, however, is less likely to cause problems than the existence of the more fundamental differences described earlier. Nevertheless, it is mandatory for both psychologists and attorneys to pursue communication gaps and conceptual differences in order to obtain a smooth working relationship.

Although the foregoing has focused on important differences between the law and psychology, there are also important points of agreement. The objective of both professions is to build a case based on verifiable evidence. This perspective especially fits a behavioral framework and an approach that includes systems variables such as archival records from community, work, or school.

Grisso (1987) has examined the guild aspects of forensic psychology and the issue of quality control of psychological services being offered in the legal system. He argues that subquality work by psychologists in the legal arena will erode confidence in the potential contributions of all social scientists. His argument has a direct bearing on the interface between psychology and the law in disasters. Psychologists, both as clinicians and as research investigators, who are ill prepared for disaster work may find themselves in the embarrassing situation of having opposing attorneys successfully attack their professional products.

TORT LAW AND DISASTERS

A brief but lucid description of tort law is provided by Melton et al. (1987, pp. 271–272). Tort law provides monetary compensation for wrongs inflicted on one party by another, and it is separate from criminal law, which is interested in prosecuting those persons who violate society's laws. Both civil and criminal systems, of course, may become engaged in the same incident. An example is the ferryboat captain whose disregard of safety codes leads to a tragic loss of life aboard ship. The captain may be prosecuted for criminal negligence (for violating safety codes) and also sued for compensatory damages by families of the deceased, and survivors who suffered injuries. On the civil side, a clinician might be asked to evaluate the extent and nature of psychological trauma suffered by the persons who were allegedly wronged, as a basis for their compensation claims against the captain. In the criminal proceedings, a mental health specialist might be used in defense of the captain if insanity or temporary loss of reality functioning were used as part of the defense.

The two types of tort cases most pertinent for psychologists working with disaster survivors are the ones concerning individual personal injury and class action suits. Although these cases may overlap considerably within the law, there are important differences between them for the psychological investigator. Class action suits, in paticular, are relevant to community disasters, where survivors may be encouraged by the legal system to pool their resources in pursuing compensation for injuries suffered.

Personal Injury

The term *tort* comes from the Latin word *tortus* (literally, *twisted*), and is closely related to the English *torture,* which connotes deliberately inflicted harm and punishment on a victim. Roughly translated, tort means injury and there are many torts described in the law (e.g., assault, slander, libel), including the ones for emotional and mental injury. The legal definition of a tort concerns the invasion of an interest that is legally protected against intentional invasion or negligent behavior, or conduct that is unintended but is subject to strict liability, even though no harm is intended (Dooley, 1977). In other words, tort concerns injury, although no crime may have been committed and the injury may not have been deliberately caused.

Following Prosser (1971), Melton et al. (1987) outlined four criteria for establishing whether a tort has been committed. The first two have to do with legal obligations and standards of conduct, and the ways in which these may be broken. As already indicated, the injurious actions may be intentional or due to negligence. The third criterion concerns *proximate cause,* and it has important implications for the psychological assessment of disaster survivors. Melton et al. characterize the concept of proximate cause as "elusive" but also as a pragmatic and reasonable determination of whether the actions of one party caused the injury of another party. Proof of injury requires not only evidence, but a logical and timely connection between the actions of one party and the effects of those actions for a second party. Determining the sources of emotional distress has been as problematic in the law as it has been for psychologists.

The legal system has relied on the importance of physical contact between the parties, the so-called impact rule, or on being physically at risk, to determine the legitimacy of claims of emotional injury ("Annotation-Immediacy," 1981). In other words it has been easier to establish an emotional or mental injury if a physical injury or some other compensable injury has also taken place. For example, a child who has been extremely frightened by a vicious dog is more likely to gain compensation for emotional distress if there was also some type of physical contact between the dog and the child. There has been a traditional reluctance to find for plaintiffs with only mental and emotional anguish (Magruder, 1935). Courts were concerned that a more liberal interpretation of personal injury statutes would produce a flood of cases and that the validity of these cases would be impossible to determine. It should be noted that recent legislation in many jurisdictions allowing for compensation for simply witnessing the death or serious injury of a loved one seems to show an easing of this traditional reluctance. This change would seem to indicate the possibility that survivors of a community disaster who are not themselves injured, but who nevertheless suffer emotional distress from watching others suffer and die, might have a greater chance of recovering compensation.

Legal Concepts

In the law, plaintiffs may recover damages for "pain and suffering," "mental anguish" and related legal concepts of emotional distress. In the benchmark Buffalo Creek disaster, plaintiffs were compensated for psychic impairment (Stern, 1976) and loss of community (Erikson, 1976). These concepts represented pain, suffering, and loss at the individual and social levels, respectively. In contrast, the legal maneuvering following the Three Mile Island nuclear reactor accident focused on the concept of stress. Following the publication of the Third Edition of the *Diagnostic and Statistical Manual for Mental Disorders* (DSM-III; APA, 1980) the concept of posttraumatic stress and the specific diagnosis of post-traumatic stress disorder (PTSD) have been utilized in legal proceedings concerning disasters.

Psychological Concepts

The choice of an organizing concept for either a clinical or research investigation of disaster survivors is very important. It provides the unifying framework for the use of data of diverse types as evidence. In addition, a well-selected psychological concept should encourage the court to accept knowledge from prior research that may have a direct bearing on the case at hand.

The major advantage of the concept of stress for legal proceedings is the body of existing research and theoretical development available to the investigating professional. It permits the alleged stress of an individual survivor or a group of survivors to be compared with other stress situations and with the effects that are known to have resulted from those situations.

The major disadvantage of the stress concept is its lack of precision. It is recognized in both psychology and the law that stress is part of ordinary living and that one must demonstrate an unusually severe or extended level of *negative* stress, in order for compensation to be possible. Put another way, it is recognized that stress varies from inconsequential amounts of short duration to extreme degrees of stress over long periods of time. The task of the court is to place the plaintiff somewhere along that continuum, and it is expected that defense and plaintiff attorneys and their supporting expert witnesses will differ on the optimal placement.

As an organizing concept, the diagnosis of post-traumatic stress disorder

(APA, 1980) has both advantages and drawbacks. It is a recognized psychiatric diagnosis which requires symptomatic behavioral criteria. Its increasing use following disasters may lead to the development of normative data for the incidence of PTSD, which in turn could guide lawyers in expectations regarding compensation.

The primary disadvantage of PTSD for some disaster populations is that a survivor may not meet the criteria for the diagnosis but still may experience emotional distress. From the plaintiff's viewpoint, PTSD as an organizing concept may be too restrictive. In these cases, alternative diagnoses with less demanding criteria may be more appropriate, for example, generalized anxiety disorder. Walker (1987) points out an important difference between adjustment disorders and PTSD—in the former, symptomatology is stronger than is deemed appropriate, whereas victims diagnosed with PTSD are reacting as expected to an unusually powerful situation. Although later research could alter the use of organizing concepts, at the present time it seems most appropriate to restrict the concept of PTSD to *individual* disaster survivors, and it is most advantageous to use the organizing concept of stress for large groups and class action suits. Finally, the difficulty in using legal-sounding terms such as mental anguish, psychic injury, and the like, is that they lack theoretical relevance in the behavioral and social sciences and are not readily placed in the body of knowledge and theory that now exists.

Measurement Issues

There are six questions that key an adequate psychological analysis of a disaster survivor's case for compensation.

1. What is the organizing concept for consideration of possible loss or harm?
2. How are the effects to be measured, so that they may be presented as evidence?
3. How are the effects linked to the individual's experience of the disaster, that is, the stressor?
4. Are the observed effects different from baseline measurements of the effect for this population?
5. What changes have occured in the life of the victim; that is, have the symptomatic effects actually produced significant life changes?
6. What future consequences can be predicted for the psychological effects observed at present?

Issues related to selection of an organizing concept have already been discussed. Problems associated with measuring psychological effects are the familiar ones—reliability and validity of the measurement instruments, plus the use of an effective design. The strongest evaluation will be one in which archival records and multiple data sources will be used, including standardized symptom scales with known psychometric properties. The investigator should keep in mind that interviews and self-report measures are subject to the strong response bias that victims may bring to the evaluation, particularly in cases involving litigation (Butcher & Harlow, 1987). The response bias is probably less often a conscious intention of victim respondents than simply a part of the way in which survivors become totally absorbed with their victim status. Thus, confirming evidence that is not subject to any response bias may be needed to balance the survivor's own appraisal. The validity of the psychologist's findings, of course, is directly related to the legal problem of establishing a preponderance of evidence for a specific legal finding in a civil case. Expert witnesses should be prepared to discuss with any member of the legal system, and especially with their attorney consultees, how data from a psychological evaluation or research project is tested for scientific soundness. These tests will be directly related to the attorney's task of testing evidence for its veracity.

Another set of problems occurs when linking the demonstrated effects to the stressor. The issues here are relevant to the proximate cause criterion for establishing tort. The psychologist who plans to testify either in court or by deposition (sworn testimony that is officially recorded) should discuss issues regarding this linkage with the attorney. In the strictest sense, the expert witness's task is to demonstrate whether or not changes have occurred in the behavioral, affective, or cognitive life of the plaintiff following the occurrence of the stressor event. In this line of thinking, it is the "finders of fact" (judges or juries) who draw the conclusions that the event caused the changes and whether they are compensable or not. On the other hand, the diagnosis of PTSD makes the inherent assumption that a stressor that is outside the range of normal human experience has produced the symptom pattern leading to the diagnosis. If the expert witness reaches too far, he or she may be accused of invading the territory belonging to the court, but too conservative a stance may not serve the best interests of the disaster survivor. In any case, the psychologist should be aware that the finding of proximate cause is a legal question in addition to a psychological one.

The finding that there have been significant changes implies the question, "From what baseline pattern?" or "As different from what behavioral norm?" Because retrospective self-report about the quality of life before the event occurred is likely to be tainted by the plaintiff's present circumstances, ancillary data in the form of records, interviews, and preevent evaluations are highly desirable. It is then up to the expert witness to place positive findings within a theoretical framework to demonstrate whether they do, or do not, fit patterns that have been found previously in persons suffering from the aftereffects of disasters.

Disasters have been found to produce two kinds of effects, ones caused by the event itself and others brought about by society's response to the disaster (Hartsough, 1985). These effects may be quite different—for example, anxiety in the form of a phobia brought about by direct exposure to a tornado, as opposed to fatigue or feelings of hopelessness brought about by the way in which victims are managed following the disaster. Depending on the legal questions involved, this difference may be important or not. Although the response-produced effects are one step further from direct causation than event-produced effects, they may still be considered compensable consequences of the disaster. It should be pointed out that these differences are often difficult to discern in psychological evaluations.

Legal decision makers such as judges and juries will be most interested in the relevance of quantitative psychological findings for the survivor's daily life. Do symptom patterns result in losses of work, relationships, or valued activities, such as hobbies or church attendance? Are the accounts of sleep disturbances confirmed by the spouse or the family physician? The consistency between psychological data and in vivo changes is important.

Finally, the investigator may be asked to state whether the effects found at present will extend into the future, that is, to predict the stability of the effects that have been discovered. The legal purpose of such requests usually concerns the expected need for future compensation, for example, for a future course of treatment.

Expert witnesses may find that they have a great reluctance to predict the future psychological effects for disaster victims, especially if there have been complications in demonstrating effects at the present time. The prediction question relates to difficulties of adapting the proximate cause thinking to a deterministic model. Although the psychologist sees many past and future variables that will be involved to varying degrees in producing future behavior, the legal question is whether the plaintiff should be awarded compensation for a condition that will exist in the future. Melton et al. recommend a conservative approach for the investigator. Rather than risking a pronouncement that the legally relevant incident is the sole or primary cause of a claimant's present or future state, the clinician should simply present evidence of a changed status on the part of the claimant and let others decide its cause. Their view stresses a division of responsibilities:

> This approach not only better reflects the clinical view of causation and the extent of clinical knowledge; it also prevents the legal decision-maker from abdicating responsibility for analyzing the causation issue and for translating expert evidence into the data that meshes with the applicable legal construct. (Melton et al. 1987, p. 282)

Whether one adopts this approach or risks making predictive statements may depend on several factors, including the empirical basis for the predictions, the fit of the case to past experience, and the legal purpose of the request.

CASE STUDY

The Illinois Central Gulf Railroad derailment in Livingston, Louisiana, will be used as a case study for exploring personal injury litigation in disasters.

After the disaster several families sued for personal injury based upon emotional consequences. Testimony from their trial is examined to illustrate some of the issues previously discussed. There was also a class action suit against the railroad by the residents of Livingston. Psychological implications of the class action suit will be described in a later section.

On September 28, 1982, at 5:12 A.M., 43 cars of a 101-car train belonging to the Illinois Central Gulf Railroad (ICG) derailed in Livingston, Louisiana, a town of 1,250 population. Of the derailed cars, 36 were tank cars and 34 of these cars contained either hazardous materials or flammable petroleum products (National Transportation Safety Board, Report No. RAR-83/05, n.d.). It was later determined that a total of 20 tank cars were punctured or breached in the derailment, and fires broke out in the wreckage, as smoke and toxic gases were released into the atmosphere in huge, black clouds. The intense heat caused two tank cars that had not been punctured to explode and rocket violently. Residents later reported hearing explosions at least 15 miles away from the accident site. Fortunately, residents were able to flee before the most violent explosions occurred, and there were no fatalities. Nearby buildings were damaged or destroyed beyond repair and evacuation of the town was required. Evacuation was a major psychological consequence of this disaster; according to the NTSB report, "About 3,000 persons living within a 5-mile radius of the derailment site were evacuated for as long as two weeks" (National Transportation Safety Board, Report No. RAR-83/05, n.d., p.1).

The Louisiana State Police took command of the incident site and coordinated the emergency response. Within an hour the immediate site was secured and shortly afterward the town was evacuated. A first major challenge was to determine the nature of the cargo, a task that was accomplished through cooperation by shippers and hazardous materials specialists. Fire suppression was not possible with water because of a metallic sodium car whose location and condition were unknown (Louisiana State Police, 1982). Cars continued to burn, vent under pressure, and bleve for the next 6 days. It was necessary to use photography and video work from a helicopter to determine placement of the damaged cars and to locate fires and unstable materials. The sky was darkened with black smoke from petroleum fires, and downwind monitoring was necessary for over a week. In addition, the ground was saturated with dangerous chemicals (Louisiana State Police, 1982). Small fires continued to burn and cars remained in a hot condition up to 2 weeks after the derailment.

The ICG Railroad assumed complete responsibility for the accident. The train was operating at excess speeds during its run from Baton Rouge to Hammond. Members of the crew had been drinking prior to the run, and blood alcohol level tests after the derailment demonstrated that the engineer was intoxicated (National Transportation Safety Board, Report No. RAR-83/05, n.d.). In addition, there was an unauthorized female operator/clerk from the railroad company in the cab. She was not only present, but actually in the engineer's seat and driving the train at the time of the derailment.

Although the accident was caused by a series of human and perhaps mechanical failures, her immediate response to an emergency was the "straw that broke the camel's back." She was unqualified to operate a locomotive, and she failed to apply the locomotive brakes correctly after the train hit a dip in Livingston. The NTSB report was highly critical of the engineer and the conductor for irresponsible behavior on the job and indirectly critical of the ICG Railroad for employing an engineer with a past history of alcohol-related accidents and irresponsible performance.

The NTSB report also praised the local fire chief for not jeopardizing the safety of his men by attacking a situation far beyond the capacities of the local department and for rapidly evacuating residents of the town. This latter was accomplished by a house-to-house canvass. The performance of the Louisiana State Police and other specialists throughout the disaster was exemplary, as indicated by the absence of casualties during the emergency (National Transportation Safety Board, Report No. RAR-83/05, n.d.).

When Livingston residents returned to the area they discovered that 19 residences and other buildings were destroyed or severely damaged. Toxic chemicals had been spilled and absorbed into the ground, resulting in long-term closure of the railroad line and an adjacent highway. Property damage was estimated to be in excess of $14 million (National Transportation Safety Board, Report No. RAR-83/05, n.d.).

Following the derailment several families independently sought counsel and sued the ICG Railroad for psychological damages. For purposes of efficiency the court requested that these cases be adjudicated in small groups of families in a jury trial. The trial testimony of a local psychologist and his cross-examination by the defense reveal a number of the issues that consistently arise in personal injury cases, including ones brought about by disaster. An examination of the record reveals several missed opportunities, especially on the part of the defense counsel who did not have the benefit of psychological consultation at the time of the trial.

The psychologist had been preparing material for a class action suit associated with the ICG Railroad disaster (to be discussed later) and was contacted by the plaintiffs' attorney shortly before the trial was to begin. The psychologist used the intervening time to administer a rather extensive battery of tests to each of the plaintiffs and had background information taken by a work associate who was a social worker. Thus, the psychologist was restricted to the psychological test results as a basis for his testimony, a fact that should have signaled a weak case to the defense but apparently did not. As indicated earlier, without a thorough understanding of a litigant's psychological history, and without knowledge of the litigant's experiences during the event in question, a mental health witness may have difficulty in speaking to the proximate cause criterion for personal injury. Psychological test results that indicate stress, anxiety, or whatever, are relatively useless by themselves until tied in some temporal or logical way to experiences during or following exposure to a trauma-inducing stimulus. Statements, for example, by the plaintiffs' counsel and the psychologist at the end of direct examination exposed the weakness of the plaintiffs' case, but it was not attacked directly by the defense. Plaintiff's attorney, after having established that psychological tests had been given and a variety of pathological results had been found on each of the family members, offered the following summary:

PLAINTIFFS' ATTORNEY: "O.K. So in your opinion, there's no doubt that, more likely than not, the train derailment, attendant stress and continuing stress relating to chemical clean up has caused these people to have the psychological problems you've seen?"

PSYCHOLOGIST: "I have no knowledge of anything else that could have caused this." *(Bridges v. Illinois Central Gulf Railroad,* 1984, p. 47).

The psychologist's response is a true statement, since he had not interviewed any of the litigants! The defense counsel here missed an opportunity to point out to the jury that the psychologist had no basis for eliminating any other rival hypothesis for the causes of the high test scores, including preevent psychopathology, intervening events, and other extraneous factors. Thus, the conclusion of the plaintiffs' attorney was allowed to stand relatively unchallenged.

On another occasion the psychologist's assumption that the test scores reflected "how the litigants have become" (since the derailment) was left unchallenged by the defense counsel as a general statement applying to all litigants. The one exception concerned one litigant who had developed an ulcer. Defense counsel had introduced medical evidence that questioned whether the ulcer had necessarily resulted from the derailment. Thus the issue of proximate cause was attacked only obliquely and the jury was not given the benefit of either conflicting testimony or argument regarding whether the derailment had, in fact, caused elevated test scores. The diagnosis of post-traumatic stress disorder (PTSD) was also cleverly introduced by the plaintiffs' psychologist without his having to document its application in each case. The plaintiffs' attorney asked about a common diagnosis for all five litigants, and was given the following reply by the psychologist.

I'm not going to offer this as a formal diagnosis but, rather, I'm going to phrase it this way: All five of these individuals have elevations in their tests which indicated underlying emotional problem [*sic*]. This emotional problem has anxiety and depression, mood changes, somatization as factors. These results I have obtained are consistent with a diagnosis given in the *Diagnostic and Statistical Manual* of the American Psychiatric Association as post-traumatic stress disorder. However, not having completed a comprehensive individual inquiry on these individuals, I cannot assign that particular diagnosis. But I can say that these tests are extremely reminiscent of this diagnosis. (*Bridges v. Illinois Central Gulf Railroad,* 1984, pp. 37–38)

This statement went unchallenged by the defense.

The above statement could have been attacked on several grounds. First, how were the tests linked to the specific diagnosis of PTSD, because none of the tests measured PTSD directly? Second, defense counsel could have challenged the foregoing statement on the basis that the criteria for PTSD, usually available only through interviews, had not been introduced as evidence at the trial. Thus, the psychologist was getting away with implying a diagnosis without having to substantiate it.

The defense counsel cross-examined the psychologist about response bias. The defense counsel correctly pointed out that self-report tests could be easily influenced by respondents who are in the process of litigation. The psychologist countered that some of the tests had a scale that would indicate exaggeration, and he was not challenged by research that indicates that litigants do, in fact, produce higher test scores than nonlitigants (Butcher & Harlow, 1987, p. 148).

The issue of proximate cause was broached again when the psychologist admitted under cross-examination that the tests did not reflect the emotional status of the litigants at the time of the event, but only at the time of testing. Thus, the opening was again there for a strenuous questioning of the relationship of the test results to the derailment and evacuation experience, but the opportunity was missed.

The court settlement of these cases awarded one litigant family $32,000, and the other family $31,000.

Class Action Suits for Personal Injury

Legal Concepts

Class action suits occur when a group of plaintiffs pool their complaints and seek compensation as one body rather than as individuals. A *class* may be defined in a number of ways, including all those persons residing in a geographical area affected by a defendant's actions, all individuals with a contractual arrangement with the defendant, or the members of a community that has been affected by the defendant. The defining characteristic of a class member is that he or she has some legal interest that has been affected. Following disasters, class action suits are instigated primarily by plaintiffs' attorneys. They organize and define the class, communicate with potential members and take the leadership to define the nature of the complaints. One of the chief advantages for members of a class action suit is the reduced cost of litigation per individual. In addition, a class action has more potential resources for carrying out the investigation and for securing expert testimony. With the increased potential size of the compensation awarded, there is more willingness on the part of plaintiffs' attorneys to finance a more thorough and comprehensive investigation and preparation. As in other endeavors, cooperative action has a number of advantages.

On the other hand, there are disadvantages to class action suits. Since members of the class may be treated more or less equally, there is less potential reward for the more severely injured individuals. Important decisions regarding both strategy and possible acceptance of out-of-court settlements are frequently made by a few members of the class in cooperation with the attorneys. In other words, the individual class member has considerably reduced decision-making responsibilities and power. Communication is also likely to be a problem especially in class action suits with a large class size.

Psychological Concepts

It is logical and efficient to organize the evidence for personal injury by using a central theme or concept. Concepts such as mental injury or psychic impairment are not recommended for marshaling psychological evidence because they are not embedded in psychological theory or measurement, even though they may be familiar concepts in the law. Instead, it is recommended that psychologists use concepts related to stress. The psychologist's task then becomes presenting research and clinical evidence related to stress, and it is the jury's or judge's task to determine whether the evidence presented constitutes a mental or emotional injury.

A class action litigation poses special problems for the selection of an organizing concept. A distinction must be made between the generalized concept of stress after a traumatic incident (posttraumatic stress) and posttraumatic stress *disorder* (PTSD) as an *individual diagnosis*. The former is conceptualized as existing on a continuum from very low or minimal stress to very high stress following a disaster and is the more generalized concept. The latter is conceptualized as a condition or status that is achieved by meeting certain behavioral criteria.

Should PTSD be used as an organizing concept for class action suits? Although this is theoretically possible, it poses a number of problems. A major logistic problem may be the requirement that each member of a class be examined for the existence of PTSD. Since class action suits usually pertain to large numbers of people, this challenge may represent a major drain on resources. It should be noted that *each* of the 625 litigants in the Buffalo Creek disaster, however, was examined by both plaintiffs and defense professional examiners (Stern, 1976). Thus, it is conceivable, that every member of a class might be examined for the purpose of determining the extent of PTSD in the class.

A second alternative that might be agreed upon by both parties would be to sample on a random basis a number of cases for the existence of PTSD. In fact, this procedure was proposed at one point in the Livingston derailment case but was not pursued further. A third alternative, and probably the least desirable one, is to argue for the existence of PTSD from grouped data that do not measure PTSD directly. Thus, other measures that bear some resemblance to the symptom criteria for PTSD might be used as a basis for estimating the extent of PTSD in the class action population. With the continued refinement of measures that purport to reflect PTSD symptoms, it may be possible to obtain either self-report or behavioral measures of PTSD in the future, although this is not possible now.

Measurement Issues

If PTSD is rejected as an organizing concept for class action suits, what other strategies are available? As indicated above, the general concept of stress is recommended, and it can be measured in several ways. Self-report symptom measures have been most frequently used, but there also have been successful attempts to use behavioral measures, including indices of health, accidents, and crime (Hartsough, 1985; Mileti, Hartsough, Madson, & Hufnagel, 1984). The Symptom Checklist-90 (SCL-90) and its variants, developed by Derogatis (1977), are useful symptom checklists that are appropriate for disaster populations. The SCL-90 yields nine subscales and a global severity index. Baum and his associates have demonstrated the utility of behavioral and psychophysiological measures of stress (Baum, Gatchel, & Schaeffer, 1983). Houts (1980) used telephone interviews to estimate stress levels following the Three Mile Island incident. Finally, archival records have been used to reflect a generalized stress response of whole communities (Mileti et al., 1984; Papperman 1984). The concept of levels of stress applies readily to groups and communities.

The most defensible strategy for demonstrating the extent of stress in a disaster population is to use a multimethod approach. It would combine an interview with standardized stress measures and behavioral or other non-reactive measurement techniques (Hartsough, 1985). A multimethod research strategy benefits plaintiffs to the extent that evidence for stress is found in each of the methods used. The argument that self-reported stress is exaggerated because the respondent is in litigation (See Butcher & Harlow, 1987) is partially countered when there is also behavioral evidence indicating stress. On the other side of the coin, the defense may be able to demonstrate through behavioral and other nonreactive measures of stress that plaintiffs' stress levels are shown only in the measures that they can consciously influence, that is, interviews and self-report scales. This finding strengthens the defense position because it weakens the plaintiffs' argument of extensive stress following the disaster.

CASE STUDY

Following the Livingston derailment disaster, a class of survivors was formed in order to instigate legal action against the railroad. The major details of the accident have already been described. This section will discuss the evidentiary basis for the plaintiffs' complaint and the role that psychologists played for both plaintiffs and defense.

A steering committee was formed by some of the Livingston residents and, through counsel, contracted for the services of a Baton Rouge private psychological clinic. Three clinical psychologists and a social worker became the principal investigators of a study of the effect of the derailment on Livingston residents (Lemoine, Rostow, Nemeth, & Ellis, 1984). Data were gathered 9 months after the accident and the study was published as a report nearly 2 years after the derailment. Neither the timing of the data gathering nor the publication of the report is unusual for disasters—even longer delays are to be expected in most cases. A static group comparison design was employed, using an experimental group from the Livingston area and a control group of 43 residents from a neighboring town not directly affected by the derailment. To construct an experimental group the investigators obtained a master list of 1,703 Livingston-area residents and sent a letter inviting participation in the survey to a random sample of 610 adults from the master list. Of these individuals, 107 residents subsequently completed all of the measures, a response rate of 18%. The control group was not randomly drawn, but instead subjects were solicited through a church in the control community. Control subjects were paid a small amount for their participation.

The investigators used several paper-and-pencil, self-report instruments to obtain evidence. A background questionnaire created by the investigators was used to gather sociodemographic information. A revised Impact of Event Scale (IES) (Horowitz, Wilner, & Alvarez, 1979) and a stress index created by the investigators were used to measure event-specific stress. The SCL-90 (Derogatis, 1977) was employed to measure psychological distress symptoms. The Million Clinical Multiaxial Inventory (MCMI) (Million, 1983) was used to measure personality dysfunction. The Wahler Physical Symptoms Inventory was used to measure physical complaints. Finally, the Shipley Institute of Living Scale (Bartz & Loy, 1970) was used to estimate cognitive impairment. All but the Wahler and the Shipley measures were also given to the control group.

Differences in the expected direction were registered for the scales reflecting event-specific stress. More generally, psychological distress symptoms were higher for the derailment subjects, as reflected by the SCL-90 scores. The largest score differences were found for anxiety, phobic anxiety, paranoid ideation, and psychoticism. Also, the magnitudes of the mean T-scores of the derailment group were substantially higher than the norms for a nonpsychiatric standardization group as indicated in the *SCL-90 Manual* (Derogatis, 1977). The test for personality dysfunction (MCMI) also demonstrated higher scores for the disaster group, especially in the clinical symptom scales for anxiety, somatoform, dysthymia, alcohol abuse, psychotic depression, and psychotic delusions. The investigators concluded that the test results demonstrated, "The Livingston residents reported a significantly higher degree of mental stress associated with the derailment incident as compared to the controls" (Lemoine et al., 1984, p. 37). They also concluded that the Livingston subjects were experiencing a greater degree of psychological distress and personality dysfunction.

The results were consistent with a finding of elevated psychological stress in the disaster population. Nevertheless, as pointed out by ICG behavioral scientist consultants, there were a number of problems with the Plaintiffs' Steering Committee Study. The most basic problem was the inability to generalize from these results to the Livingston poulation and therefore to all members of the class making up the class action suit. The low response rate of 18% indicated that a selective bias may have operated in responding to the request for participation in the survey. That is, those persons who had sustained greater stress or those with stronger interests in litigation may have also responded more readily to the survey. In addition, the control group was a sample of convenience that was not randomly selected. Because it was made clear to all respondents that the purpose of the survey was to record the psychological effects of the derailment, there was ample opportunity for response bias in filling out the self-report measures. Because the respondents knew that the purpose was for litigation, one could argue that the bias was toward amplifying or exaggerating symptoms. (The investigators argued that the MCMI results were valid and showed no tendency toward exaggeration, but this conclusion would apply only to the MCMI.) Finally, no attempt was made by the investigators to logically associate the higher symptom levels or the personality deficits of the derailment group to the experience of the derailment or the subsequent evacuation. In general the differences were presented as prima facie evidence that the Livingston respondents had, in fact, suffered a personal injury because of the derailment. The foregoing characteristics of the Plaintiffs' Steering Committee Study left it open to serious challenge by the ICG Railroad. By stretching the conclusions beyond the point at which they were credible in terms of the data and the design of the study, the investigators actually may have jeopardized the plaintiff's cause.

In contrast was a second study ordered by a district court in Louisiana, "To provide expert services in the investigation of all aspects of damage resulting from the Livingston train derailment on September 28, 1982, including the physical, sociological, economic, and ecological and psychological aspects thereof" (Siegel, Blanchard-Fields, Gottfried, & Lowe, 1984, p. iii). The psychological assessment study was conducted by four psychologists under contract by the Gulf South Research Institute (GSRI) of Baton Rouge, Louisiana. The GSRI study employed a stratified random sampling procedure and the data were collected in respondents' homes. Interviews with 133 heads of households plus 100 spouses represented a 75% acceptance rate. A Life Events Questionnaire (LEQ) (Horowitz, Schaefer, Hiroto, Wilner & Levin, 1977), the IES, and open-ended questions regarding stresses were included in a broad survey instrument detailing the respondent's disaster experience, losses, and the sociological, economic, and psychological consequences of the derailment.

By using responses to the LEQ the investigators attempted to separate baseline stresses from the ones associated only with the derailment. That is, preevent stressors and derailment stressors, plus their associated stress levels, could be compared. For life events that had occurred since the derailment, interviewers were instructed to probe whether the event was perceived by the respondent as a consequence of the derailment or not. However, they were instructed not to ask that question directly. Thus, the GSRI study attempted through its instrumentation to separate baseline from event-specific stress scores. Because this distinction has represented a troublesome problem for both disaster research and finders of fact in the courts, the GSRI solution was not only creative, but useful. Significantly, the study found zero-order correlations between baseline and derailment scores, indicating a lack of predisposition to being stressed by the derailment.

The investigators found a statistically signficant relationship between distance from the incident and level of stress. The relationship was curvilinear, with greater amounts of external event stress being experienced by persons living within 1/4 to 2 miles from the derailment site than by persons living either at a lesser or greater distance. The investigators also concluded that the Livingston sample was not "pathologically stressed" at the time that the IES was administered, but they also pointed out that 18 months had elapsed since the derailment.

The GSRI investigators were able to conclude that stress levels had become elevated as a result of the derailment. They also found that the stress scores for spouses were higher than for heads of household, especially concerning the adverse impact of the derailment on mood and emotional responses. They also found significant effects for the duration of the evacuation and the distance from the derailment.

The major deficit of the GSRI study was the lack of a comparison for the postevent measures, either through a comparison group or preevent data from the derailment population. Also, the GSRI data were restricted to self-report measures; confirming behavioral or archival information would have been useful.

The class action suit was settled out of court, with the ICG Railroad paying the 3,000 litigants approximately $3 million for all claims, including property loss, evacuation expenses, and personal injuries, including psychological or emotional injury.

Role of the Psychologist

There are two likely roles for a psychologist in personal injury litigation—as clinical investigator or research investigator, or some combination of both. In order to be effective in either role, a psychologist doing personal injury work in the context of a disaster must become familiar with the body of knowledge about the social and psychological effects of disasters. (For example, see Cohen & Ahearn, 1980; Drabek, 1986; Erikson, 1976; Figley, 1985, 1986; Gleser, Green, & Winget, 1981; Hartsough & Myers, 1985; Laube & Murphy, 1985; Mileti, Drabek, & Haas, 1975; Sowder, 1985). In the absence of familiarity with this knowledge base it is difficult to separate disaster effects from other problems, or to place the survivor's complaints, or stress findings of a disaster class, into a theoretical context.

A psychologist employed by the defense, in addition to the foregoing roles, may also serve as a research consultant. The task may be largely advisory, although preparation should be made for testifying as an expert witness. The psychologist will likely be called upon to examine critically the research on the disaster population and to inform the defense counsel as to the strengths and weaknesses of the findings. It is important to be impartial in this analysis, in order to assist the attorney in determining not only where the plaintiffs' case is solid and will likely result in compensation, but also where it is weak, so that compensation is not given for frivolous or insignificant findings.

In addition to knowing the knowledge base regarding psychological effects of disasters, it is helpful to become aware of the issues likely to arise in litigation. Many such issues concern the linkage of observed effects to antecedent conditions, principally the disaster. There are likely to be issues about how evidence was gathered, that is, the soundness of the instruments (including the interview) in the research design. Behavioral scientists and practitioners strive toward objectivity in their assessments and for this reason are valued as expert witnesses. It is sometimes difficult to maintain objectivity within the context of a working relationship with counsel, who view the situation as an adversary. It is recommended that the psychologist attempt to maintain the objective role of the clinician or research scientist, while at the same time accepting that the legal system is built upon adversarial roles for participating attorneys. This approach is consistent with the advice of Melton et al. (1987) that the psychologist not attempt to be drawn into giving an answer for the "ultimate question" which is legal in nature. For example, "Was there enough stress suffered by these litigants to merit compensation?" is not a scientific question, but one that should be answered by a judge, jury, or in negotiations between attorneys.

PUBLIC ENVIRONMENTAL POLICY AND DISASTERS

The place of psychology in public policy regarding disasters is not well defined. Public policy affecting disaster response or planning is a very broad area, including mandated relocation of citizens from high-risk residential areas and applications of federal environmental regulations to federally regulated activities, such as licensing nuclear power plants or siting hazardous waste dumps. In these situations, psychology has played a role in defining and evaluating psychological health and factors that may affect it, such as stress. In these instances clinical evaluation of an individual client is less likely than research to assess the past or potential impact of federally regulated activities on target populations. The following discussion is restricted to public policy that concerns environmental management.

Legal Concepts and Psychological Concepts

The nuclear reactor accident at Three Mile Island in March 1979 demonstrated the possibility that psychologists have a role in environmental use assessment. This came about because the federal government requires an assurance of protection of the environment where certain federal activities, such as building prisons or licensing nuclear reactor sites, have a potential impact on the environment. The question is asked, "Does the proposed activity constitute an environmental hazard?"

The method for ensuring the environmental protection is stipulated in the National Environmental Policy Act of 1969 (NEPA, 1969). An environmental impact assessment, and if necessary, a more complete and documented environmental impact statement, estimates the impact that the proposed action would have on the physical environment and the health of citizens living in the area under question. In the context of the legal maneuvering following TMI, requirements under NEPA to protect the general health were also construed to include psychological health. The decision of one court stated, "We conclude that, in the context of NEPA, health encompasses psychological health" (*People Against Nuclear Engery [PANE] v. U.S. NRC,* 1982, p. 228). What precisely constitutes psychological health was left undefined but generally referred to stress levels in the population. There are indications in other legislation that the definition of psychological impacts may be broadened to include the public confidence in the decisions of governmental bodies regarding environmental actions (Brody, 1985).

Case Study: Three Mile Island Nuclear Reactor Accident

The TMI accident attracted international attention because of its potential danger and also because of the controversy surrounding the use of nuclear energy. Conditions inside the reactor were out of control for many hours. The information coming from the plant and the media gave conflicting impressions of danger, adding to the threat already perceived by many citizens because of their unfamiliarity with nuclear energy. Radiation was accidentally released into the atmosphere, but during the first week or more of the incident, the precise amount was unknown, leading to speculation and fear. The governor of Pennsylvania issued an evacuation advisory for mothers and young children, but many more citizens evacuated the region, eventually totaling 144,000. Fortunately, it was later determined that the actual radiation released had not been life threatening and that a serious catastrophe, such as happened later at Chernobyl, had been averted.

The Metropolitan Edison Company owned two separate nuclear generating plants on TMI, and the undamaged plant was in a shutdown status for maintenance purposes at the time of the accident. The company was ordered by the Nuclear Regulatory Commission (NRC) to keep the undamaged plant inoperable until operations could be safely resumed. Included in the criteria for restart of the undamaged unit was the stipulation that restart not cause a harmful psychological reaction in the populations surrounding TMI. The company had to demonstrate not only fiscal and management soundness and plant safety, but also that no serious psychological stress would be sustained, before the restart could take place.

The primary impact of the TMI accident on the surrounding population was identified by the President's Commission on the Accident at Three Mile Island (1979) as a mental health impact, specifically psychological stress. In the years following TMI, the incident became one of the most thoroughly researched of all disasters from the standpoint of psychological stress in the affected population (Hartsough & Savitsky, 1984). The findings showed a general pattern of short-term psychological stress, distrust of both company and government actions surrounding the incident, and differential effects for different segments of the population (Hartsough and Savitsky). The long-term effects of TMI are less clear, and the clinical or functional meaning of them is uncertain. In any case, it is safe to conclude that the early high stress levels were not sustained and that these stress levels did not reach proportions recorded for patient populations (Hartsough & Savitsky).

The research on the TMI accident became a significant factor in the NRC's attempt to settle the restart question. The NRC brought together many of the TMI research investigators in order to assess the extent of psychological stress and, more importantly, to predict how much stress might be caused by a restart of the undamaged reactor. The scientists at this gathering found the prediction task extremely difficult, pointing out that these circumstances had never previously occurred, thus giving no basis for a scientific prediction (Mitre Corporation, 1982). However, the group did agree that the stress at restart would be no higher than the highest stress levels experienced in the wake of the accident, and likely would be lower (Mitre Corporation). This meeting may have represented a major step forward in the use of scientific data relating to the public policy issues regarding disasters.

The legal history of the restart issue as a public policy matter is discussed by Hartsough and Savitsky (1984). The issue was controversial in several respects, including the question as to whether psychological impacts belong in environmental policy decisions. Soon after the accident, the NRC decided to require hearings on the psychological impact issue before allowing the owners to restart the undamaged TMI reactor. The NRC raised the issue of psychological stress but could not decide whether such issues were relevant to legal proceedings. The NRC did invite intervention on the topic of psychological stress, and several organizations decided to participate in the hearings as interveners. One intervener, People Against Nuclear Energy (PANE), focused exclusively on the psychological stress issue.

The NRC's own licensing board recommended that psychological stress be considered under NEPA; the NRC, however, rejected that recommendation. PANE then appealed the NRC decision to the Second District Court of Appeals in Washington D.C. The court found in favor of PANE, ordering the NRC to prepare an environmental assessment "of the effects of the proposed TMI-1 restart on the psychological health of neighboring residents and the well-being of the surrounding communities" (*PANE v. U.S. NRC*, 1982, p. 552). This decision appeared as a landmark decision placing psychological effects of licensing activities within the purview of NEPA by relating them to general health.

The final step in this contorted legal maneuvering found the NRC appealing the Second District Court action to the Supreme Court of the United States. The Supreme Court ruled unanimously to overturn the decision of the lower court, thus, supporting NRC's original position. It did, however, leave open the possibility of some conditions under which psychological effects might be considered under NEPA. In an opinion reminiscent of previous decisions regarding emotional damages in the law, the Supreme Court found that psychological effects may only be considered by a regulatory agency when the effects are the results of *physical changes* to the environment. In other words, the existence of psychological stress among citizens cannot, by itself, curtail federal environmental use projects. The implication of the Supreme Court's decision is that *if* there had been extensive physical damage to the environment as a result of the TMI accident, then psychological stress might have been considered as an environmental impact under NEPA.

Psychological Stress and Environmental Policy Issues

One issue is whether the prospect of psychological stress, in and of itself, is sufficient to qualify as an environmental impact. The PANE decision by the Supreme Court settles the issue for the present. It holds that NEPA only requires an agency to assess the impact of environmental use projects on the physical environment (*Metropolitan Edison Co. v. PANE*, 1983). The reasoning behind this decision was expressed by Justice Brennan:

> There can be no doubt that psychological injuries are cognizable under NEPA. . . . As the court points out, however, the particular psychological injury alleged in this case did not arise, for example, out of direct sensory impact of a change in a physical environment . . . but out of a perception of risk. . . . In light of the history and policies underlying NEPA, I agree with the Court that this crucial distinction "lengthens the causal chain beyond reach" of the statute. (pp. 545–546)

A second issue concerns the use of psychological research findings as evidence for an environmental impact. What criteria should be formulated for stress studies in order that their results be considered as valid evidence? For example is it sufficient just to demonstrate a statistically significant difference on self-report measures between disaster and comparison communities? Given the deficiencies of self-report as a measuring strategy, this seems a risky criterion. Is it sufficient to show an increase in mental disorder (e.g., PTSD) in the disaster community? This chapter earlier pointed out the desirability of a multimethod approach that includes behavioral data, and if possible, a comparison of preincident data to postincident data. This is most likely possible with archival information (Papperman, 1984). The combination of psychological data from various sources is more likely to meet the legal standard of "preponderance of evidence" than findings of a single type, such as self-report, especially if these findings are subject to response bias. This issue is likely to remain ambiguous until actually tested in the public policy arena.

The final issue has to do with how psychology may be optimally employed in assessing environmental impacts. Should participation of psychologists in advocacy efforts be encouraged? The adversarial system seems an excellent way to test the soundness of both data and arguments put forth by psychologists, but it also threatens the high value placed on objectivity in the discipline. On the other hand, if psychologists are employed primarily as impartial scientists by presumably neutral agents of public policy, such as regulatory agencies, will this approach be sufficiently rigorous to allow for testing of rival hypotheses? Again, the issue may be settled by actual future cases. Developments in the profession that would assist in reducing the ambiguity around this issue include consensus agreements on the necessary and sufficient research to determine stress in a given population, and tools for its measurement.

Role of the Psychologist

The psychologist will most likely be an investigator or research consultant in environmental use cases. When the attorneys with whom one is collaborating are working for the first time on issues involving psychological stress and its assessment, an educator role is also indicated. Both psychologists and counsel will find it advisable, in the long run, to spend time and resources discussing the present state of the art regarding psychological stress. This should include the concepts of stress and PTSD, as well as the methods of measurement for these disorders. The limitations of the present state of knowledge should be addressed. This will help to build realistic expectations for both sides of the working partnership. It also helps to begin by building an understanding of how scientific concepts are to be translated into legal ones and vice versa.

Finally, it must be repeated that it is not the psychologist's task to determine whether sufficient scientific evidence exists to make a policy decision. That prerogative is reserved for members of the policy-making system or the general body politic.

CONCLUSIONS

The psychology–law interface regarding disasters is relatively recent but has already uncovered some areas for improvement. Grisso (1987) rightfully argues for greater preparation and training for psychologists entering forensic work. His warning should include clinicians who undertake assessments for personal injury litigants arising from disasters. Also, there should be better psychological consultation for attorneys to assist them in selecting meritorious cases and rejecting frivolous claims.

Research on groups of survivors and communities in disaster suffers from an inability to estimate accurately the incidence of PTSD in a defined population without interviewing each member individually. Research methods in development that could fill this gap include self-report measures and archival data sources. Perfection of such measures and the use of appropriate research designs would aid substantially in assuring fair treatment in the law of large groups of survivors.

REFERENCES

American Psychiatric Association. (1980). *Diagnostic and statistical manual of mental disorders* (3rd ed.; DSM-III). Washington, DC: Author.

Annotation-immediacy of observation of injury as affecting right to recover damages for shock or mental anguish from witnessing injury to another. (1981). *American Law Review (4th ed.), 5,* 833–851.

Bartz, W. R., & Loy, D. L. (1970). The Shipley-Hartford as a brief IQ screening device. *Journal of Clinical Psychology, 26,* 74–75.

Baum, A., Gatchel, R. J., & Schaeffer, M. A. (1983). Emotional, behavioral, and physiological effects of chronic stress at Three Mile Island. *Journal of Consulting and Clinical Psychology, 51,* 565–572.

Bridges v. Illinois Central Gulf Railroad, C. A. No. 82-1056-A (M.D. La. 1984).

Brody, J. G. (1985). New roles for psychologists in environmental impact assessment. *American Psychologist, 40,* 1057–1060.

Butcher, J. N., & Harlow, T. C. (1987). In I. B. Weiner & A. K. Hess (Eds.), *Handbook of forensic psychology.* New York: Wiley.

Cohen, R. E., & Ahearn, F. L., Jr. (1980). *Handbook for mental health care of disaster victims.* Baltimore: Johns Hopkins University Press.

Derogatis, L. R. (1977). *SCL-90: Administration, scoring and procedures manual-I for the revised version and other instruments of the psychopathology rating scale series.* Baltimore: John Hopkins University School of Medicine.

Dooley, J. (1977). *Modern tort law: Liability and litigation.* Chicago: Callaghan. (Rev. ed. by Lindahl, B. A., 1982)

Drabek, T. E. (1986). *Human system responses to disaster: An inventory of sociological findings.* New York: Springer-Verlag.

Erikson, K. T. (1976). *Everything in its path.* New York: Simon & Schuster.

Figley, C. R. (Ed.) (1985). *Trauma and its wake: Vol. I. The study and treatment of post-traumatic stress disorder.* New York: Brunner/Mazel.

Figley, C. R. (Ed.) (1986). *Trauma and its wake: Vol. II. Traumatic stress theory, research, and intervention.* New York: Brunner/Mazel.

Gleser, G. C., Green, B. L., & Winget, C. C. (1981). *Prolonged psychosocial effects of disaster: A study of Buffalo Creek.* New York: Academic Press.

Grisso, T. (1987). The economic and scientific future of forensic psychological assessment. *American Psychologist, 42,* 831–839.

Hartsough, D. M. (1985). Measurement of the psychological effects of disaster. In J. Laube & S. A. Murphy (Eds.), *Perspectives on disaster recovery* (pp. 22–60). Norwalk, CT: Appleton-Century-Crofts.

Hartsough, D. M., & Myers, D. G. (1985). *Disaster work and mental health: Prevention and control of stress among workers.* Washington, DC: National Institute of Mental Health, Center for Mental Health Studies of Emergencies.

Hartsough, D. M., & Savitsky, J. C. (1984). Three Mile Island: Psychology and environmental policy at a crossroads. *American Psychologist, 39,* 1113–1122.

Horowitz, M., Schaefer, C., Hiroto, D., Wilner, N., & Levin, B. (1977). Life event questionnaires for measuring presumptive stress. *Psychosomatic Medicine, 39,* 413–431.

Horowitz, M., Wilner, N., & Alvarez, W. (1979). Impact of event scale: A measure of subjective stress. *Psychosomatic Medicine, 41,* 209–218.

Houts, P. S. (1980). *Health-related behavioral impact of the Three Mile Island Nuclear Accident: Parts I & II.* Report to the TMI Advisory Panel on Health Research Studies, Pennsylvania Department of Health. Hershey: Pennsylvania State University College of Medicine.

Laube, J., & Murphy, S. A. (Eds.) (1985). *Perspectives on disaster recovery.* Norwalk, CT: Appleton-Century-Crofts.

Lemoine, R. L., Rostow, C. D., Nemeth, D. G., & Ellis, J. S. (1984). *The Livingston train derailment accident: An evaluation of the psychological impact on community residents.* (An evaluation report prepared for the plaintiff's steering comittee by Baton Rouge Psychological Associates, formerly the Runnymede Clinic Psychological Services.) Baton Rouge, LA: Author.

Louisiana State Police. (1982, November 10). *Illinois Gulf Central Derailment, Livingston, Louisiana.* Department of Public Safety, Office of State Police, unpublished report.

Magruder, C. (1935). Mental and emotional disturbance in the law of torts. *Harvard Law Review, 49,* 1033–1067.

Maloney, M. (1985). *A clinician's guide to forensic psychological assessment.* New York: Free Press.

Melton, G. B., Petrila, J., Poythress, N. G., & Slobogin, C. (1987). *Psychological evaluations for the courts: A handbook for mental health professionals and lawyers.* New York: Guilford.

Metropolitan Edison Co. v. People Against Nuclear Energy, 75 L. Ed. 2d 534 (1983).

Mileti, D. S., Drabek, T. E., & Haas, J. E. (1975). *Human systems in extreme environments: A sociological perspective* (Monograph 2). Boulder: University of Colorado Institute of Behavioral Science.

Mileti, D. S., Hartsough, D. M., Madson, P., & Hufnagel, R. (1984). The Three Mile Island incident: A study of behavioral indicators of human stress. *International Journal of Mass Emergencies and Disasters, 2,* 89–113.

Millon, T. (1983). *Millon Clinical Multiaxial Inventory Manual*. Minneapolis, MN: Interpretive Scoring Systems.

Mitre Corporation, M. C. (1982). *Nuclear Regulatory Commission workshop on psychological stress associated with restart of TMI-1* (Docket No. 50-289). McClean, VA: Author.

National Environmental Policy Act of 1969, 42 U.S.C. §§4321–4361 (1976).

National Transportation Safety Board (NTSB). (n.d.). *Railroad accident report: Derailment of Illinois Central Gulf Railroad Freight Train Extra 9629 East (GS-2-28) and release of hazardous materials at Livingston, Louisiana, September 28, 1982*. (NTSB/RAR-83/05). Washington, DC: Author.

Papperman, T. J. (1984). Psychosocial impact of natural disaster: An archival study (Doctoral dissertation, Purdue University, 1984). *Dissertation Abstracts International, 8423406*.

People Against Nuclear Energy (PANE) v. U.S. Nuclear Regulatory Commission, 673 F.2d 552 (D.C. Cir.), *order vacating NRC decision*, 678 F.2d 222, 235 (D.C. Cir. filed April 2, 1982), *amended interim order*, 678 F.2d 222, 228 (D.C. Cir. 1982) (Wilkey dissenting in part).

President's Commission on the Accident at Three Mile Island. (1979). *The need for change: The legacy of TMI*. Washington, DC: Office of the President Executive.

Prosser, W. (1971). *Law of torts* (4th edition). St. Paul: West.

Siegel, L., Blanchard-Fields, F., Gottfried, N. W., & Lowe, R. (1984). *Final report: Ecological, physical, economic, sociological and psychological assessment of the Illinois Central Gulf train derailment: Volume 6. Psychological assessment*. Baton Rouge, LA: Gulf South Research Institute.

Sowder, B. J. (Ed.). (1985). *Disasters and mental health: Selected contemporary perspectives*. Rockville, MD: National Institute of Mental Health.

Stern, G. M. (1976). Disaster at Buffalo Creek: From chaos to responsibility. *American Journal of Psychiatry, 133*, 300–301.

Walker, L. E. (1987). Intervention with victim/survivors. In I. B. Weiner & A. K. Hess (Eds.), *Handbook of forensic psychology* (pp. 630–649) New York: Wiley.

Weiner, I. B., & Hess, A. K. (Eds.). (1987). *Handbook of forensic psychology*. New York: Wiley.

CHAPTER 12

Research Issues in Assessing Disaster's Effects

SUSAN D. SOLOMON

This chapter highlights methodological considerations of importance in planning systematic assessments of the effects of disaster. The discussion is predicated on the assumption that the reader is familiar with basic research techniques involved in the conduct of epidemiological surveys, quasi-experimental studies, and clinical trials. The intent is therefore not to discuss how such studies should be conducted, but rather to describe when these techniques are most appropriately applied to the study of disaster and to note the likely pitfalls and opportunities awaiting the investigator of disaster's effects.

The importance of systematic disaster research, in terms of both theory development and intervention planning, cannot be overestimated. An extensive amount of research has already been conducted on the mental and physical effects of stress. However, much of the early work was conducted in a laboratory setting, using such aversive stimuli as repeated shocks or noise bursts as stressors (e.g., Glass & Singer, 1972; Roth & Bootzin, 1974). Although the theoretical contributions of such studies have been substantial, many investigators have more recently become disenchanted with the laboratory setting as an avenue for understanding reactions to "real world" stressful events, because the laboratory experiment is incapable of recreating those aspects of greatest theoretical and practical concern (e.g., the role of predictability, duration and/or scope of the event, long-term changes in physical and/or mental health, etc.; for a more detailed discussion, see Wortman, 1983; Wortman, Abbey, Holland, Silver, & Janoff-Bulman, 1980). As a consequence, investigators have increasingly turned toward investigations in natural settings as a means of enhancing the understanding of stress.

Although moving research on generalized stress into the real world may help to address many criticisms regarding external validity, it also opens

The author would like to thank Ben Locke for his thoughtful comments on an earlier draft of this chapter.

this research to a host of interpretation problems. The particular theoretical value of research on disaster lies in its ability to minimize some of the difficulties in interpretation associated with the study of more common stressful events. The amount of variance explained by exposure to common life events is typically quite small (Rabkin & Struening, 1976). Helzer (1981) suggests that if stress is an important contributor to illness, extreme events should show a stronger relationship to later outcomes than would more common stressors. Selection bias is also minimized in these studies, because respondents are identified on the basis of exposure to the disaster event rather than on the basis of, for example, health records, which may be more a measure of help-seeking behavior than illness per se (Mechanic, 1974). Further, since the occurrence of disaster is primarily outside the individual's control, these studies avoid problems of confound between the event and symptoms of illness. In studies of more common, controllable stressful events (e.g., divorce, job loss), it is difficult to assess whether an illness such as depression represents an antecedent or a consequence of the event (Dohrenwend, 1974). Disasters, because they are extreme, are unlikely to be confused with the symptoms or consequences of illness (see Helzer, 1981).

Disaster studies are not only of theoretical significance, but of great practical importance as well. It has been estimated that between 1970 and 1980 almost 2 million American households each year experienced injuries and/or damages from either fire, floods, hurricanes, tornadoes, or earthquakes (Rossi, Wright, Weber-Burdin, & Perina, 1983). Further, human-made disasters such as chemical pollution, transportation accidents, explosions, structural failures, terrorism, and the like, may pose an ever-increasing threat to physical and mental health. Although the extent of exposure to technological disaster is difficult to estimate, a 1980 Senate subcommittee concerned with only one such hazard (chemical dumps) noted that as many as 30,000 sites may be capable of causing significant health problems due to their proximity to public groundwater drinking supplies (Cohn, 1980). These estimates underline the importance of establishing the extent of psychiatric disturbance resulting from exposure to natural and human-made disaster, of identifying characteristics of events and/or individuals that put victims at high risk, and of identifying effective interventions by which to prevent or treat the mental and physical consequences of exposure to extreme stress.

This chapter attempts both to delineate dimensions of the disaster-response syndrome and to discuss some of the methodological difficulties associated with the study of psychosocial aspects of disaster. In line with Green's (1982) distinction between *actual* and *methodological* dimensions of disaster research, the discussion first addresses aspects associated with the disasters and the victims themselves which affect actual impairment and recovery rates (i.e., true scores). The focus then shifts to methodological issues that may affect estimates of these rates of impairment and recovery, emphasizing consideration of a range of reactions and consequences, as well as potential mediators of the victim's response to the stressful event. Methodological considerations pertinent to the design and execution of various types of risk factor and intervention studies are then outlined, with concluding remarks addressing constraints either inherent to disaster research or currently imposed on these studies by the state of the art.

ACTUAL DIMENSIONS OF THE DISASTER-RESPONSE SYNDROME

This section of the chapter addresses those components of the disaster experience that affect actual responses to exposure. Problems that confront researchers attempting to identify the underlying dimensions of the disaster-response syndrome include defining what constitutes a disaster, developing a taxonomy of disaster that permits cross-event comparisons, distinguishing between transient reactions and severe consequences, and identifying intervening factors that mediate individual responses to these events.

Defining Disaster

Perhaps the most immediate problem associated with the conduct of disaster research is the lack of agreement about what constitutes a disaster (see Chapter 2 and Quarentelli, 1985, for more detailed discussions). For example, Cohen and Ahearn (1980) define disasters as "extraordinary events that cause great destruction of property and may result in death, physical injury, and human suffering" (p. 5). As Baum (1986) points out, however, a definition of this nature rules out such events as the Three Mile Island nuclear reactor accident, because no observable damage to property or life ensued from that event. Barton's (1969) definition is broader, classifying disasters as a subset of "collective stress situations" that occur when a social system fails to provide many of its members with the expected conditions of life. However, this definition poses problems as well, based as it is on the concept of stress, for which a consensus of definition is also lacking (for reviews, see Burchfield, 1979; Elliott & Eisdorfer, 1982).

Stress research has been criticized as tautological: stressors are events that produce a stress response; stressors are negative because they are associated with unwanted consequences (Elliott & Eisdorfer, 1982). Disaster research, as a study of collective stress, is subject to the same criticism: an event is a disaster because its consequences are disastrous (cf. Baum, 1986).

The present discussion is based on the definition of stress adopted by the Institute of Medicine (Elliott & Eisdorfer, 1982). This definition identifies three basic components in the stress sequence: *activators/stressors* (environmental events that change an individual's present state), *reactions* (transient biological or psychosocial responses to an activator), and *consequences* (prolonged or cumulative effects of reactions). *Mediators* are defined as the modifiers that act on each of these components to produce individual variations in the stress sequence.

Types of Disaster—Defining the Stressor

Many events are potential stressors. In an effort to move the field toward the identification of the critical elements of disaster that make it a stressful experience, several taxonomies have been proposed. For example, Barton (1969) examines disasters in terms of scope of impact, speed of onset, duration of impact, and social preparedness. Berren, Beigel, and Ghertner's (1980) model uses as criteria type of disaster, duration of disaster, degree of personal impact, potential for (re)occurrence, and control over future impact. (See Chapter 2 for a more extensive discussion of disaster typology). Although the different models may emphasize somewhat different elements, they share a desire to provide some cohesion to disaster research, to enable comparisons across studies of disasters' effects.

The potential utility of a taxonomy for research on disaster is exemplified by the work of Baum and his colleagues. In a careful review of disaster literature, Baum, Fleming, and Singer (1983) contrasted the effects of technological hazards with those of natural disasters. These investigators identified several features that distinguish natural disaster from human-made catastrophes, including perceptions of control, duration of impact, presence of an identifiable low point, and the like. They inferred from their review of extant literature that technological hazards are more likely to have long-term consequences on mental health than are natural hazards.

Complicating their attempt to isolate the elements of technological disasters that account for the greater psychological consequences of these events was a confound posed by the type of events chosen for study in past investigations. Most of the natural disasters were short-term events with a recognizable low point, after which conditions slowly improved (e.g., hurricanes, floods). In contrast, the studies of technological hazards tended to focus on chronic events whose long-term consequences have been uncertain (e.g., exposure to toxic chemicals or radiation).

Baum and his colleagues used their taxonomy as a basis for designing research that would untangle this confound. Their current investigation involves multisite comparisons of disasters that differ in both origin and duration. By deliberately including chronic, natural disasters (e.g., drought, radon exposure) and acute, technological breakdowns (e.g., explosions, transportation accidents) along with the more frequently studied kinds of events (e.g., exposure to toxic waste, floods) these investigators hope to ascertain whether the component of chronicity or the component of human origin has made long-term recovery from technological hazards more difficult than the recovery from natural events. The practical significance of work such as this is potentially great: By identifying events that put victims at highest risk, this research will assist mental health practitioners in targeting their interventions toward victims in greatest need of assistance.

Types of Response—Reactions and Consequences

Taxonomies of disaster help to determine which aspects of an event make the experience stressful. However, disaster research needs to examine not only the *stressor* but also the other components of the stress sequence: *reactions* and *consequences*. Systematic attempts to separate reactions from consequences are rare and somewhat difficult to make. As noted earlier, the Institute of Medicine uses these terms to differentiate between transient responses and prolonged effects (Elliott & Eisdorfer, 1982). One interpretation of this definition suggests that the identical responses might constitute either reactions or consequences, depending on when they are measured (an issue of timing). Alternatively, the definition might be interpreted as suggesting that the type of response is also central to this distinction (an issue of both quality and severity).

These distinctions may sound academic, but scrutiny of the diagnosis of post-traumatic stress disorder (PTSD) illustrates their importance to disaster research. Post-traumatic stress disorder is the mental illness of greatest relevance to the experience of disaster (see Chapter 9 for a more detailed discussion of this syndrome). Although traumatic neurosis has been an important psychiatric concept since the turn of the century (Horowitz, 1976; Kardiner & Spiegel, 1947), the diagnosis PTSD was not recognized as a clinical entity until the recently published third version of the American Psychiatric Association's *Diagnostic and Statistical Manual of Mental Disorders* (DSM-III; APA, 1980). Earlier formulations of the manual tended to describe stress disorders as acute, transient phenomena that diminish over time, unless some premorbid character weakness is present to prolong symptom maintenance (Green, Lindy, & Grace, 1985). Thus posttraumatic stress was originally viewed as a transient reaction to a stressor.

More recent conceptualization recognizes the possibility of prolonged psychological *consequences*. Follow-up of survivors of Hiroshima and the Holocaust, as well as other victims of World War II, made it apparent that some experiences are so traumatic that even previously normal individuals suffer serious, prolonged consequences when exposed to such events (see Green, Lindy, & Grace, 1985, for a thoughtful discussion of this topic). Studies of two different disasters (fire and dam breaks) found that particular stressors present in both events (loss of a loved one, threat to one's life) increased the risk of symptomatology 2 years later, despite significant differences in levels of pathology in the two events studied (Gleser, Green, & Winget, 1981; Green, Grace, & Gleser, 1985). These studies also showed that certain stressors were associated with delayed symptoms (i.e., first appearance 2 years rather than 1 year postimpact). These findings suggest that both timing and severity of PTSD symptoms must be taken into account in studies differentiating transient reactions from consequences of disaster exposure.

Indeed, present formulations of post-traumatic stress disorder indicate that the syndrome is cyclical, with alternating periods of intrusiveness, numbing, and quiescence (Horowitz, 1976). Until the late 1960s, epidemiological studies of disaster focused primarily on the period immediately following impact (Logue, Melick, & Hansen, 1981). These studies concentrated on surveillance for outbreaks of communicable diseases and increased mortality directly resulting from disaster (e.g., suicide, cardiovascular deaths from overexertion, environmental hazards created by the event). The current understanding of post-traumatic stress disorder suggests the need for longitudinal research to capture not only the immediate physical effects of disaster but also the prolonged or delayed incidence of psychiatric disorder, as well as the natural course of such disorder when left untreated.

Even this expanded focus may be shortsighted if changes in life functioning and other early behavioral problems following disaster exposure are overlooked. These changes are important not only as potential precursors of subsequent mental disorder, but also in their own right, as building blocks in theories of stress and coping. For example, not enough is known about what constitutes good adjustment to a traumatic event (Wortman, 1983). Investigators have identified several characteristics considered indicative of good coping, such as keeping emotional distress within manageable limits, being able to function and achieve socially desired goals, and maintaining a positive attitude (e.g., Hann, 1977; Meyers, Friedman, & Weiner, 1970; see Silver & Wortman, 1980, for a review and detailed discussion). However, Wortman (1983) points out that some research evidence suggests that these factors are not always associated with effective coping. For example, Goldsmith (1955) found that individuals who were most upset by spinal cord injury made greater progress toward rehabilitation than did patients appearing to be less upset. Similarly, lack of distress following bereavement could hardly be construed as effective adjustment, because available evidence suggests that almost all bereaved are intensely distressed following their loss. Silver and Wortman note the need for normative information on how people react to similarly stressful events after varying lengths of time, as a means of assessing how well an individual is coping. This research gap can only be addressed by systematic, longitudinal studies measuring a range of reactions to traumatic events.

Mediators of Disaster Response

In addition to gaining a better understanding of the components of the stress sequence, it is also important to isolate factors that act on these components to affect the development and maintenance of prolonged consequences, as opposed to more transient reactions. Mediators are modifiers that act on the stress sequence to produce individual variations in reactions to, and consequences of, potential stressors. Mediators play a central role in determining how victims react to disaster and what physical and mental health consequences these reactions produce. Types of mediators and their differential effects at each stage of the stress sequence need to be investigated to help identify those victims likely to develop prolonged effects (Elliott & Eisdorfer, 1982).

Community Level Mediators

One important class of mediators of psychological responses to disaster relates to the community context of the event (see Chapter 1). Community-level factors that potentially affect individual response include the extent of community disruption, the scope, the centrality (e.g., an airplane crash involving a group of strangers would be peripheral rather than central; see Green, 1982, for a discussion), the setting of the community (e.g., rural vs. urban), and the nature of the community response (e.g., solidarity vs. conflict; for a discussion of this topic with regard to toxic contamination, see Edelstein & Wandersman, 1987).

Golec (1983) argues that community-level variables may be even more important than the disaster event itself in predicting individual outcomes. Her analysis of the 1976 Teton Dam collapse suggests than an unusually positive community response to the disaster resulted in remarkably rapid recovery. Despite substantial material loss and social disruption (70% of the homes in the county were severely damaged or totally destroyed), several community characteristics optimized recovery: adequate warning, a low death/injury rate, a highly integrated and homogeneous (Mormon) population, effective local disaster response, maintenance of social networks, adequate financial compensation, and a surplus of resources for immediate needs. As a result of these factors, few of what Erikson (1976) has termed *secondary disasters* ensued. Secondary disasters are adverse events occurring during the recovery period, generally of social origin. In the Teton Dam disaster, examples of secondary disaster included excessive profiteering and abuses in an unregulated construction industry and regulatory inequities in the postdisaster compensation program. The relatively few victims of these secondary disasters were more likely than other flooded residents to perceive themselves as victimized and to express greater negative affect and loss of self-esteem. Systematic comparison of communities varying in characteristics that affect the rate of recovery and incidence of secondary disaster may help identify intervening variables of importance in the prediction of individual psychological outcomes (see also Green, 1982; Logue et al., 1981).

Social Mediators

The victim's social network includes kin, friends, neighbors, and community gatekeepers (see Mitchell & Trickett, 1980; Solomon, 1986; for extensive discussions of this topic). Like community response, the immediate social environment can be an important mediator of individual outcomes following exposure to disaster. For example, the initial reactions of other family members may serve to define the severity of the event to the victim. Family members may disagree about what actions, if any, to take, thereby prolonging the uncertainty of events that are intrinsically ambiguous (e.g., exposure to toxic waste, radon contamination of the home).

Along these lines, a study currently funded by the National Institute of Mental Health (NIMH) has initial family response to disaster as its focus: Steinglass and associates at George Washington University, Washington, D.C., are examining the extent to which family disorganization in the face of disaster-initiated relocation places individuals at higher risk of long-term maladjustment than does a more coherent proximal family response to this stressor. Findings from a study by Handford, et al. (1983) illustrate the importance of initial family response as a predictor of individual consequences. In this investigation of the 1979 nuclear reactor accident at Three Mile Island (TMI), the reactions of children were not found to relate to the intensity of their parents' response. However, children of parents who disagreed in their reactions to the event were significantly more upset than children of parents who responded consistently, even when both parents were highly distressed.

Although the Handford study (Handford et al., 1983) illustrates the way in which the initial disaster reactions of family members may heighten the stress of a victim, the family's long-term adaptation may similarly affect individual consequences. Some research suggests that females may be more upset by their spouses' response to disaster than they are by the event itself (Gleser et al., 1981; Solomon, Smith, Robins, & Fischbach, 1987). The latter study examined victims of a combination of natural and/or technolgoical disasters: dioxin contamination, flooding, tornadoes, and radioactive contamination of well water. This study found that although the symptomatology of male victims (specifically, alcohol abuse and depression) increased as a result of disaster exposure, female symptomatology did not. Individuals of either sex who were both exposed to disaster and subject to substantial network demands experienced signficantly more negative psychiatric consequences than victims less heavily relied upon by persons around them. However, excellent spouse support ameliorated the negative effects of exposure for males, whereas its presence intensified the level of symptomatology in female victims. These results suggest the possibility that, for some, strong family ties may be more burdensome than supportive in times of extreme stress (see Solomon, 1986; Solomon et al., 1987).

Individual Predispositions

Another set of mediators of disaster response deserving of research attention relate to the individual characteristics of the victim. Individual characteristics most frequently studied in disasters tend to be demographic variables, such as age, sex, ethnicity, education, and income level (see Elliott & Eisdorfer, 1982, for a more extensive discussion).

Anecdotal evidence suggests that certain demographic groups may be at higher risk than others for psychological disturbance following exposure to disaster (e.g., children, elderly, the mentally ill; cf. Cohen & Ahearn, 1980, pp. 9–10). NIMH is currently funding epidemiological studies of the effects of disaster on two of these potentially high-risk groups: Smith and colleagues at Washington University in St. Louis, Missouri, are examining the responses of children to dioxin and/or flood exposure, and Norris and associates at the University of Louisville in Kentucky are investigating the effect of repeated flooding on the mental health of the elderly. Studies such as these will provide more concrete information for targeting mental health services than has been available in the past. For example, conventional wisdom regarding the special vulnerability of the elderly may in fact be wrong; it is equally possible that the elderly constitute an unusually hardy population, and that individuals with prior flood experience may be inoculated against disaster's most stressful effects.

Other individual mediators of disaster effects that have received research attention include psychiatric history and cognitive/emotional factors, such as the subjective appraisal of the event, the nature of the coping response, and attributions of blame for the event (Baum et al., 1983; Lazarus & Launier, 1978; Solomon & Fischbach, 1986).

Formal Interventions

A final category of mediators is comprised of the *formal interventions* provided to actual or potential disaster victims. Formal intervention can take place at several levels: primary prevention, secondary prevention, or treatment. *Primary prevention* efforts are directed toward the prevention of negative mental health reactions to disaster exposure. Some examples of primary prevention include techniques for building stress resistance in high-risk groups, such as rescue workers, and policies that encourage the preservation of existing support networks (e.g., relocation plans that retain natural social groups of evacuees and permit access to established transportation systems; see Solomon, 1986). *Secondary prevention* interventions are directed toward the prevention of long-term consequences in victims who display early symptoms of stress and/or behavioral dysfunction following exposure. Potential secondary interventions include arranging for participation in self-help group sessions tailed to subgroups of victims with common problems (e.g., women's groups, parent groups; see Levin, Groves, & Lurie, 1980; Solomon et al., 1987), and stress debriefing sessions for emergency workers (Mitchell, 1982). Finally, *formal treatment* for post-traumatic stress disorder includes possible interventions such as behavioral flooding techniques or pharmacotherapy using beta blocking agents that limit physiological arousal. Although the efficacy of any particular intervention technique is yet to be established, experience with one or more of these formal interventions may potentially modify the development or expression of stress responses in victims of disaster.

METHODOLOGICAL DIMENSIONS AFFECTING ESTIMATES OF DISASTER EFFECTS

The preceding discussion offers an overview of important disaster characteristics, potential outcomes, and community, social, individual, and formal mediators of responses to disaster. Although an extensive list of factors has been mentioned, the foregoing inventory is far from exhaustive. Investigators have approached this daunting array of variables in a number of different (and overlapping) ways, each of which has strengths and weaknesses.

Risk Factor Studies

Green (1982) suggests that studies regarding the psychological effects of disaster can be divided into three types, depending upon the kinds of information they are designed to yield. Some studies are prospective, epidemiological surveys (*population-based studies*), which Green characterizes as a group-focused approach designed to determine rates of psychological impairment following disaster exposure. The relation of this approach to the earlier discussion of the disaster-response syndrome is that the major focus of the design is on degrees of exposure to the *stressor*. A second kind of study is the *clinically descriptive* investigation; the intent of this work is to uncover the constellation of symptoms found in disaster victims. In terms of the disaster-response syndrome, the focus of such investigations is primarily on the *reactions or consequences* of exposure. The third kind of study identified by Green is designed to uncover factors in a particular situation that affect individual outcomes, including characteristics of the disaster itself (scope, duration, etc.), as well as intervening characteristics that mediate disaster effects (e.g., community and family response, demographics, coping style). In other words, this *process* type of investigation places relatively more emphasis on *mediators* of the disaster response. Green notes that the three types of studies are not mutually exclusive and that many studies address more than one of these goals. For purposes of the present chapter, all three kinds of studies will be termed *risk factor studies*. The following discussion addresses a number of important considerations in the design of studies of the psychosocial effects of disaster. As the foregoing analysis suggests, no single study is expected to simultaneously address all of the concerns highlighted in the discussion. Which of these considerations should be taken into account and how they should be addressed will vary according to the objectives of a particular investigation.

Population-Based Studies

Some investigators, seeking a direct assessment of risk of impairment, attempt to solve the disaster response puzzle empirically. Because the intent of the inquiry is primarily descriptive rather than explanatory, questions guiding the design are often broad and atheoretical (e.g., will disaster victims have higher rates of impairment than nonvictims?) or open-ended (e.g., which types of losses result in greatest psychological disturbance?). The study design emphasizes careful selection of the sample so as to include comparison groups varying in levels/types of exposure. The instruments employed (generally interviews and/or questionnaires) are designed to be comprehensive, so as to tap into as many of the dimensions of the disaster-response sequence as possible and to be useful in studies of a range of disaster events.

An example of this approach to disaster research is an effort undertaken by the National Institute of Mental Health. In 1983, when NIMH began a special program to fund research grants on emergencies, the inability to make comparisons across studies of different disasters was viewed as the major problem plaguing the field (see Green, 1982). Studies varied substantially in the types of emergencies examined, the nature of loss experienced by the victim, and the degree of disruption experienced by the community. Victims also varied in coping skills, in access to personal support systems, and in exposure to formal programs of assistance. Studies differed with respect to which of these situational, individual, and institutional factors were examined. Finally, almost every study employed different tools for measuring mental health effects, and different time frames for outcome assessment. All of these differences contribute to the difficulty in comparing study findings and in drawing valid conclusions regarding the extent of impairment resulting from different kinds of disaster experiences. In recognition of the problem, NIMH's Emergency/Disaster Research Program collaborated with Washington University at St. Louis, Missouri, in a project to develop an instrument for the assessment of victims' experiences and responses to a range of natural and technological emergencies (Robins & Smith, 1983). This instrument, the Diagnostic Interview Schedule/Disaster Supplement (DIS/DS), was designed to provide a comprehensive picture of the emergency experience and to be applicable across a wide range of emergencies. The instrument assesses the type of emergency, type and extent of loss, individual and family risk factors, use of formal and informal support systems, behavioral response to the traumatic event, and 15 DSM-III diagnoses selected for their potential relevance to the disaster experience. The instrument was subsequently employed in an epidemiological project which assessed mental health effects of exposure to dioxin, radioactive contamination of wells, flooding, tornadoes, and work layoffs (Robins, Fischbach, Smith, Cottler, & Solomon, 1986; Smith, 1984; Smith, Robins, Przybeck, Goldring, & Solomon, 1986). Selected portions of the instrument are also being used in other disaster research funded by NIMH, thereby enabling subsequent cross-disaster comparisons of impairment rates.

ADVANTAGES.   One strength of the population-based approach is that it is prospective in design, allowing for both direct estimates of impairment and inferences of disaster effects as they may change over time. The foregoing discussion suggests another major strength of this design: the comprehensiveness of the structured instrument. By maximizing coverage of disaster characteristics, mediators and types of outcomes, the resulting data permit both the analysis of multiple study questions and the determination of potential confounds. For example, the investigators of the St. Louis dioxin/flood disaster were concerned that respondents in the exposed and unexposed groups might differ in ways related to their impairment rates, but independent of their disaster experience. Assessment of potential confounds such as socioeconomic status and psychiatric history allowed these investigators to determine if the study results needed to be qualified by key predispositional factors (see Smith et al., 1986; Solomon et al., 1987). The comprehensiveness of the DIS/DS also serves to enhance its utility across a range of disaster events, thereby permitting the kind of standardized assessment needed for cross-study comparison of results.

PROBLEMS WITH THE POPULATION-BASED APPROACH. The comprehensive, longitudinal approach to assessing psychosocial effects of disaster has inherent shortcomings as well as strengths. At a practical level, such studies are complicated and expensive to conduct. Large sample sizes are required to detect differences in rates for disorders whose natural occurrence is rare in the general population (e.g., post-traumatic stress disorder). Further, multiple assessments over time are needed for inferences about the natural course of disorder following the traumatic event.

In addition, high response rates are needed to avoid the potential bias created by respondent self-selection. If, for example, only the victims least affected by the disaster are willing to take time to respond to the interview, no valid conclusions can be drawn about disaster exposure. A lengthy interview may work to the disadvantage of attaining high response rates by discouraging participation among those already overburdened by disaster-related demands on time and energy. Investigators may find it necessary to pay respondents a sizable sum to encourage participation in these time-consuming interviews.

Although subject payment may address the problem of response rate, it does not ensure the validity of the collected data. For example, lengthy interviews may bring about increasing reluctance on the part of the victims to admit to problems they may be experiencing at the time of reinterview, because any such admission would trigger a series of related questions designed to probe the initial response. In addition, structured instruments designed to yield psychiatric diagnoses require careful validation procedures to ensure that these diagnoses correspond to the ones that would be reached by expert clinicians interviewing the same individuals (see Burke, 1986, for a detailed discussion of this topic).

A further problem to consider in the design of population-based investigations (or indeed, in the design of any risk factor study) is the lack of baseline information on victim functioning prior to disaster exposure. Psy-

chosocial studies of disasters are typically initiated after the event has occurred, making it difficult to assess whether observed symptomatology is a
direct result of the event, or rather evidence of a preexisting psychiatric
problem.

A final problem associated with the analysis of population-based data is
known as the "fishing expedition"; that is, the problem of multiple comparisons (Saxe & Fine, 1981). In studies that employ hundreds of questions,
a small percentage of comparisons (5 out of 100), are likely to differ significantly as a result of chance, although no actual difference exists. Unanticipated findings are common in studies where large numbers of variables
have been examined. The problem imposed by "too rich" data must be
carefully addressed in both the analysis and the presentation of study findings
(see Fleiss, 1986, and Walker, 1986, for contrasting views on this issue).

SOLUTIONS.   One way of overcoming some of the problems with the
population-based approach is to capitalize on existing data bases. For example, the Epidemiologic Catchment Area (ECA) studies funded by NIMH
yielded a wealth of longitudinal information about the incidence and prevalence of 35 DSM-III mental health disorders in five sites across the country
(see Eaton & Kessler, 1985). These data are now available for public use.
In many instances these data can serve as normative information (i.e., a
comparison group) for investigators who wish to administer the DIS or
DIS/DS on a sample exposed to disaster in a demographically similar community. By eliminating the need to collect longitudinal data on a "no exposure" control group, this strategy minimizes the cost of conducting a full-
blown epidemiologic study.

Investigators interested in learning about other data sources available for
public use may wish to consult the annual DHHS Data Inventory (Department of Health and Human Services, 1985). However, researchers deciding
to employ any of the data sources listed in this inventory should proceed
cautiously. Listings do not always reflect the most current information on
these data. In addition, some of these data bases may suffer from poor
response rates, and unassessed reliability and/or validity.

Another way of capitalizing on existing data is to reanalyze longitudinal
data collected for other purposes. For example, Norris and Murrell (1987)
conducted a multiwave longitudinal study of the mental health of older Kentucky residents. When Norris noted that a substantial number of their respondents had been involved in flooding over the data collection period, she
applied for an NIMH grant to reanalyze the data, with disaster exposure as
the focus of the new analysis.

Capitalizing on existing data may serve not only to minimize the cost of
conducting population-based studies of disaster, but also to provide baseline
information about functioning prior to the experience of victimization. Few
investigators are in the fortunate position of having detailed information on
victims' psychiatric status prior to disaster impact. However, other proxy

measures of functioning may be readily available, such as records maintained by schools, employers, and medical facilities. Attaining access to such records would enable longitudinal assessments of, for example, school attendance and achievement, work performance, systolic blood pressure, number of prescriptions, and visits to physicians and/or mental health professionals. Inferences about disaster effects can be made from comparisons of these factors before and after disaster exposure, for both victims and selected comparison samples. This kind of information can be used to validate respondents' retrospective self-reports of functioning, which are open to recall bias.

Finally, the problem of too rich data can be addressed by statistical methods designed to test families of comparisons, such as the ones derived by Bonferroni, Tukey, and Scheffe (see Neter & Wasserman, 1974).

Clinical Studies

A second kind of risk factor study, the *clinical* or *case-control study,* focuses on the reactions and consequences of exposure to traumatic events. Green (1982) suggests that the goal of this kind of work is the explication of the cluster of symptoms found in disaster victims, so as to contribute to theoretical understanding of disorder and treatment. Although Green does not provide further detail, it may be inferred that studies of this nature include those with post-traumatic stress disorder as the focus of the design. In contrast to the population-based studies described above, these investigations tend to be retrospective in nature. Comparisons are made between cases and noncases, in order to discover how individuals with PTSD differ from those without the disorder in terms of precipitating events, predispositional factors, and co-occurring symptomatology.

ADVANTAGES.   The clinical investigation offers a number of advantages over the population-based study as a means of investigating the relation between stressor and disorder. Foremost among these advantages is the cost savings involved in the sampling procedure. Unlike the prospective approach, clinical investigations do not require large study populations and long periods of observation. Because the incidence of PTSD in the general population is relatively rare (depending how a case is defined; see subsequent discussion), a prospective study of the relationship of various factors to the development of the disorder requires the screening of vast numbers of people (Lilienfeld & Lilienfeld; 1980).

In contrast, retrospective studies begin with already identified cases. This procedure not only is less costly, but also eliminates the possibility that study participation will influence the development and/or reporting of disorder. For example, respondents in a prospective study of the effects of exposure to dioxin contamination may become hypervigilant about their own physical and mental health, and may change their health care behavior as a result of concerns heightened by study participation. Retrospective identification of cases removes the potential risk for this kind of response bias.

PROBLEMS WITH THE CLINICAL APPROACH.   Retrospective clinical studies have several methodological disadvantages. First, unlike population-based studies, no direct estimate can be made of incidence, that is, of the risk of developing a disorder as a result of disaster exposure. In a retrospective study, the estimate of relative risk is made indirectly on the basis of existing cases (prevalence). As Kahn (1983) notes, the most basic requirement for obtaining risk estimates in retrospective studies is that both cases and noncases in the study be representative with respect to the risk factor being investigated. Suppose, for example, that an investigator wishes to assess retrospectively the role of a local disaster as a risk factor for post-traumatic stress disorder. To do so, the investigator goes to the local private psychiatric facility and obtains lists of patients with and without PTSD and queries these individuals about their exposure, or lack of exposure, to the disaster event. What possible biases could be introduced by this strategy for the estimation of risk? Some possibilities include the following: (1) Individuals who developed PTSD may be more likely than noncases to recall exposure to disaster (i.e., to label such events as disasters). If so, the relation between exposure and PTSD will be overestimated, that is, will appear stronger than it truly is. (2) Individuals treated in a private psychiatric facility may be of a higher socioeconomic status than the community population as a whole. In turn, higher socioeconomic subgroups may have been buffered against the most stressful aspects of the disaster (e.g., they may live in well-fortified houses rather than trailers, they may have greater financial resources to draw upon for recovery from losses, etc.). If so, analysis of these cases and noncases will yield results that underestimate the relation between PTSD and disaster. (3) If the retrospective study is conducted several years after disaster impact, existing cases of PTSD are not representative of all incidence of PTSD following the disaster, since some PTSD cases may have moved, recovered, or died. For example, those with the most severe manifestations of PTSD could be unrepresented as a result of their possibly higher than average mortality from suicide, alcoholism, and the like. Loss to the study of such individuals may again yield an underestimate of the relation between PTSD and disaster exposure. As this example illustrates, obtaining access to cases and noncases that are representative of the disaster population at large may pose an insurmountable problem for retrospective clinical investigations, making it impossible to generalize the results beyond the study sample.

Another methodological hurdle for clinical investigations is the lack of an agreed-upon definition of what constitutes a case of PTSD. As noted in the earlier discussion of types of response, the definition of the disorder is still evolving. Although a revision of the DSM-III diagnosis of PTSD was recently published (APA, 1987) many of its features remain controversial. For example, the disorder is tied to "an event out of the range of usual human experience . . . that is psychologically traumatic," but it is unclear what types of experiences qualify for this definition. Further, it is not clear who must be able to make the link between the stressor and the symptoms: the respondent or the clinician. Instruments requiring that the individual be able to make this link may result in underreporting of the syndrome, in cases where symptoms of denial and numbing are predominant (Green, Lindy, & Grace, 1985). A related controversy is over the criterion that symptoms of intrusiveness and numbing co-occur within the same 6-month time period. The research of Laufer, Brett, and Gallops (1984) suggests that either a pattern of reexperiencing or one of denial will dominate the symptom picture, depending on the nature of the traumatic event. If their findings are correct, instruments that require simultaneous presentation of these symptoms for a diagnosis of PTSD may also underreport cases.

In addition to facing definitional problems, clinical studies of post-traumatic stress disorder must contend with issues of the timing of measurement. If Horowitz's (1976) view of the disorder as cyclical is valid, the symptom picture may substantially vary according to when the assessment is made. Further, assessment itself may activate otherwise quiescent symptomatology, and/or the PTSD syndrome may be delayed in expression (Green, Lindy, & Grace, 1985). Thus the nature of the disorder may, in itself, diminish chances of reliable and valid assessment.

SOLUTIONS.   There are no easy solutions to the problems associated with the conduct of clinical investigations. Given the difficulties associated with obtaining representative samples of cases with and without exposure to trauma, this methodology is not well suited to obtaining direct estimates of risk. Even within highly circumscribed subpopulations, the limits on generalizability are difficult to ascertain.

Instead, case-control studies are better applied to the explication of the clinical syndrome, through studies that explore PTSD's diagnostic specificity, symptomatology, course, and co-occurrence with other mental disorders. The definitional problems associated with identifying cases of PTSD suggest the need for research with nosology and clinical course as the focus. Evidence, primarily from studies of Vietnam veterans, suggests that individuals with PTSD typically also have at least one other diagnosis, such as substance abuse, depression, anxiety, and/or antisocial personality (Boulanger & Kadushin, 1986; Green, Lindy, & Grace, 1985). Apart from the etiological criterion, many of the specific symptoms of PTSD overlap with other disorders, indicating the need to more explicitly determine symptoms, physiological markers, and patterns of expression that distinguish this disorder from others of common co-occurrence.

An example of a clinical study that moves the field in this direction is the one by Malloy, Fairbank, and Keane (1983), who used case-control methodology to compare PTSD veterans, well-adjusted veterans, and matched psychiatric controls in terms of their psychophysiological reactivity to combat sounds versus neutral stimuli. Both these investigators and an independent research team (Blanchard, Kolb, Pallmeyer, & Gerardi, 1982) found PTSD veterans to differ from the control groups in terms of higher baseline heart rate and greater cardiac reactivity to combat stimuli. Given the controversy surrounding the diagnosis of PTSD in veterans (see Sierles, Chen, McFarland, & Taylor, 1983) and in victims of other events where litigation is a possibility, the discovery of a reliable, non-self-report assessment of the disorder is of great potential utility (Blanchard, Kolb, Gerardi, Ryan, & Pallmeyer, 1986).

The methodological problems posed by fluctuations in the diagnosis can only be addressed by repeated assessments (Green, Lindy, & Grace, 1985). Cases and controls, although identified retrospectively with respect to the event, must then be followed prospectively to assess patterns in expression of the disorder over time. Both PTSD cases and controls may be victims of the same disaster, yet have had very different experiences and symptom patterns. For example, it might be retrospectively determined that early identified PTSD cases were more likely than victim controls to have been bereaved or exposed to the grotesque. Repeated assessments over time would then permit answers to such questions as whether the control victims included delayed cases of PTSD, and/or whether individuals failed to be identified as PTSD cases because they were in the disorder's denial phase at the time of initial assessment.

Process Studies

For some investigators the key question is neither the impairment rate (how many?) nor the diagnosis (what form?), but rather the causal explanation of disaster's impact on mental health (why?). This third kind of risk factor study focuses on the development and testing of a conceptual model of the disaster-response syndrome. Emphasis in these designs is given to consideration of individual differences in response to exposure. Theoretically important mediators assume a central role in the identification of the comparison samples, groups selected by virtue of their ability to operationalize the conceptual processes of interest.

The earlier described work of Baum and his colleagues exemplifies this approach (Baum et al., 1983). Instead of comparing disaster experiences in totally objective terms (e.g., flood versus dioxin exposure, level of damage, etc.), this work translates disaster events into psychologically meaningful terms and designs studies to compare conceptual differences in experience. Noting that human-made disasters appear to induce greater psychological distress than natural catastrophes, Baum et al. hypothesized that human-made disasters pose a greater disruption of our perceptions of control, in that they represent a loss of control over expectedly controllable technology as opposed to a lack of control over natural disasters never perceived as controllable (Baum et al., 1983).

Baum and colleagues have explored these ideas with different victim populations, but most thoroughly with the victims of the Three Mile Island (TMI) nuclear reactor accident. For example, one study compares victims and nonvictims with respect to the way in which they explain the TMI event and assesses the relation between these explanations and measures of stress. Speculating that self-blame for problems following the TMI accident would lead to enhanced perceptions of control, these investigators found that victims who assumed some blame for their troubles exhibited fewer symptoms of stress than did victims who assumed no responsibility (Baum et al., 1983). These investigators are now engaged in a program of research to assess whether disasters that are relatively more disruptive to perceptions of control (i.e., technological hazards) cause more distress even when other dimensions of the event are held constant (e.g., duration).

The work of Baum and his associates, as well as that of other psychologists studying stress (e.g., Lazarus, 1966; Slovic, Fischoff, & Lichtenstein, 1981) tends to emphasize the victim's subjective interpretation or appraisal as the most significant mediator of the stress-response syndrome. As noted earlier in this chapter, many other, more objective, factors can also mediate individual response to disaster. Several investigators have elaborated complicated process models of the disaster-response syndrome that attempt to diagram the interrelations of as many mediators as possible in predicting individual outcomes (see, for example, Cohen & Ahearn, 1980, pp. 36–41). However, whether simple or complex in nature, subjective or objective in emphasis, process models provide a theoretical basis for the design and analysis of disaster data.

ADVANTAGES. The process model approach to risk factor investigation offers several advantages over the population-based and clinical strategies. Because they are guided by theory, process models can be more parsimonious than population-based studies in the number of questions asked of respondents. Similarly, because the comparisons are planned a priori, fewer respondents need to be interviewed to achieve required cell sizes. Thus process studies tend to be considerably less expensive to conduct than population-based investigations.

The process model approach also avoids the PTSD definitional problems encountered by the other two risk factor approaches. Because population-based studies are primarily concerned with impairment rates, and because clinical studies identify comparison groups in terms of cases and noncases, both of these approaches rely on arbitrary and shifting definitions of disorder that may subsequently impede cross-study comparisons of findings. Process models have greater flexibility in selecting from among a range of outcomes and may therefore express findings in terms of degree of impairment (number of symptoms) and/or type of behavioral dysfunction, rather than in terms of rates of disorder.

Finally, because causal relationships are theoretically defined and predicted prior to data collection, this research strategy avoids the statistical pitfalls posed by too rich data (see the earlier discussion of population-based studies). That is, because the comparisons are planned in advance and limited in number, the investigator has greater confidence that a given finding represents an actual difference, rather than a statistical artifact.

PROBLEMS WITH THE PROCESS MODEL APPROACH.   Although process models attempt to answer the question of why some victims suffer particularly negative effects from disaster, many researchers would argue that these studies are in fact descriptive rather than explanatory. Because naturalistic studies do not use random assignment in determining victim and control groups, the casual direction of any found association cannot be established. Process studies relying entirely on cross-sectional data are therefore especially vulnerable to this attack.

To illustrate, suppose an investigator wishes to explore the role of social support in victim response, and finds that his or her results confirm the prediction that lower levels of social support are associated with higher reported stress following disaster. Although the investigator may wish to conclude that predisaster social support acts as a buffer against disaster-induced stress, he or she cannot confidently make this inference. An alternative explanation is that poorer adjustment and lack of support are the result of social incompetence, a preexisting characterological deficit of the individual unrelated to disaster exposure. Another explanation is that the obvious suffering of a disaster victim creates feelings of vulnerability and inadequacy in others, causing them to turn away from the victim. In other words, it is not known whether disaster affects levels of social support, preexisting social support affects postdisaster adjustment, or both adjustment and support are affected by some third, unassessed factor.

Another disadvantage of process model studies is one shared by the clinical approach: it is difficult to assess the extent to which the study sample is representative of, and therefore generalizable to, the entire victim population. Because population-based studies are concerned with rates of impairment, samples are selected on a random (or stratified random) basis, allowing for direct estimates of risk in the victim population. In contrast, process models are concerned primarily with internal validity and are likely to select samples from subpopulations of particular theoretical importance (e.g., the bereaved or hospitalized). The lack of generalizability of these studies impedes the ability to compare findings across diverse study populations.

Finally, process models that attempt to specify the nature and causal direction of all possible disaster characteristics, reactions, consequences, and mediators, are too complicated to be subjected to a single test. The primary effect of such configurations may be to discourage investigators from considering disaster as a topic of research. However, as Elliott and Eisdorfer (1982) note in their discussion of stress:

Such an ever-changing, interlinking system is not only difficult to describe but also impossible to study in its entirety. For this reason, investigators inevitably try to simplify the system as much as possible by studying one small portion at a time. It is vital to remember that such studies are only partial approximations of what actually occurs. (p. 23)

SOLUTIONS.   Although random assignment is not an option available to naturalistic studies of disaster, causal inferences may yet be drawn from process studies that employ longitudinal, prospective designs. Particularly strong in this regard are studies that incorporate predisaster and/or collateral measures of the outcomes, predictors, and medicators of interest. Already mentioned in the discussion of population-based studies are archival measures that may be used to validate self-reports of functioning before and after disaster impact (e.g., systolic blood pressure, school attendance, mental health visits; see Baum, Grunberg, & Singer 1982, for an in-depth discussion of this issue). In population-based studies, where the focus is on impairment rates, verification of exposure and outcomes may be sufficient. However, in process studies mediators assume a key role, and efforts to provide collateral and/or baseline assessments of these factors may also be required for causal inference. For example, investigators studying the mediating effects of social networks may wish to interview not only victims but also members of the victims' social networks, regarding the nature of interactions pre- and postdisaster (see Sarason, Shearin, Pierce, & Sarson, 1987).

Acquiring predisaster information on less objective mediators may require considerable ingenuity. Peterson and Seligman (1987) displayed this ingenuity when they devised a method of content analysis that would allow them to infer characteristic attributional style from any 1,000-word self-referent document. This methodology permits researchers interested in causal explanations as mediators of disaster effects to predict victim responses from any spontaneously written material (e.g., letters, verbatim interviews) generated by the victim prior to the event.

With respect to generalizability, it should be noted that the problem of unrepresentativeness is not truly intrinsic to the process model approach. Given sufficient resources, process studies, like population-based studies, could be designed to include random samples representative of the entire victim population. However, unless the goal of the research is to determine rates of impairment, such an approach is not cost-effective; causal relationships can be explored with much greater parsimony by sampling from comparison groups most illustrative of the concepts under investigation. If the sample is representative of the subgroup (e.g., a random sample of the bereaved), the results may be generalized to other victims fitting the same subgroup criteria.

Concluding Remarks about Risk Factor Studies

The above discussion distinguishes among population-based, clinical, and process model studies of risk factors in an effort to highlight the purposes, strengths, and problems associated with each strategy. To some extent these distinctions have been overdrawn; in practice, there is considerable overlap among these approaches. For example, there is nothing to prevent a population-based study from *a priori* specification of a theoretical framework and related hypotheses, or from the analysis of results in terms of symptoms as well as diagnoses. The distinctions among the three types of risk factor studies are drawn primarily to illustrate the kinds of trade-offs that must be considered in making choices about various aspects of the design.

Intervention Studies

After risk factor studies have isolated the mental health consequences of different kinds of disaster experiences and identified high-risk victims, researchers must evaluate the various prevention and treatment options available to those in need of formal intervention. Many of the methodological issues raised in the discussion of risk factor studies also apply to evaluations of interventions. However, studies of formal disaster interventions also pose additional challenges to disaster researchers. Although not intended to be exhaustive, this section discusses some methodological considerations of particular relevance to the design of evaluations of interventions.

Three basic approaches are available for evaluating formal interventions for disaster-induced mental health disorders: controlled *clinical trials, field studies,* and *quasi-experimental designs*. The following discussion highlights methodological strengths and problems associated with each of these approaches.

Controlled Clinical Trials

Although random assignment of individuals to disaster events is an impossibility, random assignment of victims to interventions may be a viable option. From a scientific standpoint, randomized clinical trials (true experiments) are the method of choice in studying intervention effectiveness. However, the appropriate use of this methodology presupposes that a disordered population has already been identified by some uniform criterion. Individuals meeting this criterion are then randomly assigned to an intervention group, a no-intervention group, or other comparison group.

In comparing the outcomes of two or more groups, it is imperative that these groups not differ systematically prior to the experimental intervention. When sufficient numbers of individuals are included in the study, the random selection procedure ensures that the intervention group does not differ from the control group in terms of, for example, extent of harm, preintervention psychopathology, socioeconomic status, or any factor likely to affect outcomes other than the intervention itself (see Cook & Campbell, 1979). The strength of this approach is well recognized: a true experiment permits direct inference of cause and effect. Thus, investigators using this method can assess the extent to which a given technique (e.g., drug therapy) is successful in reducing or preventing long-term PTSD symptomatology, relative either to an alternative treatment (e.g., crisis counseling) or to a no-treatment control condition.

Unfortunately, the drawbacks of a true experiment will, in many cases, preclude the use of this method for assessing intervention effectiveness. Clinicians often express strong reservations about withholding (or delaying) treatment from individuals in immediate need of assistance. Some of these reservations may be removed by eliminating the no-intervention control group and designing the study as a comparison of two competing techniques. Given the current state of knowledge about interventions for PTSD, controlled clinical trials may be readily justified when used in this way. Comparative outcome studies on psychotherapeutic approaches to PTSD have not yet been published; the literature is still largely in the case report stage (for a review, see Ahearn & Cohen, 1984). Because it has not yet been established which, if any, of the existing therapies is effective in the treatment and prevention of post-traumatic stress disorder, random assignment of victims to two different interventions, or even to a no-intervention control group, is an ethically defensible procedure (see Saxe & Fine, 1981, for an in-depth discussion of ethical issues involved in intervention studies).

In practice, however, random assignment is likely to face opposition from clinicians who, even without supportive research evidence, feel they have a therapeutic technique of particular value to individuals suffering from posttraumatic stress. Another likely obstacle to random assignment is presented by the victims themselves, who may refuse to consent to one or another intervention technique. This kind of self-selection introduces undetectable sources and amounts of bias, thereby preventing estimation of intervention effects.

A variation of clinical trials augments that random assignment process with matching. Instead of allowing chance to minimize differences between the intervention and control groups, the investigator identifies pairs of subjects matched, for example, in terms of severity of impairment, duration of disaster exposure, and key experiences such as bereavement. Each pair is then randomly assigned to either the intervention or control condition. In this way, important differences between the subject groups are held constant, so as to minimize extraneous sources of variability that might obscure differences in intervention outcomes. Matching does not solve the access problems described earlier. On the contrary, in some cases it may be more difficult to get the kind of cooperation needed for matching than for simple random assignment, in that matched pairs are harder to locate. However, matching offers the advantage of reducing the number of participants needed to test for intervention effects.

The preceding discussion is predicated on the assumption that the investigator has ready access to a substantial population of traumatized victims who are amenable to mental health assistance. Few disasters provide this kind of opportunity for research. Perhaps for this reason, most case studies of PTSD treatment have been done on Vietnam veterans. Because this population is large, and because veterans are largely restricted, for reimbursement reasons, to the use of Veterans Administration (VA) hospitals for treatment of their mental health disorders, researchers within the VA have unusual access to large numbers of cases of PTSD. Even under these circumstances, treatment studies of VA patients have limited generalizability; cases presenting themselves for treatment are a self-selected group whose PTSD symptomatology (and therefore response to treatment) may not even be representative of Vietnam veterans as a whole, let alone of victims of other traumatic events.

Another problem potentially restricting the generalizability of clinical trials lies in the nature of the instruments employed. Most risk factor studies rely on structured survey instruments administered by lay interviewers. In contrast, clinical studies, particularly of intervention effectiveness, are more inclined to use open ended, in-depth interviews conducted by expert clinicians. Such interviews, often psychodynamic in orientation, may assess not only symptomatology, but also family history, early memories, personality structure, and so forth. Green (1982) notes that the in-depth interview, by its very nature, is likely to include the development of at least a temporary, semitherapeutic involvement of the diagnostician with the victim. In other words, even the no-treatment control group may be receiving a brief intervention not characteristically experienced by the untreated victim population. Although demand characteristics (i.e., changes in the phenomenon resulting from the act of measurement itself) are a potential problem in any experiment, their influence may be of particular concern in studies of intervention effectiveness. One way of assessing the effect of the in-depth interview would be to include a structured symptom checklist and to incorporate an additional no-treatment control group for administration of the checklist measure alone. Use of this checklist would also facilitate comparisons of the study findings with those of other disaster investigations.

Field Studies

Given the practical difficulties involved in arranging for randomized assignment of victims to treatment and no-treatment groups, investigators interested in studying interventions for PTSD and other disaster-induced psychiatric disturbances may be compelled to conduct naturalistic studies. Similar to the population-based study of risk factors, this approach involves tracking disaster victims over time; in this case, however, the long-term impairment rates of persons who seek formal assistance are compared with the rates of the ones who do not. The field study uses statistical analysis, rather than random assignment, to control for important preintervention differences.

In addition to sharing all the difficulties already discussed for population-based studies, the intervention field study also faces a major set of problems resulting from the general unwillingness of disaster victims to seek formal assistance for mental health problems (see Solomon, 1986). This reluctance translates into a need for extremely large sample sizes, because an investigator will need to follow several hundred victims in order to locate enough formally treated individuals to permit a test of intervention effects. In addition, victims are likely to seek treatment from diverse providers, rather than to use a single mental health resource. The relatively few who do seek mental health assistance may be very different from disturbed victims who avoid such services. Although some important differences between treated and untreated victims can be controlled for in the statistical analysis (e.g., level and type of impairment), other unassessed differences may still be present. Finally, respondents may underreport utilization of mental health services, due to the associated stigma.

Combining the Field Study with the Clinical Trial: Quasi-Experimental Designs

The above problems may defeat the utility of using the field study as a method of investigation of intervention effects. In some cases, a quasi-experimental approach, combining elements of both the field study and the clinical trial will be the most feasible research strategy. For example, an investigator could use field study methods to identify victims at highest risk for psychopathology, either in terms of the severity of their disaster experiences (e.g., injury, bereavement, permanent relocation) or in terms of reported levels of psychiatric disturbance. A variety of active outreach strategies could then be targeted toward these high-risk victims (e.g., media announcements, community case-finding, special efforts to reach specific groups, telephone contact; see Lindy, Grace, & Green, 1981). Individuals reached by these different methods could be referred to a particular mental health provider, who would then randomly assign victims to either of two intervention models. Because the number of victims presenting themselves for assistance is likely to be small, between-group differences could be minimized by matching victims according to levels of impairment and/or outreach strategy, prior to random assignment. This research strategy would allow for many levels of assessment within a single project: risk factor assessment, assessment of outreach efficacy, and assessment of the effectiveness of the prevention intervention. By structuring the project in this fashion, the effects of predispositional factors, disaster experiences, and the interventions themselves could be readily distinguished, eliminating problems of confound typically encountered in field studies of formal interventions. Further, the design would permit comparisons of the long-term outcomes of high-risk victims who received treatment with the outcomes untreated individuals also identified as high-risk by the initial field study.

Problems and Opportunities for Studies of Disaster

Some issues transcend the substantive nature of any disaster research. Whether a study of risk factors or one of intervention effectiveness, any investigation of disaster effects must struggle with the problems of access to victims, of human subjects' protection, of instrument validity, and of timing of measurement. Although some of these issues have already been mentioned in the context of particular research strategies, their importance suggests the need for further comment.

Access to Victims

Gaining access to disaster victims may be the greatest practical problem encountered by any study of disaster. Occasionally the investigator will be able to directly approach potential respondents, either by media announcements or by canvassing affected neighborhoods. More commonly, however, it is necessary to work through an agency with the ability to identify victims of disaster. For example, technological hazards such as toxic contamination often provide little visual evidence of damage. Victims themselves may be unaware of exposure until so advised by the government or media. An investigator wishing to enumerate these victims for sampling purposes may need to work with government organizations that have objective information about areas of exposure, such as the State Department of Health, the Environmental Protection Agency, or the Centers for Disease Control.

In cases of natural disaster, the impact of exposure may be highly visible. However, such disruptive events are likely to cause substantial dislocation of victims, and the cooperation of a victims' assistance organization like the Red Cross may be essential for locating victims in high-impact areas. Wortman et al. (1980) offer excellent practical advice on establishing a sound relationship with agencies who work with victimized populations. They note the importance of the following steps: learning about the organization, identifying key personnel, familiarizing agency staff with the project's purpose and potential benefits, enlisting agency advice and input, alleviating any potential staff burden caused by the project, and obtaining a written legal agreement that enumerates mutual responsibilities (see Wortman et al., for a detailed discussion).

Success of the project depends not only on the cooperation of victim assistance organizations but also on the cooperation of the victims themselves. Wortman et al. (1980) suggest that high respondent commitment is most likely to be obtained when the research team includes interviewers selected for strong social skills and similarity in background with the respondents. The purpose and importance of the project should be explained to respondents in sufficient detail so that they understand the potential benefits of the study both to society and to themselves (e.g., the possibility of improving intervention techniques of subsequent benefit to the victim, the opportunity to talk to a sympathetic listener, the opportunity for intellectual stimulation, the opportunity for financial remuneration). If initial participation is rejected, the interviewer should find out the victims' reasons, since many who refuse may be willing to be contacted at a later date (Wortman et al.)

Protection of Respondents

Respondents may be enlisted through a variety of means, but participation should not be secured without concern for victims' problems and needs. Investigators must guard against the use of enlistment procedures that border on coercion. They should also be sensitive to the practical problems and emotional distress of victims in the period immediately following disaster impact. Initial contact should be postponed until acute distress has subsided, and victims are able to make a reasoned choice about study participation (cf. Wortman et al., 1980).

Investigators must also carefully consider the potential impact of the interview questions. By their very nature, disaster studies are designed to explore mental health responses to a traumatic event. Answering questions about this kind of experience may be very stressful for certain victims; even interviews administered long after the event may reactivate otherwise quiescent psychiatric symptomatology. Thus, human subject protection procedures that are standard for other kinds of investigations (e.g., obtaining prior consent, assuring confidentiality, advising subjects of potential risks and of their right to terminate the interview at any time) may be insufficient for studies of traumatic events. Investigators must thoroughly pilot their instruments to identify and eliminate questions likely to induce negative psychiatric consequences. They must train their interviewers to recognize unusually negative reactions to particular questions and provide them with procedures for dealing with such distress. For example, interviewers may need to remind respondents of their right to refuse to answer upsetting questions. Investigators should also ensure that access to immediate clinical help is available and that interviewers make respondents aware of this opportunity. Finally, all respondents should be given a telephone call by a study representative on the evening following the interview to determine whether they are experiencing any negative aftereffects requiring a clinical referral.

Instrument Validity

Like problems of access and respondent protection, issues of validity also transcend the particulars of any research effort. As noted earlier, collateral and/or archival data may be used to validate self-reports of disaster exposure, as well as of functioning before and after impact. However, multiple assessments of the same factor may confront the investigator with the problem of how to handle discrepant information. For instance, the aforementioned study of disasters in St. Louis, Missouri, used government records to identify victims exposed to radioactive contamination of wells (Smith et al., 1986). Despite widespread media attention to the problem, however, few objectively identified victims reported exposure to contaminated well water. Because the accounts of actual and perceived exposure disagreed, researchers were confronted with the problem of deciding which measure to use as the basis for defining victim status (see Fischbach & Henderson, 1985, for discussion). To take another example, studies of child victims typically ask for both child self-reports and parental assessments of the child's functioning. These studies often find that children report significantly more problems and symptomatology than do their parents (see for example, Handford, et al., 1983). Although this discrepancy is often interpreted as evidence of parental underreporting, the investigator's decision to assign relatively greater validity to the child's responses must be based on judgment rather than on fact.

The issue of validity is of particular importance in the diagnosis of posttraumatic stress. The field presently disagrees about the disorder's defining characteristics, about the cyclical course of symptomatology, about the ability of the victim to link symptomatology to the traumatic event, and so forth (see Boulanger, Kadushin, Rindskopf, & Carey, 1986, and previous discussion). Consequently, existing instruments measure PTSD in markedly different ways, resulting in different rates of impairment in victim populations (Green, Lindy, & Grace, 1985). Many of these scales have been subjected to little or no assessment for reliability and validity. Given the nascent state of the art in PTSD measurement, investigators interested in determining case status may wish to incorporate three of the more extensively studied scales and define case status on the basis of a positive score on two of the three measures (see Dohrenwend & Shrout, 1981). A similar tie-breaking strategy may be used to resolve other discrepant findings (e.g., using teacher reports to resolve differences in the rates of dysfunction reported by child victims and their parents).

Timing of Assessment

The timing of the interview also affects the meaningfulness of the resultant data. Measuring victim reactions in the immediate aftermath of a disaster is questionable not only from an ethical standpoint, but from the standpoint of accuracy as well. Even if they agree to participate, individuals in acute distress are unlikely to provide complete and well-considered responses to research questions while preoccupied with concerns about shelter, transportation, and/or safety of family members. However, even if immediate assessment were desirable, it is seldom feasible given the earlier noted difficulties in gaining access to victims.

Indeed, initial assessment is more likely to take place too late in the disaster-response process than to occur too early. As Green (1982) notes, timing of assessment is often dependent on practical considerations rather than on scientific ones. Uppermost among practical constraints are the ones imposed by funding; delays in funding typically prohibit assessment of early responses. The NIMH, for example, has a 9-month grant review cycle, from time of submission to earliest possible award. The time involved in preparation of a detailed application, as well as that involved in addressing requests by peer reviewers for greater specificity, can add substantially to this 9-month time frame.

Although the length of the review process may be appropriate for other study topics, it effectively eliminates the possibility of funding studies that require the assessment of early responses to particular disaster events. Because of this problem, NIMH grant applicants are encouraged to focus their research on a particular mental health issue, rather than on a particular emergency event, thereby allowing for review, approval, and funding prior to the disaster. This review process acknowledges that, although the exact location and timing of a particular disaster cannot be predicted, the overall occurrence of emergency events is regular and frequent. Funding prior to the event is intended to allow investigators the opportunity to prepare for such events by completing the design of measures, designing analytic and sampling plans, training interviewers, and pilot-testing instruments in areas of high risk. Examples of NIMH grants that have successfully used this approach include one awarded to Peter Steinglass of George Washington University in Washington, D.C., for the study of family response to disaster-initiated relocation, and one awarded to Leonard Bickman of Vanderbilt University, Nashville, Tennessee, for the study of help seeking in the wake of disaster. In both cases, these investigators were given advance financing so that they would be prepared to begin data collection soon after disaster impact.

For important and unanticipated disasters, advance preparation is, of course, impossible. For this reason, NIMH also contributes funds to the National Science Foundation's rapid response program at the University of Colorado. This program is designed to cover nominal data collection and travel expenses for investigators desiring immediate access to a disaster site. Although the rapid response program is not designed to cover salaries, it does provide the investigator with early entry into the field, thereby allowing time for the preparation of a full-blown research application.

From a scientific perspective, early and repeated measurement is essential for understanding the course of responses to traumatic stress. Early assessment permits specification of the link between the event and patterns of acute symptomatology. Repeated, long-term measurement is needed to determine which aspects of the event and/or personal characteristics lead to chronic disorder and to ascertain whether patterns of symptomatology continue to be tied to specific environmental stimuli or instead take on a life of their own (Green, Lindy, & Grace, 1985).

CONCLUDING COMMENTS

This chapter highlights some important methodological considerations in the design of psychosocial studies of disaster. Disaster mental health is a relatively new field of research; only within the last few years have systematic theoretical and empirical advances been made. As with every important problem, there are several reasonable approaches to its study, not a singular right one. Applied research always involves a tension between practical and scientific concerns: between available resources and project goals, between empirical comprehensiveness and theoretical relevance, between standardization of instruments and their continued refinement, between research requirements and victim needs.

The foregoing discussion indicates some of the important trade-offs an investigator must make in choosing one research strategy over another. There are no easy answers; each problem may be investigated in a variety of ways, and the optimal strategy will depend on the host of factors unique to each situation. Some situations may be so fraught with practical difficulties that they are simply not amenable to systematic study; disaster investigators must hope for the wisdom to know when this is the case.

Although tests of intervention effectiveness should ideally wait until relevant measures have been perfected and high-risk groups have been identified, they cannot wait. Disasters occur daily, and victims must be helped. And although policy should wait until relevant research has been conducted, neither can it wait. Policy makers are constantly faced with decisions about how to prepare for and respond to disaster events in ways that will minimize long-term negative consequences to mental health. This chapter has outlined important problems likely to confront disaster investigators in the design of different kinds of studies. The highlighting of strategies used by some of the pioneering investigators in this area, may provide clues to the solution of some of these methodological problems. Because disaster mental health research is still in its infancy, many important topics remain unexplored, topics whose investigation will demand creative solutions yet untried. It is hoped that this book will serve to encourage new investigators to take on the challenge of disaster mental health research, for the importance of this work is undeniable.

REFERENCES

Ahearn, F. L., & Cohen, R. E. (1984). *Disasters and mental health: An annotated bibliography*. Washington, DC: National Institute of Mental Health.

American Psychiatric Association. (1980). *Diagnostic and statistical manual of mental disorders* (3rd ed.; DSM-III). Washington, DC: Author.

American Psychiatric Association. (1987). *Diagnostic and statistical manual of mental disorders* (3rd ed.–Rev.; DSM-III-R). Washington, DC: Author.

Barton, A. H. (1969). *Communities in disaster: A sociological analysis of collective stress situations*. New York: Doubleday.

Baum, A. (1986, August). *Toxins, technology and natural disaster*. Master lecture presented at the annual meeting of the American Psychological Association, Washington, DC.

Baum, A., Fleming, R., & Singer, J. E. (1983). Coping with victimization by technological disaster. *Journal of Social Issues, 39*(2), 117–138.

Baum, A., Grunberg, N. E., & Singer, J. E. (1982). The use of psychological neu-roendocrinological measurements in the study of stress. *Health Psychology, 1*(3), 217–236.

Berren, M. R., Beigel, A., & Ghertner, S. A. (1980). A typology for the classification of disasters. *Community Mental Health Journal, 16*(2), 103–111.

Blanchard, E. B., Kolb, L. C., Gerardi, R. J., Ryan, P., & Pallmeyer, T. P. (1986). Cardiac response to relevant stimuli as an adjunctive tool for diagnosing post traumatic stress disorder in Vietnam veterans. *Behavior Therapy, 17*(5) 596–606.

Blanchard, E. B., Kolb, L. C., Pallmeyer, T. P., & Gerardi, R. J. (1982). The development of a psychophysiological assessment procedure for post-traumatic stress disorder in Vietnam veterans. *Psychiatric Quarterly, 54*, 220–229.

Boulanger, G., & Kadushin, C. (Eds.). (1986). *The Vietnam veteran redefined: Fact and fiction.* Hillsdale, NJ: Erlbaum.

Boulanger, G., Kadushin, C., Rindskopf, D. M., & Carey, M. A. (1986). Post trau-matic stress disorder: A valid diagnosis? In G. Boulanger and C. Kadushin (Eds.), *The Vietnam veteran redefined: Fact and fiction* (pp. 25–35) Hillsdale, NJ: Erlbaum.

Burchfield, S. R. (1979). The stress response: A new perspective. *Psychosomatic Medicine, 41*, 661–672.

Burke, J. D. (1986). Diagnostic categorization by the Diagnostic Interview Schedule (DIS): A comparison with other methods of assessment. In J. E. Barrett & R. M. Rose (Eds.), *Mental disorders in the community* (pp. 255–279). New York: Guilford.

Cohen, R. E., & Ahearn, F. L. (1980). *Handbook for mental health care of disaster victims.* Baltimore: Johns Hopkins University Press.

Cohn, V. (1980, June 7). Waste sites may invade water supply, subcommittee told. *The Washington Post*, A2.

Cook, T. D., & Campbell, D. T. (1979). *Quasi-experimentation: Design and analysis issues for field settings.* Chicago: Rand McNally.

Department of Health and Human Services. (1985). *HHS data inventory.* Washing-ton, DC: Author.

Dohrenwend, B. P. (1974). Problems in defining and sampling the relevant population of stressful life events. In B. S. Dohrenwend & B. P. Dohrenwend (Eds.), *Stressful life events: Their nature and effects* (pp 275–310). New York: Wiley.

Dohrenwend, B. P., & Shrout, P. E. (1981). Toward the development of a two-stage procedure for case identification and classification in psychiatric epidemiology. In R. G. Simmons (Ed.), *Research in community and mental health* (Vol. 2, pp 295–323). Greenwich, CT: JAI Press.

Eaton, W. W., & Kessler, L. G. (Eds.). (1985). *Epidemiologic field methods in psychiatry: The NIMH epidemiologic catchment area program.* Orlando: Aca-demic Press.

Edelstein, M. R., & Wandersman, A. (1987). Community dynamics in coping with toxic contaminants. In I. Altman & A. Wandersman (Eds.), *Neighborhood and community environments* (pp.69–112). New York: Plenum.

Elliott, G. R., & Eisdorfer, C. (Eds.). (1982). *Stress and human health: Analysis and implications of research.* New York: Springer.

Erikson, K. T. (1976). *Everything in its path: Destruction of community in the Buffalo Creek Flood*. New York: Simon & Schuster.

Fischbach, R. L., & Henderson, P. (1985). *Exposure to dioxin and radionuclides in the public water supply: Contrast in community awareness*. Paper presented at the meeting of American Public Health Association, Washington, DC.

Fleiss, J. L. (1986). Significance tests have a role in epidemiologic research: Reactions to A. M. Walker. *American Journal of Public Health, 76*(5), 559–560.

Glass, D. C., & Singer, J. E. (1972). *Urban stress: Experiments on noise and social stressors*. New York: Academic Press.

Gleser, G. C., Green, B. L., & Winget, C. N. (1981). *Prolonged psychosocial effects of disaster: A study of Buffalo Creek*. New York: Academic Press.

Goldsmith, H. (1955). *A contribution of certain personality characteristics of male paraplegics to the degree of improvement in rehabilitation*. Unpublished doctoral dissertation, New York University.

Golec, J. A. (1983). A contextual approach to the social psychological study of disaster recovery. *International Journal of Mass Emergencies and Disasters, 1*(2), 255–276.

Green, B. L. (1982). Assessing levels of psychosocial impairment following disaster: Consideration of actual and methodological dimensions. *The Journal of Nervous and Mental Disease, 17,*(9), 544–552.

Green, B. L., Grace, M. C., & Gleser, G. C. (1985). Identifying survivors at risk: Long-term impairment following the Beverly Hills Supper Club fire. *Journal of Consulting and Clinical Psychology, 53*(5), 672–678.

Green, B. L., Lindy, J. D., & Grace, M. C. (1985). Post-traumatic stress disorder: Toward DSM-IV. *The Journal of Nervous and Mental Disease, 173*(7), 406–411.

Handford, H. A., Mayes, S. D., Mattison, R. E., Humphrey, F. J., Bagnato, S., Bixler, E. O., & Kales, J. D. (1983, December). *Three Mile Island nuclear accident: A disaster study of child and parent reaction*. Paper presented at the Conference on Methodological Issues involving the Study of Children and their Families Exposed to Disaster, sponsored by the American Academy of Child Psychiatry and the National Institute of Mental Health, Airlie House, VA.

Hann, N. (1977). *Coping and defending: Processes of self-environment organization*. New York: Academic Press.

Helzer, J. E. (1981). Methodological issues in the interpretations of the consequences of extreme situations. In B. S. Dohrenwend & B. P. Dohrenwend (Eds.), *Stressful life events and their contexts* (pp. 108–129). New York: Prodist.

Horowitz, M. I. (1976). *Stress response syndromes*. New York: Jason Aronson.

Kahn, H. A. (1983). *An introduction to epidemiologic methods*. New York: Oxford University Press.

Kardiner, A., & Spiegel, H. (1947). *War stress and neurotic illness*. New York: Paul B. Hoeber.

Laufer, R., Brett, E., & Gallops, M. (1984). Post traumatic stress disorder reconsidered: PTSD among Vietnam veterans. In B. Van Der Kolk (Ed.), *Post traumatic stress disorder, psychological and biological sequelae* (pp. 59–79). Washington, DC: American Psychiatric Press.

Lazarus, R. S. (1966). *Psychological stress and the coping process*. New York: McGraw-Hill.

Lazarus, R. S., & Launier, R. (1978). Stress-related transactions between person and environment. In L. A. Pervin and M. Lewis (Eds.), *Perspectives in interactional psychology* (pp. 287–327). New York: Plenum.

Levin, S. S., Groves, A. C., & Lurie, J. D. (1980). Sharing the move—Support groups for relocated women. *Social Work, 25*(4), 323–325.

Lilienfeld, A. M., & Lilienfeld, D. E. (1980). *Foundations of epidemiology* (2nd ed.). New York: Oxford University Press.

Lindy, J. D., Grace, M. C., & Green, B. L. (1981). Survivors: Outreach to a reluctant population. *American Journal of Orthopsychiatry, 51*(3), 468–478.

Logue, J. N., Melick, M. E., & Hansen, H. (1981). Research issues and directions in the epidemiology of health effects of disaster. *Epidemiologic Reviews, 3*, 140–162.

Malloy, P. F., Fairbank, J. A., & Keane, T. M. (1983). Validation of a multimethod assessment of post traumatic stress disorders in Vietnam veterans. *Journal of Consulting and Clinical Psychology, 51*, 488–494.

Mechanic, D. (1974). Discussion of research programs on relations between stressful life events and episode of physical illness. In B. S. Dohrenwend & B. P. Dohrenwend (Eds.), *Stressful life events: Their nature and effects* (pp. 87–97). New York: Wiley.

Meyers, B. A., Friedman, S. B., & Weiner, I. B. (1970). Coping scoliosis. *American Journal of Diseases of Children, 120*, 175–181.

Mitchell, J. T. (1982). Recovery from rescue. *Response Magazine*, Fall, 7–10.

Mitchell, R. E., & Trickett, E. J. (1980). Task force report: Social networks as mediators of social support: An analysis of the effects and determinants of social networks. *Community Mental Health Journal, 16*, 27–44.

Neter, J., & Wasserman, W. (1974). *Applied linear statistical models*. Homewood, IL: Irwin.

Norris, F. H., & Murrell, S. A. (1987). Transitory impact of life event stress on psychological symptoms in older adults. *Journal of Health and Social Behavior, 28*(2), 197–211.

Peterson, C., & Seligman, M. E. P. (1987). Explanatory style and physical illness. *Journal of Personality, 55*(2), 237–265.

Quarentelli, E. L. (1985). What is disaster? The need for clarification in definition and conceptualization in research. In B. Sowder (Ed.), *Disasters and mental health: Selected contemporary perspectives* (pp. 41–73). Rockville, MD: National Institute of Mental Health.

Rabkin, J. G., & Struening, E. L. (1976). Life events, stress, and illness. *Science, 194*, 1013–1020.

Robins, L. N., Fischbach, R. L., Smith, E. M., Cottler, L. B., & Solomon, S. D. (1986). Impact of disaster on previously assessed mental health. In J. Shore (Ed.), *Disaster stress studies: New methods and findings* (pp. 22–48). Washington, DC: American Psychiatric Press.

Robins, L. N., & Smith, E. M. (1983). *Diagnostic interview schedule/disaster supplement*. St. Louis: Washington University School of Medicine, Department of Psychiatry.

Rossi, P. H., Wright, J. D., Weber-Burdin, E., & Perina, J. (1983). Victimization by natural hazards in the United States, 1970–1980; survey estimates. *International Journal of Mass Emergencies and Disasters, 1*(3), 467–482.

Roth, S., & Bootzin, R. R. (1974). Effects of experimentally induced expectancies of external control: An investigation of learned helplessness. *Journal of Personality and Social Psychology, 29,* 253–264.

Sarason, B. R., Shearin, E. N., Pierce, G. R., & Sarason, I. G. (1987). Interrelationships of social support measures: Theoretical and practical implications. *Journal of Personality and Social Psychology 52*(4), 813–832.

Saxe, L., & Fine, M. (1981). *Social experiments: Methods for design and evaluation* (Vol. 131). Beverly Hills, CA: Sage Publications.

Sierles, F. S., Chen, J. J., McFarland, R. E., & Taylor, M. A. (1983). Posttraumatic stress disorder and concurrent psychiatric illness: A preliminary report. *American Journal of Psychiatry, 140,* 1177–1179.

Silver, R., & Wortman, C. B. (1980). Coping with undesirable life events. In J. Garber & M. E. P. Seligman (Eds.), *Human helplessness: Theory and applications* (pp. 279–375). New York: Academic Press.

Slovic, P., Fischoff, B., & Lichtenstein, S. (1981). Perception and acceptability of risk from energy systems. In A. Baum & J. E. Singer (Eds.), *Advances in environmental psychology* (Vol. 3, pp. 157–169). Hillsdale, NJ: Erlbaum.

Smith, E. M. (1984). *Chronology of disasters in eastern Missouri.* (Contract No. 83-MH-525181). Rockville, MD: National Institute of Mental Health.

Smith, E. M., Robins, L. N., Przybeck, T. R., Goldring, E., & Solomon, S. D. (1986). Psychosocial consequences of a disaster. In J. H. Shore (Ed.), *Disaster stress studies: New methods and findings.* (pp. 49–76). Washington, DC: American Psychiatric Press.

Solomon, S. D. (1986). Mobilizing social support networks in times of disaster. In C. Figley (Ed.), *Trauma and its wake,* (Vol. 2, pp. 232–263). New York: Brunner/Mazel.

Solomon, S. D., & Fischbach, R. L. (1986, August). *Control as a determinant of help-seeking following disaster exposure.* Paper presented at the annual meeting of the American Psychological Association, Washington, DC.

Solomon, S. D., Smith, E. M., Robins, L. N., & Fischbach, R. L. (1987). Social involvement as a mediator of disaster-induced stress. *Journal of Applied Social Psychology 17*(12), 1092–1112.

Walker, A. M. (1986). Reporting the results of epidemiologic studies. *American Journal of Public Health, 76*(5), 556–558.

Wortman, C. B. (1983). Coping with victimization: Conclusions and implications for research. *Journal of Social Issues, 39*(2), 195–221.

Wortman, C. B., Abbey, A., Holland, A. E., Silver, R. L., & Janoff-Bulman, R. (1980). Transitions from the laboratory to the field: Problems and progress. In L. Bickman (Ed.), *Applied Social Psychology Annual* (Vol. 1, pp. 197–233). Beverly Hills, CA: Sage Publications.

Implications for Research and Practice

RICHARD GIST AND BERNARD LUBIN

The introductory statement about the ecological viewpoint in community psychology (Introduction, this volume) suggested that an individual's responses to his or her world are largely shaped by that individual's beliefs about how that world is organized, how it functions, and how its various aspects are related. Yet life is filled with unavoidable situations, circumstances, and events that challenge those beliefs and generate disequilibrium (cf. Dohrenwend & Dohrenwend, 1974). The daily challenges of living and the adaptation to them constitute a major source of personal development but can also pose major risks for the genesis of maladaptive behaviors (Dohrenwend & Dohrenwend, 1981). The most extreme reactions to such disequilibrating situations and events have been dubbed *crises* (Caplan, 1964), and crisis intervention has become a mainstay of community mental health practice (Smith, 1977).

The representation of "crisis" in Chinese calligraphs as a blending of *danger* and *opportunity* is particularly pertinent to work with disaster victims. Disasters, by their very nature, are fraught with danger for those who must endure their wrath and adjust in the aftermath. But disasters also present unique opportunities for intervention and research. Disasters comprise a set of regularly appearing events where defined sets of stressors simultaneously affect large numbers of persons, where the major precipitators are related to clearly defined external events, and where system and community variables play important and visible roles in recovery. Disaster interventions therefore are highly instructive about community psychology in general, and about the ecological viewpoint in particular.

RECONCEPTUALIZING INTERVENTION

One important lesson concerns how interventions are conceptualized. No matter how much practitioners and researchers have questioned or even vocally rejected the traditional medical model of etiology and intervention, its patently exogenic conceptual framework permeates the language and structure of clinical work. Such terms as *treatment* and *prevention* belie protestations of independence, and may—often subtly—yield views of this work and the persons toward whom it is directed that run counter to the stated imperatives.

If the responses to disaster-engendered stress are, for the most part, normal responses to abnormal circumstances, and if, in addition, those circumstances arise from factors largely outside the control of the individual victims, then attempts to eliminate those responses or prevent their appearance are logically inconsistent. Indeed, the outcome to seek is really a matter of expediting an important set of processes, a matter of creating the climate and the vehicles through which these reactions can be most efficiently and productively experienced. It is clearly impossible to return an individual's view of the world to what it may have been before the disaster experience—nor, in point of fact, should it be attempted. It is feasible, however, to work to make the process of readjustment more tolerable and less likely to disrupt future living.

Such interventions cannot be effectively designed, researched, or evaluated under the mechanistic constraints of traditional medical metaphors. Much like the process of grieving, the processes involved in postdisaster readjustment are not in and of themselves pathological; they are not comprised of symptoms to be suppressed or avoided. They represent normal challenges confronting essentially normal persons who must find workable ways to reorder their lives in the wake of serious disruption. Psychologists cannot take the pain away or keep it from happening; they can only make it easier to experience and to grow beyond.

THE NEED FOR ALTERNATIVE APPROACHES

Attempts to deal with the normal problems of normal people require quite different modes of approach from the ones suggested by traditional models. Despite years of concerted effort to bring more people into the clinic and consulting room, the bulk of intervention work seems more likely to fall to hairdressers than to headshrinkers (Cowen, 1982). If seeking the help of a mental health professional requires one's acceptance of a schema that includes sickness or some similar concept as a central construct, it seems clear that most disaster victims never adopt such a schema (cf. Yates, Axsom, Bickman, & Howe, Chapter 7, this volume).

Wilkinson & Vera (Chapter 9, this volume) contend that virtually all persons who experience a major disaster will likely suffer at least some symptoms of post-traumatic stress disorder (PTSD) during their postdisaster adjustment. Yet Helzer, Robins, & McEvoy (1987) noted a virtual absence of fully developed cases of PTSD among disaster survivors in the general population. By one means or another, usually without organized assistance or the intervention of mental health personnel, victims apparently learn to adapt. In most cases, it may be fair to assume that their adaptation is strongly influenced by their interactions with any natural helping systems available to support them.

COMMUNITY PSYCHOLOGY AS AN INFORMATION ENTERPRISE

Naisbitt (1982) has made much note of the emergence of self-help groups and related phenomena as indicative of a substantive trend toward self-reliance and an effective rejection of professional-technological interventions in the problems of daily living. Enhancement of the effectiveness and availability of such supportive mechanisms has become a major theme in community intervention, redefining not just the role of the mental health professional in disaster response, but presenting a potential starting point for reconceptualization of many broader goals of community mental health.

The framework evolving here suggests, much in keeping with the earliest traditions of the community mental health movement, that mental health workers might more effectively view themselves as an information enterprise, defined not by actions as ministering practitioners, but rather by ability to develop and disseminate information that promotes the effective functioning of natural systems and strengthens their interrelationships. Although seeming on its surface anything but revolutionary, the subtler implications of this suggestion are worthy of consideration.

The goal of early intervention activity, for example, has historically been couched in terms of preventing the later appearance of specific pathological conditions. Accordingly, the research on which such interventions have been based has focused on such issues as the definition and etiology of specific classes of dysfunction. Evaluation of program effectiveness has similarly concentrated on seeking evidence of specific reductions in the incidence of disorders that could be directly and unequivocally linked to the programs in question. Judged along these lines, most such efforts have been notoriously unsuccessful.

These models are simply inappropriate with respect to the types of intervention contemplated here. The targets of interventions in situational crises are not persons crippled by dispositional pathologies; the goals of such interventions are not built around the suppression of specific maladaptive syndromes. Mental health workers instead pursue courses characterized by attempts to understand and support constructive processes of adaptation— not by fundamentally altering the processes or participants but by strengthening the capacity of natural systems to function effectively.

RETHINKING ROLES AND RELATIONSHIPS

Rather than assuming the need to somehow bring the ubiquitous indigenous nonprofessional into the system of service delivery (cf. Grosser, Henry, &

Kelly, 1969), the argument in this volume is that natural roles and delivery systems are inherently more effective for many situations and should remain intact. But contrary to the implicit (if sometimes subtle) assumptions of many consultation and education approaches, mental health professionals have at least as many important lessons to learn from hairdressers, bartenders, and police officers as they might learn from the professionals. It is in the exchange of *information* rather than in the exchange of *roles* that effective progress is likely to appear. And it is at the interface of these systems, rather than within the confines of either, that such progress can take place.

It is unrealistic to expect a major shift of public or professional priorities from the treatment of manifest psychopathology to the promotion of optimal adjustment in the general population. Efforts to assist persons whose maladjustment renders them incapable of adequate functioning will always assume a higher emphasis, and it is fitting that they should. Events such as disasters, however, make dramatically clear the contributions that the field can make outside the clinic, both to the applied goal of enhancing effective living and to the fundamental effort to achieve a fuller understanding of human functioning. The consistent effectiveness of ecological approaches in promoting the recovery of individuals, families, and communities in disaster's wake speaks eloquently to the practicality of the theory and challenges researchers to further its reach.

REFERENCES

Caplan, G. (1964). *Principles of preventive psychiatry*. New York: Basic Books.

Cowen, E. L. (1982). Help is where you find it. *American Psychologist, 37,* 385–395.

Dohrenwend, B. S., & Dohrenwend, B. P. (Eds.). (1974). *Stressful life events: Their nature and effects*. New York: Wiley.

Dohrenwend, B. S., & Dohrenwend, B. P. (1981). Socioenvironmental factors, stress, and psychopathology. *American Journal of Community Psychology, 9,* 128–159.

Grosser, C., Henry, W. E., & Kelly, J. G. (Eds.). (1969). *Nonprofessionals in the human services*. San Francisco: Jossey-Bass.

Helzer, J. E., Robins, L. N., & McEvoy, L. (1987). Post-traumatic stress disorder in the general population: Findings of the Epidemiologic Catchment Area Survey. *New England Journal of Medicine, 317,* 1630–1634.

Naisbitt, J. (1982). *Megatrends*. New York: Warner.

Smith, L. L. (1977). Crisis intervention theory and practice. *Community Mental Health Review, 2,* 1–14.

Author Index

Subject Index